Economic Aspects
of Television Regulation

Studies in the Regulation of Economic Activity

Economic Aspects
of Television Regulation

ROGER G. NOLL
MERTON J. PECK
JOHN J. McGOWAN

The Brookings Institution / *Washington, D.C.*

Library of Congress Cataloging in Publication Data:
Noll, Roger G
   Economic aspects of television regulation.

   (Studies in the regulation of economic activity)
   Includes bibliographical references.
   1. Television broadcasting—United States.
2. U.S. Federal Communications Commission.
3. Television—Law and legislation—United States.
I. Peck, Merton J., joint author.   II. McGowan,
John J., joint author.   III. Title.   IV. Series.
HE8700.8.N64   384.55'43   73-1086

ISBN 0-8157-6108-2
9 8 7 6 5 4 3 2

THE BROOKINGS INSTITUTION is an independent organization devoted to nonpartisan research, education, and publication in economics, government, foreign policy, and the social sciences generally. Its principal purposes are to aid in the development of sound public policies and to promote public understanding of issues of national importance.

The Institution was founded on December 8, 1927, to merge the activities of the Institute for Government Research, founded in 1916, the Institute of Economics, founded in 1922, and the Robert Brookings Graduate School of Economics and Government, founded in 1924.

The Board of Trustees is responsible for the general administration of the Institution, while the immediate direction of the policies, program, and staff is vested in the President, assisted by an advisory committee of the officers and staff. The by-laws of the Institution state, "It is the function of the Trustees to make possible the conduct of scientific research, and publication, under the most favorable conditions, and to safeguard the independence of the research staff in the pursuit of their studies and in the publication of the results of such studies. It is not a part of their function to determine, control, or influence the conduct of particular investigations or the conclusions reached."

The President bears final responsibility for the decision to publish a manuscript as a Brookings book or staff paper. In reaching his judgment on the competence, accuracy, and objectivity of each study, the President is advised by the director of the appropriate research program and weighs the views of a panel of expert outside readers who report to him in confidence on the quality of the work. Publication of a work signifies that it is deemed to be a competent treatment worthy of public consideration; such publication does not imply endorsement of conclusions or recommendations contained in the study.

The Institution maintains its position of neutrality on issues of public policy in order to safeguard the intellectual freedom of the staff. Hence interpretations or conclusions in Brookings publications should be understood to be solely those of the author or authors and should not be attributed to the Institution, to its trustees, officers, or other staff members, or to the organizations that support its research.

Foreword

THE AMERICAN TELEVISION INDUSTRY is a consummate commercial success. Most stations are profitable, and the programs they offer are regularly watched by vast audiences. On any evening, some members of most American households watch television for several hours. Public opinion surveys find that Americans regard television as the "most believable" source of news and advertising messages. But despite this success, television is widely criticized on the grounds that its reporting is biased, its advertising misleading, and its programming monotonous and tasteless.

This book examines how government policies toward television shape the performance of the industry. The authors believe that most criticism of the television industry is traceable to a single fact: The number of stations available to American communities, although greater than the number available anywhere else in the world, is smaller than the number that both advertisers and viewers would be willing to pay for. Government policy makers, particularly the Federal Communications Commission (FCC), have sought to increase the number of viewing options by encouraging the entry of more stations in the ultra high frequency (UHF) band. At the same time, they have discouraged the development of new broadcast technologies such as pay TV and cable television.

The main objective of this book is to evaluate current regulatory practices in the industry and the potential that the new technologies offer. On the basis of their evaluation, the authors conclude that conventional "free" television in the UHF band is less promising for expanding television broadcasting capacity than is each of several alternatives. They further conclude that, without explicit legislative direction, the FCC is unlikely to abandon its reliance on UHF or to become more receptive to new technologies.

The authors gratefully acknowledge the participation of a number of colleagues in preparing this study. Richard Beatty, Louis Silversin, John Herring, Elizabeth Keyser, and Susan Nelson provided research assistance;

Henry J. Aaron, Sidney S. Alexander, Harold Barnett, Robert Bruce, Robert Hartman, Leland Johnson, Rose Blyth Kemp, Newton Minow, Bruce Owen, Jack Pearce, and Douglas Webbink criticized drafts; Evelyn P. Fisher and Genevieve Wimsatt authenticated facts and citations; Mendelle T. Berenson edited the manuscript; Joan C. Culver prepared the index; and Kathryn S. Breen, Joan Gmiter, Elizabeth Keyser, Gail Schaefer, Maida Schifter, Virginia Casey, and Ann Collins provided secretarial support.

This book is the seventh of the Brookings series of Studies in the Regulation of Economic Activity. The series presents the findings of a program of research focused on public policies toward business. The program is supported by a grant from the Ford Foundation and is directed by Joseph A. Pechman, director of the Brookings Economic Studies program, and Roger G. Noll, a Brookings senior fellow. An earlier version of some of the analysis of cable television presented in this book was prepared for the Sloan Commission on Cable Communications, and appears as Appendix B of its report, *On the Cable: The Television of Abundance.* Mr. Noll's coauthors, Merton J. Peck and John J. McGowan, are, respectively, Professor of Economics and Chairman of the Department of Economics, and Associate Professor of Economics, at Yale University. Mr. Peck and Mr. McGowan are also members of the Brookings associated staff.

The views expressed in this book are solely those of the authors, and should not be attributed to the trustees, officers, or staff of the Brookings Institution or to the Ford Foundation.

KERMIT GORDON
President

March 1973
Washington, D.C.

Contents

Text Tables

Appendix Tables

Text Figures

Appendix Figures

CHAPTER ONE

The U.S. Television Industry: An Introduction

AMERICAN TELEVISION is an average-sized industry. The combined
annual revenue of television stations and networks is approximately $3
billion, about the same as such prosaic activities as the manufacture of
paperboard boxes, cotton broad-woven fabrics, or canned fruits and vege-
tables. But, because they measure only the role television plays in advertising, these revenues grossly understate the importance of the industry,
even for the economist. Most of the social value of TV arises because it is
a medium of entertainment and information. Nearly 95 percent of American homes have television sets, most of which are viewed several hours
daily. Such extensive viewing is bound to affect most Americans as consumers, voters, neighbors, and even parents. Because of this pervasive
social impact, the medium has generated persistent and voluminous criticism. The criticisms, while diverse, fall into four categories:

1. *The cultural criticism.* Television, it is said, has failed to exploit its
potential as a medium for educating, informing, and elevating tastes. The
essence of this view is that television should provide programs that educate
or inform, rather than cater to preferences for entertainment. As Robert
M. Hutchins has succinctly expressed it: "We have triumphantly invented,
perfected, and distributed . . . throughout the land one of the greatest
technical marvels in history, television, and have used it for what? To bring
Coney Island into every home. It is as though moveable type had been
devoted exclusively since Gutenberg's time to the publication of comic
books."[1]

2. *The concentration criticism.* Television is dominated by a few organizations and individuals. In a medium of such importance, these few exert

1. Quoted in Gary A. Steiner, *The People Look at Television: A Study of Audience
Attitudes* (Alfred A. Knopf, 1963), p. 235.

an enormous influence on political opinions and cultural standards. As Vice President Agnew has said, "Nowhere in our system are there fewer checks on vast power."[2]

3. *The wasteland criticism.* Because television programming consists primarily of entertainment shows appealing to large audiences, it is not sufficiently diversified to entertain such minorities as symphony lovers or motorcycle racing fans. Newton Minow, the former chairman of the Federal Communications Commission, puts it this way:

There are many people in this great country, and you must serve all of us. You will get no argument from me if you say that, given a choice between a Western and a symphony, more people will watch the Western. I like Westerns and private eyes too—but a steady diet for the whole country is obviously not in the public interest.[3]

4. *The Lawrence Welk Show criticism.* There is a limited choice even within the standard fare of commercial broadcasting. For example, complaints arose over the cancellation of the Lawrence Welk Show, a popular musical-variety series, even though it was replaced by another conventional program—presumably more popular.[4]

These four criticisms arise in part from the scarcity of television channels. Scarcity limits the educational use of television (the cultural criticism); concentrates control (the concentration criticism); encourages programming for mass audiences (the wasteland criticism); and, even for mass audiences, limits program selection (the Lawrence Welk Show criticism). Of course, the four criticisms are also directed at the way existing channels are utilized, but their scarcity profoundly influences their utilization.

Most programs are produced by firms whose quest for profits shapes television's performance. While the money-making orientation of television is not atypical of business activities,[5] its distinctive features are, first, the extent to which profit seeking in television is channeled and conditioned by regulatory policies, and, second, the fact that television gives away, rather than sells, its principal product—one of the few private enterprise activities that does.

---

2. "Address by the Vice President," printed in *Congressional Record*, Vol. 115, Pt. 25, 91 Cong. 1 sess. (1969), p. 34043.

3. Newton N. Minow, "The Vast Wasteland" (speech delivered to the National Association of Broadcasters, May 9, 1961), reprinted in Newton N. Minow, *Equal Time: The Private Broadcaster and the Public Interest* (Atheneum, 1964), p. 55.

4. *New York Times*, March 20, 1971.

5. The commercial orientation of the U.S. broadcasting system is, however, not typical of broadcasting in other countries. See Chapter 8.

Technological changes have created new opportunities for restructuring the industry in ways that may respond, in part, to the criticisms just cited. This book examines the economics of the television industry, the regulatory policies that shape it, and the technical and economic viability of the promising innovations that could significantly alter its future.

The Structure of the Television Industry

The structure of the broadcasting industry is a result of congressional actions, the policies of the Federal Communications Commission (FCC), economic forces, and a rapidly changing technology.

The FCC and Television Station Assignments

Most television programs are delivered by over-the-air broadcasting. Television broadcasting occupies a band of frequencies in the electromagnetic spectrum. The amount of spectrum required by an electronic communication is determined by the amount of information transmitted and the method by which the signal is impressed on the electromagnetic wave. Television requires the transmission of a vastly greater quantity of information per unit of time than do most other types of emissions. The frequency space required for a single television channel could accommodate 600 amplitude modulation (AM), 30 frequency modulation (FM), or 240 land mobile radio channels.[6]

Since no two transmissions, whether of the same or different kinds, can use the same frequency at the same time in the same geographic areas, frequencies are assigned by the Federal Communications Commission. In 1945, the FCC set aside thirteen very high frequency (VHF) channels for television, one of which was subsequently turned over to land two-way radio service. Eventually the twelve remaining channels accommodated 529 station assignments through careful control of geographical separation, antenna height, and transmitter power. About a fifth of the VHF assignments were reserved for noncommercial licensees, who must be nonprofit organizations and cannot sell advertising.[7]

6. For example, the entire AM radio band, containing all AM assignments, takes up less than 20 percent of the spectrum space taken by one television channel. See Federal Aviation Administration, Frequency Management Division, "The Electromagnetic Spectrum," Chart SPP-F-1000 (February 1969).

7. The public broadcasting allocations are discussed in Chapter 8.

Table 1-1. Status of VHF and UHF Television Channel Assignments, September 1, 1971

Status	Commercial		Noncommercial	
	Very high frequency	*Ultra high frequency*	*Very high frequency*	*Ultra high frequency*
Stations on the air	511	186	87	115
Authorized stations not on the air	15	81	4	16
Channels available for authorization	67	395	32	392
Total channels authorized or available	593	662	123	523

Sources: Federal Communications Commission, Broadcast Bureau, Rules and Standards Commission, unpublished data on allocations; *Broadcasting*, Vol. 81 (September 27, 1971), p. 60.

As early as 1948, the FCC recognized that the number of VHF stations was insufficient for adequate competition and for a reasonable range of choice for much of the population. After four years of hearings and deliberations, the commission issued the Sixth Report and Order, allocating seventy ultra high frequency (UHF) channels.[8] These channels (14–83) provided 1,433 additional station assignments; only 11 percent of the UHF assignments were reserved for noncommercial use. The FCC issued an altered allocation plan in 1966 which illustrated the diminishing availability of VHF allocations, the increasing importance of educational broadcasting, and the underutilization of the UHF frequencies. The number of UHF allocations was decreased to 1,098, of which noncommercial users were reserved a whopping 46 percent, while total VHF allocations grew to 658.[9] Allocations have changed little in the intervening years.

As Table 1-1 indicates, 37 percent of the commercial assignments (85 percent of them in the UHF band) remain unclaimed, while 66 percent of the noncommercial assignments (92 percent of them UHF) are unclaimed. UHF stations have several disadvantages compared to VHF. Not all sets can receive UHF, and most of those that can have a cumbersome UHF

8. Federal Communications Commission, Sixth Report and Order (Dockets 8736, 8975, 8976, 9175), adopted April 11, 1952, published in *Federal Register*, Vol. 17 (May 2, 1952), pp. 3905–4100. For a summary of the report, see FCC, *Eighteenth Annual Report, Fiscal Year Ended June 30, 1952*, pp. 107–13. The report also appears in Pike and Fischer, *Radio Regulation*, Vol. 1, Pt. 3, pp. 91:599–1112, and is summarized in Pike and Fischer, *Radio Regulation Comprehensive Digest*, Vol. 2, pars. 53:606–07, pp. M-3625–M-3738a.

9. Douglas W. Webbink, "The Impact of UHF Promotion: The All-Channel Television Receiver Law," *Law and Contemporary Problems*, Vol. 34 (1969), pp. 538, 547.

tuning system. Furthermore, higher frequency assignments are less suitable for television use, making the quality of received signals lower.[10]

In its licensing policy the FCC has attempted to provide as many communities as possible with at least one local station—defined as a station that originates programs in that locality. The local service policy is not a necessity for widely available television, for this purpose could be achieved with powerful regional stations. Rather, according to a key FCC opinion, "In the Commission's view as many communities as possible should have the opportunity of enjoying the advantages that derive from having local outlets that will be responsive to local needs."[11]

Networks, Independents, and Group Ownership

While FCC policy emphasizes local stations, the most important programming sources are the three national networks—Columbia Broadcasting System (CBS), National Broadcasting Company (NBC), and American Broadcasting Companies (ABC). The networks provide local affiliates with programs that carry advertising that is sold by the networks. The network pays the affiliate about one-third of the advertising revenues that are earned in the affiliate's market.[12]

Except for news, sports, and daytime shows, networks produce few programs; instead they purchase them from producing companies. About one hundred firms have succeeded in selling a prime-time series to a network in the past few years, and no firm has had more than 20 percent of the market in any one year.[13]

The advantage of networks arises in the various economies of national distribution. The cost of producing a half-hour prime-time program currently averages almost $120,000.[14] Only a large audience, which nationwide networks can most easily provide, can yield advertising revenues sufficient to support such costs.[15] But with only three networks, program decisions

10. For a further discussion of UHF disadvantages, see Chapter 3.

11. Sixth Report and Order, par. 79; in Pike and Fischer, *Radio Regulation*, Vol. 1, Pt. 3, p. 91:624.

12. Chapter 3 discusses these arrangements in detail.

13. See Arthur D. Little, Inc., *Television Program Production, Procurement and Syndication: An Economic Analysis Relating to the Federal Communications Commission's Proposed Rule in Docket No. 12782* (ADL, 1966), Vol. 2, Tables 33, 34; *Broadcasting*, Vol. 80 (April 5, 1971), pp. 32–33, and Vol. 82 (April 10, 1972), pp. 28–29.

14. *Broadcasting*, Vol. 80 (April 5, 1971), pp. 32–33.

15. The economics of networks is discussed in detail in Chapter 3.

become highly centralized, thus vitiating the objective of local outlets responsive to local needs.

In addition to the networks and their affiliates, many larger communities have one or more "independents"—stations that have no network affiliation. Independent programming consists largely of "syndications"—usually filmed or taped shows sold directly to local stations by program packagers. (On occasion affiliates also buy syndications as an alternative to network programs and independents broadcast network programs that are not broadcast by the affiliates.) Syndications offer an alternative to networking as a means of achieving large multicommunity audiences to cover program costs. While many syndications are reruns of network shows or movies, a growing number are produced especially for the independent market, and some are live productions. In the past most live syndications have been sports events, but, starting in 1971, a few prime-time entertainment programs have been syndicated for live broadcast after being rejected by the networks.

The remaining stations are noncommercial broadcasters of two types. One group broadcasts largely instructional programs on frequencies that can be received only by specialized television sets owned by schools and other institutions. Most of these stations are owned and operated by local school systems, universities, or state education departments.[16]

The second group of noncommercial broadcasters uses the same range of frequencies as commercial broadcasters. In the past this group has relied upon their most successful stations—in Boston, Los Angeles, New York, and San Francisco—for most of its programming. Prior to 1968, National Educational Television (NET) acted as a clearing house for tapes and films, many of which were produced by its own New York station. In 1968 NET was supplanted by the Corporation for Public Broadcasting (CPB), which began to develop a network of public broadcast stations modeled after the commercial systems. CPB provides financial support for program production, and the Public Broadcasting Service, established by CPB in 1969, distributes these and other programs to public broadcasting stations. For the first time, noncommercial television now uses microwave interconnections among stations. This means that noncommercial stations all over the nation, like network affiliates, broadcast many programs, some of which are live, in the same time slot on the same day.

The combination of networks, independent stations, and noncommercial

16. See Appendix C.

television has meant that viewers in the United States have more television programs from which to choose than do viewers in any other country. Still, choice is more limited than in all other communications media except local newspapers. Fewer than half the homes in America can receive more than five channels.[17]

Technological Developments

About 7.5 percent of the homes with television sets subscribe to community antenna or cable television (CATV).[18] CATV systems carry signals from a central station to homes via coaxial cable, thereby making possible improved reception of local over-the-air television and also more stations, through the importation of signals from other cities using master antennas or microwave relays.[19]

Two further technical possibilities are in an experimental stage—subscription television and home video players. The first, known as STV, takes the box office approach: Viewers pay for individual programs or for access to a particular channel. Home video systems play prerecorded programs that are sold or rented like records or books.[20]

Policy Issues

Five key issues have confronted the federal government in recent years:
The economic viability of UHF. Virtually all of the UHF stations without network affiliation lose money, and even among UHF network affiliates, about half are in the red.[21] Since UHF constitutes the major pos-

17. Herman W. Land Associates, *Television and the Wired City: A Study of the Implications of a Change in the Mode of Transmission* (Washington: National Association of Broadcasters, 1968), p. 119.

18. *Broadcasting*, Vol. 80 (April 12, 1971), p. 60.

19. A single cable can carry as many as twenty to twenty-five channels and several cables can be placed side by side and connected to the same receiving device. Some channels can be used by the CATV system to originate its own programs. Current home television sets can receive twelve CATV channels without any technical change and twenty-four channels with an adapter costing $15 to $20. All twenty-four have better picture quality than over-the-air VHF. CATV systems make a monthly charge to their subscribers for the use of the cable. A complete discussion of cable television is contained in Chapters 6 and 7.

20. The first videocassette players in the early 1970s were priced at about $800 (see Chapter 9).

21. FCC, *37th Annual Report, Fiscal Year 1971*, p. 158. By contrast, 38 percent of VHF independents and 16 percent of VHF affiliates are not profitable. *Ibid.*

sibility for expansion of over-the-air television, the prospect for substantial growth in the number of commercial stations appears bleak, as is illustrated more completely in Chapter 3.

Noncommercial television financing. Most of the educational stations have led a perilous financial existence with very limited funds for programming, making it difficult to start new stations to utilize the many channels the FCC has reserved for noncommercial use. The bright future for public television foreseen in the fifties has only barely begun to be realized.

Criteria for granting and renewing licenses. The FCC has periodically wrestled with the problem of giving concrete meaning to the public service requirement it has imposed on broadcasters so that some solid basis could be laid for awarding licenses. While occasionally a license is not renewed, it is still fair to say that the commission has not yet developed clear standards of performance for judging licensees.

The role of subscription television. Despite the enthusiasm several entrepreneurs have displayed for STV since the late fifties, the huge potential stakes involved and the political pressures that they evoke have so far deprived this new form of television of permanent operating rules. In the 1969–70 session of Congress, twenty-three bills were introduced that would prohibit or curtail STV.

The future of cable television. From 1961 to 1971, the number of CATV subscribers increased eightfold to about 6 million homes.[22] Broadcasters regard cable as a competitive threat to local, over-the-air, advertiser-supported stations, largely because cable systems can bring in programs of stations in distant communities.

Behind these issues are the more fundamental questions of program content, advertising, concentration of control, and profitability.

Program Content

For the individual viewer, what matters is the number, variety, and quality of available programs. We shall consider three dimensions of programming: the number of options, diversity in program types, and program "tone," which refers to the social effects of program content and the objectivity of public affairs and news programming.

The term *options* denotes the number of programs that are simultaneously available, whether or not these are of different program types. Even

22. Television Digest, Inc., *Television Factbook, Services Volume, 1970–1971 Edition* (Washington: TD, 1970), p. 66a.

Table 1-2. Type of Television Programs Available, Viewing Pattern, and Type Viewers Desire Expanded, New York City, 1960

Percent

Type of program	Program availability[a]	Actual viewing pattern[b]	Percent of viewers desiring more programs in category[c]
Action	16	22	14
Comedy and variety	20	19	22
Light drama	8	7	7
Light music	5	4	10
Sports	8	3	6
Regular news	5	29	1
Information and public affairs	9	5	17
Heavy drama	6	4	6
Religion	2	0	5
Movies	22	6	1
Heavy music	0	0	1
All other	...	...	11
Total	100	100	100

Sources: Gary A. Steiner, *The People Look at Television: A Study of Audience Attitudes*, pp. 146, 163, 166. Copyright 1963 by Alfred A. Knopf, Inc.; data reprinted with their permission. The figures on availability and viewing patterns are derived from American Research Bureau samples between September 20, 1959, and March 7, 1960. The figures on changes desired in programming are derived from an independent sampling in March and April 1960. Figures are rounded and may not add to 100.

a. Unduplicated minutes of programming devoted to category from 6:00 P.M. to sign-off weekdays and all day Saturday and Sunday as percentage of total number of minutes available.

b. Number of programs i n category watched by viewers from 6:00 P.M. to sign-off weekdays and all day Saturday and Sunday as percentage of total number of programs viewed.

c. First-mentioned request for additional programming in category as percentage of total requests.

if programs are similar, the number of options still matters, for viewers, who are the ultimate judges, are not indifferent among programs in the same category. If more programs of a given type are offered, a viewer is more likely to find a program he likes.[23]

A survey by Gary Steiner indicated that the greatest unfilled demand is for just those types of programming that already dominate the program schedule. His data, shown in Table 1-2, compare program availability, the actual viewing pattern, and the distribution of preferences for more programs for a sample of New York City residents. The actual viewing pattern matches the menu provided except for regular news broadcasts and movies.

23. See Edward Greenberg and Harold J. Barnett, "TV Program Diversity—New Evidence and Old Theories," in American Economic Association, *Papers and Proceedings of the Eighty-third Annual Meeting, 1970* (*American Economic Review*, Vol. 61, May 1971), pp. 89–93. Among the conclusions of this study are that "program characteristics other than 'type' are significant for viewers," and that "choice within types may be as valuable to many viewers as diversity across types" (p. 93).

Given the technical limits on the number of programs that can be shown, commercial broadcasting appears to do a good job in matching its offerings to actual viewing preferences. The problem is that the menu has so few options. Most people want more options in each category, including those now well represented. In fact, the distribution of responses in the last column indicates that the program types most heavily supplied are the very ones for which the strongest unsatisfied demand exists.[24]

Increasing the number of channels to provide more options cannot be classified as an absolute goal. Such a move would fragment the audience and thereby reduce the resources available to each broadcaster for programming. More generally, additional channels become less and less valuable; that is, an expansion from one channel to three is worth more to society than an expansion from three to five. Viewed in terms of the best use of society's resources, the goal should be to add channels until the additional benefits no longer exceed the additional costs. Despite the simplicity of this general proposition, the complexities of television make the goal difficult to quantify. The problem will be considered subsequently and repeatedly in this volume.

Diversity refers to the number of categories in which programs are offered—family series, sports, drama, and many others. Deciding upon the extent of diversity presents problems that are similar to those arising in choosing the appropriate number of options.[25] Given the number of options, the price of greater diversity is a reduction in the choice within categories.

The sale of advertising now governs the extent of diversity on commercial television. Because the price of television advertising, and hence the broadcaster's revenue, is determined by the number of viewers, and because the addition of another viewer imposes no further cost on an existing broadcast, profit-maximizing behavior on the part of broadcasters implies audience-maximizing behavior as well.[26]

24. It should be emphasized that this demand pattern emerges when all programs are shown at a zero price to the viewer. Whether and to what extent the imposition of positive (and variable) prices would change the pattern are questions to which we address ourselves directly in Chapter 5.

25. Analytically the number of options and the amount of diversity would be determined simultaneously since the optimal number of options is a function of, among other things, the degree of diversity desired. For purposes of exposition, however, we treat the two problems separately.

26. Two factors make the objectives of broadcasters more complicated than simple maximization of audience size: (1) To the extent that broadcasters can attract additional viewers only by spending more on programs, the marginal cost of a viewer is greater

Table 1-3. Relation between Market Size and Diversity in TV Programs, Levin and Land Studies, Late 1960s

	Average number of program options per time period		
Number of stations	Levin,[a] prime time	Land[b]	
		Prime time	Full day
1	1.00	1.00	1.00
2	1.74	1.72	1.71
3	2.40	2.44	2.31
4	2.89	3.14	2.66
5	3.40	3.61	3.10
6	4.10	4.13	3.38

Source: Harvey J. Levin, "Program Duplication, Diversity, and Effective Viewer Choices: Some Empirical Findings," in American Economic Association, *Papers and Proceedings of the Eighty-third Annual Meeting, 1970 (American Economic Review*, Vol. 61, May 1971), p. 85. The Land results are included in the Levin paper.
a. For a sample of eighty-eight markets during the week of February 25–March 4, 1967.
b. For a sample of fifty-nine markets during the week of April 27–May 3, 1968.

Different program types are associated with different expected audience sizes. If, in selecting a program for a time slot in which his competitor is showing a program designed for the mass audience, a broadcaster chooses a similar program, he will have to compete for a share of the mass audience. Or, he can have a specialty audience all to himself by opting for a program catering to a minority taste; however, as a general rule, the latter strategy will produce a much smaller audience.[27]

The relationship between greater diversity and more options has been explored in statistical studies by Herman W. Land Associates and Harvey J. Levin, summarized in Table 1-3. Diversity, as they define it, grows with the number of stations but as this number grows larger, the additional programs are increasingly likely to be within a popular category already available rather than in a new category.

---

than zero, and broadcasters will increase audience size only to the point where the advertising revenue derived from an additional viewer equals the cost of attracting him; and (2) government regulations encourage commercial broadcasters to carry some public service and other programming that attracts only small audiences and thus possesses only limited profitability. While the assumption that broadcasters maximize audience size distorts reality, it facilitates the discussion and does not lead the analysis too far from the actual operations of commercial television.

27. For a more detailed version of this argument, see Chapter 2.

Table 1-4. Percentage of Households Viewing Documentary Specials Telecast in Prime Time between October 1967 and April 1968, and Ranking with Programs on the Other Two Networks at the Same Time

Program	Percent of homes viewing	Rank in time period
Dean Rusk Senate Hearings	10.3	3
Gold Crisis	10.8	3
Dr. Barnard/Heart Transplant	15.5	2
America and The Americans	12.3	3
Can You Hear Me?	12.1	3
Childhood of Timmy	9.5	3
Confrontation	8.9	3
The Actor	6.5	3

Source: Herman W. Land Associates, *Television and the Wired City: A Study of the Implications of a Change in the Mode of Transmission* (Washington: National Association of Broadcasters, 1968), p. 127.

These results reflect the limited size of the audience for diversified programming—public affairs, serious drama, concerts, and the like. Of the various kinds of diversified programming, the one that fares best is the documentary special shown on one of the three networks. And that "best" is none too good: Only one of eight network documentaries shown during the 1967–68 season drew as many as 15 percent of the homes, the share that is considered the minimum acceptable for a network program (see Table 1-4). The Warren Report on the assassination of President Kennedy, shown in 1967, drew an unusually large audience; it was viewed by 21.7 percent of the television homes.[28] Many popular entertainment programs regularly draw larger audiences.

When diversified programming is shown by stations not affiliated with networks, ratings are apt to be lower. In New York City, four out of ten relatively high-cost documentaries scored last place in audience share, with about half the normal ratings of independents.[29] Before the establishment of the Corporation for Public Broadcasting, programs on noncommercial television fared worse, averaging about 1 percent of television homes, with a range of 0.3 percent to 2.6 percent.[30]

The historical record on viewer tastes and broadcasting profits indicates that a significant broadening of program types is unlikely to attract enough

28. Land Associates, *Television and the Wired City*, p. 127.
29. *Ibid.*, p. 128.
30. American Research Bureau, *1968 Television Market Analysis* (New York: ARB, no date), pp. 9–11, 53.

viewers to make it successful within the present commercial system. To stimulate diversity by other means, two specific policies have been devised. The first is the imposition of a public service obligation on commercial broadcasters. The provision of the Communications Act of 1934 that ordered broadcast licenses to be awarded to serve "public interest, convenience, or necessity" has been interpreted as requiring programs that have a high educational or cultural content. Public affairs and serious drama, however, account for less than 5 percent of network prime time simply because they are not as profitable as light entertainment.

The second policy has been the promotion of public, noncommercial television. But this policy has met obstacles in the small size of the audience, the precarious financial life its stations lead, and the costliness of extensive noncommercial television. As one remedy, the Carnegie Commission on Educational Television set forth a plan for substantial expansion that would maintain about 200 noncommercial stations at a cost of $270 million annually.[31] An alternative route is to require the present commercial system to carry more public service programs, or to link the support of noncommercial television to a revenue-producing system like CATV, pay television, or domestic satellites. The issues in these and other proposals are whether the benefits of public service broadcasting are worth the costs, and, if so, who should pay the bill.

Tone refers to the social consequences of television. Many contend that television now has undesirable social effects. Forty percent of the respondents in Steiner's survey cited television violence as a bad influence on children; too much sex was also mentioned, although it ran a distant second.[32] The obvious solution—control over viewing by concerned parents —is apparently unrealistic in light of Steiner's finding that only 4 to 7 percent of parents attempt to regulate the viewing of their children with respect to violence.[33] But to resolve the issue at its TV source is also difficult because a full schedule of television programming appropriate for children would make a bland diet indeed for adults.

Another issue of tone is the relation of television to the political system. Despite limited public affairs programming, television is an extremely effective news medium. In a 1970 poll, television ranked far ahead of news-

---

31. *Public Television: A Program for Action*, The Report and Recommendations of the Carnegie Commission on Educational Television (Bantam Books, 1967), pp. 159, 164.
32. Steiner, *The People Look at Television*, p. 91.
33. *Ibid.*, pp. 97–98.

papers, magazines, and radio as the most important source of news and as "the most believable source."[34] Another poll showed TV advertising to be the most authoritative, believable, entertaining, exciting, and influential.[35]

The FCC has recognized television's impact on public opinion by establishing the now famous "fairness doctrine":

> In . . . [the] presentation of news and comment the public interest requires that the licensee must operate on a basis of overall fairness, making his facilities available for the expression of the contrasting views of all responsible elements in the community on the various issues which arise.[36]

While widely accepted, the fairness doctrine is difficult to apply because it cannot be precisely defined. No one argues that it should be applied to publications like the *New Republic* or the *National Review*, or for that matter to this book. Fairness in print is presumed to be assured by competing books and magazines, and in this way the noneconomic issue of fairness becomes linked to the economic issues of numbers of competitors and ease of entry. This kind of competitive solution is now precluded in television by the limited number of channels.[37]

Another issue is the "equal time" rule that guarantees rival political candidates equal access to television. In political campaigns television is often a key element—witness the $13.5 million the two presidential candidates spent on television in 1968.[38] With the use of television spreading to statewide and primary campaigns, fund-raising activities begin to dominate American politics—so much so that the ability to raise money has become a criterion for success. The equal-time rule does not solve the problem. It requires that stations make available the same amount of time, at the same price, to all candidates for the same office. In practice, the rule guarantees only that a candidate can buy as much time as his opponents bought—if he can afford it.

34. R. H. Bruskin and Associates poll. See *Broadcasting*, Vol. 79 (November 2, 1970), p. 48.

35. Bruskin poll, reported in *Broadcasting*, Vol. 79 (November 23, 1970), pp. 40–41.

36. FCC, Editorializing by Broadcast Licensees (Docket 8516), in *Federal Communications Commission Reports*, Vol. 13 (July 1, 1948–June 30, 1949), p. 1250.

37. For a discussion of the doctrine, see Lee Loevinger, "The FCC and Program Regulation," in David M. White and Richard Averson (eds.), *Sight, Sound, and Society: Motion Pictures and Television in America* (Beacon Press, 1968); and *Fairness Doctrine*, Hearings before the Special Subcommittee on Investigations of the House Committee on Interstate and Foreign Commerce, 90 Cong. 2 sess. (1968).

38. Congressional Quarterly, Inc., *Weekly Report*, Vol. 27 (September 12, 1969), pp. 1701–02, quoting figures released by the FCC on August 27, 1969. Estimated production costs account for an additional $3 million to $4 million.

Television as an Advertising Medium

Much of the economic literature about television is focused on the industry's most visible output—its programs. Yet television's other output—advertising—is more than the way programming happens to be financed; it is also a key input in the marketing of many products.

The rapid growth of television advertising suggests that, for certain goods, it is a very useful promotional medium. Television's share of all advertising expenditures increased from 1 percent in 1949 to 12 percent in 1956, and then, at a much slower rate, to 19 percent in 1970.[39] After commercial television in the United Kingdom began to be significant in the mid-1950s, there developed a similar pattern of rapid expansion followed by slower growth.[40] Television advertising raises several issues relevant to public policy: (1) the effects of advertising on consumer behavior; (2) the equity and efficiency of using advertising to finance television; and (3) the effect of television on competition among producers of advertised products. These issues are discussed in Chapter 2.

Concentration of Control and Profitability

Concern with concentration of economic power has always been a characteristic of American public policy. Some of this concern is based on the desire to achieve the presumed benefits of competition—prices and quantities responsive to demand and supply, adaptation to technological and market opportunities, and prevention of monopoly profits. Yet it also reflects a dedication to decentralization of power per se. This particular objective ranks high for communications media because of their social and political importance.

CONCENTRATION. Television is a highly concentrated activity. The three networks originate about 85 percent of evening prime-time programming and 60 percent of all programming for affiliated stations, which account for 87 percent of all stations.[41] While the three networks pay close attention

39. Land Associates, *Television and the Wired City*, p. 81; U.S. Bureau of the Census, *Statistical Abstract of the United States, 1971* (1971), p. 746.
40. Sydney Caine, *Paying for TV?* Hobart Paper 43 (London: Institute of Economic Affairs, 1968), p. 27.
41. Arthur D. Little, Inc., *Television Program Production, Procurement, Distribution and Scheduling* (ADL, 1969), p. 180; Broadcasting Publications, Inc., *1972 Broadcasting Yearbook* (Washington: BP, 1972), p. 75; FCC, *Annual Report, 1971*, p. 158.

to audience ratings, which are rough measures of the tastes of viewers, they nevertheless have the initiative in deciding what is offered.

Concentration also manifests itself in station ownership. Each of the networks owns the legal maximum of five VHF stations. Since these are in the largest cities, networks reach 25 to 30 percent of all TV homes with their own stations.[42] Other chains are also significant. In the top twenty-five television markets, which cover 60 percent of television homes, 70 percent of the stations are part of a multiple ownership system.[43]

Cross-media ownership produces another form of concentration. Thirty percent of the television stations are owned by daily newspapers, which, theoretically, offer TV the closest competition, at least with respect to news.[44] Joint ownership of radio and television stations is also extremely common, and is often accompanied by newspaper ownership. The most extreme degree of media concentration exists in seventy-three communities in which one firm owns all the local broadcast and newspaper properties.[45] Often mentioned as another policy problem is the ownership of television stations by conglomerates—enterprises operating in a wide range of industries. The alleged dangers are that program policy will be shaped to promote or protect the interests of the other activities of the conglomerate.

TELEVISION PROFITS. In 1969, television profits, before federal income tax, were about $554 million, representing a 20 percent return on sales.[46] By comparison, all manufacturing corporations earned about 8 percent.[47] The profit rate before taxes on the book value of tangible broadcast property was 73 percent,[48] more than three times that prevailing among manufacturing corporations elsewhere in the economy. While 1969 was a good year, 1970 was lean by industry standards. Profits before taxes fell to $454 million, 16 percent of sales and 54 percent of tangible investment if the latter was worth 10 percent more than in the previous year (a generous assumption).[49] Returns of this magnitude have persisted since the fifties.[50]

42. Hyman H. Goldin, "The Television Overlords," *Atlantic*, Vol. 224 (July 1969), p. 88.

43. Lee Loevinger, "Broadcasting and the Journalistic Function," in Harry J. Skornia and Jack W. Kitson (eds.), *Problems and Controversies in Television and Radio* (Pacific Books, 1968), p. 324.

44. *Ibid.*, p. 323.

45. "The American Media Baronies," *Atlantic*, Vol. 224 (July 1969), p. 83.

46. FCC, *36th Annual Report, Fiscal Year 1970*, p. 153.

47. *Economic Report of the President, February 1971*, p. 283.

48. FCC, *Annual Report, 1970*, pp. 153, 164.

49. *Broadcasting*, Vol. 81 (September 6, 1971), pp. 56–57.

50. Tangible property, on which these profit rates are calculated, does not include the

One objection to high profits is that the revenues are greater than is necessary to maintain the industry. Yet this objection is not very compelling. If television profits were down to, say, $175 million, yielding a rate of return on investment comparable to that in manufacturing, the cost of the commercial television industry in 1970 would have been $2.5 billion instead of $2.8 billion.[51] A $300 million gain is trivial for an economy with a gross national product of $1 trillion. Rather, high profits are important as an indicator that competition is less rigorous in television than elsewhere in the economy and hence that resources allocated to the industry are inadequate, at least from the standpoint of advertisers.

In using profit rates as indicators of resource misallocation, three additional points must be noted. First, in the early years of television, networks and many stations incurred substantial losses, whose inclusion as part of initial investment would render profit rates a little more modest. Second, at least some of the high profits reflect the fact that television obtains one of its key resources—scarce spectrum or frequency allocations —without significant charge, and at the sacrifice of alternative uses—land mobile communications, intercity microwave relays, and domestic satellites, to name a few. A third qualification is that the average profit rates cloak a division between high- and low-profit sectors. The highest profits are earned by the networks. In 1969, they and the fifteen stations they owned earned 41 percent of the industry profits, and their profit rate, before taxes, on net tangible broadcast property was 134 percent.[52] Among stations, VHF broadcasters (most of which are network affiliates) received the remaining industry profits and a rate of return of 78 percent on net tangible broadcast property. Among this group, profitability was widely divergent, with 17 percent having losses. The largest cities provide affiliates with their highest profits. Indeed, in 1970, 70 percent of network profits came from the five affiliates each owns in the largest cities. The rate of return for affiliates in the largest cities must be very high—perhaps 200 or 300 percent on tangible investment. The low profit component is composed primarily of the UHF stations; 96 percent of nonaffiliated UHF stations

---

value of the broadcast license, an important asset of every station. While each station owner includes the value of the license in calculating his investment in the station, the licenses are, from the point of view of society, not a "real" asset since they have no production costs. The price of the license is the capitalized value of the profits of the station above a normal return to tangible investment.

51. *Ibid.*, p. 57.

52. All figures in this paragraph are computed from FCC, *Annual Report, 1970*, pp. 152–64, and *Broadcasting*, Vol. 81 (September 6, 1971), pp. 56–57.

had losses in 1969, as did 49 percent of the affiliates, while in 1970 the corresponding figures were 90 percent and 57 percent.

Objectives of the Book

The aim of this book is a critical examination of public policies that determine the structure of the American television industry. The discussion thus far has emphasized four objectives commonly assigned to regulatory policy: more program options, more program diversity, fewer anticompetitive effects from television advertising, and greater attention to the social aspects of television. The key issues raised in the past few years can be viewed in terms of these objectives. Each objective involves balancing incremental gains against costs.

The problem of describing a better television system is a complex one. Chapter 2 explores this question in some detail, formulating it in terms of welfare economics.

Chapter 3 reviews the economics of commercial television, the starting point for considering the impact of newer forms of television on the financial health of the existing system. It also assesses the prospect of further expansion of commercial television to provide more diversity and options. Chapter 4 looks at the FCC policies designed to achieve these ends.

Chapter 5 examines subscription or pay television; Chapters 6 and 7, cable television; and Chapter 8, public television. Chapter 9 evaluates other new technologies, such as direct satellite-to-home television and videocassette players.

The final chapter reviews the four criticisms listed at the outset and considers how changes in regulatory policy might help the industry to respond to them.

The topics listed above make clear that this book approaches television primarily from one perspective, that of economics. We think that perspective is an important one, a view confirmed by Fred Friendly: "One of the problems of broadcasting is that the economic literature is so scanty, and that most of what does exist has been written by special-interest parties in order to create a climate for favorable congressional or FCC action."[53]

Yet we recognize that the basis of the criticisms listed at the outset are noneconomic and many of the issues of television are cultural or even

53. Fred W. Friendly, *Due to Circumstances Beyond Our Control* (Random House, 1967), p. 293.

philosophical. While at times we venture beyond economics in our policy judgments, we do not intend, nor are we competent, to present in this volume the full range of considerations that should determine the role of television in American society. Thus we omit many important topics: the process by which political candidates gain access to the mass audience of television; the proposition that commercial television promotes a materialistic life style by representing consumption as the source of human satisfaction; the effect of televised violence; the proposal that television be required to carry "counter-advertising" to balance the message about controversial goods that, in their use or production, create problems such as pollution and congestion; and numerous others.

CHAPTER TWO

Television and Consumer Welfare

THROUGHOUT THIS BOOK alternative structures and regulatory environments are evaluated in terms of their effect on broadcasting costs, income distribution, and the dimensions of programming defined in Chapter 1—options (the number of program alternatives), diversity (the range of types and qualities among the options), and tone (social, cultural, and political effects). This chapter pinpoints the issues on which normative judgments have to be made if the performance of the television broadcast industry is to be assessed definitively, and shows why the present structure of the industry probably produces programming that falls short of reasonably attainable policy objectives.[1]

Income Distribution

Economists conventionally neglect the income redistribution effects of a change in government policy unless they are its explicit objective. Analysis is normally confined to the effects of policy on allocative efficiency; it asks, Will the policy change bring about a more beneficial use of resources? The basis for analyzing income distribution separately from resource allocation is the assumption that if society is dissatisfied with the way income is distributed, the tax-transfer powers of government can be used to redistribute it without affecting allocative efficiency.[2]

1. We assume throughout that the composition of national income, rather than the total, is the issue in the debate over broadcast policy; we assume also that fiscal, monetary, and mobility policies will prevent alterations in broadcast policy from changing total employment, and that they will do so at a cost sufficiently small that it can be neglected.

2. The classic reference on this topic is Paul A. Samuelson, "The Pure Theory of Public Expenditure," *Review of Economics and Statistics*, Vol. 36 (November 1954), pp. 387–89.

As a practical matter, the effects of policy changes on income redistribution cannot be ignored. First, even if society wanted to offset these effects, alterations of the tax-transfer system entail costs, especially if firms in a particular industry or consumers of a particular product are to be affected differentially; the small amount of allocative efficiency obtained may not be worth the costs of the income redistribution that must be made after it is secured. Second, taxation and income transfers affect resource allocation, except in the case of "inescapable" head taxes; the pristine purity of a system that allocates resources optimally generally cannot be preserved if taxes and transfers are necessary.[3] Third, society does not have, and is probably incapable of establishing, a coherent, consistent income distribution policy; as a consequence, rarely are all of the income redistribution effects of policy changes thoroughly investigated, and almost never are compensations made through changes in the tax-transfer system. Fourth, the probability that a policy change—even one with highly beneficial effects on allocative efficiency—will clear all the political hurdles necessary for adoption varies with its income redistribution effects, as proponents of less fettered markets in international trade, agriculture, transportation, and the broadcast spectrum can testify.

We assume, then, that effects of changes in broadcast policy on income redistribution will not necessarily be compensated through the tax-transfer system, and, consequently, that both the distributive and allocative consequences of policy changes are relevant to the public debate. For example, the fears of low-income groups that pay TV will price them out of the television viewing market should not be dismissed summarily as an irrelevant issue of income distribution, but should be analyzed and evaluated in policy formulation.

The Value of Television

The income distribution aspects of television are particularly critical because the present free system generates an enormous amount of consumer satisfaction. Any significant alteration in the distribution of the benefits derived from television viewing would have a major effect upon income distribution. The precise magnitude of the benefits to consumers

3. See William J. Baumol and David F. Bradford, "Optimal Departures from Marginal Cost Pricing," and Avinash K. Dixit, "On the Optimum Structure of Commodity Taxes," both in *American Economic Review*, Vol. 60 (June 1970), pp. 265–72, and 295–301, respectively.

from the present system is difficult to measure since television viewing normally is not sold, and hence consumers are rarely required to express the intensity of their desire by forgoing some income for the privilege of viewing.

Cable television is the principal exception to this generalization. It collects an installation charge and a monthly fee from a viewer in return for connecting his television set to a cable carrying several channels that cannot be received, or can be received only poorly, through the viewer's over-the-air reception system. The monthly fee generally varies from $4 to $7. The installation fee is much more variable, generally ranging from zero to $35. In areas with little or no television, cable systems have little trouble inducing households to subscribe to their service: Where there is no over-the-air network affiliate, or only one, more than 80 percent of the households adjacent to a cable usually subscribe to it.[4] Judged by the experience of cables, the absolute minimum amount all households would be willing to pay rather than forgo advertiser-supported television is about $2.9 billion annually, or $5 a month from 48 million households. If such payments were collected, it would double the revenues of the television industry, yet this is an absolute minimum estimate. It neglects the price that the 20 percent of households who do not subscribe to cable service at the going fees would be willing to pay rather than give up television. Furthermore, cable systems in areas with little or no over-the-air reception probably charge less than the profit-maximizing price, since the same range of subscription fees is charged in areas where several strong VHF signals can be received without cable service. Because the former systems offer more service, it is likely that consumers value them more highly.

Another source of information about the value of various viewing options is a statistical analysis of the operating experiences of a sample of large cable systems reported in Appendix A. According to the results of the analysis, the estimated value of the third network is roughly $100 per household, or about $5.8 billion nationally.[5] In addition, the first independent station is valued at $65 per household, or $3.8 billion nationally. If the other two networks are valued the same as the third, the total estimated value of a three-network, one-independent system, the typical over-the-air offering, is about $21 billion. This is a conservative estimate, for the first network is certainly of greater value than the third. A direct valuation

    4. See Chapter 6 and Appendix A for a thorough discussion of cable prices and penetration.
    5. These estimates are based on 1966–67 data, and so are conservative.

of the first and second network options (also derived in the appendix and reported in another context in Table 2-4) implies that over-the-air television is worth about $33 billion, which is roughly ten times the total advertising revenue of television. This may be an overestimate. The functional form of the demand for cable subscription used in the appendix attributes considerable value to the first option. While it works well for the range of data available, this function may not adequately represent the shape of the demand function for extremely sparse (or abundant) offerings of television service. No cable television system offers only one or two channels, so no data are available for estimating the valuation consumers would place on such service.[6]

The preceding suggests that a realistic estimate of the value of free, over-the-air television to Americans is at least $20 billion—$25 per month per TV household, or about 4 percent of after-tax household income. This is about seven times the present revenues of television.

Distribution of Benefits

The $20 billion benefit of television is not spread equally among all households regardless of income, age, and other socioeconomic characteristics, since the amount of viewing, and the ability to pay for it should the need arise, differs widely. To assess the distribution of this $20 billion requires information on the pattern of demand for TV viewing.

Table 2-1 shows the number of hours spent viewing television according to various socioeconomic characteristics of the household. As the table shows, low-income individuals spend considerably more hours viewing TV than those with higher income, probably in part because of greater sensitivity to prices of other entertainment. When low-income households have

6. One other estimate places this figure much higher. In "The Social and Economic Benefits of Television Broadcasting" (prepared for the Association of Maximum Service Telecasters, Inc., RRNA, 1969; processed, p. 43), Robert R. Nathan Associates estimates that the price the public would be willing to pay rather than do without television is approximately $100 billion. The primary basis for this estimate is the price viewers would have to pay to spend as much time in moving picture theaters as they spend viewing television. Obviously this figure is a substantial overestimate. Viewers have revealed that they prefer free television to movies in theaters; they have not indicated that if television were just as expensive as the movies they would be indifferent among the following three options: (1) to have no television; (2) to watch television as much as they do currently at the same price charged for admission to motion pictures; (3) to spend as many hours at the movies (at present theater prices) as they now spend watching television.

had the opportunity to purchase increments to their viewing options through cable or subscription television systems, they have been considerably less willing than the more affluent to do so, as the data from the Hartford subscription TV (STV) experiment reveal (Table 2-2). According to these data, the middle-income group is most willing to pay for an additional television

Table 2-1. Hours of Television Viewing per Week, by Socioeconomic Characteristic, 1969

Characteristic	Estimated hours viewed per week
Age of viewer	
Adults	
Under 35	
Men	20
Women	26
35–49	
Men	22
Women	28
50 and over	
Men	27
Women	33
Children	
2–5	28
6–11	23
12–17	
Boys	20
Girls	20
Annual income of household[a]	
Under $5,000	26
$5,000–9,999	21
$10,000–14,999	19
Over $15,000	19
Years of schooling of male head of household	
0–8	22
High school	
1–3	24
4	22
College	
1–3	18

Source: A. C. Nielsen Company, *Nielsen Television, '70* (Chicago: Nielsen, 1970), pp. 13, 15.

option, at least for the recent movies and otherwise untelevised sports events that were the main fare of Hartford STV. The figures suggest, but by no means prove, that middle-income groups would be willing to pay much more for the present system than either the rich or the poor. Assuming that the value of television is proportional to the expenditures on increments to viewing indicated in Table 2-2, weighted by the amount of free TV each income group watches, the estimated $20 billion value of free television is distributed by income groups as shown in Table 2-3.

For purposes of comparison, Table 2-3 also has estimates of the distribution of television benefits by income according to various assumptions about the relationship of income to the willingness to pay for television. In each case the income elasticity of demand for television is assumed to be equal to a particular value, which is to say that if, for example, the income elasticity is assumed to be equal to e, then a p percentage increase in income increases the amount a household is willing to pay for television by ep percent. The first case assumes an income elasticity of 0.5, the second an elasticity of 1, and the third an elasticity of 2. (An elasticity of zero suggests that all groups, regardless of income, are willing to pay the same amount per household for TV.)

These calculations are estimates of what each income group would pay rather than have free TV disappear, not of the amount of income viewers would lose if it did. For low-income households especially, the latter is probably much larger than the former. The existence of free television

Table 2-2. Response of Households to Hartford Subscription Television Experiment, by Income Group, 1963–65

Annual income	Percent of subscribers	Percent of U.S. households, 1965[a]	Average weekly STV purchase[b]
Under $4,000	1.5	33.6	$0.99
$4,000–6,999	40.8	25.2	1.25
$7,000–9,999	43.3	20.6	1.23
$10,000 and over	14.4	20.5	1.18
All groups	100.0	100.0	1.22

Sources: *Subscription Television*, Hearings before the Subcommittee on Communications and Power of the House Committee on Interstate and Foreign Commerce, 90 Cong. 1 sess. (1967), p. 265; U.S. Bureau of the Census, *Current Population Reports*, Series P-60, No. 51, "Income in 1965 of Families and Persons in the United States" (1967), p. 18. Figures are rounded and may not add to totals.
   a. The FCC report in the hearings cited here contains a distribution of income among families that has a smaller fraction of the total in the low-income categories.
   b. In addition, subscribers paid $0.95 weekly to cover a decoder rental fee and, on an annuity basis, the weekly value of the decoder installation.

Economic Aspects of Television Regulation

Table 2-3. Estimated Value of Free Television to Consumers, by Income Group, 1965

Dollars

| | Based on Hartford data | | Based on selected income elasticities | | | | | |
| | | | 0.5 | | 1.0 | | 2.0 | |
Annual income	Total (thousands)	Per household	Total (thousands)	Per household	Total (thousands)	Per household	Total (thousands)	Per household
Under $4,000	240	13	3,980	210	2,520	130	650	34
$4,000–6,999	8,310	580	6,940	480	5,160	360	2,000	140
$7,000–9,999	8,680	740	6,810	580	6,390	540	4,430	380
$10,000 and over	2,770	240	8,610	730	11,380	970	17,030	1,450
All groups	20,000	350	20,000	350	20,000	350	20,000	350

Sources: Derived by authors. The Hartford estimates are based on Table 2-2, weighted by the proportions for free TV viewing.

considerably augments the real income of all viewers, but especially the poor. The amount a low-income household would be willing to pay for any commodity (including television) if its real income in that form were taken away is almost certain to be less than the payment that would be necessary to compensate them for the loss, since at a lower income they would be forced to cut back on their consumption expenditures. Thus Table 2-3 probably grossly underestimates the value to low-income groups of free TV, though it is more reliable for the other groups since the fraction of their real income attributable to free TV is much smaller.

The object of the preceding calculations is to reveal the magnitude of the stake that the viewing public has in the structure of the television industry. To put the matter in perspective, even our admittedly low estimate of the value of television to poor households greatly exceeds the profits currently being extracted by the industry. Significant changes in the broadcast delivery system can cause changes in the real income of consumers amounting to several hundred dollars per household. This amount dwarfs the stake of the industry in these changes and creates a strong rationale for weighing the effects on income redistribution in judging proposed changes in the structure of the industry.

Allocative Efficiency of Television Broadcasting

The allocative efficiency of any industry measures the extent to which the industry uses its scarce resources to the best social advantage. According to this principle, an industry is operating efficiently if (1) all of the resources it uses are employed as effectively as possible—that is, the industry could not produce its present output with fewer resources or expand its output without more; (2) society would not be better off if resources were transferred into or out of the industry; and (3) the industry produces the amount of each possible qualitative variant of its product that is most beneficial to society.[7] The television industry probably does not satisfy the second and third criteria, and may embody some inefficiencies of the first type. The structure and operation of the industry are the sources of these inefficiencies.

Television stations produce only a small fraction of the programs they broadcast. Most prime-time television programs, especially, are bought by networks from reasonably competitive independent producers. In preparation for the 1972–73 season, twenty-four companies produced about seventy pilots for consideration by the networks as possible weekly television series.[8] In addition, movies produced by all of the major motion picture companies—several made especially for television—were broadcast in network prime time. Most of the programming that networks produce for themselves is in the news-documentary-public service category, although some of it is music-variety programs and movies.

Because the television industry is so complex, it is useful to begin examining the efficiency of the industry by considering separately each of its four components—broadcasters, program producers, advertisers, and viewers. We shall discuss, in turn, the efficiency aspects of television as a consumer good, an advertising medium, a customer of program producers, and a user of electromagnetic spectrum.

Television as a Consumer Good

Because television programs are not sold to viewers, it is difficult to estimate the value of various types of programming. Yet such an evaluation is essential to determining whether the number, quality, and diversity of programs are satisfactory. The efficiency criteria listed above are satisfied when the social benefits associated with producing and consuming the last unit of output of a good or service are equal to the social costs of doing so. For commodities that are sold in a market, that provide benefits only to the individual consumer, and that create costs only in the direct

7. With a sufficiently narrow definition of an industry, the second and third criteria are the same.
8. *Broadcasting*, Vol. 82 (January 17, 1972), pp. 14–18.

resource requirements of production and distribution, the efficiency criteria are met if all consumer demand at the going price is satisfied and if price equals the direct long-run incremental cost of the commodity,[9] that is, the costs that must be covered by sales revenue if the industry is to produce at the same rate indefinitely. The price of the commodity then represents its resource costs to society, and consumers buy it up to the point where the value of each unit to the consumer equals the value of resources used to produce it.

Since the price of television viewing is zero (neglecting operating costs of a receiving set), viewers seek to watch each type of program until its marginal benefit to them is also zero. Similarly, because of the zero price the networks have no incentive to broadcast programs that provide benefits to the viewers more than incrementally above zero, since they collect no greater fee from those who are satisfied beyond the level necessary to induce them to watch the program in the first place. This arrangement implies that a large number of viewers regard the benefits from an increment to viewing time in general as negligible, but regard the benefits of additional hours of certain types of programming as very great. Since every type of program arouses the desire for more on the part of at least some viewers, the value of more programming of any type is positive, even though the value of more total viewing may be equal to the price, zero. The divergence between the incremental value of viewing and the incremental benefits of particular program types is the source of the "wasteland" and "Lawrence Welk Show" criticisms discussed in Chapter 1.[10]

The fact that the benefits of more programming of a particular type exceed the zero price is not sufficient evidence that more of it should be produced, since the zero price does not measure the marginal cost of programs. Programming of a given type can be expanded in two ways: (1) by substituting it for another type of program on a currently operating station; and (2) by creating a new station. For a substitution to be worthwhile,

9. The actual requirement for efficiency is that all prices diverge from marginal cost in a systematic way, related to the price elasticities of supply and demand for the product and the amount of taxes and transfers required to make total revenues exactly cover total costs for every industry. See Baumol and Bradford, "Optimal Departures," and Dixit, "Optimum Structure."

10. Perhaps this point was made most clearly by one respondent to a survey of television preferences. Referring to the Lawrence Welk Show, he said, "Of course, I wouldn't watch it exclusively, but I could still listen to it for three or four hours." Quoted in Gary A. Steiner, *The People Look at Television: A Study of Audience Attitudes* (Knopf, 1963), p. 144.

the sum of the benefits of the new program to all viewers and the costs of producing the old program must exceed the sum of the benefits of the old program to all viewers and the production costs of the new program. For a new station to be worthwhile, the additional benefits to all viewers from its programming must exceed the sum of the production costs of the new programs and the operating costs of the new station (including the annualized costs of the capital investment). A definitive statement that the number and composition of television options fall short of the social optimum depends on a comparison of the marginal costs and benefits of more programs.

Television programming has been subjected to market tests in three distinct ways. First, cable television systems charge for giving viewers access to a larger number of television stations than can be received over the air. Second, programming options not available on a conventional television station have been made available by fee through subscription television. Third, some cable television systems have devoted a few channels on the cable to original programming and have offered access to these channels for an increment to the basic price of attaching to the cable system. These three "tests" have yielded some indication of the price viewers are willing to pay for more viewing options and for more programs of specific types.

Consumer Demand for Cable Service

Existing cable systems provide information on the intensity of demand for different types and numbers of stations. The typical system competes with few over-the-air viewing alternatives, either because few stations operate in the area or because the topography prevents good reception of all or most channels. Cable systems earn revenue by selling access to a larger number of signals of good quality. Presumably the greater the improvement cable offers compared with over-the-air options, the higher the price viewers will pay for it. From the data about cable systems, and assumptions about the consumer's utility function, estimates can be made of the value of additional options of conventional television to households. The model for these estimates is presented in Appendix A and the results in value per viewer are summarized in Table 2-4. These results have the following implications:

1. Networks are more highly valued than independents (not surprisingly, considering their relative popularity).

2. Value increases, but at a rapidly diminishing rate, with the addition of networks or independent stations.

3. If there were four networks, and no independents, viewers would value

another independent station about as highly as a fifth network. While the programming of independents and networks do not differ radically, the mix of program types could vary enough to make this a rational result.

4. Most important, additional television is highly valued. The average household, which has access to three networks and an independent, would pay $68 annually to receive another network, implying an annual total of $4.2 billion. Since annual network and station revenues are approaching $3.5 billion, these numbers suggest that, by traditional criteria of consumer welfare, not only another network but a very large expansion of television is warranted. Despite the possibility of major errors in the estimate and despite the unrealistic assumption that all of the incremental value could be collected, the relative magnitudes validate the conclusion that expansion of television is worth the costs.

Expansion is precluded partly by regulatory policies and partly by the more fundamental fact that revenues to support additional television are determined by advertisers, who value it less than viewers do. The most obvious demonstration of this point is the fact that many viewers like a program but will never buy the product; for example, an elderly Christian Scientist may be a Lawrence Welk fan but will never use Geritol.

Pay TV and the Value of Specific Program Types

The calculations above yield the value of more television generally. The Hartford pay TV experiment, described more fully in Chapter 5, points to

Table 2-4. Estimated Consumer Surplus from Various Levels of Free Television Service

Annual surplus per television home in dollars

	Type of station			
	Network		Independent[a]	
Number of stations	Total surplus	Marginal surplus	Total surplus	Marginal surplus
1	234	234	60	60
2	365	131	96	36
3	456	91	121	24
4	525	68	140	19
5	581	56	156	16

Source: Derived by authors. See Appendix A for a description of the model. As explained there, the surplus for combinations of network and independent stations cannot be obtained simply by adding the relevant surpluses in this table. Calculations are based on household income of $9,000 in 1968 prices.
a. Assumes existence of three networks.

the kinds of expanded programming that would be highly valued. Because the experiment was limited to a single station, the system could afford only relatively inexpensive programs, which consequently, with the exception of a few sports events, consisted of movies and entertainment produced for other media—nightclubs, theaters, concert halls—or for free broadcasts in other cities. The programming was thus much less varied and of lower quality than could be provided even in a single large city (the Hartford market is about one-tenth the size of the market in New York, and about one-sixth the size of the Los Angeles market). Nevertheless, the Hartford programs, competing with the free over-the-air networks, generated revenues that, when scaled to a national audience, are comparable with the production costs of regular network programming. Table 2-5 shows, by program type, the revenue that would have been collected nationally had the fraction of the national television audience that viewed the program been the same as

Table 2-5. Program Values Established by Hartford Subscription Television Test, by Program Type, July 1962–July 1964

Program type	Average charge[a]	Audience rating, all showings[b] (percent)	Estimated national revenue[c] (thousands)
Movies	$1.03	20.1	$ 559
Sports	1.37	9.8	363
Championship boxing	2.06	63.3	3,521
College basketball	0.81	13.6	297
High school basketball	0.25	10.7	72
Professional basketball	1.00	6.6	178
College football	1.05	6.2	176
Professional hockey	1.07	5.3	153
Entertainment	1.60	8.7	376
Concerts, opera, ballet	1.50	12.4	502
Popular music and variety	1.48	13.1	523
Broadway plays, other drama	1.62	7.5	328
Miscellaneous specials	2.40	1.7	110
Educational	0.71	0.8	15
Medical[d]	1.50	18.7[d]	n.a.

Sources: From, or estimated from, data in *Subscription Television*, Hearings (1967), pp. 241–335.
a. Second year of test only.
b. Percent of subscribing homes that watched the program. Since most programs were offered more than once, the audience rating per showing was much less—5.6 percent for movies, for example.
c. Based on 4.5 percent of 60 million television homes.
d. Programs offered to 100 subscribing doctors. The audience rating is the percent of subscribing doctors that watched the program.
n.a. Not available.

that in Hartford.[11] Because of the Hartford station's UHF handicap, the figures in the last column should be at least doubled to measure the value of these programs on VHF. At the time of the Hartford experiment only about half of all TV sets could receive UHF, and UHF stations, when competing with VHF stations, were capturing audiences less than half as large as those of comparable VHF stations.

Two of the five types of programs in greatest demand—boxing and serious music—were categories generally missing from free television. The other three—movies, amateur basketball, and light entertainment—were available in substantial doses on free television, but were also in great demand on Hartford STV. Perhaps the demand for the two categories arose from the more sophisticated programs offered on STV, but it seems likely to have stemmed in part from a greater intensity of demand that free TV does not measure. Of course, the weekly series was not tried in Hartford, so that estimates cannot be made of the unsatisfied demand for this staple of free TV.

The available evidence from both STV and cable experience suggests the existence of considerable unfulfilled demand for television programming, both of the conventional type and of a few categories not well represented in the present program logs. The value to consumers of additional television options appears great enough to warrant expansion, even if it were not economically justified within the advertiser-supported system.

Efficiency Aspects of Zero Price

To be an optimum, a social arrangement must make it impossible to make one member of society better off without making another worse off. An arrangement satisfying this condition is called by economists a Pareto optimum.

A television system that charges a zero price for viewing provides neither the incentive to broadcasters to produce programs that evoke the greatest viewer satisfaction, nor the information on which to determine the most desired types of programming. Presumably a small audience with an intense desire to see a particular program could bribe a mass audience with a mild desire for conventional programming to forgo the standard fare so that the program with the smaller audience could be broadcast. If such is

11. In Hartford about 4.5 percent of the homes that watched the station before it converted to pay TV had subscription television descrambling devices; the percentages of audience share used to calculate potential national revenues are percentages of 4.5 percent of the television households.

the case, the present television system diverges from a Pareto optimum (because its framework is not hospitable to a mutually beneficial exchange between the groups of viewers) and is therefore inefficient.

Establishing a price for broadcasts forces broadcasters to take account of the intensity of demand, but it introduces another kind of inefficiency. Viewers who would be willing to pay a lower price than the one set would be excluded, even though including them imposes no cost on anyone else. Thus, once again Pareto optimality is not satisfied.

Unfortunately, there is no escape from this dilemma. Barring God-like prescience on the part of the broadcaster, a zero price is inconsistent with efficient allocation of television resources among program types, while a positive price is inconsistent with efficient total viewing by the entire population. This inherent allocative inefficiency is not unique to the television industry, but occurs whenever the cost of providing one more unit of consumption is always below the average cost, either because the product has the characteristics of a pure public good (in which case the cost of additional consumption is zero) or because of persistent, pervasive economies of scale in producing a private good. In many instances society permits, or at least does not interfere with, situations in which prices equal average costs; magazines, concerts, local public transportation, and public utilities are examples. In other instances, the costs of establishing a market and setting prices are so high that society maintains the zero price and uses the tax-subsidy system to cover the costs—national defense is the prime example.

The decision between fees for viewing and indirect support through advertising or government subsidy as the general approach to financing television depends on the value of one efficiency advantage relative to the other. The solution is difficult, for as the preceding sections have shown, the stake of viewers in the free system is high, but so is the gain from gearing television more closely to audience demand. The implication is that an intermediate solution, involving some free and some pay television, could prove best if the costs of implementing it are not too much above those of adopting either system exclusively.

Welfare Implications of Advertiser-supported Television

Reliance on advertising to support television raises two questions: (1) whether the television industry serves its sponsor-customers efficiently, and (2) whether television advertising has more general effects on society, imposing costs beyond the resources used to produce viewer minutes, and generating benefits beyond increased sales for advertisers. In the first case, the television industry would serve advertisers efficiently if viewer minutes are supplied in that quantity for which price was equal to marginal cost—that is, the additional cost of supplying one more viewer minute. Certain aspects of the supply and demand for television advertising make it difficult to satisfy this requirement, even in the absence of external costs and benefits. And, in the second case, it is highly unlikely that the industry would ever take adequate account of social benefits and costs.

The Supply of and Demand for TV Advertising

The factors governing supply and demand in television advertising are in several ways unique. From the standpoint of the individual advertiser, television is a substitute for other media, so that his demand for television advertising, all other things being equal, is highly elastic—that is, a small percentage change in price leads to a large percentage change in demand—at a price per household comparable with prices in other media (corrected for differences among the media in the productivity per household of advertising). In this range, advertisers switch rapidly from other media to television as the (relative) price of television advertising per viewer-minute falls. Eventually, however, each advertiser either regards the advantages of substituting further television advertising in other media as minimal, or, because he has already devoted most of his advertising budget to it, can substitute television for other media no further. In either event, the demand for viewer-minutes of television advertising becomes less elastic. At the same time, in television—more than in any other medium—the value of advertising to the advertiser is sensitive to the total amount and proportion of advertising in the medium. This is true because an increase in the fraction of broadcast time devoted to advertising reduces both viewership and the attention viewers pay to a given commercial. As a result, for television, the initial range of elastic demand is smaller and less elastic, while the slope of the demand curve in the inelastic range is even steeper, than would otherwise be the case. The market demand for viewer-minutes of advertising resulting from these influences resembles the demand curve DD^1 in Figure 2-1.

The supply of advertising viewer-minutes by the television industry is governed by the number of broadcasters, the relationship between advertising minutes and total operating costs, and the demand for advertising. Since the effect of expanded total advertising on demand is already

Figure 2-1. Equilibrium Price and Output for Viewer-minutes of Television Advertising[a]

Price and cost of viewer-minutes

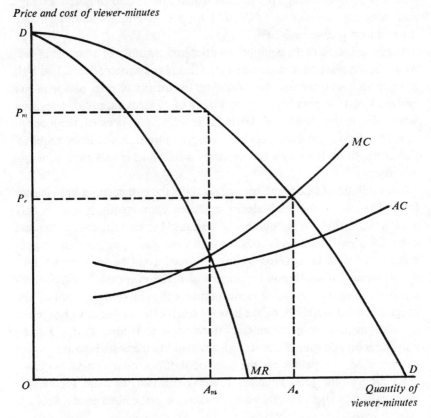

a. A monopolist broadcaster will supply A_m viewer-minutes and charge price P_m, whereas the efficient level of output is A_e sold at price P_e. MR = marginal revenue curve. See text for other definitions.

incorporated into the demand curve in Figure 2-1, the remaining supply considerations relate to the direct cost of producing viewer-minutes. For a given number of hours of broadcasting, more viewer-minutes can be achieved by increasing (1) the time devoted to advertising, and (2) audience size. Since advertisers normally produce television commercials, the first method costs the broadcaster the difference between the advertising value of viewers alienated by the greater frequency of commercials and the costs saved by shortening programs. The costs of the second method are the additional expenditures occasioned by the higher program quality required to attract larger audiences. In the long run a profit-maximizing broadcaster will alter production quality and the number of commercial minutes so that the cost of producing an additional viewer-minute is the same no matter how it is accomplished. This process would give rise to long-run average and marginal cost curves (AC, MC) for viewer-minutes somewhat like those shown in Figure 2-1.[12]

Figure 2-1 depicts the equilibrium price and quantity of advertising that would be supplied by a monopolist television broadcaster (P_m, A_m), as well as the price and quantity, corresponding to equality of price and long-run marginal cost, that satisfy the conditions of efficient supply of television advertising in the absence of external effects (P_e, A_e). As usual, the monopolist broadcaster produces less and charges more than efficiency requires. But competition from new broadcasters would not, in this case, promote efficiency.

The addition of stations to the system shifts the cost curves a broadcaster faces. The size of the total television audience apparently is not strongly affected by changes in the number of stations,[13] so that the shift in the cost curve for viewer-minutes is most pronounced: $n + 1$, rather than n, program costs must be covered by the revenues from the same number of viewer minutes if another station enters an n-station system. For the industry, the average cost curve of viewer-minutes thereby shifts upward by the program cost undertaken by the new station (corrected for any change the old stations make in program costs in response to the new entry). For an individual broadcaster, the cost of viewer-minutes increases because he now has one more competitor for the *same* pool of potential viewers.

As long as the total audience remains constant, demand for viewer-minutes is unlikely to be affected by an increase in the number of stations.[14]

---

12. Whether there is a region of decreasing long-run average and marginal cost may be debatable, but both curves must ultimately rise if for no other reason than that broadcast hours and viewers are finite in number. There also may be levels of output of viewer-minutes at which *short-run* marginal cost is negative. This will be the case in a range where the effect of an increase in commercial minutes on the size of the audience for programs of given cost and quality is so small that viewer-minutes increase. However, efficient production of viewer-minutes requires that their marginal cost be the same whether they are produced by altering program costs at the margin or by altering the number of commercial minutes at the margin. Since program costs are never negative, long-run marginal costs cannot be negative.

13. Although it is not completely convincing, evidence to support this assertion can be found in the staff report to the FCC, "The Economics of the TV-CATV Interface," prepared by the Research Branch, Broadcast Bureau (1970; processed). Additional evidence presented later in this chapter suggests that once two stations are available, the total audience is insensitive to a change in the number of stations.

14. If a new station stimulates more viewing, a decline occurs in the fraction of broadcast time that must be devoted to advertising to produce any given amount of

As a result, additional competition leads to a change in the quantity of viewer-minutes supplied and brings marginal costs and price closer together, while reducing profits. But the equation of price and marginal cost would be bought at the price of raising industry costs for all levels of output, including the one at which price and marginal cost are equal. Since competition cannot bring about *both* an equation of price and marginal costs *and* production at least cost, television advertising is a "natural monopoly" in the same class as public utilities (power, water, telephone). In the absence of price or rate-of-return regulation, it will either earn excess profits derived from a "scarcity" of channels for TV advertising (relative to demand), or produce viewer-minutes at excessive cost. The existence of these "external effects"—that is, costs from added competition that are not paid by the new competitor—detracts from the efficiency of a free market in providing television advertising.

Anticompetitive Effects of Television Advertising

Another external effect in broadcasting operates through the impact that television advertising has on market competition generally. In recent years the alleged effect of television advertising on the structure of markets for advertised products has become an important antitrust issue. The path-breaking event was a ruling by the Federal Trade Commission (FTC) in 1960 that a merger between Clorox and Procter and Gamble should not be allowed. According to the FTC, the merger would confer an unfair competitive advantage since the enlarged corporation could purchase national television advertising at a lower price than its competitors. The decision was subsequently upheld by the Supreme Court, and has been cited as a precedent in several subsequent antitrust actions.[15]

The basis for the Clorox decision was the network policy of granting "volume discounts" to firms purchasing large amounts of advertising in a

---

viewer-minutes. This increases the demand for viewer-minutes; however, this effect is not likely to be important in the contemporary American broadcasting system. Thus the industry demand curve can be assumed to be independent of the number of stations.

15. A substantial volume of literature has appeared arguing the merits of the Clorox decision. Perhaps the best work supporting the decision is Harlan M. Blake and Jack A. Blum, "Network Television Rate Practices: A Case Study in the Failure of Social Control of Price Discrimination," *Yale Law Journal*, Vol. 74 (July 1965), pp. 1339–1401; and criticizing it, John L. Peterman, "The Clorox Case and the Television Rate Structures," *Journal of Law and Economics*, Vol. 11 (October 1968), pp. 321–422. For a complete description of the pricing system employed by television networks before and during the Clorox litigation, see John L. Peterman, "The Structure of National Time Rates in the Television Broadcasting Industry," *Journal of Law and Economics*, Vol. 8 (October 1965), pp. 77–131.

Table 2-6. Network Advertising Costs, for Conventional Purchases and
for Participations, by Advertisers Ranked by Evening Outlays on CBS
Television Network, First Quarter 1965

Dollars

	Costs of network advertising per 1,000 homes	
Group of advertisers[a]	*Conventional purchases*[b]	*Participations*[c]
A	3.52	3.82
B	3.96	3.44
C	4.10	3.17
D	d	3.55
E	4.93	3.47
F	4.58	3.56

Source: David M. Blank, "Television Advertising: The Great Discount Illusion, or Tonypandy Revisited," *Journal of Business*, Vol. 41 (January 1968), p. 31. Copyright 1968 by the University of Chicago. All rights reserved; reprinted with permission.

a. All evening advertisers ranked from largest (A) to smallest (F) in groups of ten, except group F, which has thirteen advertisers.

b. Purchases of all or part of the advertising on a particular program.

c. Purchases of minutes of advertising.

d. There were no purchases in this group.

particular television year. The discounts applied primarily to "conventional" and "time-only" sales, both of which are, in effect, purchases of all or part of a particular television program. The other mode of advertising sales, "participations," is the sale of minutes of advertising rather than periods of broadcasting that include the program itself; volume discounts were much smaller and less common for participations. The extent of the impact of network selling practices is shown in Table 2-6.

By the 1968–69 season, nearly all television advertising was sold as participations—97 percent in the daytime, 92 percent in the evening.[16] But this shift was not accompanied by more discounting of participations. In fact, volume discounts were virtually eliminated from the network price structure.[17]

16. A. C. Nielsen Company, *The Television Audience/1969* (Chicago: Nielsen, 1969), pp. 49, 51. Many factors contributed to the shift to participations. Among those usually cited is the greater opportunity they provide for hedging against uncertainty over audience size. Of course, participations do not provide the strong identification of program and product that the sponsorship system offers. However, the rising costs of television programs during the 1960s may have shifted the tradeoffs between participations and sponsorships in favor of the former.

17. The impact of the Clorox case, in which television networks were made responsible for antitrust judgments against their best customers, was not the only reason for this change. The growing demand for television advertising made special concessions to large purchasers unnecessary.

In spite of these changes, two aspects of television advertising can—in principle at least—adversely affect competition in the markets for advertised products. The first is the discount—a small one of a few percent—offered for year-long advertising commitments. A fifty-two-week commitment to sponsorship of a particular program, or at a particular time of day, transfers the risk of program unpopularity from the network to the advertiser. Only firms with large advertising budgets, spent throughout the television schedule, can afford to run the risk of committing themselves to a full year of commercials in a period that might have a small audience. Consequently, they have the most incentive to take advantage of this discount offer.

Second, regardless of price structure, television advertising can reduce competition by creating a cost barrier to firms in industries that depend on advertising. Because the number of television viewers is so large, even a low per-viewer cost means high total expenditures. In an industry in which television advertising is particularly effective, firms must have a large advertising budget—and hence a large volume of business—to compete.[18] While a cost barrier is present in all forms of advertising, it is most pronounced in television, the medium in which complete-coverage, mass-circulation advertising is almost the only option available. This high total cost of television advertising could be overcome only by fragmenting viewers through a vast increase in the number of television stations.

Other Effects of Television Advertising

Some claim that advertising is beneficial since it transmits information from sellers to potential buyers. Others claim it is harmful since it transmits useless, incorrect, or irrelevant information; since it generates demands that, when met, provide little or no consumer satisfaction yet still absorb scarce resources; and since it clutters the desired product—a newspaper, the daily mail, or a radio or TV program—with undesirable huckstering. While these and other arguments about the intrinsic worth of advertising are not evaluated here, they are pertinent to the assessment of various

---

18. A large fraction of a local market is adequate, for television advertising on a particular station can be purchased on the spot market. The value of local advertising for local companies competing against nationally advertised products is lessened somewhat by the costs of producing commercials: A local firm must either produce commercials of lower quality, run a given commercial more often, or spend more on commercial production per viewer reached.

mechanisms, including advertising, for supporting television. One highly relevant issue is the extent to which television advertising swells the total amount of advertising. To the extent that television drains advertising revenues from other media, production of other forms of communication declines. If television advertising is more pernicious (or beneficial) than other forms, social costs (or benefits) of advertising rise with the switch. To the extent that television generates new advertising, the social costs (or benefits) associated with advertising are increased.

The existence of television has probably increased the total demand for advertising for several reasons. The object of advertising is to carry a message to potential purchasers, so that a new communications medium that reaches potential buyers who were not accessible to existing media opens up new advertising opportunities. Unlike other media, television has greater appeal to the lower and lower middle socioeconomic classes. Furthermore, attitudes toward television and television advertising are quite different from those toward other media, thus influencing the extent to which advertising actually motivates expenditures. According to public opinion surveys, television is generally regarded as the "most believable" communications medium. Individuals also exhibit an extraordinarily high degree of interest in television advertising. In a broad survey, admittedly containing a disproportionately large fraction of well-educated individuals of higher socioeconomic status, an average of only 15.5 percent of viewers were found to pay no attention to commercials during their entire showing (see Table 2-7). In other media (particularly print) the problem is to attract the interest of the individual, and the solution is often flashy, eye-catching advertisements. In television, advertisers have found that offensive commercials can be highly productive.

Television commercials can be regarded as a technological change in

Table 2-7. Attention of Viewers to Television Programs and Commercials, 1964 Survey[a]

Percent of all viewers

Level of attention	Behavior just before commercial	Behavior during commercial
Full	71.0	48.0
Partial	21.6	36.5
None	7.2	15.5
Total	100.0	100.0

Source: Gary A. Steiner, "The People Look at Commercials: A Study of Audience Behavior," *Journal of Business*, Vol. 39 (April 1966), p. 278. Copyright 1966 by the University of Chicago. All rights reserved; reprinted with permission. Figures are rounded and may not add to totals.

a. The viewer survey was conducted among the families of 325 Chicago-area college students.

advertising that, like other such changes, raises the productivity (that is, the sales impact) of advertising expenditures. The profit-maximizing advertiser, purchasing advertising until the last dollar of expenditure increases net income (excluding advertising costs) by one dollar, will respond to this technological change by increasing his total expenditures (if by less than the total expenditure on television), although the imperfections in the television broadcasting and program production industries interfere with this process. The limitations to entry and to competition in broadcasting tend to award the gains of the higher productivity of television advertising to broadcasters, rather than to advertisers through lower prices on television advertising, as discussed above. Viewer loyalties and the uniqueness of the popular television program, analyzed more thoroughly below, tend to make programming costs adjust upward to capture the benefits from the large audiences of the most successful programs, passing the benefits of the high productivity of advertising on these programs to performers, writers, and other artists, rather than to advertisers.

There is no obvious best test of how much television advertising substitutes for other media as opposed to how much it adds to total advertising. To estimate this division requires a reasonably accurate specification of the relationship between advertising and sales, which is very difficult to establish because it need have no particular functional form. Certainly income is important in determining responsiveness to advertising, since higher income groups spend much more on discretionary consumer goods, whose purchase is heavily influenced by taste and style. Yet education and security, which also rise with income, probably dampen the effectiveness of advertising.

Table 2-8 gives one plausible expression relating advertising expenditures

Table 2-8. Relationship between Household Characteristics and Media Advertising Expenditures[a]

Independent variable	Coefficient	t-statistic[b]
Constant (intercept)	−2,761.01	13.58
Non-TV advertising expenditures[c]	1.12	22.48
GNP per household	55.78	3.76
GNP per capita	−1.08	2.28
Number of TV homes[c]	19.3	7.02

Source: Derived by authors, based on 1947–68 data from U.S. Bureau of the Census, *Statistical Abstract of the United States*, various years.

a. The dependent variable is total annual advertising expenditures for all media. All expenditure and income data are expressed in constant (1968) dollars.

b. Significantly greater than zero at 95 percent confidence level. $\bar{R}^2$ is 1.00 and the Durbin-Watson statistic is 1.81.

c. In millions.

to average household income, per capita income, and the number of homes with television. Household and per capita income are both included since the demand for advertised products may (for example, toothpaste) or may not (for example, television sets) be closely related to the number of individuals in the household. An estimate of the fraction of television advertising that is a substitute for other media can be derived from this equation. The equation indicates that nearly half of television advertising is a net addition to total advertising outlay: One more TV home is worth about $40 to broadcasters,[19] but, according to the equation, adds $19 to total advertising expenditures (both figures in 1968 dollars). These figures are roughly consistent with the effect of the ban, effective in 1971, on broadcast advertising by cigarette manufacturers. Of the $211 million the cigarette companies spent on broadcast advertising in 1970, about 63 percent was shifted to other media in 1971, while 37 percent went to a reduction in total advertising expenditures.[20]

The preceding analysis suggests that the existence of television added about $1½ billion to total advertising expenditures in 1971—roughly 7 percent of all advertising and about $23 per television household. This makes the choice of mechanisms for financing television particularly sensitive to the estimate of the social costs and benefits of advertising.

Advertising as a Method of Financing Television

Resources allocated to television must ultimately be drawn out of the production of other goods and services. The required reallocation of resources is not carried out directly but rather is a by-product of the process by which those who in the end compensate the resources used in television reduce their expenditures on other goods and services.

Institutional arrangements for financing television differ in three important ways: (1) their impact on the allocation of resources—that is, on the composition of goods and services that are given up in favor of television; (2) the incidence of the costs, and distribution of the benefits, of television among various individuals and groups in society; (3) collection costs.[21]

19. Calculated from data in FCC, *37th Annual Report, Fiscal Year 1971*, p. 153, and Television Digest, Inc., *Television Factbook, Services Volume, 1970–1971 Edition* (Washington: TD, 1970), p. 25-a.
20. *Broadcasting*, Vol. 82 (January 24, 1972), pp. 40–41.
21. The method of financing also affects the amount and composition of television programming, discussed earlier in this chapter. The effects mentioned here can be investigated separately.

The main alternatives to the present system are pay television, cable television, and public television, whose efficiency as financing mechanisms are discussed in separate chapters.

The unique impact of television advertising on the composition of output stems from the substitutability of advertising among media. Deprived of revenues by the existence of television (as noted above), sellers of competing media—magazines, newspapers, and radio—accordingly raise their prices or lower their output (or both), thus reducing the net benefit to readers and listeners. For some, of course, the benefits lost are at least offset by those that television affords. But undoubtedly some former subscribers to *Collier's* and some radio mystery fans feel deprived, and there is no way of knowing whether society as a whole is better off than it would have been without television, particularly when advertising demand, not viewer tastes, determines the output of the television industry.

Through the way it allocates costs by income groups, the choice of a mechanism for financing the television system has still another effect on income distribution. Lees and Yang, who have estimated the distribution of the costs of television advertising by income groups assuming that all advertising costs are passed on as price increases in advertised products,[22] suggest that in 1963 families with incomes of less than $3,000 spent $21.20 on the advertising costs of goods purchased, as against $51.73 for families with incomes of more than $10,000. Since the two groups view television about the same amount, a program costs the upper income group two and a half times what the lower income group pays, and is therefore unlike market commodities, which are priced the same for all. By comparison, a television system financed out of a proportional increase in everyone's federal income tax would make the cost per program more than ten times as high for the upper income group; as a system, television advertising is, like other "sales tax" mechanisms, regressive (that is, costs rise less than proportionately to income). On the other hand, financing television through a tax related to viewing—such as a tax on TV sets—would be even more regressive than the advertising option.

22. Francis A. Lees and Charles Y. Yang, "The Redistributional Effect of Television Advertising," *Economic Journal*, Vol. 76 (June 1966), pp. 328–36. They also estimate the net income redistribution from the television system, assuming that the value of television to a viewer is equal to the per-viewer cost of the program watched. Thus, their net redistribution to a given family is the difference between the per-viewer cost of television programs watched by the family and the expenditures of the family on the advertising costs of goods. Since the measure ignores the intensity of demand by the household—that is, how much they value the program being watched—the relevance of the calculation of net benefit is not clear.

In comparing advertising to alternative support systems, one must recognize that, if advertisers were denied access to it, half of the advertising on television would shift to other media, and would still have to be paid for by all income groups. The true net cost of the television system to each income group is therefore about one-half of the estimates by Lees and Yang plus the benefits that would be derived from expansion in other media in response to an elimination of television advertising.

The final cost of advertiser-supported television is the direct cost of revenue collection. Just like pay TV systems, advertising-supported television incurs collection costs. These costs are difficult to separate from other costs of advertising; however, the selling expenses incurred by networks and stations, as well as at least part of the 15 percent media commission paid to agencies, do represent pure collection costs. If all agency fees paid by stations and networks are counted as collection costs, along with selling costs incurred by broadcasters, total collection costs amounted to $700 million in 1970.[23] Since one-half of the expenditures for TV advertising would be made if TV did not exist, the net direct collection cost of an advertiser-supported television system is at least $350 million annually, or about $5 per television home, assuming TV selling costs are the same as the average for other media. It must be reemphasized that this is only the direct cost, and includes no allowance for the effects on income distribution that are not compensated, for the social consequences of advertising, or for reductions in revenues to other media resulting from an advertiser-supported television system. Finally, if no TV-created advertising has any value, production costs of commercials would also have to be included.

The Program Production System

The market for new programs oriented toward a national viewing audience is highly imperfect. The demand rests almost entirely with the three large television networks. On the supply side, the program production industry has a reasonably competitive structure; during 1959–64, sixty-five to seventy firms sold a regular series to a major network. The largest firm rarely accounts for more than 10 percent of network series programming. Mortality in the industry is high: About 40 percent of the firms produce programs for only one season.[24]

23. *Broadcasting*, Vol. 81 (September 6, 1971), p. 56.

24. Arthur D. Little, Inc., *Television Program Production, Procurement and Syndication: An Economic Analysis Relating to the Federal Communications Commission's Proposed Rule in Docket 12782* (ADL, 1966), Vol. 1, pp. 32, 35.

Despite the large number of firms, the supply side of the industry also has imperfections. Television programs are not homogeneous products; viewers (and hence advertisers) have strong preferences for certain programs. To some extent the degree of success is predictable. A series can expect to be more popular, on the average, if it stars a well-known entertainer than it can with an unknown, but exceptions are common. Once a program has gained audience loyalty, tinkering with the "formula"—cast, writers, primary production personnel, and format—is risky. Rarely can major changes in cast or writers be made without significant erosion of the audience, thereby conferring upon a popular program a degree of monopoly power. The profit that would be lost if a major production component were changed can be captured from the broadcasters by the production firm and talent responsible for the program's unusual popularity.

Because of the special character of the production market, the price of a program is determined by different influences at different stages of its life. Initially, the dominant market position of the network forces the price to be roughly equal to production costs—which in this case reflect the income program personnel could earn in other media.

If the program is highly successful, attracting large advertising revenues, the program producer is no longer simply one among many competitors dealing with oligopolists; he becomes a monopolist dealing with three competing networks. The success of the program permits its owners to share in the extra revenue that it generates. The limits to the range of bargaining, their determinants, and the success of producers in bargaining with the networks are discussed more fully in the next chapter.

Statistical analysis validates the preceding description of the market for television programs. In 1968–69, each point above an audience rating of 15 accounted for about $1,555 in the costs per half-hour of a weekly episode of regularly scheduled television series. Since the most successful programs obtained weekly ratings of between 25 and 30, more than $15,000 per half-hour per episode of the costs of these programs was attributable to their success in the ratings. The costs of series averaged between $85,000 and $90,000 per half-hour per episode, and about three-fourths of the regularly scheduled programs attained an audience rating above 15.

The following equation was used to derive this estimate:

$$C = \sum_{j=1}^{k} a_j T_j + bR,$$

where

C = the cost per half-hour of one episode of a program

T_j = a dummy variable taking the value of 1 if the program is of program type j and zero otherwise (programs were grouped according to the duration of an individual episode and the general category of program; for example, half-hour situation comedies were one type, and hour-long westerns were another)

R = zero if the program is new; otherwise, the rating in the previous year minus fifteen

a_j and b = constants estimated by least squares.

The values for program costs and the standard errors are shown in Table 2-9.

In an analogy to other industries, the market imperfections in program production result in scarcities of programs deemed most desirable by the viewers. The frequency and length of a program are, with few exceptions, determined permanently before its first broadcast, and thereby are independent of its popularity. In a perfectly competitive television industry in which all the components of a program (including the actors) could be reproduced at will at some fixed cost, a popular program might be broadcast more frequently than those that attract fewer viewers. Often it is not technically feasible to broadcast new episodes of series, dramas, and comedies more frequently than once a week because the principal actors are not freely available for filming. Nevertheless, more frequent showings have occasionally been tried by expanding the cast and rationing the principals among episodes—Peyton Place and The Man from Uncle are examples. In the case of variety programs, such as the Dean Martin Show or Laugh-In, programs broadcast more than once a week or much longer single programs offer possibilities. And the same episode of one of the most popular programs could probably be broadcast twice weekly and still have an above-average audience for each broadcast.

Neither means for increasing the exposure of popular programs is apt to be invoked as long as market imperfections offer profit incentives for maintaining their scarcity. Producers are interested in devising programs that can more than hold their own against the average new program that challenges their place in the network's schedule. The excess profits of the program producer and of the principal talents depend upon audience ratings above the new-program average. Broadcasting more or longer epi-

Table 2-9. Estimated Costs per Half-hour of Episodes of Network Prime-time Entertainment Programs, 1968–69[a]

Thousands of dollars

Type of program and length and rating	Cost per half-hour per episode	Standard error
Adventure		
½ hour	78.7	5.1
1 hour	88.8	2.5
Comedy		
½ hour	83.8	2.3
1 hour	95.0	6.2
Variety		
1 hour	88.7	2.8
Western		
½ hour	81.0	8.8
1 hour	88.2	3.9
1½ hours	80.8	9.1
Drama		
½ hour	85.9	8.8
1 hour	84.4	8.8
Children's		
½ hour	73.2	9.0
1 hour	86.2	5.2
Quiz		
½ hour	65.9[b]	5.1
Excess of program rating over 15	1.555[c]	0.338

Source: Authors' estimates based on ratings data for the 1967–68 season and costs for the 1968–69 season from *Television Magazine*, Vol. 25 (March 1968), pp. 52–55, and Broadcasting Publications, Inc., "Television Magazine's Telecast: The 1968–69 Season" (May 1968).

a. $R^2 = 0.484$; degrees of freedom = 56; F ratio = 533.0.

b. Only half-hour quiz programs differ significantly from the group mean.

c. Average value per half-hour episode to the program owners of each rating point in excess of 15. Significantly greater than zero at 99 percent level.

sodes of a popular program erodes the audience size per episode, and thereby the potential monopoly profits that the successful producer can earn. To the desire of the successful program producer to limit exposure of his product, the networks offer no strong opposition, for their bargaining strength insures their share in the revenues generated by highly successful programs.[25]

The network has a strong interest in expanding the average audience for

25. Evidence of such sharing is presented in Chapter 3. Briefly, a successful program is paid a higher fee, but the fee is a lower percentage of the revenue the program generates.

new programs so as to narrow the spread between it and the audience of a successful program and thus to weaken the bargaining position of the latter's producers. If the network succeeds in this aim (for which it pays a price determined by the potential earnings of talent in other media, principally movies), costs of average programs are unaffected, but costs of successful programs, which now enjoy less profit advantage over average programs, fall, and therefore network profits increase.[26]

The effects the imperfections in the market have on the efficiency of program production are complicated and to some degree offsetting. First, viewers of popular programs can see them less often than they could if broadcasting and program production were both perfectly competitive industries. But, by the same token, those whose tastes run to less popular programs have more options per network than they would if the most successful programs were broadcast as frequently as their popularity would dictate. As in any other case in which the characteristics of a product can not be perfectly duplicated by a competitor, the contrived scarcity in the most popular product types benefits those who prefer less popular types at the expense of those who prefer more popular ones. Because television programs are free, and, therefore, intensity of demand for programs is not an important factor in program success, there is a strong presumption that a market imperfection resulting in more diversity may, in fact, increase aggregate consumer satisfaction. To offer a concrete example, the 9 percent of the TV households who viewed CBS News Hour in the 1967–68 season each week may, in sum, have derived more satisfaction than would the audience of an additional weekly episode of Bonanza, then in its heyday, that might otherwise have occupied the time slot.

The major deleterious effect on programming and diversity of the way the market for program production is now organized is that it makes the entry of new television networks more difficult. This works in two ways. First, a new network cannot survive simply on the strength of a few very popular shows, because, by threatening to transfer their programs to another network, producers of these shows can to some degree capture the excess profit their work generates. Second, a new network can gain the rights to a successful program only by bidding against established networks for the entire twenty-six-week set of weekly episodes, rather than settling

26. Not surprisingly, networks concentrate their preseason publicity and advertising on the new, not the renewed, programs. Perhaps this concentration reflects a judgment that the audience of an old program cannot be increased significantly, but it is also consistent with the argument developed above.

for an occasional "extra" episode. This second problem is probably more important, since a major difficulty of new stations is attracting audiences to an unfamiliar channel (perhaps UHF with all its attendant problems) with unfamiliar programs and personalities. A more open and competitive market for programs would have ways of providing some familiar programming short of buying an entire—and expensive—popular series.

The significance of imperfections in the market for programs for the structure of television programming cannot be assessed independently of the other components of the economics of broadcasting—the costs and revenues of stations and networks—which are discussed in Chapter 3. Nevertheless, as one tentative conclusion, the nature of the market for television programs probably contributes to the diversity of options on the existing system, but it also helps to prevent the entry of new stations, particularly national networks. Whether, on balance, these imperfections are beneficial or detrimental depends upon the importance of the first relative to the second; if, in the absence of market imperfections in program production, more television stations, including another national network, would not be economically viable, the presumption is strong that the imperfections are, on balance, beneficial.[27]

The Broadcasting System

The present system for delivering television programs creates two types of inefficiencies: limitations on program diversity and misuse of an unpriced but valuable resource, the electromagnetic spectrum.

Industry Structure and Diversity

The present three-network system tends to produce programming for a mass audience, neglecting the demands of viewers with special tastes.[28] This need not cause concern if the value of special programs to minority audiences is small compared with the value of mass-audience programs to

27. The effects on income distribution in this case are probably of no special concern and, therefore, are unlikely to affect this conclusion, since, in the absence of more competitors, the market imperfections affect distribution between two very affluent groups: star performers and television broadcasters.

28. See Peter O. Steiner, "Program Patterns and Preferences, and the Workability of Competition in Radio Broadcasting," *Quarterly Journal of Economics*, Vol. 66 (May 1952), pp. 194–223.

the majority. Because television is unpriced, however, the groups deriving the greatest satisfaction from the programming they rate highest have no means of expressing the intensity of their feelings through bidding for scarce television resources.

Beyond the fact that programs are unpriced, the concentration of television programs in the mass-audience category is a consequence of the current number of national television networks. Stations and advertisers seek large audiences, and as long as the share a network has of the mass audience exceeds that which it could attract with specialty programming, it will tend to broadcast mass-audience programs. This tendency is easily illustrated. Suppose a society consisting of 450 viewers is divided according to the intensity of demand for four types of programs. Table 2-10 shows how many individuals from each group would watch each program type if it were offered in a given time period. All four groups would, to some degree, watch mass-audience programming (M), but three groups would, in significantly greater numbers, watch some specific specialty program type (A, B, or C).

A one-network system will obviously broadcast program type M, capturing an audience of 330 viewers. If a second network enters the industry, the best it can do by offering specialty programs is to broadcast program type A for 101 viewers; however, if it broadcasts program type M, duplicating the first network's offering, it can share the larger audience, attracting (in principle) 165 viewers. In a three-network system, the third network also decides to broadcast type M since a one-third share of the large audience, 110 viewers, is better than the best specialty option, type A. But when a fourth network enters, a one-fourth share of the mass market is no longer the best option (82 viewers, compared with 101 for program type A).

Table 2-10. A Model of the Distribution of Viewer Tastes

Number of viewers watching particular program in given time slot

	Program preference groups			
Program type	I	II	III	IV
Specialty, A	101	0	0	0
Specialty, B	0	100	0	0
Specialty, C	0	0	99	0
Mass-audience, M	60[a]	60[a]	60[a]	150

Source: Prepared by authors. See text for discussion.

a. Number of viewers if type of program preferred by group is not offered; if group preference is broadcast, number watching M from special-taste group is zero.

Furthermore, if one of the four networks begins broadcasting type A programming, a one-third share of the remaining mass audience (90 viewers) is not as attractive as that obtainable by broadcasting specialty type B (100 viewers). A four-network system will thus broadcast A, B, and M twice (105 viewers to each M-broadcaster, compared with 99 for type C). Finally, a five-network system will broadcast all types, with two stations broadcasting M for an audience of 75 viewers each.

The preceding example assumes competitive behavior among the networks. Interestingly, collusion aimed at maximizing joint profits, or monopoly behavior, will, in this example, produce more diversity than the competitive solution. A monopolist is interested in maximizing the audience of the entire television system, not that of a particular channel. Consequently, in a two- rather than a one-network system the monopolist will not duplicate programming type M; he can expand the total audience only by broadcasting a specialty program on the second network. Thus a monopolist will show program M on one channel, A on the second, B on the third, and C on the fourth, in each instance providing more diversity than a competitive system with the same number of channels.

The preceding model is highly simplified and should not be used by itself to evaluate or formulate policy toward broadcasting. It takes no account of the effect of showing a given type of program at one time on the audience another program can command at another time, nor of the fact that viewers value options as well as diversity.

Some evidence that viewers value more options as well as diversity is worth mentioning—a statistical analysis of affiliated station audiences. For a random sample of sixty-five network affiliates, audience size, S_A, as measured by the percentage of television homes in the stations' "area of dominant influence" actually watching the station during prime time, was found to be given by[29]

$$S_A = 0.427D_1 + 0.445D_2 + 0.420D_3 - 0.036U$$
$$(0.027) \quad (0.029) \quad (0.029) \quad (0.030)$$
$$- 0.209 \ln (1 + N_A) - 0.14 \ln (1 + N_I).$$
$$(0.028) \qquad\qquad (0.027)$$
$$R^2 = 0.915.$$

In this equation, N_A is the number of *competing* network affiliates in the station's market and N_I is the number of independent stations; U is a

29. The numbers in parentheses are standard errors.

dummy that takes the value of 1 when the station is UHF and 0 when it is VHF. Each of the variables D_1, D_2, D_3 is a dummy representing the affiliation status of the station. Thus, for example, D_1 is unity if the station is an ABC affiliate and zero if the station is affiliated with either CBS or NBC. Likewise, D_2 or D_3 is unity only if the station is affiliated with CBS or NBC, respectively. The regression coefficients imply that a single affiliate will attract between 42 and 45 percent of the potential viewers in its market. In a market with two stations, the total audience would be between 55 and 58 percent of the potential, depending upon the affiliation status of the stations. Finally, in a market with an affiliate of each network, the total audience is 60 percent of potential.

These figures suggest that the second network is highly valued and that a two-channel monopolist would probably not find it profitable to behave much differently from the existing networks. The probable behavior of a three-channel monopolist is less certain. Assuming he used all three channels, he would not behave the way the third network actually does unless there are no new program types (like A, B, or C in the example) that can attract more than 2 percent of viewers. This seems unlikely.[30]

The principal point of the preceding analysis is to demonstrate how a television industry in which the number of networks is small will tend to concentrate programming in the mass-audience type of program, even if total viewing would be increased by diversification. It also shows that in a competitive television industry, new entry cannot be expected to generate diversity until the last entrant's share of the mass market is smaller than the largest audience obtainable for specialty programming. This explains why the development of the American Broadcasting Companies to full schedule network status in the late 1950s did not contribute to diversity, and why the emerging loose networks for syndicated programs, built around such multistation systems as Group W and Metromedia, appear to be following the same audience path, emphasizing variety, talk, and game shows.

Network special-interest programming usually has drawn between 15 and 20 percent of the television audience,[31] indicating that a system of

30. The assumption that all of the third channel would be used may be faulty, for perhaps no new program types can attract audiences large enough to generate advertising revenue sufficient to cover their production costs. If that is the case, the three-channel monopolist would increase neither diversity nor options above present levels, but would reduce costs by not broadcasting on the third channel.

31. Normally about 55 percent of the potential audience is watching television. ABC Stage 67, a recent attempt at high-quality drama in a regular series by a commercial net-

perhaps five, but more likely six, networks would be required to ensure an audience for specialty programs comparable with a single network's share of the mass audience; obviously, in a three-network system in which each network can achieve one-third of the audience by mass programming, specialty programs will be few and far between.

Spectrum Allocation and Use

Aside from the scarcity of television options arising from the present institutional structure of the broadcasting industry, another inefficiency stems from the method of allocating a vital component of over-the-air broadcasting—electromagnetic frequency space. Broadcasting rights are bestowed by the Federal Communications Commission at virtually no cost, yet their value is, obviously, very high. Levin estimates that approximately 40 percent of the net worth of thirty-one television stations sold during 1960 represented the value of the broadcast license. Undoubtedly this ratio has increased since 1960 along with the profitability of television stations.[32]

The failure to charge for spectrum rights—given frequencies at a given place during a given time—has several important consequences. First, and most obvious, are the high profits of broadcasters, which could, at least in part, be captured by auctions for broadcast rights. Second, broadcasters have no motive to conserve spectrum beyond the loose limits imposed by the FCC on the "inputs" to broadcasting, such as power, antenna height, and antenna directionalization; the periods of the day in which the broadcaster may operate; and the amount of band-width (or spread of adjacent frequencies) that the station's signal may occupy. Within these constraints, the interest of the broadcaster is to make his signal heard as far away as possible as long as the costs are incidental. He has no interest in using

---

work, attracted about 10 percent of the potential audience, or 18 percent of the viewing audience. First Tuesday (renamed Chronolog, then NBC Reports) and Sixty Minutes, television counterparts to news-feature magazines, averaged 10 percent of the potential audience in the 1970–71 season (A. C. Nielsen Co., *Television Audience, 1971*, p. 63). The regularly scheduled in-depth news program, CBS Reports, averaged 8 percent of the potential, or 15 percent of the actual, viewing audience in the 1971–72 season (Nielsen, *Television Audience, 1972*, p. 71). Special informational programs tend to draw slightly larger audiences; for example, Search For The Nile averaged 13 percent, the Undersea World of Jacques Cousteau 11 percent, and National Geographic specials 20 percent of the potential audience in 1971–72 (Nielsen, *1971–1972 Specials: Spring, Summer vs. Fall, Winter Comparison*, Nielsen, 1972; pp. 70, 74–75).

32. Harvey J. Levin, "Economic Effects of Broadcast Licensing," *Journal of Political Economy*, Vol. 72 (April 1964), pp. 151–62.

even less band-width than prescribed by the FCC, for to do so is more expensive, nor to limit the geographical area reached by his signal any more than the FCC requires. If its use were priced, the broadcaster would have an incentive to use spectrum space only to the extent that was economically justified. If, for example, the going price made it cheaper to buy better broadcasting equipment than to use a broader band-width with inferior equipment, the station would have an incentive to conserve spectrum space.

The third consequence of nonmarket allocation of spectrum is that it provides no assessment of the economic value of alternative uses. While a television station is one of the most profitable uses of spectrum, it also consumes more spectrum space than most other individual users—several hundred times as much as a local radio station or land mobile user. Whether competitive bidding among various types of users would make more or less spectrum available for television than does the current system is not clear. In an auction, the profitability of television might be offset by the amount of spectrum it would have to buy and by the availability of an alternative—cable delivery—at a fairly low cost, at least part of which can easily be passed on to viewers. It *is* clear, however, that the present method of allocation is not based on highest and best use, and that industries with good substitutes for spectrum space are given no incentive to vacate it for use by others who have poor substitutes.

Developing a workable mechanism for marketing spectrum rests on the solution to several difficult technical problems, the discussion of which is beyond the scope of this book.[33] But they are not insurmountable, and a rational system of spectrum allocation requires either a market, or some form of market simulation, to supply usable estimates of the economic value of alternative uses of the spectrum.

The Problem of Tone

Of the characteristics of broadcasts, the most difficult to control through a commercial broadcast system is program tone—the aspects of program content that alter behavior in ways affecting others. Among the knotty regulatory issues in the category of program tone are the "fairness" doc-

33. For a discussion of these problems, see Harvey J. Levin, "Spectrum Allocation without Market," *American Economic Review*, Vol. 60 (May 1970), pp. 209–18, and discussion papers, pp. 219–24.

trine regarding politically controversial issues, and limitations on violence, language, and scenes of allegedly pornographic character.

Some believe that certain types of television programs incite antisocial behavior and that others improve the contribution of the individual to society. Thus nonviewers of a program pay costs and reap benefits according to the tone of a program. For example, the Kennedy-Nixon debates could be alleged to have helped those who saw them to make a wiser choice of candidate, thus making their votes more meaningful and benefiting themselves and nonviewers alike. Or the debates could be regarded primarily as entertainment, in which the personalities and physical appearances of the candidates obscured the substantive issues, thereby reducing the ability of viewers to cast a well-informed ballot and damaging nonviewers.

A commercial television system will not take adequate account of its broader, societal effects since, whether it is financed by advertising or subscription, its revenues will not depend on the costs or benefits society at large derives from its programming. Nonviewers contribute neither to advertising revenues nor to pay-TV fees. Even a dedicated viewer, in choosing a program, would weigh the social effects scarcely at all relative to its other characteristics. Because few extra viewers, and therefore little additional revenue, can be garnered through improving the social effects of broadcasts, commercial programming can be expected to create more social costs and fewer social benefits than would be optimal. This is particularly true if the elements creating social costs also generate increased private satisfaction, as is perhaps the case with violence; or conversely, if socially beneficial components of tone lower private satisfaction with programs.

To make decisions about tone that reflect social consequences calls for collective action, through either direct regulations or fines and subsidies. But, in the absence of a purely objective way to determine the proper content of programming with respect to program tone, an essentially political decision must be taken on the appropriate public goals. Certainly, objective evidence about the effect of televised violence on individual behavior, of the political orientation of broadcasts on viewer attitudes, and of other aspects of program content on social welfare is relevant to the decision about these goals. But evaluations of these effects are inherently subjective, and do not produce analyzable artifacts through a price system. The only certainty is that if any aspect of program content does generate significant social benefits (or costs), it follows that too little (or too much) of that aspect is included in program content. If one can reach the qualitative judgment that, for example, political information broadcasts are socially beneficial, it follows that the existing television system, in the absence of governmental regulations or subsidies, will produce too little such programming.

Conclusions

The viewing public has an enormous stake in the structure and performance of the television industry. Television generates consumer satisfactions that far exceed its costs in resources. Yet a substantial demand for many types of television programs remains unsatisfied. While much could be lost from a change that seriously eroded the consumer satisfaction generated by the present system, much could be gained from a broadening of program options and diversity.

This chapter has raised a number of issues that are relevant to evaluating alternative structures of the television industry and the public policies necessary to produce structural changes. Each alternative must be gauged on the basis of its uncompensated effects on income redistribution, its contribution to consumer satisfaction, its direct resource costs of implementation (both for changes in programming and for collecting the revenues necessary to pay for the resources committed to the system), and its implications for the welfare of society at large. The evidence suggests that the present advertiser-supported, free broadcasting system creates an enormous benefit for the middle and lower income groups. It also harbors a number of inefficiencies: an insensitivity to intensely felt demands of a large minority for particular types of programs; a scarcity of the most popular mass-audience programs; an absence of incentives to be alert to the social consequences of programming and of advertising; anticompetitive effects on the markets for advertised products; and less advertising than demand and cost conditions justify. In addition, because total advertising expenditures apparently have risen with the advent of television, the process of collecting revenues to support it probably costs about $1½ billion annually, depending upon assumptions about the effects of advertising on product costs and on society generally. On the other side of the ledger, television generates enormous consumer satisfaction, satisfies the important efficiency condition that the price of viewing equal its true marginal resource cost (in this case zero), and subsists in large measure by shifts in advertising revenues from other media, implying a concomitant decline in resources committed to other advertising media that may or may not offset the benefits of television.

A judgment on the present television system must await answers to these same questions of efficiency about alternative structures of the industry. In addition, the analysis must expand to include the probable development of the present structure in the future. This, in turn, requires examination of the trends in costs and revenues of the advertiser-supported system to assess the likelihood of overcoming some of its defects, particularly with regard to options and diversity.

An examination of the alternative structures of the television industry should allow for one important point: The nature of a television broadcast precludes a solution that meets all of the efficiency criteria as satisfactorily as does a perfectly competitive industry producing a private good. Leaving aside the problem of income distribution, no structure will both insure equality of price and marginal cost and produce the socially most desirable mix and number of programs. And no system will be free of fairly high costs of collecting the revenues necessary to reward the resources committed to television. Consequently, a significant number of viewers will always be dissatisfied with the performance of the television industry, regardless of its structure and of public policy toward it.

CHAPTER THREE

Expanding Commercial Television

EXPANDING OVER-THE-AIR commercial television is one obvious way to meet the demand for more options in standard entertainment fare and for more programs to suit minority tastes. This chapter examines the obstacles to such an expansion and assesses the role of economically feasible expansion for a better television industry.

The common belief that expansion is prevented by limited spectrum space for over-the-air television broadcasting offers only a superficial explanation, for, as pointed out in Chapter 1, many ultra high frequency (UHF) channels are unused. While the signal disadvantage under which UHF labors helps to explain its slow development, a more fundamental problem is the lack of attractive programming for UHF broadcasters. This chapter, therefore, focuses on the economics of program supply. Since the three national networks provide most of the programming to local stations, acting as intermediaries between independent program packagers and network affiliates, the first section explores the economics of the relationship among these three groups. The second section examines the terms on which nonnetwork programming is available to local stations. The analyses in these sections are then used to assess the prospects of policies for expanding commercial television.

The Economics of Networking

In its most rudimentary form a broadcast network is merely a group of interconnected stations. Interconnection provides a means of distributing programs from a central source, either for simultaneous broadcast in several communities or for recording, storage, and rebroadcast at the discretion of the local station.

Program distribution, however, is a minor activity of the networks. Indeed, the technical facilities for achieving interconnection are provided by the American Telephone and Telegraph Company (AT&T) and other communications common carriers, not by the networks themselves. Networks occupy the dominant position in American broadcasting by supplying an audience for national advertisers and by originating much of the programming broadcast by local television stations.

The economic origin of this position is the ability of networks to reduce the costs of broadcasters, advertisers, and program suppliers. First, the networks serve to economize on the costs of arranging for nationwide advertising by employing a single agent to deal with national advertisers and granting him exclusive rights to the sale of prespecified blocks of time. Similarly, by supplying programs that are broadcast nationwide, the network simplifies the guesses advertisers must make about audience sizes.[1]

Second, further economies can be achieved through centralized program procurement. Without it, the program owner would be required to negotiate with every station separately in order to maximize his return, thus raising transaction costs for both program owners and broadcasters. In addition, concentrating program procurement in three networks unbalances market power, converting a competitive situation into an oligopolistic one favoring broadcasters. By passing some of the gains from market power on to stations, networks provide broadcasters with an incentive not to deal directly with program producers.

Both the economics of supplying national advertising time and the economics of program procurement thus provide advantages to centralized decision making in commercial television broadcasting. Because of regulatory restrictions on multiple ownership, centralization must be achieved, for the most part, through contractual agreements between the networks and their local affiliates. The terms of these agreements are important factors in the economics of commercial broadcasting because they serve as one determinant of the distribution of revenues among networks, affiliates, and program suppliers.

The agreements, in turn, reflect two elements: (1) the costs of labor and capital in the broadcasting industry, and (2) rents—the portion of pay-

---

1. With nationwide programs, economy in decision making is purchased at the cost of diminished opportunities to select a diversified advertising portfolio since the number of independent program alternatives falls with nationwide programming. But such costs seem insignificant relative to the savings in information processing, particularly since many opportunities for diversification remain.

ments reflecting the scarcity value of talent, broadcasting licenses, and so forth. Rents can also be viewed as payments to induce owners of unreproducible resources to take one action rather than another. Thus fees are paid to local stations for carrying network rather than nonnetwork programs, or to program owners for selling their programs to networks rather than directly to stations. These payments have no necessary relation to social costs—that is, the resources used—in the various alternatives.

An economic analysis of broadcasting requires estimates of the size of rents in the industry. Changes in policy will alter the strategic positions and scarcity values of unique resources, thereby affecting rents, but since these payments for market positions exceed the amount necessary to draw a resource into the television business, such shifts will not change the actual resources available to it. The next sections focus on the size and distribution of rents in the broadcasting industry.

Network-Affiliate Relations

The essence of the network-affiliate relationship can be captured in a somewhat abstract statement of the economic interest of each party. An affiliate will carry a network program if its share in the total advertising revenue generated by the program is greater than the profit from broadcasting a nonnetwork program.[2] Since the total advertising revenue of a program is directly proportional to the size of its audience, the relative attractiveness of a network vis-à-vis a nonnetwork program depends on (1) the size of the audiences of the two programs, and (2) the terms on which the station shares in the advertising revenues of each. These factors interact; the greater the popularity of network programs the smaller the share of revenue required to make them more profitable to a station.[3]

2. The algebraic relationship that must hold among the various factors in order to make it more profitable to carry the network program is developed in Appendix B, which provides a complete mathematical statement of the relationships among networks, affiliates, and program suppliers discussed in this and the following section. The reader who is not interested in a detailed exposition of the relationships among producers, networks, and stations can skip to the section, "FCC Policy and the Performance of Commercial Braodcasting," beginning on page 79. The intervening material provides support for the conclusions on the economic viability of a significant expansion in commercial UHF stations offered at the end of this chapter.

3. Minimization of the share of revenue given up to affiliates would require a different sharing proportion for each program, with the share declining as the popularity of the program increases. Such a structure would be costly to implement since the shares would have to be renegotiated with each affiliate every year as programs and their audiences changed. In addition, the full exercise of network monopoly power implied by such

The basis of network control over the share of revenues affiliates take is the superior audience appeal of its programming. Using its economic advantage, a network can offer a program owner more favorable terms than, acting independently, he could obtain from stations. Networks thus acquire, and offer to affiliates, programming more appealing than that available from nonnetwork sources, and do so at prices that afford them a profit representing the value of the scale economies and of their market power. But a potential for profits beyond this amount exists and its magnitude can be influenced by the terms on which networks compensate affiliates for clearing network programs.

During most regularly scheduled network entertainment programs, three minutes per half hour are set aside for network commercial messages; movies have four network commercial minutes per half hour. Network program schedules also allow for varying amounts of additional time at the hour and at the half hour during which local stations identify themselves and broadcast commercials for local, regional, and national advertisers. In the 1968–69 season the net result of these practices was an average of 3.8 minutes of commercials for each half-hour segment of prime-time network television, 83.7 percent of which was allotted to the networks and the balance to affiliates.[4] Thus, one way in which a network compensates its affiliates is by allowing them to share in potential advertising revenue through the commercial time it makes available to them within and adjacent to its programs. Assuming affiliates sell all of the time made available and that they receive the same aggregate revenue per viewer per commercial minute as the network, the value of the commercial time to them is equal to 16.3 percent of the total revenue from a network broadcast.

Affiliates also receive compensation directly from the networks. The terms vary somewhat among the networks and among the affiliates but the basic agreement contains two provisions. First, no compensation is paid on the first 21 to 24 hours of prime-time programs carried each month. Second, for each network commercial minute carried beyond the

---

behavior would be likely to incur regulatory wrath. These considerations suggest the prudence of a simpler, though perhaps less efficient, structure of sharing ratios that, for many programs, will make the actual ratio exceed the minimum required.

4. Figures in this paragraph are based on (1) data on network-affiliate commercial time in *Broadcasting*, Vol. 77 (November 24, 1969), p. 70, and Vol. 77 (December 29, 1969), p. 47; (2) assumptions that all three networks allot essentially the same commercial time per half-hour to affiliates and that 2 seconds per commercial is for station identification and technical requirements; and (3) the 1968–69 network schedule shown in *Television Magazine*, Vol. 25 (August 1968).

minimum number of program hours, the network agrees to pay each station approximately 30 percent of its so-called station rate.[5] Station rates were formerly used as the basis for computing charges for network time to national advertisers for the programs they sponsored. However, with the shift from sponsorship of whole programs to purchase of commercial minutes within programs supplied by the networks, the station rates have come to be used almost exclusively as a basis for determining network compensation to affiliates.[6] The station rates are negotiated between each affiliate and its network, and a network's charge to a national advertiser for a commercial minute differs substantially from the sum of the station rates of the affiliates over which the commercial message is broadcast.

In practice network compensation in the years 1965 through 1969 averaged 20.3 percent of total network revenue.[7] Since an affiliate carrying the full network schedule received no compensation for approximately 21 percent of network programs carried, it would require compensation at an effective rate of very nearly 26 percent of network revenues on those hours for which compensation was paid to produce an overall average share of 20.3 percent. Since affiliates were granted 16.3 percent of advertising time during all network programs, an affiliate carrying the full network line-up received 16.3 percent of potential broadcast revenue during 21 percent of the network hours, and 42 percent on the balance, for an average share of approximately 36 percent.

In response to an increase in AT&T rates for network interconnection, the terms on which affiliates participate in potential program revenues were changed by CBS and NBC early in 1970 and by ABC later that year. Again, there were variations among networks, but the basic adjustment consisted

5. For a discussion of the structure of national time rates, see John L. Peterman, "The Structure of National Time Rates in the Television Broadcasting Industry," *Journal of Law and Economics*, Vol. 8 (October 1965), pp. 77–131. The basic contractual arrangements and variations are presented in *Monopoly Problems in Regulated Industries*, Pt. 2, *Television*, Hearings before the Antitrust Subcommittee of the House Committee on the Judiciary, 84 Cong. 2 sess. (1957), Vols. 3 and 4, pp. 4781–83, 5786–883, and 6356–433. Industry sources report little change in the nature of affiliation agreements since the mid-1950s except as noted in the following paragraph.

6. The changes in network selling and pricing practices leading to the limited role of station rates are described in David M. Blank, "Television Advertising: The Great Discount Illusion, or Tonypandy Revisited," *Journal of Business*, Vol. 41 (January 1968), pp. 10–38, especially pp. 20–22.

7. The affiliates' share in network advertising revenue in these years ranged from a high of 23.2 in 1965 to a low of 19.2 in 1969. Figures are based on data in the FCC annual reports and represent network compensation including payments to owned and operated stations as a percent of network advertising revenue less commissions to agencies.

of a 6.5 percent reduction in direct compensation coupled with a roughly 10 percent increase in the amount of time within the network schedule made available to affiliates for their own commercials.[8] Since there was no compensating reduction in network commercial time, the changes increased the supply of commercial minutes and therefore potential broadcast revenue. Despite the changes, the average share of affiliates in potential broadcast revenues remained very close to 36 percent.

Network-Program Producer Relations

Just as the need to induce stations to carry network programs establishes the share of revenue that the network must pay them, so the share required to induce program producers to sell their products to the network governs payments to them.[9] The network then stands in the middle between two groups—the program owners and the stations—and must make payments to each determined by their nonnetwork alternatives. Obviously, the magnitude of the two payments interact; specifically, the larger the share of revenue networks give up to affiliates the smaller the share program owners will be able to extract. This follows because the bargaining power of program owners is limited by the attractiveness of nonnetwork alternatives.[10] The higher the share affiliates have in revenue from network programs, the higher the share a program owner must allow them to retain in order to dislodge the network offerings.

The program owner's disadvantage in dealing with the network is wors-

8. See *Broadcasting*, Vol. 77 (November 24, 1969), pp. 70, 72, and Vol. 77 (December 29, 1969), pp. 47–48.

9. If the owner of a program were to withdraw it from the network line-up, the network would replace it with another, probably less popular, program. Affiliates would continue to clear all of the other network programs but would also clear the replacement unless the withdrawn program was offered to them by syndicators at fees low enough to make it the more profitable of the two. The full implications of this relationship are developed in Appendix B.

10. Even though networks usually acquire exclusive rights to purchase programs for terms of five years, they still have strong incentives to put checks on the bargaining power of producers of established programs. One reason is that it is the most popular programs that will come up for renegotiation at the end of the original five-year contract. Another is that the practice of using five-year contracts with built-in escalations for each time the program is renewed probably survives only because the rewards it produces are, for most shows, reasonable approximations of what annual renegotiation would produce net of its higher transaction costs. The instances when networks have been found to renegotiate contracts prior to expiration because stars in hit programs refused to work on the terms originally accepted provide some indication that standard contracts persist only because they are an acceptable substitute for annual renegotiation in most cases.

ened by the arrangements through which affiliates are compensated. Any program that an owner withdrew from the network would have to compete with the less attractive network offerings that an affiliate screens beyond the minimum it carries without compensation, for these are the ones it would be most willing to drop. But the network fixes a relatively high share of revenues for the affiliates to induce them to show these programs, thereby discouraging them from dealing with program owners. For the network, this share is not too expensive, on balance, for its total payments to affiliates are held to the level it considers necessary to induce them to carry the schedule it deems desirable by the requirement to carry a certain minimum number of hours without any compensation at all.

The upper limit on the affiliate share for the least popular network programs that is useful to the networks in dealing with producers is governed by the true (that is, rent-free) resource costs of production. This is the bare minimum a network must be willing to pay program producers, so they cannot set the affiliates' share so high that this minimum cannot be met.

The uncertainties surrounding program production further restrain networks in limiting the bargaining power of program owners. The size of the audience that any individual program will attract cannot be predicted exactly. One device for dealing with this uncertainty is the series, in which the cast of characters and general themes are relatively constant from episode to episode. Another device is the "pilot"—a single trial show—on which the network can judge the potential audience and base its decision. Another technique for reducing uncertainty in recent years has been the "made-for-TV" movie as a vehicle for testing a series idea. Still a fourth is the practice of ordering only a limited number of episodes of a new series.[11] These devices facilitate sequential decision making, which reduces the risk of failure, since the audiences attracted by each set of episodes provide information to decide whether to produce more.

A producer of a potential network series usually must first produce the pilot, financed partly with his own or borrowed money and partly by the network. Thus he bears considerable uncertainty both at the outset and even after acceptance, because the size of audience and length of the network run remain unknown. In the presence of these uncertainties, the producer's decision to invest in a pilot rests on an estimate of the expected return. While every producer thinks of his program as unique, he—or his

11. Normally only twelve or thirteen episodes are purchased at a time. The decision to continue a series after these episodes are broadcast is based on the audience rating of the program in its first few weeks.

financial backers—recognizes the historical rates of return for established programs. Producers are unlikely to invest in new pilots if experience indicates that the expected returns are too small to justify their costs. Since networks are interested in promoting new pilots, they must also consider how the terms on which they deal with the producers of current programs may affect the future supply of pilots and hence of new series. Even if the advertising revenues substantially reduce the risk to producers and networks of investing in a pilot, they do not eliminate it, since the series can still fail and be canceled after its first set of episodes is broadcast.

All of the uncertainties surrounding program success present a very difficult bargaining problem for the networks and the program producers. In Appendix B the theory of this bargaining relationship is analyzed and its outcome in practice is estimated. The results of that analysis bear, first, on the form of the bargain. Networks have an incentive to bargain for a share of the off-network syndication rights (the revenue from reruns and runs abroad) at the time they accept a program. Taking such a share, they can profit from successful programs, yet not jeopardize the supply of new programs by too hard a bargain at the early stages. By negotiating a share in syndication profits at the outset, when their bargaining power is greatest, the networks hedge against the bargaining power owners accumulate with a program's success.

The data in Table 3-1 illustrate the outcome of this bargaining process and allow an estimate of the extent to which payments to program producers exceed the real resource costs they incur. The data and estimation procedures used to construct the table are described in detail in Appendix B. The table is constructed on the assumption that an expected after-tax rate of return of 12 percent would make investment in pilots competitive with alternative opportunities.[12] The rate is slightly more than the average return on stockholders' equity in manufacturing corporations over the period studied. Since this is an expected return, the computation recognizes the probabilities that some programs will not recoup their investment. Although it might be argued that television production is more risky than

---

12. The estimates also assume that pilot production costs are financed by the producer. In recent years it has been common for the networks to underwrite some or all of the pilot costs. To the extent pilot production costs are underwritten by a network, even the minimum required shares of broadcast revenue shown in Table 3-1 overstate the actual minimum required shares. The shares shown in Table 3-1 are nevertheless of interest since, as noted below, they show that actual shares have been more than sufficient to offer an attractive investment alternative even in the absence of the added attraction of network financing of the pilot costs.

Table 3-1. Networks' Share in Syndicated Profits and Required and Actual Average Shares of Program Producers in Total Broadcast Income, 1960–68

Year	Average network share in syndication profits	Minimum required by producers with networks sharing in syndication profits[a]	Producers' average actual share	Minimum required if networks' share of syndication profits were zero[a]
1960	0.284	0.331	0.316	0.326
1961	0.272	0.321	0.336	0.314
1962	0.249	0.317	0.351	0.310
1963	0.222	0.300	0.353	0.292
1964	0.221	0.318	0.350	0.308
1965	0.251	0.320	0.362	0.306
1966	0.252	0.328	0.398	0.311
1967	0.231	0.327	0.438	0.308
1968	0.224	0.364	0.406	0.342

Source: See Appendix Table B-1, and accompanying source notes.
a. Assumes 12 percent after-tax rate of return.

other activities, the gap between actual returns and the benchmark of 12 percent is so large that adding a substantial risk premium would not change the central conclusion.

The first column of Table 3-1 shows the average share in syndication profits that networks have obtained in the programs purchased during the 1960s. The second column presents estimates of the minimum share of revenue networks would have had to give up in order to insure program owners an expected 12 percent after-tax rate of return on pilots, given the network shares in syndication profits shown in column one, while the third column shows the average share of revenues actually given up. The last column presents estimates of the share that networks would have had to give up to guarantee an expected after-tax rate of return of 12 percent if they had not obtained shares in syndication profits.

The table shows that, on the average, the networks have not completely suppressed the bargaining power of program owners even though they have obtained shares in profits from off-network syndication. Over the entire period the share of revenue paid out for the typical program has exceeded the minimum required by more than 4 percentage points. Prior to 1966, the excess share averaged about 3 percentage points, compared with 7 during 1966–68. This means that from 7 to 17 percent of the amount actually paid for regular series entertainment programming represents *rents* extracted by program owners—payments in excess of those necessary to cover the cost of resources devoted to program production.

Appendix B reports estimates of the rents paid to program owners relative to the potential rent, given the program's rating, for network programs in the 1967–68 season. On average, program owners were able to extract slightly more than one-half of the rents generated by programs, although the variation among programs was great.

In summary, the networks have been able to bargain rather effectively in procuring entertainment series. Nevertheless, a considerable proportion of the payments they make to program owners—approaching 20 percent of the total in recent years—is rent. As a result, the expected rate of return to investment in television pilots has been substantially greater than that available in other sectors of the economy.

Sources and Costs of Nonseries Network Programming

Movies are the primary alternative to entertainment series during prime time. Prime time devoted to movies rose from two hours per week in 1961 to eighteen hours per week in 1971–72. Furthermore, movies have consistently drawn better than average audiences. The average rating in the 1972–73 season was 21–22 percent of television homes.[13] The standard alternative is more new series with expected ratings of 16.2—the rating for new shows of the 1968–69 season[14]—so the maximum share of broadcast revenue that owners of movies could extract from the networks is 0.453.[15] Since 1967–68 the share of expected revenues that networks have pledged to movie owners has averaged 0.405, relatively close to the estimated maximum.[16]

13. Data on the time devoted to movies are from Arthur D. Little, Inc., *Television Program Production, Procurement, Distribution and Scheduling* (ADL, 1969), p. 16 (henceforth referred to as *Television Program Production*), and *Broadcasting*, Vol. 80 (April 5, 1971), pp. 32–33. Data on ratings of movies are from *Broadcasting*, Vol. 84 (January 15, 1973), p. 42. Ratings of other programs are given in various issues of *Television Magazine*.

14. A. C. Nielsen Company, *The Television Audience/1969* (Chicago: Nielsen, 1969), p. 61.

15. The maximum share is determined by three factors: (1) the audience of movies relative to new series; (2) the affiliate's share in broadcast income at the margin; and (3) the commissions charged by distributors of syndicated programming. The exact relationship between the maximum share program owners can extract from the network and the foregoing determinants is developed in Appendix B.

16. The average share varied from 0.381 in 1967–68 to 0.410 in 1971–72. The shares were computed by dividing the price per movie (usually $750,000) by the estimated expected revenue per movie. The latter was calculated from the prices per minute asked by the networks, and assumes that each movie is shown twice.

Sports are a major alternative to series outside of prime time.[17] Of the television sports, professional football has been the most important, with the three networks paying a total of $47.0 million for professional football broadcast rights for the 1971 season.[18]

According to the prices they asked, ABC agreed to pay 38.8 percent of total expected broadcast income for rights to prime-time football games and CBS 37.3 percent for its nonprime-time games. These payments compare with estimated maximum extractable shares of 41 percent and 48 percent, respectively.[19]

Football and movies receive an actual share of broadcast income that is closer to the estimated maximum than that accorded regular series. Since *all* of the income from broadcast rights is rent in both cases, these figures indicate that the bargaining power of movie owners and the football leagues vis-à-vis the networks is much stronger than that of the typical producer of a network entertainment series. This conclusion is not surprising since both sports and movies could find ready outlets through syndication or the sale of local broadcast rights. In procuring programming that has viable, well-established alternatives to network broadcasting, networks have limited bargaining power beyond their ability to economize on distribution costs, and normally will pay fees for broadcast rights that are close to the maximum that could be extracted. Furthermore, both sports and motion pictures are concentrated industries, whose own market power reduces that of the networks.

The remaining types of programming are entertainment specials, the majority of which are produced by the same firms that make series, and news and public affairs programming, which are produced predominantly by networks.[20] For most of these, syndication is not a feasible alternative to

17. Until ABC introduced football into prime time in the 1970–71 season, relatively little of it was devoted to sports. For example from September 1, 1964, to August 31, 1965, only 25 hours of prime-time programming were devoted to sports. This number had risen to 95 hours in 1967–68. See *Television Program Production*, Table 5, p. 14.

18. *Broadcasting*, Vol. 81 (July 19, 1971), p. 36. These figures do not include amounts paid by the networks for announcers and other personnel and resources devoted to football broadcasts.

19. The maximum shares have been calculated assuming that the ABC football games obtained an average rating of 18.5 compared with an average 16.3 for new prime-time series. The calculation for CBS uses an average National Football League rating of 15.9 and an average CBS rating of 9.7 for programs between noon and 6 P.M.

20. In 1967–68, 55.9 percent of entertainment specials were licensed from packagers and 31 percent were supplied by advertisers. See *Television Program Production*, p. 15.

network exhibition, so that other considerations determine the fees paid for them.

Entertainment specials are usually built around one or more well-known show business personalities who command high fees outside of television, and demand like rewards to appear on television. Wanting to capitalize on the very large audiences—much above the average for series—that these few superstars attract, networks are apt to pay suppliers of these specials a share of broadcast revenue that closely approaches the maximum.

News and public affairs, as well as educational and cultural specials, typically draw audiences below the average for entertainment series. Thus they are unprofitable to networks unless their producers accept below-average shares of broadcast revenue. The probable outcome of this process is an effort to limit production costs so that net revenue to the network for such programs is not lower than average. Even though the attempts are probably not always successful, the networks do not necessarily suffer an out-of-pocket loss on such broadcasts. Nevertheless, their net revenues are lower than they would have been if a typical episode in an entertainment series had been broadcast.

The foregoing considerations suggest that neither entertainment specials, news, nor public affairs specials are profitable, and thus probably explain the relatively small amount of time devoted to them. In 1967–68, for example, entertainment specials accounted for 6.8 percent of total network broadcasting between 6 and 11 P.M., while news and public affairs specials accounted for 11.8 percent.[21]

Sources and Costs of Nonnetwork Programming

Feature films and reruns of old television series account for more than half of the programming by independent stations, as well as by network affiliates when they are not carrying network-originated programming. These two types of programming do not involve the consumption of additional resources except those used in distributing and broadcasting, yet revenues from them must more than cover these additional costs. For either type, a minimum fee, or residual, amounting to a fixed percent of base salaries paid to the performers during the original production, is due them upon release of a television program for a second showing and of a movie for its first television showing. The minimum residual fee for a series previ-

21. See *Television Program Production*, Table 5, p. 14.

ously shown twice on network television is 30 percent of the base salaries.[22] Moreover, this payment is due as soon as the series is shown anywhere in the country, even though the rerun has not yet appeared everywhere. Feature movies are subject to almost the same residual provisions, except that the fee is determined by the total revenue earned through syndication sales rather than by the number of nonnetwork showings.

As a result of these residual provisions, the owners of a program or film will not release it for nonnetwork exhibition unless they expect to be able to recover both the residual fees and the costs of distribution. Once an owner has made the release, he should be willing to sell broadcast rights to any station that will cover distribution costs at least. But over the long run earnings from syndication must cover residuals as well, and the supply of off-network series and syndicated feature films will adjust to ensure that they do so.

The remaining nonnetwork programming consists largely of series originally produced for nonnetwork television, generally referred to as first-run syndications, and programming produced by local stations. As additions to the stock of available programming, both involve the consumption of additional resources, and hence are generally more costly per unit of broadcast time than feature films and network reruns.[23]

Market Structure and Prices for Syndicated Programming

The effects of market structure on the quantity and prices of syndicated programming can be conveniently analyzed in the simplified situations portrayed in the panels of Figure 3-1. In both cases a single station has a total available broadcast time of $\bar{h}$ half-hours and a single type of programming—perhaps network reruns—is available. The marginal cost to syndicators of this programming, consisting of residual fees and distribution

22. For schedules of minimum residual fees for reruns of television programs, see Herman W. Land Associates, *Television and the Wired City: A Study of the Implications of a Change in the Mode of Transmission* (Washington: National Association of Broadcasters, 1968), pp. 102–06.

23. In addition to the sources of programming mentioned in the text, government agencies and various public service organizations provide some programming free of charge to local stations. Some advertisers now offer programming comparable with first-run syndications to stations on a quasi-free basis. The programs cost nothing, for the advertisers pay for production and distribution; but they insert their own messages in one-half of the commercial time per half-hour, leaving one-half to the station. In effect, stations receive one-half the potential broadcast revenue for these programs, which exceeds the share normally offered by networks.

Figure 3-1. Illustrative Division of Broadcast Revenue[a]

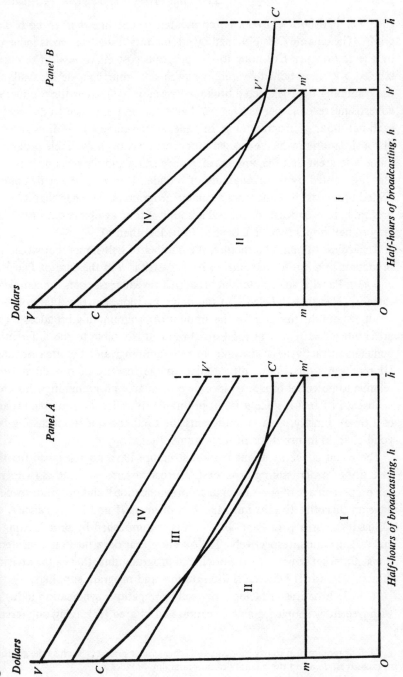

a. I = residual fees and distribution costs; II = rents attributable to differential audience size; III = rents attributable to scarcity of broadcast time; IV = costs of broadcasting other than program costs.

costs per half-hour episode, is represented by the line mm' in both diagrams. The curve CC' is obtained by adding total broadcast costs incurred by the station per half-hour to the program cost curve mm'. The curve labeled VV' is obtained by ranking each half-hour episode of available programming by its expected broadcast revenue, defined as the product of advertising revenue per viewer per half-hour and expected audience for each half-hour of programming. In Panel A, the curve VV' is drawn to depict a situation in which expected broadcast revenue of available programming is so great that the amount of broadcasting and the revenue it generates are limited by the availability of broadcast time. In Panel B, the expected broadcast revenue from available programming is such that it is not profitable to broadcast for the full amount of time available but rather for only h' half-hours (which is defined to be less than $\bar{h}$).

Regardless of market structure, the number of half-hours that would be broadcast by a profit-maximizing broadcaster is $\bar{h}$ in the case of Panel A and h' in Panel B since potential broadcast revenue less costs is maximized thereby. The areas labeled I in the diagrams represent the total cost for residuals and distribution for the amount of programming broadcast. The areas labeled II represent total quasi-rents attributable to the differential audience attractiveness of available programming, and the area denoted III represents quasi-rents attributable to the scarcity of broadcast time relative to potential broadcast income of available programming (this area is absent in Panel B since it is not profitable to utilize all available broadcast time). Finally, area IV represents the total costs of braodcasting beyond charges incurred for programming.

The usual concerns about market structure have no relevance for the quantity of programming broadcast.[24] Broadcasters, syndicators (who receive a percentage of gross revenue from syndication), and program owners have an incentive to maximize the sum of areas II and III in Panel A or to maximize area II in Panel B, which is accomplished by broadcasting $\bar{h}$ and h' half-hours, respectively. The question that does turn on considerations of market structure is the pricing of programming, that is, the division of areas II and III between station owners and program suppliers.

A single broadcaster facing a perfectly competitive syndication industry with free entry should be able to capture all of area II, leaving only area I

24. The requirement to pay residuals and other similar practices, such as the granting of exclusives, do affect the quantity of programming broadcast.

for syndicators and program owners, by paying a price equal to residual charges plus distribution costs for every half-hour episode regardless of its potential broadcast revenue. Of a single broadcaster facing a monopolist in syndicated programming, little can be said about the likely outcome.

Cases involving a large number of competing broadcasters (providing together the same total number of half-hours, $\bar{h}$) can be analyzed within the framework of Figure 3-1 by ignoring the cost curve CC' and taking a horizontal straight line through the point C' as the long-run average cost of broadcasting when programming is priced at its marginal cost. If the syndication industry were a monopoly, all of areas II and III would be captured by the syndicator and program owners. On the other hand, if both syndication and broadcasting were competitive, area II would probably be captured by syndicators and program owners and area III by broadcasters; in a regime of unrestricted entry into broadcasting, however, $\bar{h}$ would increase, area III would eventually disappear, and the other areas would expand. In any event, in the overall competitive regime, prices for programs per half-hour episode would not all be the same but would adjust to reflect their relative audience attractiveness.

Even though the actual markets in which broadcasters and syndicators meet are more complex than the simple situation analyzed here, the existence of program types with differing costs and audience potentials, for example, could be easily incorporated into the analysis. The only additional insight that this elaboration would yield is that in equilibrium broadcasters would purchase and broadcast the mixture of program types that equates the profit earned on the last unit of each. But here, too, market structure would affect neither the total amount of broadcasting nor its composition, although it would influence the price structure and division of rents.

Another complication arises from the existence of many geographical markets. The degree of competition may differ among markets and the costs attributable to royalty fees as well as some of the syndicators' operating costs are not allocable to individual markets. At the margin a syndicator would be willing to sell programming so long as the price covered the costs directly attributable to providing it in a given market. In addition, the potential broadcast income of a series varies from market to market with the number of television homes and the number of stations. As a result of both these phenomena—differing market size and nonallocable costs—the price of a given program will vary from market to market and generally will be greater the larger the market.

Table 3-2. Concentration in the Domestic Television Syndication Market, 1964 and 1967

Percent of domestic sales

	TV series		Feature films		Total	
Type of distributor	1964	1967	1964	1967	1964	1967
Largest distributors[a]	45.0	46.4	79.6	90.1	67.7	69.7
Next largest distributors[b]	21.8	21.4	3.9	1.6	10.1	10.8
Network company	7.0	8.3	...	...	2.4	3.9
Network company	6.8	7.2	...	...	2.3	3.4
Network company	5.5	2.6	...	...	1.9	1.2
Other	14.0	14.1	16.4	8.2	15.6	11.0
Total	100.0	100.0	100.0	100.0	100.0	100.0
Total number of distributors	36	55	n.a.	n.a.	n.a.	n.a.

Source: Computed from Arthur D. Little, Inc., *Television Program Production, Procurement, Distribution and Scheduling* (ADL, 1969), pp. 103, 106, 113, 114. Figures are rounded and may not add to totals.
a. Six in 1964, seven in 1967.
b. Three in 1964, four in 1967.
n.a. Not available.

Market Structure in the Domestic Syndication Industry

Both broadcasting and program syndication are structurally oligopolistic, but broadcasting is more so. All of the one hundred largest television audience markets, which account for 87 percent of television homes, have three-network service although in six of these areas one of the affiliates is in a nearby city. Two-thirds of the top one hundred markets have three VHF affiliates. Fifteen of these markets have at least one VHF independent, while Seattle-Tacoma has two, New York three, and Los Angeles four; twenty-three other markets in the top one hundred have one or more UHF independents. Outside these top markets, thirty-one have three network affiliates, thirty-three have two, and forty-three have only one. There are only three independent stations in all of these smaller markets.[25] Competition is therefore quite limited. The small number of potential purchasers of programming and the concentration of network affiliates among them tend to tip the balance of market power in favor of broadcasters.

By comparison with broadcasting, syndication appears to have a relatively competitive structure. Table 3-2 presents data on concentration based on domestic sales of series, both off-network and first run, and of feature

25. Broadcasting Publications, Inc., *1972 Broadcasting Yearbook* (Washington: BP, 1972), pp. 12–39.

movies for 1964 and 1967. Concentration appears low, at least by standards of manufacturing industry. The general picture is one of a limited number of distributors accounting for roughly equal shares of 85 percent of the market for TV series syndication in the range of 3 to 8 percent each and a number of very small distributors on the fringe. While these companies together accounted for about 86 percent of total series sales in both years, they accounted for only one-half of new first-run and off-network series introduced from 1957 through 1968, which suggests that they managed to acquire distribution rights to the more attractive programming.[26] Syndication sales of feature movies are decidedly more concentrated, with the seven largest distributors accounting for 80–90 percent of total sales, most of which is attributable to four or five distributors.[27]

Pricing and the Division of Rents

While data on prices paid for syndicated programming are scant, those available suggest, as did the examination of market structure, that the balance of market power probably rests with stations.

In 1968, the average price per half-hour episode was $3.50 per thousand viewing homes for off-network series reruns and $3.75 per thousand for first-run syndicated series. The prices were subject to considerable variation, ranging from less than $1.50 to more than $10.00 for first-run series and from less than $1.00 to more than $10.00 for off-network series. Slightly more than 55 percent of off-network series, and slightly more than 60 percent of first-run series, sold at prices per thousand within 50 percent of their respective means. These figures suggest that, on average, syndication revenues for series amounted to 30 percent of the broadcast revenue they generated.[28]

The absence of information on distribution and production costs for first-run syndications makes it difficult to estimate the extent to which this

26. The share of new titles accounted for by these distributors was calculated from *Television Program Production*, Table 44, pp. 96–107.

27. *Television Magazine*, Vol. 24 (September 1967), pp. 76–86, and Vol. 25 (June 1968), pp. 42–47.

28. Average prices per thousand per half-hour were calculated from *Television Program Production*, p. 122. The estimate of average share of syndicators in broadcast income from these series is based on estimated broadcast revenue of roughly $13.50 per thousand viewing homes. This figure, in turn, derives from average network revenue per half-hour episode per thousand homes of $10.00 in prime time adjusted for the fact that, on average, network gross revenue accounts for 83.7 percent of the total revenue from a program (see text, p. 61).

estimated 30 percent of broadcast revenue exceeds the share required to cover costs. However, for network reruns at least, there are two ways in which an upper bound may be estimated.

All network reruns in syndication in the 1968 season would have been produced at least two years previously, so their average cost per episode would have been no more than $65,500 per half-hour. Assuming payments to performers amount, on average, to 15 percent of total costs and applying the minimum 30 percent residual charge to this basis, residual fees per half-hour episode are slightly less than $3,000.[29] At an effective price of $3.50 per thousand viewing homes, an off-network series must then be viewed by 1 million homes to generate broadcast revenue equal to residual fees. Since such programming probably draws at least 5 percent of the television homes in the market areas in which it is broadcast during prime time on a VHF station, it would generate sufficient revenue to cover residuals if it were broadcast in markets encompassing no more than 20 million TV homes, or 33 percent of the total. If it is assumed that the typical program will, eventually, receive a showing in every market—surely an optimistic estimate—it would draw three times the viewers necessary to cover residuals. This suggests that payments in excess of residuals would amount to two-thirds of the 30 percent of broadcast revenue that such a series generated, or 20 percent of total broadcast revenue, ignoring distribution costs.

An alternative estimate can be derived from data on network revenue arising from the profits of syndicated network reruns.[30] In 1967 these revenues amounted to $4.3 million. Since the network share during the sixties averaged about 25 percent, total profits (foreign and domestic) from syndication of network reruns can be put at roughly $17 million in 1967, which is 17 percent of total sales. Sales to domestic stations in that year amounted to $43 million, so profits from domestic syndication shared by networks and program producers may be placed at $7.3 million. In addition, distributors' commissions amounted on average to 38.3 percent of gross revenue, or $16.5 million. The total of $23.8 million earned by program owners and syndicators is in excess of residuals and some distribution costs such as

29. The estimate of actors' salaries as a percent of total costs is based on data appearing in John A. Dimling, Jr., and others, *Identification and Analysis of the Alternatives for Achieving Greater Television Program Diversity in the United States*, Prepared for the President's Task Force on Communications Policy (Lexington, Ky.: Spindletop Research, 1968), Appendix F, p. F-3.

30. Data on average network shares and on domestic syndication revenues used in the calculations in this chapter are taken from *Television Program Production*, Table 19, p. 49, and Table 47, p. 114.

those for prints and shipping. Thus, their combined share in total syndication revenues can be estimated at over 55 percent. Based on the earlier estimate that total syndication revenues amount to 30 percent of broadcast revenue for network reruns, this estimate suggests that 17 percent of the broadcast revenue generated by syndications of network reruns is captured by syndicators and program owners.

Thus, the rents that program owners and syndicators can extract for syndicated network reruns account for 17 to 20 percent of the broadcast revenue they generate, while 10 to 13 percent covers residuals and distribution costs.

As noted earlier, payments for first-run syndications also appear to be approximately 30 percent of the broadcast revenue they generate. First-run syndications probably incur the same distribution costs and pay no residuals, but must, over the long run, cover production costs. This suggests that, in the existing regime, few first-run syndicated programs do more than meet their production and distribution costs, a suggestion that appears to be borne out by industry behavior during the 1960s. The number of first-run syndicated programs introduced each year and the number of equivalent half-hours of such programming increased quite steadily during the period, yet of all the series introduced, only 13 percent were produced for more than one season and less than 3 percent for more than two.[31]

The record of movies as audience attractions and the relatively few competitors in the movie distribution industry suggest that they would earn greater profits than off-network syndications do. No data on prices paid by local stations for movies are available with which to determine directly the share of broadcast revenue that owners and syndicators of movies claim. More roundabout procedures indicate that movie owners receive only a slightly larger share of broadcast revenue than do owners of off-network series; however, because old movies have lower residuals and larger audiences, their owners probably earn much higher profits.

In 1967 the average local station devoted 94 percent as much of its broadcast time to movies as it did to off-network and first-run syndications.[32] On average, movies broadcast on networks in the 1966–67 season in prime time drew audiences 15 percent larger than the average for entertainment series. Taken together these factors indicate that the broadcast revenue gen-

31. Derived from *Television Program Production*, Table 35, p. 76.
32. See Broadcasting Publications, Inc., *1969 Broadcasting Yearbook* (BP, 1969), p. D-61. Time devoted to syndicated programming was taken to be hours of syndicated videotape programming plus hours of nonnetwork film made especially for television.

erated by movies shown on local stations is 1.08 (= 0.94 × 1.15) times the broadcast revenue generated by off-network and first-run syndicated series. If movie distributors extract the same 30 percent share of broadcast revenue as series do, total expenditures by stations for movie exhibition rights would be 11 percent greater than their expenditures for series. In fact, in 1967, expenditures for movies were almost 15 percent greater than those for series.[33] This suggests that owners of movies may on average obtain between 31 and 32 percent of the broadcast revenue they generate, or one to two percentage points more than other syndications.

Overall, syndicated program types do not appear to differ according to share of broadcast revenue, and as a result the prices paid per episode per viewer tend to be equal for the three types. Yet, markets differ in the shares of broadcast revenue extracted by syndicated programming and hence the prices paid per episode. The theoretical discussion above suggests that the price per episode of a syndicated program in any market might be given by

$$P_j = D + \lambda(va_j - D),$$

where

P_j = price per episode
D = cost of distributing a series to any station
λ = syndicator's share in program quasi-rents
v = broadcast revenue per half-hour per thousand viewing homes
a_j = thousands of homes expected to view the series in the market ($\bar{a}$ is the mean).

If a_j is a function of total TV homes in the market, H_j, expected audience may be written as

$$a_j = (\bar{a} + u_j)H_j,$$

where u_j is a random error term with zero mean and constant variance.

Combining these two equations gives

$$P_j = (1 - \lambda)D + \lambda v\bar{a}H_j + \lambda vH_ju_j.$$

In this form the equation is not suitable for estimation by ordinary least squares because the error term vH_ju_j does not have constant variance. This, however, is easily rectified by dividing by H_j:

$$\frac{P_j}{H_j} = \frac{(1 - \lambda)D}{H_j} + \lambda v\bar{a} + w_j,$$

where w_j is a disturbance term with zero mean and constant variance. Table 3-3 presents estimates of the parameters of the last equation for off-network

33. See *Television Program Production*, Table 45, p. 109.

Table 3-3. Regression Estimates of the Relation of Prices Paid per Episode for Syndicated Programs to Market Size, and Implicit Estimates of λ and *D*

Type of program	Regression coefficients[a]		Syndicator's share[b] λ	Distribution cost[b] (dollars) *D*
	λv$\bar{a}$	*D(1 − λ)*		
30-minute first-run syndication	0.185 (0.024)	29.3 (1.84)	0.24–0.37	38–46
30-minute off-network	0.161 (0.016)	22.3 (1.22)	0.21–0.27	28–31
60-minute off-network	0.312 (0.028)	26.4 (2.18)	0.20–0.26	33–36

Source: Derived from equation on p. 78. Data are based on average prices for market group sizes in 1968, computed from *Television Program Production*, Table 48, pp. 115–16.

a. The R^2 in all cases is 0.935 or better but in interpreting that number it must be remembered that the observations are group means. In each case there are twelve such observations. The numbers in parentheses are standard errors.

b. To estimate the range of values taken by λ and *D*, $\bar{a}$ was assumed to be between 0.050 and 0.065.

and first-run syndications of various lengths based on average prices for market group sizes in 1968. The table also gives implied estimates of λ and *D* that have been derived by using extraneous estimates of *v* ($12.00 per thousand homes per half-hour) and $\bar{a}$ (5.0 to 6.5 percent of television homes in the station's area of dominant influence) reported above. These estimates indicate that, on average, programs cost stations at least $30 plus 20 to 30 percent of their expected broadcast revenue. As a result, stations in the smaller markets pay most of their broadcast revenue for programming, while those in the large markets give up only about a quarter of broadcast revenue for purchased programming. Assuming that a syndicated program captures 5 percent of the local potential audience and that a viewer home is worth 1¼ cents per half-hour in advertising revenues, a station in a market with 60,000 TV homes will pay roughly $45 for a program generating $60 in revenues. A station in a market with 1,000,000 TV homes will receive $600 in revenues for a program that costs approximately $180.

FCC Policy and the Performance of Commercial Broadcasting

Throughout the fifties and sixties the FCC recognized the desirability of expanding commercial broadcasting. To promote such expansion the commission relied exclusively on the development of UHF broadcasting with its special advantages over alternative means such as cable television: (1) It is the only technologically feasible means of increasing over-the-air viewing alternatives while preserving the concept of the local station—another policy objective, discussed in the next chapter; and (2) it preserves an advertiser-supported system that might be threatened by the alternatives. At the outset UHF presents problems in its inferior signal and its lack of attractive programming. Further, it may not be the best alternative if it would make a smaller contribution to diversity than the others. The following sections assess, first, the probable impact of full UHF development on diversity, and then its economic limits.

The Effect of UHF Development on Diversity

If all UHF and VHF commercial assignments operated, in effect doubling the supply of programs to viewers, the average audience size per program would be halved unless total viewing increased. If broadened options induced a rise in prime-time viewing from its present 60 percent to 90 percent of television homes, the average audience would be three-quarters its present size. Reducing audiences means reducing the opportunity cost of broadcast time, so that, to be broadcast, a program need not attract as large a minimum audience. An expanded system, then, would assuredly cater to smaller average audiences than the present system does. Yet even an expansion of the commercial system on the order envisioned here would beget only minor changes in the composition of programming, according to an examination of audience sizes for light entertainment versus more serious entertainment, news, and public affairs programming.

Full UHF development would give the typical television home choice among four to seven commercial channels. With the exception of a few large cities, it would at best raise viewing alternatives to the current number of VHF stations in Los Angeles and New York. During prime time the VHF independents in these cities draw average audiences of about 5 and 4 percent of television homes, respectively, with a range of 3 to 9 percent in the former and 2.5 to 6 percent in the latter.[34] Compared with network affiliates, which generally attract audiences of about 18 percent of television homes, these independent stations cater to minority audiences. Their most common programming is movies and syndications, most of which, even

34. American Research Bureau, *1968 Television Market Analysis* (New York: ARB, no date), pp. 17, 50.

when they are not reruns of network series, are so similar to network offerings that the greater viewing alternatives mean simply a longer menu of the standard network entertainment fare.

The characteristics of programming in the markets with the greatest number of viewing alternatives thus lay no foundation for the belief that full UHF development would significantly alter the composition of programming. Rather, any such expectation must be based on a belief that expansion will affect the economics of program production and supply in such a way as to encourage broadcasters to gratify minority tastes.

Full UHF development would call for considerably more original programming, either through syndication or through one or more new networks. But the bulk of it would be very similar to present network fare.

A fourth, and perhaps a fifth, network would be able to assemble a large number of conventional programs only slightly less attractive than those currently available. At present the average audience size for prime-time network shows is slightly greater than 18 percent of television homes, while the marginal audience—the minimum a program must attract to be retained in the schedule—is generally about 16 percent.[35] Data on replacements indicate that a large volume of programming can be produced that attracts only slightly smaller audiences than the marginal programs in the present system. Of the 40 percent of programs that are replaced each year, most are only slightly less popular than is necessary for survival: Fewer than 5 percent have audience ratings below 10, and almost all are between 11 and 15. If total prime-time viewing did not increase as the number of alternatives rose from three to four or five, and if the composition of programming remained unchanged, average prime-time audiences per program would fall to 10 to 14 percent of television homes, and the minimum acceptable audience would fall to 9 to 12 percent. Expansion on this order would, therefore, affect the composition of programming only to the extent that serious entertainment or nonentertainment programming could be viable even if it attracted only 9 percent of television homes.

In a catchall sample of sixteen network news and public affairs specials that had an average rating of 11 percent, two-thirds had ratings greater than 9 percent;[36] the more popular programs focused on events of fairly widespread current interest. Regularly scheduled programming with similar content attracts smaller audiences; CBS Reports, the CBS News Hour, and

35. Nielsen, *The Television Audience/1969*, contains the information in this paragraph.
36. Land Associates, *Television and the Wired City*, p. 127.

Bell Telephone Hour typically attracted only 7 to 10 percent of television homes,[37] and a sample of documentary programs shown on independent VHF stations in New York in prime time averaged less than 3 percent.[38] Finally, the average prime-time audiences of VHF public television stations in the ten largest cities are about 1 percent of television homes, covering a range from a low of 0.6 percent in Chicago to nearly 2 percent in Boston, San Francisco, Pittsburgh, and Miami. In New York—the only market in which a VHF public television station competes with approximately the same number of VHF commercial stations as might exist in an expanded system—the average prime-time audience of the public television station is about 1 percent of television homes.[39]

The bulk of the more serious programming would probably draw smaller audiences than the least popular of the original entertainment programs that might be broadcast in a system reflecting full UHF development. Indeed, much of the network's programming aimed at *minority* tastes seems unable to attract audiences any larger than the programs for *conventional* tastes offered by VHF independent stations.

Although expansion would bring some programs for special audiences close to the point of broadcast, their status would be marginal at best. News and public affairs specials might be broadcast somewhat more frequently than at present, and in a few very large markets with many channels and many potential viewers, so would serious entertainment and informational programming. But the conclusion that full UHF development would serve largely to broaden the range of choice among light entertainment programs is inescapable.

Such a conclusion does not in itself imply that the FCC's goal to expand advertiser-supported UHF broadcasting is an undesirable regulatory objective, for, as noted in Chapter 2, broadened choice within customary broadcast fare is greatly valued. But success in achieving this objective depends upon the economic feasibility of substantial UHF development.

The FCC has realized that the crux of economic feasibility for UHF is better programming for local stations, which, in turn, requires an expansion of the program production industry. The assumption that this expansion can be induced by raising the prospective profitability of program production underlies many of the commission's actions and proposals.

A leading example is the prime-time access rule, which (1) limits to three

37. *Television Magazine*, March issues for 1966–68.
38. Land Associates, *Television and the Wired City*, p. 128.
39. American Research Bureau, *1968 Television Market Analysis*, pp. 9, 53.

hours per night the programming that a local station in the fifty largest
markets can obtain from a national network; (2) prohibits networks from
acquiring shares in potential syndication and merchandising profits; and
(3) bars networks from acting as distributors of syndicated material other
than that which they have produced themselves.[40] The first provision aims
at expanding the demand for nonnetwork programming and thereby at
enhancing the expected profitability of first-run syndications. The second
tries to make producing for sale to networks more appealing by increasing the expected profits from off-network syndication. The third attempts
to overcome a presumed competitive advantage of the networks over nonnetwork distributors in selling syndicated material to network affiliates.

In addition to the prime-time access rule, the commission favors a policy
observing "program exclusivity" (the practice of a broadcast station to contract exclusive rights in its market through a network or through syndication) and requiring cable television systems to pay royalties on the programming of the over-the-air stations that they carry.[41] These positions reflect,
in part, a belief either that failure to observe exclusivity and pay royalties
would curtail the profitability and hence the supply of programming, or
that maintaining these practices will increase profitability and hence the
supply of programming.

The actual, as opposed to the presumed, effects of these policies on the
program production industry depend upon two factors: (1) the effect on
profitability, and (2) the response of supply to profitability.

Effect of Prime-time Access Rule on Production for Network Exhibition

Some industry observers argue that prohibiting networks from sharing
in syndication and merchandising revenues will have no effect on the
profitability of programming because the networks will negate the rule by
reducing the prices they pay for the network run. That argument overlooks
the fact that, despite their strong bargaining position, the networks have
been unable to hold the shares of broadcast income claimed by program
owners (so-called "packagers") to the minimal levels required to bring forth
an adequate supply of programs. The data presented in Table 3-1 indicate

40. See FCC, *Annual Report, Fiscal Year 1970*, pp. 38–39. The commission's concern
about network dominance of the industry, pointed out earlier, also finds expression in
the prime-time access rule.

41. *Federal Register*, Vol. 37 (February 12, 1972), Pt. 2, pp. 3260–61, 3267, especially
par. 104.

that the average share of broadcast income given by the networks to pack-agers in the late 1960s was roughly 7 percentage points greater than neces-sary to ensure an expected return that would approximate the real cost of resources employed in program production. This suggests that packagers' shares of broadcast income may not decline at all under the prime-time access rule, or at most will not decline enough to offset the larger shares of syndication revenue they will be able to retain.

Even if packagers' share of broadcast income remains unchanged as a result of the rule, the expected rate of return on investment in pilots for network series will not necessarily rise. The prime-time access rule effec-tively reduces the demand by networks for programming. This reduction should lower the probability that a pilot will be accepted, and thus expected profits. While it is possible that the profitability of program production for network exhibition will rise in the wake of the prime-time access rule, such a rise is by no means certain.

Even less predictable is the effect of any change in the expected after-tax rate of return on investment in pilots. Table 3-1 indicates that this return has persistently and significantly exceeded 12 percent, or indeed any bench-mark that was up to twice that.[42] In the logic of economic theory, if invest-ment in pilots were sensitive to expected return, the number produced should have risen until the probability of acceptance fell to the point where expected return was equal to returns in other industries. Failure of this adjustment to emerge suggests that further increases in the expected rate of return are unlikely to draw additional resources into the industry. The reasons are fairly clear.

Although pilot production is the stage at which the explicit investment of funds takes place, it is not the very beginning of the process of producing a series. Artistic and entrepreneurial activity aimed at developing the format of the series, securing tentative commitments from writers and actors, and convincing a network or another investor that the pilot would have a reasonable chance of procuring an order for the series, all precede its actual production. Persistence of above-average expected rates of return in program production reflects decisions not to proceed beyond the pre-pilot stage. These decisions, in turn, must betoken a scarcity of ideas and talent for developing more pilots that have a chance of becoming successful network series, given the limited number of programs the networks require.

---

42. Note that the 12 percent return is on the overall invéstment. To the extent that the owners can borrow part of the capital at less than 12 percent, the return will be higher.

To the extent the prime-time access rule has any effect on production for network exhibition, it will be to enable producers of accepted pilots to retain a larger share of broadcast revenue and to earn even larger profits.

Prime-time Access Rule and the Supply of Syndicated Programming

Two factors have limited the expected profitability of investment in first-run syndicated programming. First, the existence of the networks and the nature of their relationships with affiliates have generally restricted the market for first-run syndicated material in prime time to independent stations. As a result, a syndicated series that was shown in every market with a VHF independent would reach only 33 percent of TV homes in the country. Markets containing another 24 percent of TV homes could be covered by sales to UHF independents,[43] but limited UHF reception capability suggests inclusion of only one-half to three-quarters of the homes in these markets in the potential audience. Thus, the potential audience for syndicated programs has been restricted to less than half of the TV homes in the country. Second, first-run syndications have had to compete with off-network syndications and movies, which have been generally available at prices equivalent to about 30 percent of potential broadcast revenue (see the previous section).

Together these characteristics imply that the gross revenues in syndication of a program with a given expected audience rating might be less than one-third its potential on the network. Under these conditions, it can be profitable to invest only in first-run syndicated programs in which the cost per episode is substantially lower than that for network programming. (In turn, however, lower-cost production often leads to lower ratings.)

A statistical analysis of audiences attracted to syndicated programs shown in prime time indicated no significant difference in the share of television homes attracted to first-run and off-network syndications. In either case the typical audience for a showing on a VHF station was roughly one-third the share of television homes attracted to the typical network program.

The prime-time access rule modifies both of the factors underlying the conditions in the first-run syndication market just outlined. First, it expands the demand for nonnetwork programming by limiting the networks to three hours nightly in prime time. Second, after the first two seasons

43. Derived from American Research Bureau, *1968 Television Market Analysis*, pp. 9–14, 50–52, and *1971 Broadcasting Yearbook*, pp. 17–44.

under the rule, it requires affiliates to fill the time released by the networks with programming other than off-network syndications. These measures will undoubtedly stimulate demand and thus augment the supply of first-run syndicated programming. The important questions, however, are whether this increase will abet the development of UHF and how the change will affect the nature of programs offered by the networks and their affiliates.

The 10.5 hours of prime time per week by which total programming by all of the three networks must be reduced could be filled by half-hour weekly episodes of twenty-one series. Proponents of the rule obviously hope that competition among producers will lead to the production of substantially more programming than this minimum requirement. In the markets where a series is not sold to an affiliate, its producers will be willing to sell to VHF or UHF independents. In this way, if at all, the prime-time access rule will supposedly increase the supply of first-run programming to UHF stations in particular and independent stations in general.

The following analysis investigates the probable impact of the prime-time access rule. In the equation, the total number of weekly hours of first-run syndicated programming is $10.5N$ (N is the ratio of total weekly hours to 10.5, the minimum necessary for compliance with the prime-time access rule). If it is assumed that (1) a series is certain to be purchased by some station in markets with at least one independent station; and (2) a series has a $1/N$ chance of being purchased by an affiliate in markets without an independent station, the expected potential audience for any first-run syndication can be expressed as $[(N + 1)/2N]H_p$, where H_p is the total number of television homes in the country, since the total of television homes is about equally divided between the two types of markets. The producer's expected revenue per episode will be given by

$$R = \eta(1 + s)\alpha V\left(\frac{N + 1}{2N}\right)H_p,$$

where

V = broadcast revenue per viewer per half-hour

η = producer's share of broadcast revenue

α = share of potential audience that the series attracts on its first run

s = second-run audience as a fraction of first-run audience.

Since new series will be produced only if they are expected to produce revenues in excess of production costs, an upper bound on N is provided by setting R equal to C, production cost per episode.

Table 3-4. Estimates of Minimum Values of the Share of Potential
Audience for First-run Syndicated Programming, on Selected Assumptions

	First-run share of potential audience α			
Value of N[a]	$\eta^{b} = 0.3$ $C^{c} = \$25,000$	$\eta = 0.3$ $C = \$45,000$	$\eta = 0.5$ $C = \$25,000$	$\eta = 0.5$ $C = \$45,000$
1	0.064[d]	0.116[d]	0.039	0.070[d]
2	0.086	0.154[d]	0.051	0.093[d]
3	0.096	0.174	0.058	0.104[d]
4	0.103	0.185	0.062	0.111[d]
5	0.107	0.193	0.064	0.116[d]
∞	0.129	0.231	0.077	0.139

Source: Derived by authors from method described in the text.
a. N = ratio of total weekly hours of first-run syndicated programming to 10.5, the minimum hours required by the prime-time access rule (for example, a value of 2 for N signifies 21/10.5).
b. η = producer's share of broadcast income.
c. C = producer's cost.
d. These figures are probably the only possible outcomes, as explained in the text.

Table 3-4 presents estimates of the values of α, the first-run share of potential audience, consistent with various values of N under alternative
assumptions as to the value of η and C. The assumed alternative values of
η are 0.3 and 0.5, the lower representing the average share of broadcast
revenue now paid for first-run and off-network syndications and for syndicated movies and the higher the effective share of broadcast revenue stations
give up for syndicated programs supplied by advertisers. Of the values
assumed for costs per episode, the lower figure of $25,000 is the average
cost of half-hour episodes produced for noncommercial television stations,
which is probably somewhat below the average cost per episode of first-run
syndications in the years preceding the prime-time access rule. The higher
figure of $45,000 represents about 40 percent of the typical cost per episode
for new network series. It is also reported to be the cost per episode of the
most expensive of the syndicated series offered in 1971–72, the first season
in which the prime-time access rule was in effect.[44] In all of the calculations
the value of s is assumed to be 0.6, which is slightly less than the average
ratio of second- to first-run audiences for network series; the value of H_{p}
is taken as 60 million homes, the approximate number of TV homes in
1970; and the value of V as 0.0135 per thousand homes, a realistic value of
advertising revenue per viewer.

44. *Broadcasting*, Vol. 80 (May 3, 1971), p. 21, quotes a representative of Group W
to the effect that none of its new syndicated programming costs more than $45,000 per
half-hour episode.

Most of the outcomes tabulated in Table 3-4 can be judged extremely unlikely based on past experience. All of the outcomes in the first column, with the possible exception of $N = 1$, $\alpha = 0.064$, can be ruled out because the average cost per episode of first-run syndications produced in years immediately prior to 1971 was almost certainly greater than $25,000 and their average audience on a VHF station in prime time was less than 6 percent of the potential.[45] Similarly, all of the outcomes in the second column, with the exception of $N = 1$, $\alpha = 0.116$ and perhaps $N = 2$, $\alpha = 0.154$, can be ruled out. Programs capable of attracting more than 17 percent of the potential audience would be bid away by the networks, replacing one of the many continuing series with a lower rating. In addition, it is not likely that many programs that would attract network-size audiences could be produced at less than half the typical $120,000 cost of network programs. All of the outcomes in the third column can be ruled out because the audiences are, at best, comparable with the average audiences for off-network syndications and movies, which are available at prices equivalent to 30 percent, rather than 50 percent, of broadcast revenue.

The implication of the analysis is that the prime-time access rule will not induce a sizable expansion in the amount of first-run syndicated material for independent stations except under the circumstances assumed in the fourth column of the table. Significant expansion requires that syndicators produce programming capable of attracting 10 to 12 percent of television homes at a cost of $45,000 per episode, and that they sell the programming at prices equivalent to 50 percent of broadcast revenue.

The likelihood that even column four outcomes can be achieved does not seem great. Past deletions of network programs suggest that programming capable of attracting 10 to 15 percent of television homes could be produced in quantities implied by $N = 5$ (that is, about 52 hours per week). But these deleted programs typically cost more than twice the assumed $45,000 per half-hour. Only if the audience for these programs is insensitive to costs can the prime-time access rule accomplish expansion in the supply of first-run syndicated programming to independent stations.

While costs of producing marginal network programming might be cut without jeopardizing audience size, a reduction by more than half seems highly unlikely. The high rents from the networks that would allow room

45. The average prime-time audience of first-run syndications on UHF stations was derived from audience data appearing in American Research Bureau, *Syndicated Program Analysis, Fall 1968* (New York: ARB, revised May 2, 1969), and market television household figures in ARB, *1968 Television Market Analysis*, pp. 9–14.

for such a drastic cut characterize few programs attracting audiences in the size ranges under consideration.

The data in Table 3-4 make allowance neither for return to producers beyond recovery of production costs nor for distribution costs. More realistic assumptions about these elements, coupled with the unlikelihood of marked reductions in production costs, dim the prospect for a substantial expansion brought on by the prime-time access rule.

More likely to result is a level of production of new first-run syndicated programming barely above that required to enable affiliates to comply with the rule. Production costs of these programs will be much lower than those for the network programs that are replaced, a development achieved through concentrating on relatively cheap programs, such as quiz and talk shows, and through employing less elaborate settings, fewer retakes, and the like. The probable decline in viewer satisfaction, however, conceivably could be offset if the rule stimulated an increase in the number of viewing alternatives, which in practice is synonymous with an increase in the number of UHF independents on the air.

The Prospects for UHF Development

The disadvantages UHF stations suffer in competing with VHF stations stem from their smaller potential audiences and from their inability to acquire equally popular programming. Time and the all-channel receiver law of 1962 are the means by which the commission hopes to overcome the former; the prime-time access rule is designed to redress the latter. But neither policy is likely to be as effective as the commission apparently believes. This section attempts a closer estimate of the effectiveness of these policies. Such an attempt requires a number of assumptions, which in general demand a more hospitable environment for UHF development than is likely to exist.

The first assumption is that the potential audience of UHF stations will be no different from that of VHF stations once ownership of UHF sets becomes universal. This assumption is overly optimistic, for even in the conditional circumstance, UHF will labor under the handicap of signals of inferior quality unless reception capability is improved or UHF stations are allowed to increase their power substantially.

A second assumption involves the costs of operating television stations. The breakdown of the costs of existing stations shown in Table 3-5 reveals striking differences among stations. Big-city affiliates, such as those owned

Table 3-5. Number and Costs of Television Stations, by Type, 1970

Dollar amounts in thousands

Station type	Number of stations*	Average original cost of capital equipment*	Average programming costs	Average nonprogramming costs
Network-owned affiliates	15	$5,246	$6,518	$6,491
VHF affiliates	409 ⎫	2,038	719[b]	1,090
VHF independents	29 ⎭		2,841	2,252
UHF affiliates	98 ⎫	1,114	260[b]	546
UHF independents	48 ⎭		733	1,005

Source: FCC, *37th Annual Report, Fiscal Year 1971*, pp. 160, 163. Capital investment data are from a different, but largely overlapping, sample of stations, except for the network-owned affiliates. The number of stations reporting capital costs was 491 for VHF and 180 for UHF.

    a. Excludes part-year and satellite stations, and those with less than $25,000 in time sales.

    b. Affiliates receive most of their programming from the networks at no charge except for the share of advertising revenue the network retains, as explained in the text. Consequently, the programming costs are not comparable between affiliates and independents.

by the networks, spend twelve times as much on nonprogramming costs and twenty-five times as much on programming as do UHF affiliates, most of which are in small markets. Fees for programming vary with the size of market in which it is to be broadcast. Further, stations may indulge in many discretionary types of expenditure. No well-defined and invariant production function relates inputs and outputs of television stations, nor are inputs and outputs exchanged in perfectly competitive markets. Consequently, a statistical cost function for television stations is difficult to conceptualize and impossible to estimate from available data. As an alternative, the present analysis employs engineering cost estimates for four types of stations that differ from each other in the amounts of programming they produce. These estimates are combined with information developed earlier on the costs of purchased programming to obtain relationships between total annual cost and market size for each of the station types. They can also be loosely compared for reasonableness with the figures in Table 3-5.

    The estimates of costs other than those for purchased programming are taken from data presented in the report of the Carnegie Commission on Educational Television, relating to what the report calls Key, Flag, Standard, and Basic television stations.[46] All types of stations were assumed to operate for a total of 95 hours per week throughout the year, or about 13.5 hours per day on average.

    46. See Sidney S. Alexander, "Costs of a Nationwide Educational Television System," in *Public Television: A Program for Action*, Report and Recommendations of the Carnegie Commission on Educational Television (Bantam Books, 1967), pp. 135–91.

The main differences among these four types of stations are in the amount and quality of programming they produce, which govern differences in the amount of capital and operating expenses. Key stations are assumed to produce eleven hours of programming a week, one hour of which is of a quality comparable to nationally distributed programs. Only the key stations are capable of color productions, although all four types can broadcast films, tapes, and network offerings that are delivered to the station in color.

Flag stations produce ten hours a week of black-and-white programming, all of which is intended for local or regional showing. The programming would be of much lower quality: Compared with key stations, flag stations spend one-third as much on film production, less than one-third as much on program creation, a little over half as much on operating crews, and 40 percent as much on studio and mobile equipment.

Standard stations produce half as much programming as flag stations, and of even lower quality. The sum of the costs of operating crews, program creation, film production, and amortization of studio and mobile equipment is one-third as much for standard as for flag stations, indicating a cost per program on standard stations of about two-thirds the cost of flag stations.

The basic station is nothing more than a conduit for national programming, producing less than fifteen minutes of programming per day.

The amount of programming produced by the station itself and some of the financial characteristics for each type of station are shown in Table 3-6.

Table 3-6. Characteristics of Hypothetical Television Stations

Dollar amounts in thousands

Type of station[a]	Hours of programming produced per week[b]	Capital investment	Annual operating costs excluding purchased programming[c]	Revenue required to provide 10 percent after-tax rate of return[d]
Key	11	$6,220	$3,593	$622
Flag	10	3,294	1,458	329
Standard	5	1,690	651	169
Basic	1–1.5	1,262	286	126

Source: Sidney S. Alexander, "Costs of a Nationwide Educational Television System," in *Public Television: A Program for Action*, Report and Recommendations of the Carnegie Commission on Educational Television (Bantam Books, 1967), pp. 142, 182–83.

a. Station categories are defined in the text.

b. Only key stations can originate color programs. All others can produce only black-and-white programs.

c. Includes depreciation. While different assets are assumed to have different useful lives, total annual depreciation averages about 10 percent of investment, for an average useful life of ten years.

d. Assumes 50 percent corporate income tax. Since average depreciated book value of stations is roughly half of initial cost, a 10 percent average after-tax profit is equivalent to a 10 percent before-tax return on the total investment.

In addition to the amounts shown in the table, stations would incur costs for purchased programming to fill out their broadcast schedules, in amounts depending on the size of the station's market. On the basis of the data in Table 3-6 and costs per episode of purchased programming based on the regression coefficients for 60 minutes of network programming reported in Table 3-3, required revenues for each of the station types are as follows:

$$C_k = 4330 + 1.36\,H_p$$
$$C_f = 1904 + 1.38\,H_p$$
$$C_s = 944 + 1.46\,H_p$$
$$C_b = 540 + 1.51\,H_p,$$

where C_k, C_f, C_s, and C_b are the required revenues in thousands of dollars for key, flag, standard, and basic stations, respectively, and H_p is potential audience or market size in thousands of television homes.

The annual costs of these stations, including programming, in markets of various sizes are shown below in millions of dollars.[47]

	Size of market (hundred thousand households)		
Type of station	1,000	500	150
Key	5.7	5.0	4.5
Flag	3.3	2.6	2.1
Standard	2.4	1.7	1.2
Basic	2.1	1.3	0.8

Comparison of Tables 3-5 and 3-6 suggests that a key station is probably very much like the existing VHF independents. Its annual operating costs of over $3.5 million exceed the average for VHF independents of $2.25 million, but include roughly $1.5 million in program production costs that are covered by the nearly $3 million of programming costs of the average VHF independent. No capital cost data are available for VHF independents, but those for big-city affiliates are probably not much different. The key station has capital costs about 20 percent higher than the average network-owned affiliate, which is as close a representation of big-city affiliates as is available, but this difference is due at least in part to the fact that most of the latter were built many years ago. The cost of building a new station would be greater than the original cost of an existing station with the same characteristics.

47. Of the 224 television markets of the country, ten have 1 million households; a market of 500,000 households would rank twenty-fifth; and one of 150,000 would rank eighty-ninth.

The costs of flag stations are quite similar to those of VHF affiliates and UHF independents. In addition, the ten hours of local programming they produce corresponds roughly to the local program production among existing stations.[48] The major difference is that flag stations are assumed to produce only black-and-white programs, whereas some color capability is common among existing commercial stations.

The standard station is the counterpart of the UHF affiliate, having very similar cost conditions and serving almost entirely as a conduit for national programming. Only about 5 percent of the standard station's broadcast time is devoted to local programming, which is in the lower range among existing commercial stations. UHF affiliates survive because they offer the highly attractive network programming, not because of the quality of the service they offer themselves. UHF independents spend more than twice as much as UHF affiliates but draw much smaller audiences.

The basic station, with essentially no program origination and with nonprogramming costs about half those of UHF affiliates, represents the minimum in station service. A nation of basic stations would be essentially equivalent to completely national broadcasting. If this is the service to be offered, it is much cheaper to provide it through powerful regional stations or even through direct national broadcasts from satellite than through a large number of relatively weak local stations.

Given the FCC's dissatisfaction with the amount of local programming now offered by commercial broadcasters, a point discussed more fully in Chapter 4, both the basic and the standard stations probably would not satisfy the agency's programming objectives. The policy to promote UHF development would be regarded as a success only if most, if not all, of the stations were of the key and flag types.

The viability of each type of station can be determined by comparing its revenues and its costs. To assess the future prospects of UHF development, estimates of revenues must be made for each type of station, again assuming that UHF independents attain parity with their VHF counterparts.

For any station annual revenue can be stated simply as a function of potential audience. Broadcast revenue per thousand homes per year net of agency commissions was $43,840 in 1968, the appropriate year for comparison with the cost data. The average audience share of independent VHF

48. Chapter 4 contains a more complete discussion of the present extent of local programming. In general, few stations devote as much as 20 percent of their broadcast hours to programs they have produced, and more than a third produce less than 10 percent. The key and flag stations are both assumed to produce more than 10 percent.

stations competing with three network affiliates was 12.1 percent of viewing homes in their market, compared with 2.9 percent for independent UHFs. Thus, viewing of UHF independents might reach 12.1 percent of total viewing. Broadcast revenue of a UHF independent would be the same percent of total market broadcast income if the station had signals of VHF quality, gained access to the same kinds of programming available to VHF independents, and received the same revenue per viewing household as other stations. (The last, too, is optimistic, since the audience share of independents is higher outside of prime time, when the revenue per household is lower.) The potential annual revenue of a station under these assumptions is then given by

$$R = 5.30 \ H_p.$$

Equating the revenue and cost relationship for each type of station points to the minimum market size for viable operation of a station. For a key station, this minimum size is 1,100,000 households, or larger than all but eight markets in the nation in 1968. For a flag station, the minimum market is 486,000 households; there were twenty-six such markets in 1968. Standard and basic stations could survive in areas with 267,000 and 151,000 households, respectively, roughly the size of the 1968 markets ranked sixtieth and eighty-eighth according to potential audience.[49] Of 662 commercial UHF channel assignments by the commission, only 100, or about 15 percent, are in markets sufficient for a flag station by the standards employed here.[50] Finally, it should be noted that of the twenty-three VHF independent stations in operation in 1968 only seventeen are located in markets large enough to support a flag station. FCC statistics show that at most seventeen VHF independents are earning profits great enough to provide a 10 percent after-tax rate of return on the invested capital of a flag station.[51]

All of these considerations strongly attest to the almost certain realization of the gloomy future projected for UHF unless its stations eventually can attract larger audiences than independent VHF stations now do or can act solely as conduits for national programming.

49. For data on market size, see *Television Factbook, Services Volume*, 1969–70 edition, pp. 54a–56a. Potential audience is the area of dominant influence. Market sizes in 1968 were used to maintain consistency with cost and revenue data.

50. Using different procedures, Greenberg too has reached the conclusion that FCC allocation policies are overly optimistic about the viability of UHF. See Edward Greenberg, "Television Station Profitability and FCC Regulatory Policies," *Journal of Industrial Economics*, Vol. 17 (July 1969), pp. 210–38.

51. FCC, *Annual Report, 1970*, p. 159.

What is needed to make UHF development feasible is some way of putting UHF independents on an equal footing with VHF affiliates. Suppose that programming could be distributed among competing stations so that all received equal shares of total viewing, and hence of total broadcast revenue in their market. Under such an assumption the potential revenue function would become

$$R = \frac{43.84 H_p}{N},$$

where N is the number of stations in the market. By combining this modified potential revenue function with the required revenue function for each type of station, minimum market sizes can be calculated for various levels of N. Under these assumptions six flag stations would be viable in the top forty-four markets, five could survive in markets 45 through 54, and four would be viable in markets 55 to 69. Six standard stations would be viable in markets down to the eightieth and four standard stations could survive in a market as small as number 113. Thus, it would be possible to provide six-station service, producing roughly the present average amount of local programming, in nearly all of the top fifty markets. Six stations providing some local programming could survive in thirty-five additional markets, so that roughly 75 percent of the population could have six-station service with probably no diminution in the local program origination that is offered them. The remaining markets would be served much as they are now, except with three or four stations devoted almost entirely to national programming, rather than two or three as at present.[51]

Perhaps a system such as this is what the FCC has hoped might emerge and has sought to promote for the past twenty years. To justify the channel assignments the commission has made and most of the other actions it has taken in the name of promoting UHF development requires belief in the feasibility of essentially equalizing audience sizes among competing stations. Such a belief seems entirely without foundation, short of a complete dismantling and reorganization of the present structure of the commercial television industry. Since it is unreasonable to expect any regulatory agency to work such changes by direct action, the commission has behaved as though they could be brought about through an evolutionary, rather than

51. If, as argued above, a substantial part of program costs are rents to the entrepreneurs and talent in the program production business, more competition in broadcasting would lead to reductions in program costs. This development would permit slightly greater expansion of television options than these estimates predict.

a revolutionary, process—and one that could be unleashed by minor changes in the regulatory climate.

The difficulty with the evolutionary approach is that it will take too long. Even if six stations were operating in each of the top 100 markets today, some years would pass before, say, three new networks had their fair share of highly rated programs. Since these programs are the major sources of profits for networks and local stations, the new networks and their affiliates would experience substantial losses for some undetermined but significant period of time, as did the early entrants into commercial television. This prospect would seem fair enough but for one difference between the two cases: The early entrants were induced to suffer losses by the hope of very large future profit, which the six-channel system envisioned here does not offer. The initial investment to provide the six-channel service and to start the evolutionary process would not be forthcoming if the prospects for profit were as low as those predicted here.

This is not to say that the six-channel system, or a similar system, is impossible to achieve; it says only that to bring it about demands a bolder regulatory approach, involving considerable intervention in the industry. Exact details of such a policy need not be discussed, since it is not at all clear that a six-channel system should be the permanent objective of public policy. Nor would the six-channel system envisioned here do much to further the goal of localism in programming to which, as the next chapter shows, the commission attaches great importance.

CHAPTER FOUR

FCC Policies toward Television

THE PRESENT COMMERCIAL BROADCASTING system is, to a large extent, the outcome of the regulatory policies pursued by the Federal Communications Commission (FCC). The distinguishing feature of FCC policies has been an emphasis on local service. In the FCC's words, the present allocation of stations "protects the interests of the public residing in smaller cities and rural areas more adequately than any other system."[1] This chapter evaluates the local service policy, as well as the general approach the FCC has taken toward regulation. The specific policies associated with subscription television, cable television, and public television, treated in subsequent chapters, are all better understood against the background of the FCC's "local service" doctrine.

The Legislative Origins of TV Regulation

Television broadcasting is generally considered to be a regulated industry, but the scope of its regulation differs radically from that in other industries. The reason lies partly in the structure of the broadcast industry and partly in the origins of broadcast regulation. In most industries the ostensible reason for regulation was a concern over excessively high or discriminatory prices, and a related concern over inadequate competition and high profits. As an alternative explanation of America's regulatory experience, revisionist economic historians have emphasized producers' desires to protect themselves against competition and uncertainty.[2] Neither rationale alone accurately explains broadcast regulation.

1. Federal Communications Commission, Sixth Report and Order (Dockets 8736, 8975, 8976, 9175), adopted April 11, 1952, published in *Federal Register*, Vol. 17 (May 2, 1952), p. 3905, par. 68.
2. See, for example, Lance E. Davis and Douglass C. North, *Institutional Change and American Economic Growth* (Cambridge, England: Cambridge University Press, 1971).

The regulation of radio broadcasting was a response to the problem of frequency assignment. Initially, radio broadcasting was open to all comers, who obtained licenses from the Department of Commerce, but the department did not have the power to regulate the broadcasters. By 1922, only two years after the first commercial broadcast, interference had become a vexing problem that agreements about time allocation among local broadcasters failed to solve. After a number of years of studying proposals for regulating radio broadcasting, Congress passed the Radio Act of 1927, creating the Federal Radio Commission. Among other provisions, the commission was given the power to assign wavelengths and determine the power and location of transmitters. Licenses were to be granted for three years, but only if the commission determined that the award would serve the "public convenience, interest, or necessity."[3] When more than one group applied for a given frequency assignment, the public interest was to guide the commission's decision among them; licenses could be transferred only with the commission's approval and could be revoked for misconduct, but censorship powers and control of program content were specifically denied the commission.[4] In 1934 the Federal Radio Commission became the Federal Communications Commission as the power to regulate telecommunications was added to the agency's responsibilities; however, its licensing powers were maintained virtually intact.[5]

The distinctive feature of broadcast regulation is the focus on licensing as the essential regulatory power. While regulatory agencies such as the transportation and power commissions exerted control over entry by requiring proof of usefulness or need, the "certificates of convenience or necessity" they issued not only were for indefinite terms, but also were secondary to the regulation of profits and prices. The emphasis on licensing results partly from the fact that the FCC is specifically denied, with respect to broadcasting,[6] the power to regulate rates or profits that is the central feature of the conventional regulatory approach—indeed, of its own approach to its other regulatory responsibilities.

The Communications Act of 1934 also expressly applies the antitrust

3. See R. H. Coase, "The Federal Communications Commission," *Journal of Law and Economics*, Vol. 2 (October 1959), pp. 1–7. The quote is from Radio Act of 1927, sec. 9 (44 Stat. 1166).

4. *Ibid.*, secs. 9, 12, 14, 29, respectively (44 Stat. 1166–68, 1172–73).

5. Communications Act of 1934 (48 Stat. 1064, 1081–84).

6. But not with respect to other forms of telecommunication. *Ibid.*, sec. 2b (48 Stat. 1065).

laws to broadcasting and provides for the preservation of competition.[7] Other regulated industries are statutorily exempted from antitrust prosecution for specific types of transactions.[8] Together with the limitation on rate regulation, this provision indicates that Congress intended a greater role for competition in broadcasting than in other regulated industries. The Supreme Court has explicitly noted this intention:

The sections [in the Communications Act] dealing with broadcasting demonstrate that Congress has not, in its regulatory scheme, abandoned the principle of free competition, as it has done in the case of railroads, in respect of which regulation involves the suppression of wasteful practices due to competition, the regulation of rates and charges, and other measures which are unnecessary if free competition is to be permitted.[9]

The geographic distribution of licenses also drew legislative attention. In 1928, Congress passed an amendment to the Radio Act of 1927 that required "equality" of radio reception and transmission in each of the five broadcast zones set up in the original act.[10] This amendment was replaced in 1934 with a requirement that the FCC distribute licenses so as to provide "equality of radio broadcasting service" to "each of the States and the District of Columbia."[11]

This provision underlies what has come to be known as the FCC's "local service" objective—establishment of stations in as many localities as possible. From the power to grant licenses in the public interest originated two other FCC objectives—achievement of an acceptable level of diversity in program content and fulfillment of broadcasting's role as public servant. As noted above, the FCC's fourth major objective is the maintenance of an acceptable level of competition. The problem is that these four objectives are conflicting. Recognition of this conflict is crucial to comprehension of the dilemmas the FCC has faced.

The Primacy of the Local Service Objective

An idealized view of FCC policy making would put all four objectives on a par, with the FCC making difficult tradeoffs between them in each of its

7. *Ibid.*, secs. 313, 314 (48 Stat. 1087–88).
8. For an extensive investigation of the applicability of procompetitive policies and laws to regulated industries, see Almarin Phillips (ed.), "Competitive Policies in Regulated Industries," manuscript in preparation for the Brookings Institution.
9. *FCC* v. *O. Sanders Bros. Radio Station*, 309 U.S. 470, 474–75 (1940).
10. 45 Stat. 373.
11. Communications Act of 1934, sec. 307b (48 Stat. 1084).

decisions. But the record shows little willingness to subordinate the local service objective to any of the other goals. In dogged pursuit of localism the FCC has paid a high price in terms of its other objectives.

The FCC Vision of Television

The primacy of local service reflects a deep-seated view of how television ought to be organized. Although the view arose out of legislation, the statute, couched in general language and containing admonitions toward other goals, cannot alone explain it.

The FCC's vision of broadcasting developed gradually, reaching maturity only in the 1950s. It foresaw a local television station in as many communities as possible. Larger communities would have several stations, but only to the extent that channels were available for small communities as well. Stations would be owned and managed by local residents, and would devote considerable broadcast time to information and commentary on important local issues. The stations would be instruments for community enlightenment and cohesion, much like the hometown newspaper of an earlier era.[12]

From this vision sprang three specific FCC policies: (1) reservation of channel allocations for many communities where, for a long time, no entrepreneur was willing to launch a station; (2) encouragement of the development of ultra high frequency (UHF) to provide more local stations; and (3) concern about the ownership of stations.

Localism and Station Assignments

The localism doctrine began with the granting of radio licenses. While a few high-power, "clear-channel," regional stations were authorized, the vast majority were low-power operations whose daytime signal carried only a few miles. The localism tradition was applied even more strongly to television. Beginning in 1945, the FCC allocated the very high frequency (VHF) spectrum in such a way that as many cities as possible had stations, and regional stations were permitted only in the sparsely populated Moun-

---

12. In Britain, the view of broadcasting was diametrically the opposite. National programming was established as the policy objective on grounds of economic efficiency and social purpose. See R. H. Coase, *British Broadcasting: A Study in Monopoly* (Harvard University Press for the London School of Economics and Political Science, 1950), pp. 46–60.

tain States. By 1948, the frequencies then available for television were fully allocated, and for the next four years no licenses were granted while a master allocation plan was devised.

The key issue was the choice between local and regional television stations, forced by the limited amount of VHF spectrum allocated to TV. The concept of regional stations centered around powerful transmitters receivable over a large area, providing most of the country with as many as seven VHF channels. The local station concept, on the other hand, would reduce the power of each station, permitting many more communities to have their own stations but reducing the number of channels any given viewer could receive. Localism won out.

The new allocation plan was challenged by DuMont. In attempting to establish a fourth national network, DuMont was stymied by an inadequate number of VHF affiliates, as well as by doubts that advertising revenues would be sufficient to support four networks. DuMont proposed the sacrifice of some local stations so that regional stations could be established to carry its network programming. This meant more competition: A viewer could choose among four national networks on VHF. But it also meant a reduction in the number of stations identified with a particular community. The FCC made its preference clear:

. . . the Commission cannot agree with the DuMont principle than an overriding and paramount objective of a national television assignment plan should be the assignment of four commercial VHF stations to as many of the major markets as possible. . . .

In the Commission's view as many communities as possible should have the opportunity of enjoying the advantages that derive from having local outlets that will be responsive to local needs.[13]

To put the issue another way, the commission decided that the public interest was better served by three networks carried by local stations than four networks, some of which would be available from regional stations. Greater value was attached to more local stations than to more options via another network.

The Promotion of UHF

The only way simultaneously to have more options *and* localism is, of course, to have more stations. The shortage of VHF assignments meant that additional stations had to be located in another part of the electromagnetic

13. FCC, Sixth Report and Order, pars. 77, 79; in Pike and Fischer, *Radio Regulation*, Vol. 1, Pt. 3, p. 91:624.

spectrum. In 1952 the FCC announced a new station allocation plan, which added UHF stations to communities already having VHF stations. The difficulties of UHF, discussed in Chapters 1 and 3, were recognized from the outset: Most sets were built for VHF reception, UHF tuning was more difficult, its signals were poorer. Still the commission had faith that economic growth and technical improvements would solve the problem:

. . . we are convinced that the UHF band will be fully utilized and that UHF stations will eventually compete on a favorable basis with stations in the VHF. . . .

We are persuaded that the differences in propagation characteristics will not prevent UHF stations from becoming an integral part of a single service. . . .

Further, there is no reason to believe that American science will not produce the equipment necessary for the fullest development of the UHF.[14]

UHF began auspiciously. In 1954, 121 commercial television stations, over one-third of the total, were UHF, but by 1960, 46 of these had gone off the air.[15] Although the data are not strictly comparable, another indication of the declining importance of UHF lies in the fact that in 1954, 13 percent of the television sets in use could receive UHF, but by 1961, only 5 percent of the new sets being produced could receive it.[16]

In the face of the early failures of UHF, the commission toyed with "deintermixture," which would eliminate competition between UHF and VHF stations. While some communities would have all their stations in the UHF band, others would have theirs in the VHF band. Areas where only UHF was available would experience a mass conversion of sets to UHF reception since sets would be useless without it. The UHF stations naturally were in favor of deintermixture, and in 1955, UHF broadcasters brought five cases requesting that the commission eliminate commercial VHF channel assignments in their areas. The American Broadcasting Companies (ABC), which had a large number of UHF affiliates, supported the proposal, but the other two networks and the VHF stations were opposed.[17]

---

14. *Ibid.*, pars. 197–99; Pike and Fischer, p. 91:664. The FCC was not alone in its enthusiasm for UHF. As late as 1966, an eminent economist said that UHF would make cable television less attractive and unprofitable in many markets. See Franklin M. Fisher, "Community Antenna Television Systems and the Regulation of Television Broadcasting," in American Economic Association, *Papers and Proceedings of the Seventy-eighth Annual Meeting, 1965 (American Economic Review*, Vol. 56, May 1966), p. 328.

15. Television Digest, Inc., *Television Factbook, Stations Volume, 1970–1971 Edition* (Washington: TD, 1970), p. 59a.

16. FCC, *20th Annual Report, Fiscal Year Ended June 30, 1954*, p. 109, and *28th Annual Report, Fiscal Year Ended June 30, 1962*, p. 62.

17. See Douglas W. Webbink, "The Impact of UHF Promotion: The All-Channel

Despite the controversial nature of deintermixture, the FCC continued to test the policy selectively until 1962.[18] The FCC even proposed a study of shifting all television to the UHF band, but this generated neither enthusiasm nor action.[19]

As the result of another commission attempt to solve the UHF problem, the all-channel receiver act of 1962,[20] almost all sets will soon be able to receive UHF.[21] Nevertheless, UHF still suffers technical disadvantages. Some claim that the "continuous" tuner, similar to that used on radios, discourages UHF viewing, and now "click" tuning of UHF channels must be incorporated into all new sets by July 1, 1974.[22] A far more serious problem is the inability to receive a good UHF picture more than a few miles from the transmitter even if the station is permitted to use several times as much power as a VHF station.[23] The fundamental economic problems of UHF stations are small audiences and low revenues, and, hence, the inability to provide better than low-budget programming.

The deep-seated nature of the UHF problem is suggested by the fact that almost all independent UHF stations suffer substantial losses. In 1970, of forty-eight stations reporting, forty-three had losses; thirty-three were of $200,000 or more, and of these, twenty-eight were over $400,000.[24] As Chapter 3 demonstrated, UHF stations cannot be financially viable unless commercial television is drastically reorganized. And yet this financially troubled sector of television has been the FCC's major instrument for providing more program options, more diversity, and more competition for the VHF network affiliates. Furthermore, the implementation of the all-

---

Television Receiver Law," *Law and Contemporary Problems*, Vol. 34 (Summer 1969), pp. 543–44, and Note, "The Darkened Channels: UHF Television and the FCC," *Harvard Law Review*, Vol. 75 (June 1962), pp. 1583–91. The testimony of the various parties at interest can be found in *All-Channel Television Receivers and Deintermixture*, Hearings before the House Committee on Interstate and Foreign Commerce, 87 Cong. 2 sess. (1962).

18. Webbink, "Impact of UHF Promotion," pp. 543–44.

19. *Ibid.*, p. 544.

20. 76 Stat. 150.

21. Not until 1969 did over half of the homes in the United States have UHF reception capability. By 1971, almost 80 percent of television homes could receive UHF. See National Association of Broadcasters, *1971 Dimensions of Television* (NAB, 1971), p. 10.

22. FCC, *37th Annual Report, Fiscal Year 1971*, p. 37.

23. Cable television eliminates all of the signal and tuning disadvantages of UHF, but increases the share of the audience of a typical UHF independent only from 1 percent over the air to 2 percent on the cable. See Chapter 6.

24. FCC, *37th Annual Report, 1971*, p. 158.

VF

channel receiver act imposed a cost estimated at $100 million a year on pur-
chasers of new television sets in order that the modest achievements of
UHF could be realized.[25]

Station Ownership

The pursuit of localism has given rise to a regulatory concern with who
owns a station. The FCC appears to conceive of the station owner as a kind
of latter-day Mark Twain who understands the needs and concerns of his
community in an imaginative and sensitive way. Given this conception,
the ownership of the local station is crucial.

The "integration doctrine" reflects most directly the FCC's interest in
ownership. It holds that in a contest among applicants for a single license,
preference should be given to an owner-manager, who it is believed will be
more sensitive to the community's needs than a manager reporting to an
absentee owner.

GROUP OWNERSHIP. The integration doctrine is related to FCC limitations
on group ownership. No more than seven AM, seven FM, and seven TV
stations (only five of which may be in the VHF band) may have common
ownership.[26] This rule simply places upper bounds on group ownership,
within which it is increasing, as Table 4-1 indicates.

The group ownership rule represents a compromise between the commission's desire to limit concentration of ownership and the competitive
power of group owners vis-à-vis single market owners, and its recognition
that multiple owners might more easily provide resources for balanced,
high-quality broadcasting than might single owners. Espousal of multiple
ownership is perhaps best characterized as a reluctant abandonment by the
FCC of the objective of completely local ownership.

A preference for individual station ownership implies the belief that station groups can out-compete single local stations through the greater
bargaining power multiple ownership affords. In comparing the behavior

25. Webbink, "Impact of UHF Promotion," p. 552.
26. From 1965 to 1968, the FCC experimented with an even more stringent rule. No
group was permitted to acquire VHF stations in the top fifty markets if it already owned
two such stations. This rule was rescinded because groups could circumvent it by buying
existing stations rather than constructing new ones. The FCC was unwilling to police
license transfers as closely as it did new license awards. See FCC, "Interim Policy Concerning Acquisition of Broadcast Stations," Public Notice 68788 (June 21, 1965), and
"Commission to Designate for Hearing Applications to Acquire Interests in a Second
VHF Station in Major Markets," Public Notice 60894 (December 18, 1964).

Table 4-1. Multiple- and Single-owner Commercial Television Stations, by Size of Market, 1956 and 1965

Number of stations

Size of television market	Multiple ownership		Single ownership	
	1956	*1965*	*1956*	*1965*
Top 50	91	134	71	59
51–100	49	112	86	52
101–150	32	82	59	40
150–200	20	47	26	28
Below 200	13	16	10	17
Total	205	391	252	196

Source: Harvey J. Levin, "Competition, Diversity, and the Television Group Ownership Rule," *Columbia Law Review*, Vol. 70 (May 1970), pp. 826–27.

of group-owned and single-owner stations, Harvey Levin found these elements:[27]

1. No major differences in national spot rates, suggesting that groups cannot use their multiple ownership to obtain higher rates.
2. No major differences in network time charges, suggesting that groups have little differential bargaining power with the networks.
3. Only slight differences in station profit margins, indicating little cost advantage to group ownership.
4. Only slight differences in station sales prices, indicating that the group or nongroup character of the station has little influence on buyers.

According to Levin's statistical tests, group stations fare no better than individually owned stations. This is not surprising. The limited number of possible VHF allocations, the decisive role of the networks, and the limited number of stations in each market are all far more important than any competitive advantages of multiple ownership. We agree with Levin: "Decisive elements in industry structure appear to forestall the possibility of abuse of market power by non-network TV groups."[28]

In evaluating group ownership, several conflicting factors must be considered. The major benefit conferred by strong groups—like Metromedia, Group W, RKO General, AVCO Broadcasting, and Taft Broadcasting—is the nucleus they form for additional networks. This nucleus could be

27. Harvey J. Levin, "Competition, Diversity, and the Television Group Ownership Rule," *Columbia Law Review*, Vol. 70 (May 1970), pp. 791–835.

28. *Ibid.*, p. 794.

achieved through the emergence of more groups with audience coverage— and the secure base it implies—comparable with that of the networks (each of which owns five VHF stations in the largest markets which are seen in 14 million television homes, 24 percent of the nation's total). Even under the present rules, such groups have been formed: Three nonnetwork groups reach some 8 million homes each week, and two others reach 3 million homes.[29]

The cost of group ownership is the sacrifice of dispersed station control and of the local ownership it entails. These costs are mainly noneconomic, paid in political and social distaste for concentrating control of a mass medium in a few hands.

To make a policy judgment with respect to group ownership involves weighing the benefits and costs. The question is whether the potential program supply to independent stations, and the nascent networks that group ownership has begun to provide, is worth more than broader dispersion of station ownership and more localized ownership. A more restrictive policy on group ownership also faces the difficulty that it would solidify the commanding position the networks hold by virtue of their ownership of VHF stations in the five top markets.

CROSS-MEDIA OWNERSHIP. The localism issue is also present in the prevalence of cross-media ownership. Often the most capable and eager local group seeking a television station license has been a local newspaper or radio station. Thus it is not surprising that 30 percent of the commercial stations in the top one hundred markets are affiliated with newspaper or magazine ownership; that about 10 percent of the radio stations are affiliated with a newspaper; that thirty of the top fifty markets contain at least one station with newspaper ownership and seven multimedia conglomerates control more than half of these; or that several major publishers— Cowles, McGraw-Hill, Newsweek—as well as the three networks also own groups of radio and television stations.[30]

The situation these statistics portray developed out of policies that the FCC has haltingly, and often inconsistently, applied. As Judge Henry Friendly has noted:

On some occasions the Commission has preferred a non-newspaper-owner, on grounds of diversification, over a newspaper applicant at least as well or better qualified. On other occasions it has awarded licenses to newspaper-owning

29. Calculated from *Television Factbook, Stations Volume, 1970–1971 Edition*.
30. Data in this paragraph are from *1972 Broadcasting Yearbook*, and Christopher H. Sterling, "Newspaper Ownership of Broadcast Stations, 1920–68," *Journalism Quarterly*, Vol. 46 (Summer 1969), p. 235.

or -affiliated applicants despite the availability of other well-qualified contenders without newspaper affiliation. On still other occasions it has chosen between applicants both of which had heavy dosages of newspaper affiliation—and of radio broadcasting as well.[31]

In response to continuing criticism of cross-media ownership, the FCC in 1970 adopted a rule forbidding any party to acquire more than one full-time broadcast license in any single market. This rule would not disturb existing ownership, but the FCC is considering requiring that present licensees reduce their holdings in any one market to no more than one of the following: a television station, an AM-FM combination, or a newspaper, a change so drastic that it is unlikely to be implemented. In FCC concern with the restrictions to be imposed on cable ownership,[32] the issues also have been group ownership and cross-media ownership in the same locality.

Concentration of media ownership in a locality does represent a potential hazard, not only to market competition for advertising but, more important, to the free flow of ideas. As Rosse, Owen, and Grey note, "Any concentration of media ownership—especially in local markets—increases the potential for the exercise of control over information, ideas, and opinions in the hands of a few and decreases the potential for diversity in sources of information, ideas and opinions."[33]

FCC Commissioner Nicholas Johnson makes an eloquent case for what is practically a prohibition of cross-media ownership per se:

In general, I would urge the minimal standard that no accumulation of media should be permitted without a specific and convincing showing of a continuing countervailing social benefit. For no one has a higher calling in an increasingly complex free society bent on self-government than he who informs and moves the people. Personal prejudice, ignorance, social pressure, and advertiser pressure are in large measure inevitable. But a nation that depends upon the rational dialogue of an informed electorate simply cannot take any unnecessary risk of polluting the stream of information and opinion that sustains it. At the very least, the burden of proving the social utility of doing otherwise should be upon him who seeks the power and profit which will result.[34]

31. Henry J. Friendly, *The Federal Administrative Agencies: The Need for Better Definition of Standards* (Harvard University Press, 1962), pp. 66–67.

32. FCC, Notice of Proposed Rule Making and of Inquiry, Docket 18891, July 1, 1970, and FCC, Second Report and Order, Docket 18397, June 24, 1970.

33. James N. Rosse, Bruce M. Owen, and David L. Grey, "Economic Issues in the Joint Ownership of Newspaper and Television Media: Comments in Response to 'Further Notice of Proposed Rule-Making,' Federal Communications Commission, Docket 18110," Studies in the Economics of Mass Communication, Memorandum 97 (Stanford University, Research Center in Economic Growth, May 1970; processed), p. 3.

34. Nicholas Johnson, *How to Talk Back to Your Television Set* (Bantam Books edition, 1970), p. 66.

While this position arouses sympathy and the rhetoric is persuasive, the very existence of the problem is due in substantial measure to the FCC's persistent emphasis on localism. Owning and operating a television station requires substantial capital, whose sources in a given community are likely to be a limited circle of local capitalists or corporations that quite probably include a newspaper. Furthermore, the traditions of the American press make the newspaper one of the few potential station owners that could conceive of operating a television station as a higher calling, rather than as simply a very profitable business.

In principle, the maintenance of numerous independent sources of information and opinion is a worthwhile undertaking, but here the FCC has sacrificed wider options to localism by prohibiting regional stations. As long as viewing options are few, dissolving cross-media ownerships makes only a minor contribution to diversity compared with the likely effect of abandoning localism in favor of regional stations. And there is a good chance that alternative local private owners will be less public-spirited than newspapers have been.

The Benefits of Localism

The benefits of localism have proved to be relatively small. The objectives sought are summed up in a statement by Commissioners Cox and Johnson:

Congress created the present scheme in order to promote specific policies and specific kinds of programs. A system of locally based stations was deemed necessary to ensure that broadcasting would be attentive to the specific needs and interests of each local community. It was also considered a guarantee to local groups and leaders that they would have adequate opportunity for expression. Ultimately, our broadcasting system is premised on concern that the very identity of local states and cities might be destroyed by a mass communications system with an exclusively national focus.[35]

These fears notwithstanding, the fact remains that almost all of the programming broadcast over the local station has a national focus. The network affiliates, which constitute the vast majority of VHF stations, rely on the networks for 82 percent of their prime-time programming.[36] Of the

35. Kenneth A. Cox and Nicholas Johnson, "Broadcasting in America and the FCC's License Renewal Process: an Oklahoma Case Study" (FCC, 1968; processed), p. 3 (henceforth referred to as the "Oklahoma Report").

36. Arthur D. Little, Inc., *Television Program Production, Procurement, Distribution and Scheduling* (ADL, 1969), p. 180.

remaining 18 percent, a high proportion is devoted to nonnetwork films and other national programming. Outside of prime time, the reliance is less —particularly for affiliates of ABC, which offers less daytime network programming—but the pattern is much the same.[37] Few local programs other than local news and weather and sports are offered.

Independent stations are not much different. Most of their programming is new or rerun syndications and movies, and many, particularly in the UHF band, go off the air in the daytime and late evening rather than broadcast local programs.

The nature of television programming was revealed by Commissioners Cox and Johnson in their examination of television stations in Oklahoma, New York, the District of Columbia, Maryland, Virginia, and West Virginia. Among the ten stations in Oklahoma, local programming consumed less than 20 percent of prime time and about 10 percent of daytime hours;[38] half of the total, and almost all of the prime-time local hours, was news, weather, and sports. The additional local service included a weekly average of one and one-half hours of religious broadcasting, primarily on Sunday morning (when the impious are asleep and the pious are in church), some daytime talk shows, and a single local entertainment program. All the Tulsa stations presented public affairs: In a composite week one of its stations presented three two-minute editorials, another a daily half-hour talk show, and a third a daily fifteen-minute discussion program in the afternoon.

The commission had held hearings in Chicago and Omaha in 1962 and 1963 that showed, according to Commissioners Cox and Johnson, that metropolitan TV stations originated relatively little programming of their own, and that most of it was news, weather, and sports. In light of these hearings, Commissioners Cox and Johnson concluded that Oklahoma was not atypical:

As far as Oklahoma broadcasting is concerned, the concept of local service is largely a myth. With a few exceptions, Oklahoma stations provide almost literally no programming that can meaningfully be described as "local expression." They provide very little that can be considered tailored to specific needs of their individual communities. . . .

[This conclusion is not necessarily] an indictment of the broadcasters of this particular state; it is unlikely that their performance differs greatly from the performance of broadcasters in other states.[39]

37. See Chapter 3.
38. "Oklahoma Report," pp. 45–54.
39. *Ibid.*, pp. 13, 15.

The two commissioners later found similar patterns in New York. Only four of the twenty-four stations in the state devoted over 20 percent of their broadcast time to programs other than entertainment and sports.[40] They also reported other findings on programming in the mid-Atlantic region that showed that only two of thirty-two stations devoted more than 20 percent of their broadcast time to locally originated programming, with thirteen below 10 percent.[41] These data reinforce the conclusion expressed in the first Cox and Johnson study that local service is a myth.

One other rationale for local stations is that they serve as an advertising medium for local merchants. Here the localism role is somewhat more important, but the broadcasters still earn 80 percent of their revenue from either network or spot messages of national advertisers.[42] Paradoxically, independent stations earn more of their revenue from national advertising than do network affiliates.

Local Program Profitability

The reasons for the failure of the original FCC vision are not hard to find. Local programming is not as profitable for station owners as national programming. The difference in profitability simply reflects the fact that a program of the same quality shown nationally is obviously much cheaper per viewer. A typical half-hour evening network show costs at least $90,000 to produce, but, with an average share of the nationwide audience, this amounts to less than one cent per viewing home.[43] At the same cost per viewer, and with the same share of the local audience, the individual station in a market with a million homes can afford only $1,500 for program costs —an amount sufficient to produce only a low-quality talk show with minimum salaries for production and performing talent and with guests who are generally volunteers. For the most part the viewing audience prefers highly professional talent—professional football rather than local high school games, for example. Locally produced programs, therefore, have low audience ratings, and their advertising revenues are correspondingly low. Con-

40. Kenneth A. Cox and Nicholas Johnson, "New York State License Renewals" (FCC, May 29, 1969; processed), Table 9.

41. Ralph L. Stavens, "Television in the Mid-Atlantic Region: An Analysis and Statistical Account," appended to Kenneth A. Cox and Nicholas Johnson, "Renewal Standards: the District of Columbia, Maryland, Virginia and West Virginia License Renewals (October 1, 1969)," FCC 42255 (December 31, 1969), Table 24, p. 125.

42. FCC, *Annual Report, 1971*, p. 167.

43. See Chapter 3.

sequently, they must operate on very small budgets—which act further to reduce their audiences—even though they are often much more expensive per viewer than national programming.

This combination of significantly higher costs and lower revenues means that station owners are attracted to the more profitable national programs. The exception is local news and weather, which often draws good audiences, is cheap to produce, and, hence, is reasonably profitable.

Who Defines the Public Interest?

The premise of localism is that more local programming serves the public interest. But this is not as obvious as its adherents imply. The viewers, by their program choices, have clearly voted for national programming. It typically outdraws its local competitors by many orders of magnitude. Rather than stirring worry, such a record should excite applause—for giving customers what they want. Why, then, the concern on the part of the commission and other observers?

Some argue that television is fundamentally different from most products or services and that consumer sovereignty should not apply. Local programming is different from other products because it does more than fulfill consumer wants; it serves an allegedly important public function. Commissioners Cox and Johnson are eloquent on this subject:

The greatest challenge before the American people today is the challenge of restoring and reinvigorating local democracy. That challenge cannot be met without a working system of local broadcast media actively serving the needs of each community for information about its affairs, serving the interests of all members of the community, and allowing all to confront the listening public with their problems and their proposals.[44]

The minimal local programming now available hardly serves this purpose. To make stations broadcast more local programming even in prime time would not alleviate the problem, since most viewers would turn to competitive channels that offered network programming. The effective way to assure that the local program is seen by a large fraction of the population would be to set aside certain prime-time hours in which *all* channels must carry local programming. The FCC's 1970 decision, discussed in Chapter 3, to limit the amount of prime-time programming by networks is a step in this direction, although it was also designed to improve the market for non-network national syndication.

44. "Oklahoma Report," p. 10.

We have considerable doubts about obligatory local programming and about making viewing, in effect, semicompulsory by withdrawing the alternatives. Yet anything less seems unlikely to further the grand objective that local programming is supposed to serve. The harsh reality is that most viewers do not want to sacrifice even a small fraction of national entertainment to their obligation as local citizens. The present television stations give most viewers the kind of programming they want. If the wish of the vast majority of viewers is that local stations serve primarily as conduits for national programming, the FCC's promotion of localism is highly questionable. Localism *has* produced tiny benefits. But even if its objective— more local programming—were achieved, it *could* produce only very little more since the local programs would reach very few viewers.

The FCC Practice in Television Licensing

Localism has obviously run aground on the hard rocks of economic reality. While this foundering is most apparent in programming, it is also reflected in the practice of FCC licensing.

If the FCC followed its stated principles, broadcast licenses would be awarded to groups promising more local and public affairs programming, and owned by residents of the locality in which the station operates. But practice does not concide with theory, at least as revealed by FCC decisions in contested applications for licenses to construct new stations. During the 1967–70 period, at least sixteen new television licenses were awarded after hearings evaluating more than one applicant. The FCC received forty-five applications for the sixteen assignments, of which seventeen (two applicants merged while competing) were successful. The stations licensed were all UHF independents or VHFs in small cities.

An application for a broadcasting license requests detailed information about the prospective owners of the station, the costs of constructing the station and operating it for one year, the capital available to the applying group, the expected revenues of the station during its first year, and the programming the applicants expect to offer. This information is more than adequate to permit a test of the hypothesis that local ownership, public affairs programming, and local program origination are actually favored by the FCC in making license awards.

Table 4-2 shows the results of a regression analysis designed to identify the determinants of the success of a license application. The dependent variable took the value of one if a license was granted, zero if it was not, or the fraction of ownership in the final licensee if during the hearings one original applicant merged with another to present a new, unified, successful application (a practice that seems reasonable since the FCC encourages mergers among applicants it views as worthy licensees). The explanatory variables were the inverse of the number of competing applications for the license, the planned amount of various types of programming, the characteristics of the applying group—possession of other broadcast licenses, a connection to a newspaper, and the participation of local residents—and its financial backing.

The statistical analysis reveals that the FCC has abandoned its stated policy objectives in granting licenses. Local ownership, news and public affairs programming, and local program origination all *detract* from the

Table 4-2. Relation of Characteristics Revealed by Applications and Broadcast Licenses Awarded by the Federal Communications Commission[a]

Characteristic (explanatory variable)	Coefficient[b]	t-statistic[c]
Inverse of number of applicants	0.70	1.64
Total programming hours[d]	1.40	3.38
News and public affairs programming[d]	−1.09	3.29
Local origination[d]	−0.44	2.25
Newspaper ownership	−0.76	3.52
Local ownership	−0.25	1.77
Other broadcast interests	0.16	0.98
Total available capital[d]	0.25	1.14

Source: Derived by authors from forty-five applications for sixteen broadcast licenses awarded by the Federal Communications Commission during the 1967–70 period.

a. $R^2 = 0.38$; standard error = 0.37171.

b. The actual dependent variable predicted by this estimated equation is a position on the normal distribution with mean zero and variance of one. The estimated probability that an application will be successful is the probability that an observation of the $N(0,1)$ distribution will be less than the predicted value of the dependent variable. See Arthur S. Goldberger, *Econometric Theory* (Wiley, 1964), pp. 248–51.

c. With 37 degrees of freedom, a coefficient is significantly positive or negative at the 95 percent confidence level if its t-statistic exceeds 1.69. The t-values for the 90 and 80 percent confidence levels are 1.30 and 0.85, respectively.

d. These variables are expressed as fractions of the values of the underlying variable for the applicant that promised the most for the same license. For example, a given value of the "local origination" variable will be the ratio of that applicant's total locally originated programming to the local origination promise of the applicant for the same license that promised the most local origination. Thus, these variables take on values from zero—in which case the applicant promised nothing—to one—in which case the applicant promised the most of all applicants for that particular license. This scaling of the variables is justified because the relevant consideration to the FCC is the quality of applicants in relation to their competition, not to applicants for other licenses. Stations in areas with relatively low population are likely to spend less and promise less public service than more profitable stations in larger areas. The coefficients of these variables can be interpreted as roughly the change in the likelihood that an application will be successful, expressed in percent, from a 1 percent change in the promise of an applicant in relation to the promise of other applicants for a given variable.

likely success of an application.[45] An applicant promising 10 percent *more* news and public affairs than his competitors was approximately 11 percentage points *less* likely to be granted a license. An applicant promising 10 percent *more* local programming than his competitors was about 4 percenage points *less* likely to receive a license. And an applicant that listed local residents as owners was 25 percentage points *less* likely to be granted a license than a competing applicant with no local representation.

The only variable that appears especially important in adding to the success of an application is the number of hours of programming to be offered each week. To offer 10 percent *more* programming hours than another applicant makes the award of the license 14 percentage points *more* likely.

The FCC is apparently actively pursuing its policy against cross-media ownership. Connections with a newspaper virtually ring the death knell for an applicant. In a competitive license award, such an applicant has a probability of receiving a license that is 0.76 lower than it otherwise would be— in essence, the applicant has no chance against even a minimally competent competitor. Other broadcast interests are apparently not so prejudicial to an application. While the coefficient on whether the applicant owned other stations was not statistically significant by conventional standards, it was positive. The best estimate of the effect of broadcasting experience is that an experienced applicant is about 16 percentage points more likely to receive a license than an inexperienced applicant. Finally, the coefficient of the total capital available to the applicant, including loan commitments, while not statistically significant by normal standards, is also positive. It suggests that 10 percent more capital improves the chances of an application by 2.5 percentage points.

The explanation for this seemingly perverse licensing behavior probably is that the commission has succumbed to the economic realities that work against localism. Because all of the recent new stations have been either UHF, or VHF in small cities, they consequently are likely to be in precarious financial positions. Emphasis on commercial programming and

45. In 1965, the FCC rejected the straightforward rivalry on promised hours of local and public service programming that was a feature of television licensing proceedings. See FCC, "Policy Statement on Comparative Broadcast Hearings," Public Notice 71120 (July 28, 1965), in Pike and Fischer, *Radio Regulation*, Vol. 5 (2nd ed., 1965), pp. 1901–20. For a description of the process, see Louis L. Jaffe, "WHDH: The FCC and Broadcasting License Renewals," *Harvard Law Review*, Vol. 82 (June 1969), p. 1695.

connections to other profitable broadcast interests improve the financial picture of the new station, at least in the eyes of the commission.

The FCC has failed to use the one sanction it has—refusal to renew a license —to enforce the local service policy. The reasons seem fairly straightforward.

First, failure to renew a license is an extremely serious sanction for many of the licensees, particularly VHF affiliates in good-sized cities. The stations are often worth millions of dollars; all stations in the top fifty markets have been valued at $4 billion.[46] Every three years the licensee must subject this very valuable asset to administrative review with the hazard of nonrenewal. Until recently, the hazard has been a theoretical one, for renewals have rarely been denied in the absence of serious misconduct.[47] However, in 1971 the District of Columbia Court of Appeals ruled that a broadcasting licensee applying for renewal had no advantage over rival applicants.[48] Presumably this means that an applicant that promised more local programming could supplant an existing licensee whose record was deficient in this respect. This decision caused a considerable outcry at the FCC and in the industry, and the introduction into Congress of a bill to make license renewals nearly automatic.[49]

The second reason the FCC has eschewed the sanction of nonrenewal is its failure to arrive at clear criteria for "sufficient" local programming. Programs vary in quality and cost, so that hours alone are not a good measure of the contribution. Furthermore, any across-the-board requirement has to be a minimal one to allow for the wide variation in station profitability. Beyond this, the FCC traditionally has been loath to prescribe programming content.

Nor has the commission attempted to evaluate the fitness of new owners of an existing station. License transfers are virtually automatic as long as the old licensee can show that he did not "traffic" in the license—that is,

46. Estimate by M. H. Seiden and Associates, in "An Economic Analysis of the Impact of License Forfeiture on the Television and Radio Broadcasting Industry," submitted to the FCC as part of Docket 18110 (Seiden, January 1969; processed).

47. Only Lamar Life Broadcasting Company and WHDH, Inc., have been denied renewals. See Jaffe, "WHDH: The FCC and Broadcasting License Renewals," pp. 1693, 1696–97.

48. See *Broadcasting*, Vol. 80 (June 21, 1971), pp. 28–29.

49. The bill (S. 2004) was introduced by Senator John O. Pastore in early 1970. See *Broadcasting*, Vol. 78 (January 12, 1970), pp. 36–38, and Vol. 78 (January 19, 1970), pp. 21–23, for the industry's viewpoint on the WHDH ruling, the Pastore bill, and the FCC's reaction.

obtain a license solely for the purpose of selling it. The reason for the passive transfer policy is, again, the financial stake: Owners should be permitted, according to the FCC, to liquidate their assets. Of course, passive transfer policies provide a loophole that renders untenable strong policies on any other kind of license grant—new or renewal.

The Costs of Localism

Although there are twelve VHF channels, no more than seven can be used for transmitting broadcasts for any given location, since the remaining five must be left vacant to prevent interference from adjacent channels (a single receiver can receive adjacent channels as long as the transmitters are separated geographically). Stations using the same channel must also be substantially separated geographically to prevent co-channel interference. These twin requirements place technological limits on the number of VHF signals that can be broadcast if each community is to be able both to receive and to transmit signals different from those in nearby communities.

Abandonment of localism in television broadcasting would make reception of at least six VHF signals technically feasible for all homes in the country.[50] At the present, such service is enjoyed only by residents of Los Angeles and New York; no other city receives more than five channels. Any one of the channels in such a system would carry the same programming throughout the country. From a central origination point for each, programming would be delivered by coaxial cable, microwave links, or satellites to local transmitters, which would replace the local stations in the present system. This standardization and centralization of programming for each channel does not mean that all six need be programmed from the same geographic location. Thus, one might envision the assignment of an origination point to each region of the country, and the orientation of some of the programming to the station's home area. Nationwide broadcasting might well be more geographically decentralized than the present system of networks, all of which are headquartered in New York, but less so than present local programming.

50. With a direct satellite-to-home system, all twelve VHF channels could be independently programmed for each of several regions in the nation. With ground transmitters, judicious grouping and spacing of regional stations could provide virtually all of the country with six simultaneously programmed networks. Or, if networks are to have less than national coverage, as many as eight or nine VHF signals could be delivered over the air to each home.

The Economic Feasibility of a Six-channel Nationwide System

A six-channel nationwide system would differ from the existing system in the following ways:

1. Since no program would be locally originated, no television advertising would be local. Local broadcast facilities, except for basic transmitters, would be unnecessary. Beyond the costs associated with transmission, all expenses of local stations—studio, programming, selling, administrative, and general costs—would be eliminated. If some regional programming were desired, a few broadcasting studios scattered across the country in the largest cities would be needed, but even in this case virtually all of the costs now incurred by local stations could be avoided.

2. Additional transmitters would be required to deliver the six channels throughout the country. Each channel would incur expenditures for origination, interconnection, selling, administrative, and general expenses on the order of those incurred by the existing three networks.

3. Each channel would incur expenses for the purchase or production of programming. This need not inflate the real resources devoted to program production beyond the levels for the present system. Three channels could carry on as the present three networks while the others broadcast the best programming—which is to say, that with the highest audience appeal—currently available on the stronger VHF independents.

Programming expenditures would differ from their costs in the present system for reasons explained in detail in Chapter 3. Briefly, this difference would arise because the advertising revenue that any program would generate in the six-channel system would probably fall short of its revenues in the existing system and thus the rents to program owners and talent that constitute some of the expense of current programming also would fall.

Estimated revenues, costs, and profits of the six-channel system are presented and compared with those of the present system in Table 4-3. The notes to that table provide more detailed information on the derivation of the estimates.

If history could be rewritten so that the FCC had set localism aside and created a nationwide broadcasting system, that system might well be the kind that Table 4-3 reports. The estimates indicate that it would have been more profitable and less costly to the economy than the present system of local stations. And viewers would have six rather than three networks to choose among.

The Value of Increased Viewing Options

The analysis of the demand for television options presented in Chapter 2 and developed further in Appendix A underlies estimates of the value consumers would derive if all communities had six channels of viewing options comparable with those available to residents of New York. Table 4-4 indicates that the additional consumer surplus would amount to more than 1 percent of personal income or, in 1972 prices, to about $10 billion.

Table 4-3. Economic Feasibility Analysis of a Six-channel Nationwide Television System

Millions of dollars, based on 1968 costs of the present system

Revenue, cost, or profit	Present system	Six-channel system	Change
Total revenue	2,520.9	2,227.7[a]	−293.2
Total costs	2,000.2	1,505.5	−494.7
Signal distribution	192.1	185.4[b]	−6.7
Programming	1,265.5	1,113.9[c]	−151.6
Selling	155.6	55.1[d]	−100.5
Administrative and general	387.0	151.1[d]	−235.9
Profit	520.7	722.2	+201.5

Sources: Present system—FCC, *35th Annual Report, Fiscal Year 1969*, pp. 135, 137; six-channel system and change—derived by authors, as explained in detailed notes below. New York viewers, number of television households, and prime-time audience are from American Research Bureau, *1968 Television Market Analysis* (New York: ARB, no date), pp. 9, 14, 17, 24; number of TV communities—Broadcasting Publications, Inc., *1971 Broadcasting Yearbook* (Washington: BP, 1971), p. 52; transmitter costs—*Public Television: A Program for Action*, The Report and Recommendations of the Carnegie Commission on Educational Television (Bantam Books, 1967), pp. 145–46, 174.

a. Total revenues of the present system, exclusive of local advertising, were approximately $2,123 million in 1968, while the average prime-time audience was 34.5 million homes (57.5 million homes owned a TV receiver). Thus each full-time equivalent prime-time viewing home was worth $61.54 in national advertising revenue per year to the system. The six VHF channels in New York attracted, on average, 63 percent of television homes in the New York area of dominant influence. Thus the national audience of the six-channel system is estimated at 36.2 million homes (0.63 times 57.5). National revenue of the system is thus estimated at 36.2 times $61.54, or $2,227.7 million per year.

b. The first element of this estimate represents the annual cost of six transmitters in each of the 204 communities that contain 100 percent of the TV homes in the country. At an annual cost for depreciation, maintenance, and operation of $85,000, the system cost for transmitters is $104 million (204 times 6 times 85,000). The second element represents an estimate of signal origination costs. In the existing system the three networks incurred technical costs of $40.7 million in 1968 (FCC, *35th Annual Report*, p. 137). These costs for the six-channel system were estimated as double this amount. Together, these estimates imply signal distribution costs of $185.4 million for the six-channel system.

c. The text argued that reported programming costs will be highly responsive to potential revenue. In the present system payments for programming are equivalent to one-half total revenue, and this is the basis of the estimate of $1,113.9 million for the six-channel system. Programming expenditures might, however, be higher than this. In particular, they might rise to 60 percent of revenue, the proportion paid for programming by the three networks in the existing system. However, this outcome would be likely only if there were an increase in the supply of network-type programming, which might be expected to lead to higher revenue as well as higher costs. In any event, it seems likely that, for the level of expenditures estimated here, programming of the quality now available in New York, which attracts 63 percent of local TV homes, could be acquired by the six-channel system.

d. Selling, administrative, and general expenses were estimated at twice the corresponding expenditures by the existing networks. An alternative procedure would be to base the estimates on the ratio of such expenditures to total sales for the networks in the existing system, which leads to slightly lower estimates.

Table 4-4. Estimated Value to Consumers of Replacing Current VHF Viewing Options with a Six-channel Television System, 1970

Current VHF options		Percentage of television households (2)	Consumer surplus as percentage of personal income (3)	Gain in consumer surplus as percentage of personal income (4)	Weighted gain in consumer surplus as percentage of personal income[a] (5)
Number of networks receivable (1a)	Number of independents receivable (1b)				
3	4	5.3	6.47	−0.19	−0.0101
3	3	9.5	6.28	0	0
3	2	1.2	6.03	0.25	0.0030
3	1	17.8	5.68	0.60	0.1068
3	0	57.7	5.07	1.21	0.6982
2	0	6.0	4.06	2.22	0.1332
1	0	2.6	2.60	3.68	0.0957
Total	...	100.0	...	...	1.0268

Sources: Columns 1 and 2—*1972 Broadcasting Yearbook*, pp. 12–39; column 3—derived from Appendix A, where an example is given; column 4—consumer surplus with three networks and three independents (column 3) minus the subject surplus; column 5—column 2 times column 4. Figures may not add to totals due to rounding.
a. The gain resulting from the six-channel system weighted by television households.

For several reasons, this estimate may be biased upward, but at least a lower bound on the estimate of the value of additional viewing options can be derived from the experience of a cable system in San Diego, California. The San Diego experience indicates that, on a national basis, consumers would find four additional viewing options of the quality of Los Angeles independents worth $2.4 billion per year.[51] Thus it seems reasonable to place the value to viewers—and hence the cost of localism in terms of the value of forgone viewing alternatives—at $2 billion to $12 billion annually. At the midpoint of this range, the annual cost of localism exceeds $100 per television home.

This $100, in effect, purchases the nightly local newscasts and a modest amount of local programming. The first draw about half the viewership of network programs, though they appear earlier in the evening (in part because they are considered less popular). Other local programs seem to draw

51. The principal advantage of cable subscription compared with a good rooftop antenna in San Diego is that the cable system carries four independent stations from Los Angeles. The San Diego cable systems have been quite successful, achieving ultimate penetration of 60 percent of the potential subscribers. If 60 percent of the nation's TV homes value four independents at $66 a year, the total value is $2.4 billion. This calculation, of course, assumes that the remaining 40 percent of TV homes would place no value on this additional service.

substantially fewer viewers than the newscasts, and, as noted earlier, they absorb few hours of the weekly programming. We frankly doubt that families in every television home in the country regard the present level of local programming as worth $100 per year, or, alternatively, that many families would pay a multiple of $100 to offset those who would pay nothing. This sum is equivalent to the amount collected in 1968 from the controversial income tax surtax that Congress took almost a year to pass, and is about 15 percent of current family expenditures on recreation.

The FCC does not defend its emphasis on localism on the grounds that it contributes to viewer satisfaction. Rather it holds localism to have major social benefits—enhancing the political process and community cohesion—that have turned out to be illusory. Meanwhile, it ignores the social benefits in reducing the present power of the three networks by providing three new competitors.

The FCC and Regulatory Change

The preceding analysis is quite critical of the FCC's emphasis on localism and the costs it imposes on society in limitations on viewer choice and the lack of competition for networks and affiliates. Yet the policy itself is understandable in terms of the legislative origins of broadcast regulation. What is less obvious is the rationale behind the FCC's continued adherence to localism in face of the heavy cost it exacts in diversity and the paucity of local programming undertaken by the stations themselves.

To find the rationale requires an understanding of the common resistance of regulatory agencies to change.[52] What is needed is at least the beginnings of a formal theory of the regulatory agency so that the positions taken by regulators can be better understood and perhaps even predicted.

A Theory of FCC Behavior

The following analysis is based on two assumptions.[53] First, the FCC's decisions are the result of rational, optimizing behavior. Given the informa-

52. William M. Capron (ed.), *Technological Change in Regulated Industries* (Brookings Institution, 1971), contains numerous criticisms of the reluctance of regulatory agencies to accept change in transportation and electric power generation, as well as in communications.
53. The analysis in this section is based upon points raised by James M. Buchanan and Gordon Tullock, *The Calculus of Consent: Logical Foundations of Constitutional*

tion available to them, the commissioners attempt through their decisions to maximize some objective function, including the welfare of the commissioners as individuals and of groups affected by their decisions, and the survival and growth of the regulatory agency. All other things being equal, it is assumed that the commissioners prefer to advance the commonweal; but they are also interested in protecting and augmenting their own and their agency's stature and power. This assumption does not demean the FCC. By long tradition, economists examine business behavior as profit maximization; they are now beginning to analyze the behavior of government officials in similar terms.

The second assumption is that the potential for economic gain motivates not only purely economic behavior but much of political behavior as well. As a result, the operation of social institutions and the process by which they are altered are highly sensitive to the magnitude and distribution of existing and potential economic interests.

The actual decisions of the FCC respond to the environment in which it operates. Among the important characteristics of that environment are the following:

1. The budget of the FCC is very small compared with the total amount of funds appropriated by Congress. In 1971 the FCC budget was $25 million in a $200 billion total.[54] Even for congressmen who are members of the subcommittee with special responsibilities for monitoring the FCC, evaluating its performance is only a tiny fraction of their overall responsibility. Furthermore, the low budget means that the FCC does not attract the attention of relatively remote interest groups that, in the competition for federal funds, focus on the major items. Thus, one important constraint on the FCC's operations—its budget—is easily lost in the shuffle of congressional business.

2. The FCC normally finds itself exercising a quasi-judicial role in an issue that pits the special interest of the strong, well-represented broadcasting industry against the general public interest. The latter is represented sometimes by staff members of the agency assigned to the task, and sometimes not at all.

3. The volume of the day-to-day business of the FCC has grown through

Democracy (University of Michigan Press, 1962); Davis and North, _Institutional Change and American Economic Growth;_ Anthony Downs, _An Economic Theory of Democracy_ (Harper, 1957), and _Inside Bureaucracy_ (Little, Brown, 1967); and William H. Riker, _The Theory of Political Coalitions_ (Yale University Press, 1962).

54. _The Budget of the United States Government, Fiscal Year 1971,_ p. 466.

time, as the industry has grown and become more complex and as technological and institutional changes have proliferated. Regulating radio evolved into the more difficult task of regulating television and, more recently, cable and subscription TV. Furthermore, the number of firms in each part of the broadcasting industry has grown. In response to its expanding responsibilities, the agency has "automated" decision making through an ever-lengthening list of rules for the regulated, and has increased incentives for staff members to settle regulatory issues so that formal hearings become unnecessary or perfunctory. One example is the recent proposal to make most license renewals virtually automatic.[55] This is formal recognition of an accomplished fact. Commissioners Cox and Johnson describe renewals as follows: "We [the commission] simply 'note' that the staff has completed its processing of the applications, doing little more than nod to the sketchy memoranda as they pass our desks."[56] Another aspect of automated decisions is that they make for cumbersome and costly procedures that insulate the agency from groups with insufficient resources to represent themselves effectively. Thus, in March 1971, the FCC had open hearings on cable TV policies. Because the costs of appearing at the hearings were not borne by the FCC, only the special interests could afford to be heard. Of the sixty-five witnesses, forty-four represented special private interests, eight spoke for public broadcasters, and four for local governments. (The remaining nine could be viewed as having no special interest.[57])

4. Much of the FCC's activity is insulated from external review and judgment. The three principal theaters in which the performance of an organization can be judged are the marketplace, the hearing room (including both courts and commissions), and the political arena.[58] An external economic, legal, or political test of an agency decision generally comes only

55. *Broadcasting*, Vol. 78 (January 19, 1970), pp. 21–23.

56. "Oklahoma Report," p. 6.

57. *Federal Communications Commission Reports*, Vol. 27, 2d Series (March 26, 1971), pp. 933–37.

58. Downs defines a bureau as an organization that, among other things, does not sell its output in a market (see *Inside Bureaucracy*, p. 26). A more restrictive definition, which depends on the absence of any external tests—economic, legal, and political—of the agency's output, has considerable merit. The activities of elected bodies and of organizations and agencies such as the antitrust division of the Justice Department are subject to an objective discipline similar to the market test of a firm. The external judgment on the organization causes a firm-like concern for efficiency in a broad sense; for any given access to resources, agencies whose activities require the voluntary acquiescence of individuals external to the agency will attempt to do as well as the given resources permit in the theater of external judgment.

as a direct consequence of some action by the agency that directly invites it or that causes some interest group to appeal the decision. As one example, the FCC could test the economic validity of its spectrum allocation policies by auctioning at least some rights to use the electromagnetic spectrum, but such a test cannot be forced on the commission except by law. Legal and political tests are the recourse of the losers in the proceedings of the regulatory agency. Agency decisions can be appealed through the federal courts, through direct pressure on congressmen, and through a political issue raised with the general public.

5. Few regulators devote their entire professional life to government service. More typically, commissioners and high-level staff members serve for a few years, and then move on to private industry. In the FCC, as in most other regulatory commissions, the main source of job opportunities is the regulated industry. Table 4-5 shows the extent to which FCC commissioners and top staff personnel were recruited from the regulated sector, or after a time moved on to jobs in it. While many of the FCC decision makers have had experience in the communications business, the data mainly demonstrate that for most a high-level FCC job is an entry into a career in the industry. These data do not imply that FCC officials are

Table 4-5. Affiliation of FCC Commissioners and Other Officials with Communications Industry, 1945–70[a]

Status of affiliation	Number of commissioners[b]	Number of other high-level staff officials[c]
Total number holding positions	33	32
Affiliation with communications industry[d]		
Before FCC service	4	8
After FCC service	21	13
Never[e]	11	11[f]

Sources: FCC, *37th Annual Report, Fiscal Year 1971*, p. 125; FCC, unpublished records; various professional directories.

a. All officials whose date of departure from the FCC fell within the 1945–70 period are included.

b. Three commissioners who were affiliated with the communications industry both before and after FCC service are counted in both groups. Therefore the components of this column add to three more than the total number of commissioners.

c. Includes the following positions: executive director, general counsel, chief engineer, chiefs of bureaus, chairman of review board, chief hearing examiner, chief of the office of opinions and review, and chief of reports and information.

d. Affiliation with communications industry means employment by a firm regulated by the FCC, either as a full-time employee or as an engineering or legal consultant. Former officials acting as lawyers representing communications firms before the FCC are considered to be affiliated with the industry.

e. Most with no affiliation after FCC service left the FCC to retire.

f. Includes three officials whose post-FCC status is unknown, but who were not affiliated with the communications industry before FCC service.

corrupt; rather, they reveal the inclinations, attitudes, and perspectives of the persons who are politically acceptable appointees to important jobs in the commission. They also suggest that most of these people must find themselves—at least some of the time—in the difficult position of sorting out the public interest from their own interests as future employees of regulated firms.

6. Regulatory decisions create powerful interest groups. The FCC's emphasis on local stations, and the station assignments that were its result, naturally created a group of station owners with a strong interest in the policy of localism. Had regional stations been licensed, there would now be a strong group interested in maintaining that form of organization of broadcasting. Regulatory policies can not only allocate, but also create profits that quickly become capitalized into the asset value of regulated firms; in effect they can create wealth.

Given these characteristics of the FCC's environment, the preferred state for regulators is one that minimizes visibility and change. If there is no external evidence (in the form of court cases or political pressures) that the agency is performing badly, its budget is likely to sail through Congress with only cursory review; new laws constraining its behavior are unlikely to be passed, while those extending its authority, should they be proposed, will probably be looked upon more favorably. Agency personnel will prosper, and still be confident—in the absence of an organized attack on their decisions—that they are serving the public interest.

Unfortunately, this confidence may not be justified, particularly when the agency makes a decision in response to a significant change in the regulated sector. The motivation to make decisions that minimize the chance of unfavorable external judgments begets several behavior patterns that inhibit socially desirable change.

First, the agency will be more receptive to groups with a high *per capita* interest in the decision than to those with a low per capita interest, even if the latter add up to a higher *cumulative* interest. A small group of individuals whose welfare depends vitally on a particular regulatory decision will be more likely to commit time, money, and political support to lobbying for a favorable decision. A large group with a small per capita interest in the decision may be composed of individuals not sufficiently interested in the issue to pay the costs of organizing and running an effective lobbying operation, even though their cumulative stake exceeds that of a small group whose members have high individual stakes in the outcome. The agency will then eschew the maximization of net social welfare to avert the wrath of an effective organization willing to appeal the decision legally and politically. In matters of broadcast policy, the small but intensely interested group is composed of stations and networks. The FCC, then, is likely to make decisions favorable to broadcasters in all but two types of instance: (a) when an issue has potential political importance—the "fairness doctrine" relating to political broadcasts is one example—that occasions close scrutiny of FCC decisions by politicians and other mass media; and (b) when an issue arises in which a special interest group other than broadcasters has a major stake in the outcome.

Second, when several special interest groups have a stake in an issue, the agency will tend to seek compromises among the competing powerful interests to a greater extent than is justified by social efficiency. Since the agency can only lose if a special interest is sufficiently antagonized to carry the battle to an external theater, it is motivated to parcel out some gains to all interests. This practice acts to weaken the desire to appeal the decision, to create the illusion among objective observers of "fairness," and to establish a potential loss to all interests from a change in the agency's decision imposed as a result of an appeal to an external judgment. For instance, the agency is likely to split the benefits of a technological change between the innovators and the firms whose welfare will be reduced by the innovation by forcing the former to subsidize the latter, either directly by making them share the innovation or indirectly by holding back the rate of its adoption to preserve the market of the noninnovating firm. The 1971 decision by the FCC on the importation of distant signals by cable systems in big cities is an ideal example of such a compromise.[59] Local broadcasters got some protection against competition and cable owners some leeway to offer a more attractive product. Yet neither received what they wanted—no importation (broadcasters) or unlimited importation (cable owners). As subsequent chapters will discuss, the compromise between the special interest groups was probably contrary to the interests of viewers, which, in this case, closely parallel that of the cable owner.

Third, when faced with an issue that is very likely to involve an appeal to an external judgment no matter what the decision, the agency will employ two tactics: (1) It will engage in interminably long information-collection proceedings, not only to delay the unhappy day when its decision must be defended, but also to try exhaustingly to find a conflict-avoiding compromise and to test the resolve of various interest groups and their willingness

59. See *Federal Register*, Vol. 37 (February 12, 1972), Pt. 2, pp. 3260–69.

to spend money and political capital to support their point of view; and (2) it will attempt to shift responsibility for the decision outside the agency by appealing to the Congress, the courts, other regulatory agencies, or the executive to provide direction. In the fifteen-year consideration of subscription television, the FCC practiced both techniques. First, it "experimented" with a few licensees for ten years; then it turned to the courts and Congress to decide the issue. Decisions on cable TV were similarly protracted. The chronology of the UHF allocation proceedings provides a striking illustration: The FCC first considered the possibilities of UHF in the late forties; its 1952 allocation plan included UHF intermixed with VHF, although pressure immediately arose to consider deintermixture. In June 1955 it began hearings on five deintermixture cases. In June 1956 it issued a general report and order which included a recommendation for research and development to determine the feasibility of moving all television to the UHF band. Such a move had been declared contrary to the public interest by commission spokesmen in 1952 and 1954. In February 1957 it issued deintermixture orders making five small areas all-UHF, but later reversed itself on one area. In all, by 1962 the selective deintermixture policy of the FCC had led to the decisions to make six markets all-UHF. No more was ever heard of this proposal, its application becoming unnecessary with the passage of the all-channel receiver legislation. Technically, however, deintermixture still remains to be carried out.[60]

All of these tendencies are likely to become more pronounced through time as the agency staff tries harder to keep yet unresolved issues from reaching the commissioners and as the rules and procedures—the devices for automating decisions—become more numerous, more time-consuming, and more costly to abide by. The rising costs of obtaining agency permission to make technological and institutional innovations will form an ever-larger impediment to change.

Forces for Change in Regulatory Policy

The propositions just explored support the conclusion that change in regulatory policy will come very slowly. But, by similar reasoning, four forces might occasionally overcome this inertia.

60. *Broadcasting·Telecasting*, Vol. 49 (July 4, 1955), Vol. 50 (June 11, June 25, 1956), Vol. 51 (July 2, 1956), and Vol. 52 (March 4, 1957); *Harvard Law Review*, Vol. 75 (June 1962), pp. 1583, 1588–89; FCC, Second Report on Deintermixture, issued June 26, 1956, published in Pike and Fischer, *Radio Regulation*, Vol. 13, p. 1571.

First, a business firm might envision large profits from a change in regulatory policy. Such visions animate those involved in both the STV and the cable proceedings to provide the legal and political capital necessary to keep them going. If it is sufficiently powerful, a special interest group acting for change can, in time, overcome one that stands for the status quo. Nevertheless, promoters of change suffer two disadvantages: (1) Their profits are highly uncertain and accrue (if at all) in the future—that is, their operations are not securely based on current profits; and (2) the innovators are only a small fraction of those who eventually will prosper as a result of regulatory change—as in most innovations, the secondary wave of followers will realize the greater part of the benefits of change.

As a second force working for change, "public interest" lobbyists occasionally carry a battle to a regulatory commission. In FCC hearings, comments have been submitted by such diverse groups as the American Civil Liberties Union, the Broadcasting and Film Commission of the National Council of Churches, and the authors of this book. Such groups are more active in television regulation than in many regulatory issues because television is rightly considered an influential factor in the political and moral attitudes of the society. Whether these groups are effective remains a question.

Third, some commissioners and staff members are impatient with limited reforms and compromises designed to meet what they view as major problems. The dilemma inherent in such reforms is that they can reduce the profits of the established industry yet leave unsatisfied the critics or the innovators, and so please no one. (The corresponding benefit, on the other hand, is that no one may be so dissatisfied that he seeks major rectifying legislation.) The dissatisfaction with restricted reform may be reflected in the dissent FCC Chairman Dean Burch entered to the prime-time access rule. Chairman Burch defined the issue as the need to make diverse programming available to the public. After concluding that the rule would at best make a minor contribution, he argued that instead of "spending years on a rule of this nature, the Commission must concentrate on the obvious alternatives which have a different economic base and thus may make a genuine contribution to diversity."[61] He went on to mention subscription television, cables, and public broadcasting, the topics treated in the next four chapters.

Fourth, there breathes in some commissioners and staff members an

---

61. "Dissenting Statement of Chairman Dean Burch in Which Commissioner Wells Concurs," p. 6, part of Docket 12782, FCC 70–466, May 4, 1970.

entrepreneurial spirit that runs counter to the more pervasive tendency to minimize external criticism and review. Such individuals, like their counterparts in business, wish to be known by the reforms they have instituted during their tenure in office. They are willing to sacrifice the prospect of a good job in the regulated industry when their government career draws to a close by courting the criticism and turmoil that accompanies a record of reform. Commissioner Nicholas Johnson probably fits this mold. Still, such men are nearly always in a small minority within any established commission, including the FCC. Just as the realities of the economic and political power of special interests influence agency decisions, so, too, do they affect the choice of commissioners. While the broadcasting industry does not have enough power to choose new FCC commissioners, it normally can prevent the appointment of a potential enemy. Commissioner Johnson's positions, which broadcasters regarded as threatening, made his reappointment highly unlikely.[62]

It is difficult to predict a priori which of the competing forces of change and inertia will be stronger. In general, inertia appears to prevail enough of the time to inhibit both technological and institutional change. Those changes that occur reflect mostly the emergence of a new special interest. Recognition of this tendency of the agencies is necessary not only to explaining their behavior and predicting their decisions, but also to steering them more in the direction of the public interest. In the case of the FCC, reforms in the structure of broadcasting are far more likely if some protection can be afforded to the existing interests and if some other existing, powerful special interest can be made to regard its own welfare as coincident with the public interest in the change. It is against this backdrop that we investigate the potential reforms of broadcasting offered by subscription television, cables, satellites, videocassettes, and public television.

---

62. *Broadcasting* periodically comments on his likely departure—see Vol. 82 (March 13, 1972), pp. 7, 40, 74.

CHAPTER FIVE

The Possibilities of Subscription Television

SUBSCRIPTION TELEVISION (STV), sometimes known as pay TV, is a system in which viewers pay either for each program or for continuing access to additional channels. STV introduces the box office concept into television and shifts the financing, at least in part, from advertisers to viewers.

Subscription television has been debated for over fifteen years. It has been the subject of several congressional hearings, numerous legislative proposals, repeated Federal Communications Commission (FCC) proceedings, and even a constitutional amendment in the State of California.[1] The debate has been so intense, so extended, and so inconclusive, because the potential stakes appear to be so immense. The possibility of placing STV on cable has now raised the debate to a new pitch.

Opponents say that STV threatens the survival of free television and the enormous consumer satisfaction that Americans derive from it (as de-

---

1. See *Television Inquiry*, Hearings before the Senate Committee on Interstate and Foreign Commerce, 84 Cong. 2 sess. (1956), Pt. 3; *Subscription Television*, Hearings before the Subcommittee on Communications and Power of the House Committee on Interstate and Foreign Commerce, 90 Cong. 1 sess. (1967); and *Subscription Television—1969*, Hearings before the same committee, 91 Cong. 1 sess. (1969). Over sixty bills in the House and one in the Senate have been introduced to amend the Communications Act of 1934 so as to prohibit STV. For a complete listing of these bills see the yearly *Congressional Quarterly Almanac* (Washington: Congressional Quarterly, Inc.), since 1956. A short history of FCC proceedings on STV can be found in *Subscription Television*, Hearings (1967), pp. 246–48, cited above, hereafter referred to as *Subscription Television* (1967). For the history of the constitutional amendment in California, see issues of the magazine, *Broadcasting*, between September 21 and November 9, 1964, and the issues for May 24, 1965, and March 7, 1966. The amendment, which would have prohibited STV, was passed by a referendum in November 1964 and in March 1966 was found unconstitutional and overturned by a 6–1 decision of the Supreme Court of the State of California.

scribed in Chapter 2). They argue that the principal effect of STV will be the introduction of payments for existing programming.

Proponents argue that STV will allow viewer preferences to be registered more efficiently. In the present commercial system, television is geared to advertising revenues and viewers influence programming only by their numbers. With a charge per program, both their numbers and the intensity of their desires could be reflected. A program that draws few viewers at a high price could compete for broadcast time with mass programming that attracts a large audience at a low price. In addition, if advertising were banned from pay TV, viewers who find it offensive would have an opportunity to escape it without sacrificing television entertainment.

The empirical evidence is too meager to provide a solid estimate of the potential economic performance of subscription television. Only three STV systems have had as many as several thousand subscribers—one in Etobicoke, a Toronto suburb, one in Los Angeles and San Francisco, and another in Hartford, Connecticut. In the fifties and early sixties, smaller systems operated for a short time in San Francisco, Los Angeles, Palm Springs, Chicago, and Bartlesville, Oklahoma.[2] With actual experience so limited, a discussion of STV is necessarily speculative and must rest largely on inferences from knowledge of present commercial television and of other media.

The Gains and Losses from an All-STV System

Subscription television probably would be politically feasible only as a supplement to the current advertiser-supported system. Americans value the present system of "free" television too highly ever to permit a completely pay system; indeed, most of the political opposition to even a modest amount of STV arises from fears that free television will be injured. Yet analysis of a universal STV system is worthwhile because it throws into bold relief the benefits and limitations of the proposal for pay TV.

The principal presumed gain from STV would be a more accurate reflection of consumer preferences. Minasian has made the point well:

2. Information on the STV systems in Toronto, Hartford, and Los Angeles-San Francisco is contained in David M. Blank, "The Quest for Quantity and Diversity in Television Programming," in American Economic Association, *Papers and Proceedings of the Seventy-eighth Annual Meeting, 1965* (*American Economic Review*, Vol. 56, May 1966), pp. 451–54.

In an advertising-supported system . . . the program results reflect an all-or-nothing type of voting since votes take weights of either one (viewer) or zero (nonviewer). In contrast, a subscription system allows proportional representation, since votes take different weights (different prices paid for different kinds of programs) and reveal the voters' subjective evaluations of the program. Therefore, a subscription system can be expected to yield a more diversified program menu than an advertising system, because the former enables individuals, by concentrating their dollar votes, to overcome the "unpopularity" of their tastes.[3]

A weighted voting system requires different prices for different programs. With respect to the sort of prime-time entertainment programming that appears on the three existing networks, widespread price differences would be unlikely in an all-STV system. The financial success of programs would still differ, owing to varying popularity, but this is not the salient issue in pricing decisions. Rather, the responsiveness of audience size to price variations—the price elasticity—is the critical factor that would permit the intensity of demand to be measured against mere numbers of viewers at a going price (whether the price is at or above zero).

Price elasticities may indeed differ among programs. But even if they do, the networks would be unlikely to set prices accordingly. The popularity of a new program could not be predicted at the beginning of a season, when the pricing decision would be made. Moreover, the popularity of an estab-lished program would be likely to change, even during a season. The effect of uncertainty about audience size would be compounded by the quest for highly successful shows. The demand for a new show would be a function of, among other things, the number of people who have been exposed to it (at least once). Hence, the pricing decision would determine not only the initial audience, but future demand as well. Given all these uncertainties, the best strategy might be to avoid price premiums on the popular programs. Industries that face similar problems—newspapers, movies, books, phonograph records, the theater—exhibit very little price variation in relation to the popularity of the offering.

An additional factor peculiar to broadcasting is that some part of the big audience of a popular show will watch the following show on the same station simply out of viewer inertia. This gain from "adjacency" would probably appear also with STV, though viewers might be more discriminating after the imposition of prices.

Just as networks would not charge a premium price for popular pro-

3. Jora R. Minasian, "Television Pricing and the Theory of Public Goods," *Journal of Law and Economics*, Vol. 7 (October 1964), p. 75.

grams, neither would they cut prices on the less popular programs. Because television is a highly concentrated industry, the three networks serve their individual interests by limiting price competition, for price cuts would be self-defeating. The marginal program would probably gain little from a price cut, for if it succeeded in attracting many viewers, the other two networks, losing significant audience and revenue, would respond by lowering prices on competing programs. Instead of inducing price cuts, unpopular programs would be removed from the schedule, just as is now the case, since launching a potentially successful program would be a more profitable use of the time. The outcome would be prices that reflect the general intensity of demand for television (capturing monopoly-like profits for the industry) but not the relative costs and popularity of programs.

The implications of such a price policy are quite striking for the argument that STV will change programming. If all mass entertainment were offered at roughly the same price, incentives to the networks would remain unchanged. Networks would soon pick that mix of popular programming that maximized audience size. Indeed, the only difference from the present system would be that the single price would be positive instead of zero. Network profits would rise significantly, particularly if advertising were still allowed.

Proponents may dismiss the preceding argument as unrelated to the purpose they see in STV, and as expressed by Minasian. The means through which STV would increase program diversity is visualized not as a change in the mix among situation comedies or among mystery-adventure series, but rather as a shift of some programming from mass entertainment to programs of higher quality—public affairs and serious entertainment with high prices, appealing to a small group.[4] Ignoring the cost differences, "heavy" programs would have to carry a price at least twice that of "light" programs to yield equivalent profits. The Hartford and California STV experiments did not attempt to attach premium prices to heavy programming. In Hartford, the prices for concerts, opera, ballet, variety, and popular music averaged about $1.50; movies, $1.03; and educational programs about $0.70. In California, specials were about $1.20 and educational programs about $0.80, whereas movies were $1.40. Audience disparity

---

4. Audiences for present public affairs and cultural programming are one-fourth to one-half of those for entertainment. See John A. Dimling, Jr., and others, *Identification and Analysis of the Alternatives for Achieving Greater Television Program Diversity in the United States*, Prepared for the President's Task Force on Communications Policy (Lexington, Ky.: Spindletop Research, 1968), p. B-15.

among program types was, if anything, larger in the two STV experiments than on commercial television. In Hartford, Broadway plays and drama were seen by 7.5 percent of the subscribers, concerts, opera, and ballet by 12.4 percent, and educational programs by 0.8 percent, as compared with 18 percent for older feature films and 27 percent for the newer films.[5] The ratings of California programs followed the same pattern.

Still, many people believe that STV could permit minority programming. One difficulty of this view is that in supporting it most proponents compare minority programs on STV with popular entertainment on free channels. Thus, Minasian states:

To gain some perspective, note that programs which are currently discarded may have had as many as 15–20 million viewers. Network programs do not become "profitable" before passing the 20 million mark, and popular shows command 30–50 million viewers, according to the rating services. *A nonpopular show by current standards, if viewers are willing to pay a quarter on subscription television, needs an audience of less than a million to compete with a current show with 30 million viewers on advertising-supported television* (many of the current popular programs cost only a few pennies per family) [emphasis added].[6]

Minasian compares a minority program on STV with a majority program on free television. Yet without restrictions on entry, the popular program could switch to STV, altering the comparison. Restated in terms of television homes rather than viewers, his example suggests that a popular show draws 15 million homes. The likely STV charges for such a show are, say, 10 cents per half hour, yielding a revenue of $1,500,000. To realize the same revenue as the popular program, a minority program with a *realized* potential of 1 million homes would require a charge of $1.50. Minority viewers might well pay the quarter of Professor Minasian's example; but, at $1.50, all the potential is unlikely to be realized. Assuming that only half of it was, the price would have to be $3.00 if the revenue of a popular program were to be matched. To illustrate in another way, the mass audience of 15 million homes would have to pay less than $0.02 each—roughly the price adver-

5. Readers of this volume may not be surprised to learn that on Hartford pay TV precisely *one* viewer chose to watch "You and the Economy," a program featuring Yale economists. The Hartford data are from, or derived from, FCC, "Joint Comments of Zenith Radio Corporation and Teco, Inc., in Support of Petition for Nation-wide Authorization of Subscription Television," Docket 11279, March 10, 1965, reproduced in *Subscription Television* (1967). Data for Toronto, Los Angeles, and San Francisco are in Oxtoby-Smith, Inc., "Study of Consumer Response to Pay TV" (Oxtoby-Smith, 1965; processed).

6. Minasian, "Television Pricing," pp. 75–76.

tisers now pay—to outbid the one million homes willing to pay $0.25 for *their* choice. Thus, it seems unrealistic to expect "small" minorities—in this case, almost four million people—to outbid majorities for network time.

STV is most likely to promote diversity through independent stations, the most successful of which attract 5 to 10 percent of the television homes. One can imagine Professor Minasian's minority program capturing 1 percent of TV homes at 10 cents a home (five times the advertiser price for standard programming), hence yielding revenues equal to current advertising revenues of independents.[7] Of course, this is the efficient way to obtain diversity—to supplant the *least*, rather than the *most*, popular programming. The difficulty is that one-third of the television homes, including those in five of the twelve largest markets, do not have access to very high frequency (VHF) independents.[8]

STV could have a second effect:

The total resources used in broadcasting will be different in that the profitability of the broadcast station depends upon the system of payment for its services. It is plausible to expect that viewers would subscribe to see current programs at a higher price than a few pennies per family, as measured by the advertising expenditures. This, in turn, could be expected to induce more resources to be drawn to the industry.[9]

As shown in Chapter 3, the bottleneck to expansion of television is VHF channel space, not profitability. Unused channels are available on the ultra high frequency (UHF) band, but they present problems of signal quality. Both more independent stations and STV might be profitable on VHF while neither could survive on UHF. Cable transmission eliminates the UHF disadvantage, and indeed the availability of cable channels has revived the STV debate. Only on cable is this potential effect of STV likely to be felt, although STV is not the only viable means to increase television diversity. An alternative is more standard commercial stations on the cable.

The Costs of an All-STV System

The cost of the all-STV system is the inherent inefficiency of pricing for television programs noted in Chapter 2. While a positive price will exclude some viewers, this does not conserve any resources, for the marginal cost of another viewer of an existing program is, in effect, zero.

7. Five percent at two cents equals 1 percent at ten cents.
8. See Television Digest, Inc., *Television Factbook, Services Volume, 1970–1971 Edition* (Washington: TD, 1970), p. 42a.
9. Minasian, "Television Pricing," p. 76.

The Hartford experiment demonstrated that it is the lowest income groups (under $4,000) who would be excluded from an STV system.[10] Even some families earning $5,000 to $10,000 would probably restrict their viewing as nightly television became a large item in their budget.

The most significant loss is the massive income transfer from consumers to the television industry. Viewers would watch the same kinds of programs, but they would be poorer by several billion dollars. Unless the number of channels were significantly increased, most of this vast sum would flow to the present networks and program producers.

Upper-income groups would also benefit from an all-STV system. They are not, in general, avid television watchers, and STV charges would not be burdensome for them. At the same time, they are the group most interested in more diversity, which STV to some degree would provide.

Evaluation of All-STV

If individual satisfaction is the measure of an all-STV system, the losers far outnumber the beneficiaries. If dollars are the measure, the sum TV viewers of standard programs will pay the networks—the vast bulk of STV payments—swamps the sum devoted to program diversity and new stations, which are the presumed benefits from STV. Hence, an all-STV system is an inefficient way to achieve these aims. This conclusion suggests the essence of a desirable STV system—the preservation of free television together with STV for revenue to support more options and diversity.

A look at an exclusively subscription television system underlines the sources of popular opposition to STV and makes dubious its allure for economists. As to the first, the networks quite apparently do a good job in selecting programs that maximize audience size. Most people recognize that to pay for exactly the same programs now financed through advertising would mean a massive reduction in their welfare.

Because an all-STV system is politically infeasible, the argument surrounding STV in whatever form has not been rigorous. Its proponents have tended to ignore its income redistribution aspects, the oligopolistic character of competition among the networks, and the limited number of VHF channels, all of which cast doubt on the expectation that the system would provide a more accurate reflection of consumer tastes. Of more significance, concentration on the abstract advantages of a price system has precluded

10. See Table 2-2, p. 25.

serious examination of the problems of a mixed STV and advertiser-supported television industry.

The Mixed Over-the-air System

STV will emerge, if at all, alongside present advertiser-supported television. Political constraints dictate that the three networks will continue to function on their present basis. But even in their absence the highly profitable networks would probably find STV unattractive as long as free television were possible.

The Socially Efficient Combination

If STV offered only programs now unavailable on free television and if free television retained all its existing programs, STV would represent an unambiguous gain in consumer welfare. Those who watched—and paid for —STV would do so only if it contributed to their satisfaction. Others could watch the free programs they now watch and be no worse off. All would be at least as well off as before.

The conclusion that a mixed system is unambiguously preferable rests critically on the assumption that free TV remains unchanged—that is, that it would present the programs that can be shown profitably with advertiser financing. To show such programs on STV would imply that viewers would pay for what they could receive free. Conversely, STV ought to carry only programs that are unprofitable for free TV but that, with positive prices, are profitable on STV.[11] This criterion, which insures additional options and precludes welfare losses, we call the *program rule*.

The two threats to the program rule are audience diversion from advertiser to viewer-supported programs and program diversion from free to subscription TV.

Audience diversion matters because each home that shifts to an STV program reduces the revenues of commercial television by about three cents an hour. Because the network systems realize substantial profits, and producers of the most popular shows earn significant rents, the diversion of some viewers to STV, and the resulting fall in advertising revenues, could

11. These programs are unprofitable in the sense that, given the limited availability of air time, they are less profitable than the least successful programs being shown, so their airing would entail a reduction in profits. Also, it should be noted that STV makes "adult" entertainment possible because children can more easily be excluded from watching it.

be absorbed without a major change in commercial TV programming. The most likely casualties would be a few public service offerings on the networks, which rarely cover costs even now.

Demand and Costs for Over-the-air STV

The nature of the threat to the program rule (in the absence of regulation) depends on the demand and costs for STV and the extent of the STV system that would emerge. One such system was tried in the Hartford experiment.

Cost and revenue data supplied by Zenith Radio Corporation and its subsidiary, Teco, Inc., participants in the Hartford experiment, underlie Table 5-1. At the assumed revenue per viewer of $106, the system needed 20,000 subscribers to break even. A before-tax rate of return of 18 percent —roughly the average for manufacturing corporations—would require 75,000 subscribers, compared with the 3,000 to 5,000—about 4 percent of the Hartford market—the system had during most of its life.[12] On a national scale, if 8 percent of the television homes subscribed to STV, an operation based on the Hartford model could realize this rate of profit only in the ten largest markets.[13]

STV's costs on an expanded basis would probably be different from those in the Hartford experiment. For example, some STV operators may not need the assistance in promoting the system and in developing programming that Zenith's subsidiary, Teco, provided in exchange for a franchise fee, and thus the fee may not be necessary. Furthermore, the $300,000 shown as payment for station time may include the alternative value—say, $100,000—of a UHF station in regular commercial television, not just the operating costs. These two adjustments would bring the estimate of costs down about 10 percent. Finally, programming costs per viewer would be much lower with more stations and a larger viewing audience.

The revenue per subscriber based on the Hartford experience is also open

12. This was a very good performance, considering that the STV station was a UHF independent, and that the experiment began before the all-channel receiver law of 1962 took effect.

13. The 8 percent is based on an assumption that Hartford's UHF handicap halved the penetration of the system. To achieve 75,000 subscribers, a market of 900,000 TV homes would be required. According to *Television Factbook, Services Volume, 1970–1971 Edition*, p. 42a, only ten markets are larger than this. They contain about one-third of all TV homes.

Table 5-1. Restatement on a Per-subscriber Basis of Zenith-Teco's Breakeven Projection for Subscription Television System

Expense item	Dollar amount
Variable income and expense items	*Per subscriber*
Income	
Programs	65.00
Decoder rental	39.00
Installation	2.00[a]
Total income	106.00[b]
Expenses	
Program product	22.75
Sales and commissions	8.15
Franchise fee[c]	5.20
Technical	7.93
Taxes (other than federal)	2.22
Supplies, truck, bad debts, other	3.10
Depreciation[d]	27.09
Total variable expense	76.44
Gross margin before fixed expense	29.56
Fixed expense items[e]	*Per station*
Station time	300,000
Administrative salaries	94,000
Program staff	23,000
Lines and facilities	32,000
Fees to Broadcast Music, Inc., and American Society of Composers, Authors, and Publishers	18,000
IBM equipment rental	88,000
Rent	15,000
Legal, audit, insurance, travel, telephone, utilities, dues, maintenance	20,000
Total fixed expenses	590,000

Breakeven point: $590,000 ÷ $29.56 = 20,000 subscribers

Source: Prepared by the Federal Communications Commission staff as part of Docket 11279 on subscription television service, from data supplied by Zenith Radio Corporation and Teco, Inc., on the basis of the Hartford subscription television experiment. Reproduced in *Subscription Television*, Hearings before the Subcommittee on Communications and Power of the House Committee on Interstate and Foreign Commerce, 90 Cong. 1 sess. (1967), p. 131.

a. Zenith-Teco assumes 20 percent turnover, or 4,000 per year. This gives a total of $40,000 installation income, or $2 per subscriber (of which there are 20,000 at the breakeven point).

b. The figure is somewhat lower than the 1962–64 average because it counts on lower installation revenues in the long run.

c. Five percent of program and rental income.

d. Primarily for decoders.

e. Some fixed expenses increase slightly with increased income.

to question. Ideally, this information should come from a demand curve for STV, relating price and usage, but the Hartford station did not experiment with prices. Such information as is available arises from the fact that various STV systems followed different price policies (see the last column of

Table 5-2. Penetration and Average Expenditure for Four Subscription Television Systems, Various Years, 1962–64

STV system and year	Penetration[a] (percent)	Average annual expenditure (dollars)	Annual charge
Etobicoke, 1962	45	33	No
Etobicoke, 1964	12	65	Yes
Hartford, 1963	3.5	100	Yes
Los Angeles, 1964	31	60	No
San Francisco, 1964	20	61	No

Source: Oxtoby-Smith, "Consumer Response to Pay TV—An Interim Report on the Conclusion of a Study in Los Angeles Three Months after STV Initiation" (New York: Oxtoby-Smith, Inc., 1965; processed), p. 29.
a. Penetration is the proportion of households in the service area that subscribe.

Table 5-2). STV charges were divided between the specific program charge and the annual charge for the decoder. The range for the first typically was $0.25 to $1.50, depending on an estimate of the program appeal, with higher prices charged for live sports events.[14] In the Etobicoke operations, movies of comparable quality were available at $1.00 and $1.25. It was reported that the "25% increase in price for motion pictures of high critical merit ... proved to be no deterrent."[15] The audience penetration was about 20 percent for the $1.25 movies and 23 percent for the $1.00 movies, a statistically insignificant difference that, in any event, led to higher revenues at the higher prices. Prices for hockey games were increased from $1.00 to $1.50 with no change in audience. These data suggest that, within the range of prices charged in the experiments, higher program charges might well increase revenues and profits.

The major price deterrent to the popularity of STV appears to be the annual charge. As Table 5-2 suggests, systems that have none appear to achieve the higher rates of penetration. In the Etobicoke experiment, the introduction of an annual charge—lower than Hartford's—was associated with a significant loss of subscribers.[16] The annual charge penalizes the less

14. Statistical data in the remainder of this paragraph are from *Subscription Television* (1967), pp. 370–71.
15. *Ibid.*, p. 370.
16. *Ibid.*, p. 369. Prior to the annual charge, the system had as many as 5,500 subscribers; after its introduction, subscriptions dropped to 2,500, even though the area served by the cable had been expanded. Use of STV, however, was much greater by the smaller group.

frequent user and forces the viewer to place a value on a year's subscription in advance.

The fixed annual charge was designed to cover the high expense of the decoder, which precludes nonpayers from viewing and serves to record selections. In Hartford, over a third of total costs were attributable to the decoder.

High collection costs not only discourage use, but also reduce the social contribution of STV, since so much of its resources must be expended in that manner. The benefits of a price system conceivably could be so considerable that high collection costs would be justified. And it may be that with a larger market, costs for decoders might decline as the result of either the accumulation of production experience or the development of cheaper collection systems.

The Outlook for Over-the-air STV

An extrapolation of the Hartford experience suggests that, whether broadcast on VHF or UHF channels, STV would be profitable in only a few of the nation's largest markets.

PROGRAM DIVERSION. If STV operated on UHF and in only a few cities, it would not threaten a general diversion of present programming. Most programs would continue on commercial television simply because STV could not offer comparable payments to their producers. The Hartford experience suggests that STV programming would have three main elements:

1. Programs that draw such low audiences that they now do not appear on the networks.
2. Recent movies and sports that do not now appear on television. Motion picture companies and sports promoters keep these programs off television for fear of jeopardizing box office receipts. Shown on STV, such programs would have lower audiences, and thus less effect on box office revenues. In addition, STV revenues typically are shared with teams and movie makers, so that box office diversion would be offset.
3. Special events—particularly in sports—that occur infrequently but that evoke intense demand by certain fans. Here premium prices can be charged. In Hartford, 63 percent of the subscribers watched the February 1964 Clay-Liston championship fight at a price of $3—more than double the normal charge for an STV program.

AUDIENCE DIVERSION. Hartford STV captured only 1 percent of the audience for its most successful regular program, current movies. Only if several STV stations were operating would audience diversion even be noticeable, and such an eventuality is not possible given the limited availability of channel assignments.

Only the special STV programs could significantly diminish commercial television audiences. The $3 price of the Clay-Liston fight was more than fifty times its advertising value, which means that not all subscribers would have to pay the higher price to outbid the network. Such cream skimming is not a major problem for the networks, for it has already largely occurred through closed-circuit theater TV to which major boxing matches, the Indianapolis "500," and even some home games of teams who have sold out their stadiums have already been diverted. Were these programs to switch to STV, neither the networks nor the fans would be harmed significantly, and the fans would probably benefit. Should the remaining major televised events—the World Series or the Super Bowl, for example—switch, sports fans would experience substantial loss in welfare. This one difficulty could be cured by specific restrictions laid down by the FCC.

Over-the-air STV is, then, a paper tiger of a threat to commercial television. There is little merit in prohibiting the spread of the Hartford type especially if the program rule serves as a constraint on STV development. The importance of over-the-air STV is surely going to be small as long as regulation reserves a large number of channels for free TV.

Most of the broadcasting industry sees little future for this kind of STV. The principal exception is Zenith Radio Corporation, the manufacturer of electrical products related to broadcasting, which in 1972 bid for UHF stations in Los Angeles and Chicago that it plans to operate on a subscription basis.[17]

Cable STV

The prospects for cable STV are significantly brighter than those for the type of system described in the preceding section.[18] The UHF signal disadvantage does not apply to cable, and STV, as only one of several cable services, bears only part of the cost of the entire system. With the renewal

17. *Broadcasting*, Vol. 82 (March 13, 1972), p. 37.

18. Several firms have recently entered the "pay-cable" field, and experimental systems are already under way. See *Broadcasting*, Vol. 82 (May 22, 1972), pp. 8, 21–22.

of interest in STV occasioned by the development of cable has come stronger opposition to it.

Revived interest in STV appears to us to be justified. If the FCC permits the development of a national cable system serving half the homes, the chances are excellent that an economically viable STV system can be instituted. STV on cable presents problems somewhat different from those involved in over-the-air STV, requiring a separate examination of demand and costs.

The Demand for STV

As argued above, consumers probably would be willing to pay a substantial amount for more viewing options, even when provided a full complement of free network and independent stations. According to the estimates of the demand for viewing options described in Appendix A, if cable systems provided three networks, at least four independent stations, and a public broadcasting station, they could further increase the number of subscribers by 9 million, generating additional revenues of about $600 million, by providing access to another channel with programming similar to that shown by the existing three networks. Even a fifth strong independent station on cable would draw 2 million more subscribers, or about $130 million additional revenues.[19] These figures provide rough estimates of the amount cable subscribers would be willing to pay for STV.

Despite all its limitations, the Hartford experiment also suggests considerable demand for more viewing options. Between 1962 and 1964, subscribers paid, on the average, $2.17 a week (or about $113 annually) for STV. In 1971 dollars, this figure would be $147 annually. If cable were permitted to develop to the extent predicted by the economic and statistical analysis in Chapter 6, reaching 50 percent penetration of all TV homes (about 30 million), and if, as in Hartford, 4 percent of the homes with cable service subscribed to an STV service charging the same prices as did the Hartford system (corrected for inflation), the revenues for the subscription service would be about $175 million. (The Hartford STV station was UHF, which, of course, limited demand for it.)

A detailed breakdown of the revenues generated by specific program types indicates that the strongest unfilled consumer demand is in categories similar to those that dominate current network schedules. The last column of Table 5-3 shows the estimated revenue per showing on a national cable

19. These figures are based on a $65 annual fee for cable service.

Table 5-3. Hartford STV Programs and Revenues, by Category, June 1962–June 1964

Program category	Average charge[a]	Distribution of separate features		Distribution of all broadcasts		Audience ratings		Revenue per program for all showings on a national cable (thousands of 1963 dollars)
		Number of programs	Percent of programs	Number of showings	Percent of showings	Percent of subscribers viewing each showing	Percent of subscribers viewing all showings	
Movies	$1.03	432	72.1	1,537	86.5	5.6	20.1	$ 497
Sports	1.37	79	13.2	79	4.4	9.8	9.8	322
Championship boxing	2.06	6	1.0	6	0.3	63.3	63.3	3,130
College basketball	0.81	2	0.3	2	0.1	13.6	13.6	264
High school basketball	0.25	1	0.2	1	0.1	10.7	10.7	64
Professional basketball	1.00	21	3.5	21	1.2	6.6	6.6	158
College football	1.05	5	0.8	5	0.3	6.2	6.2	156
Professional hockey	1.07	44	7.3	44	2.5	5.3	5.3	136
Entertainment productions	1.60	35	5.8	97[b]	5.5	3.1	8.7	334
Concerts, opera, and ballet	1.50	6	1.0	13	0.7	10.6	12.4	446
Popular music and variety	1.48	15	2.5	48	2.7	4.1	13.1	465
Broadway plays and other drama	1.62	11	1.8	34	1.9	2.4	7.5	292
Miscellaneous	2.40	3	0.5	3	0.2	1.7	1.7	98
Educational features	0.71	50	8.3	57	3.2	0.7	0.8	14
Medical presentations (limited to 100 subscribing doctors)	1.50	3	0.5	6	0.3	9.3[c]	18.7[c]	…
All	1.08	599	100.0	1,776	100.0	5.5	16.4	425

Source: From, or derived from, data in "Joint Comments of Zenith Radio Corporation and Teco, Inc.," in *Subscription Television* (1967), pp. 255 ff. Figures may not add to totals due to rounding.

a. Average charge during the second year of operation.
b. In cited source, total number of entertainment showings adds to 98, but summary table lists 97.
c. Percentage of the 100 doctor-subscribers; the 100 doctors were about 2 percent of all subscribers.

system (encompassing half the homes) of each type of program on the Hartford system, assuming that, on a cable system serving half the television homes, 8 percent of the viewers subscribe to STV.[20] Recent movies, boxing, and several entertainment categories were the most popular of the STV offerings; only boxing is not offered regularly on free TV. A fairly recent movie shown three or four times generated revenues of about $500,-000 on a cable STV system of national scale. An average concert produced revenues from all performances of $140,000; an average ballet or opera, $530,000; and a typical nightclub performance, $290,000 (all in 1963 prices).

Considering the characteristics of the Hartford STV operation, it did remarkably well. First, Hartford STV was broadcast by a UHF station, with all its problems. Since, all other things being equal, a UHF station will attract about half as large an audience as a VHF station, STV on cables could be expected to do twice as well. Second, as the only STV station, the Hartford operation could not afford to purchase programming especially for broadcast on STV, just as no single television station—particularly one capable of reaching a maximum of only 100,000 homes—can afford to produce programs of the same quality as network programming. As a result, the Hartford STV station relied primarily on programs produced for other media. Third, the station used did not devote itself exclusively to STV. Except for the two or three STV programs daily in prime time, it carried free, advertiser-supported television; hence, its total revenues were higher than those strictly from STV operation. Fourth, and perhaps most important, the Hartford experiment was limited by the FCC to 5,000 subscribers. The operators of the experiment did not attempt to maximize the penetration of their system, thus placing a severe limit on the revenues of the system and on the programs it could afford.[21] For all these reasons, Hartford STV did not offer programming of network quality. It was more akin to a strong independent, which makes the revenues it generated consistent with the estimates from data on cable penetration.

All of these factors, plus the likelihood that the 30 percent growth in real per capita personal income since the Hartford experiment has increased the amount consumers would be willing to spend on STV, suggest that $175 million is now too low an estimate of the revenues that could be generated by a strong, national STV service on cable.

20. The full 8 percent is assumed because the handicap UHF imposes is lifted. The table is similar to Table 2-5; it is based on fewer potential viewers but more subscribers.
21. See *Subscription Television* (1967), p. 292.

Two other factors would detract from the potential demand of a Hartford-like system. Viewers on cables will already be paying $60 to $90 annually for the basic cable services, and will be provided at least seven commercial channels, whereas Hartford subscribers had only the three networks. The willingness to spend on STV would be reduced by both the commitment to cable payments and the greater availability of free television.

Costs of a Cable STV System

Networks currently spend about $175 million each on production, including both programs produced by the network and purchases from independent companies. Because the hope is that STV programs will be similar in quality to those on existing networks, these figures are a good place to start in estimating the program costs for an STV system.

Programming costs have considerable flexibility, particularly over several years; as Chapter 3 discussed, much of the present costs are rents—the capturing of program popularity in talent fees. Hence, the fees paid to program producers will depend to some extent on the success of the system. The minimum programming cost is the lowest price that must be paid to induce individuals to work in television rather than elsewhere. Judging from the costs of series that are in their first year or that are marginally successful, these minimum costs are probably under $150 million annually for a full STV system. Of course, for this amount STV could offer full daytime and news service similar to the programming now offered by networks; a prime-time, entertainment-only STV system would cost substantially less.

The Hartford experiment indicates that movies, boxing, opera, concerts, ballet, variety and nightclub programs, and perhaps drama, would be likely to generate revenues more than sufficient to cover costs on national cable STV. This list, containing both heavy and light entertainment, emphasizes a dual role for STV, one aspect of which generally has not been recognized.

First, opera and ballet did well in Hartford. Drama, however, had only mixed success: The average program, shown three times, generated about $290,000 in revenues on a national scale, slightly less than the cost of made-for-TV movies. A few programs did very well, such as lighter Broadway productions ("Wake Up Darling" and "Tchin-Tchin"), while most of the more serious plays (such as "Hedda Gabbler" and "Androcles and the Lion") drew very small audiences.

To film and broadcast properly a single performance of the Metropolitan

Opera, neglecting payments to the performers, would cost on the order of $50,000 to $100,000, while the Met could earn revenues several times these figures on a national STV system. And even a series of symphony concerts, featuring three broadcasts each of ten separate concerts of the leading orchestras, might generate revenues in excess of production costs of at least $1.5 million. How much of this would actually go to the orchestra management and how much to performers is, of course, inestimable. Most likely, the performers would gain most, at least as long as philanthropic interests are willing to underwrite symphony losses.

The second aspect of STV, generally neglected, is the overwhelming support for several categories of lighter entertainment. The Hartford station, with its low budget, could not experiment with the staple of free TV, the regular series, but all other categories found in the usual TV fare did very well, earning revenues that easily would cover production costs.

PAYMENTS TO AFFILIATES. In a cable STV system, payments to cable owners for a channel would be the counterpart to the $80 million each network now annually pays its affiliates.[22] Historically, broadcasters have not had to pay to have their signals carried by cable systems. Regulation has largely dictated which signals can be carried and has determined that cable owners benefit more from carrying signals than broadcasters do from using cable.

Cable STV would be quite a different matter. A channel charging Hartford prices would not deepen penetration very much (the increase in consumer welfare from one more channel would be largely offset by the higher price). The cable system would therefore have to be induced to broadcast STV, particularly in view of the collection costs. A sharing of the profit, much like that between networks and affiliates, probably would develop between cable owners and STV; however, this is not a true "cost" to STV, for any payment slightly above collection costs would induce cable owners to carry it.

TRANSMISSION. If, like the networks, STV were to use the existing long-distance microwave links, the costs would be roughly $20 million, about what each network now pays.[23] STV probably will not pay this much, for a satellite system can provide the same capacity more cheaply and reach all parts of the nation, including those not served by microwave where cable is now more common. A system consisting of a few earth stations that can send signals to the satellite and several thousand stations that can receive signals from it could probably be operated at a total annual cost of about

22. FCC, *37th Annual Report, Fiscal Year 1971*, p. 153.
23. *Ibid.*, p. 157.

$13 million;[24] furthermore, this cost will decline as technology improves and use expands. In addition, cable systems will spend about $5 million annually to transmit the received signal.

COLLECTION COST. The costs of preventing viewing without fee will be substantial. Using the most expensive technology, the Hartford experiment broadcast scrambled signals, which required the installation of a descrambling device on each subscriber's television receiver. Even if produced in large numbers, these devices would cost $100 each. Over their three-year expected life, they would raise the annual cost of operating an STV system over cables by about $40 per home, or about $100 million for a system reaching 8 percent of the cable subscribers.

The Prospects for Profitable STV

The total of the components discussed above suggests that a minimum STV system using scrambled signals would cost at most about $250 million annually. Given the demand estimates outlined above, the system would probably be viable. Should the fraction of cable homes that subscribe to STV be twice that in Hartford—the likely result because Hartford STV was UHF—revenues would be about $350 million. Profits thus would be about $100 million annually, more than the three existing networks combined earn, and almost as much as a single network and all of its affiliates earn.

The STV collection cost could be reduced substantially by making the revenue collection process more like periodical subscriptions than theater admissions. In this version a subscriber would pay a monthly fee to equip his set to receive an additional channel on the cable system. In light of the Etobicoke experience of resistance to high fixed costs among potential subscribers, this system looks especially attractive. Its cost is much lower if the receiving capability is built into the television receiver; however, to convert an existing set to this type of service costs about $20, assuming mass production. This lowers the total costs of a cable STV system well below $200 million, making it clearly viable—with substantial profits—even at Hartford penetration rates.

Under this STV arrangement, for $5.50 monthly (including the amortized installation fee), a subscriber could receive the three networks, at least four independents, and public broadcasting. For an additional fee, he could have access to service including one channel programmed much like the existing networks or Hartford STV, but free of advertising. According to the Hart-

24. See Chapter 9.

ford results, a monthly fee of around $12 would induce at least 4 percent of the homes receiving the first service to purchase the second. But a more likely result would be that virtually all of the cable subscribers would pay $1 a month for the extra service, generating revenues of $350 million (far above the costs of the system).

In the fixed-fee system, prices for individual programs, an advantage of STV that many economists find so attractive, would be lost. The more accurate measurement of consumer preferences provided by a full-scale pricing system can be purchased only at the cost of a complicated collection system that might absorb a third of the revenues. The monthly charge for a program package also reduces the problem of cream skimming noted earlier, for very popular specials could no longer be sold at a premium price and in that way diverted from advertiser-supported television.

Regulation and the Pay-TV Threat

Just because cable STV appears to be easily worth its costs is no guarantee that the FCC or Congress will allow it to develop. In addition to impediments that might be placed on the expansion of cable service to 50 percent of all TV homes, cable STV may be made illegal or so burdened with restrictions as to make it commercially unviable. Legislation introduced in the Congress and proposals put forth by the Federal Communications Commission would limit both cable and over-the-air STV to programming types not now broadcast on free TV.[25] Banned would be regular series, all but first-run movies, and sporting events broadcast in recent years on free TV. Outright bans on STV have been introduced in the Congress, and several local governments have enacted legislation banning STV from cable franchises.

The spirit behind the FCC proposals is to permit STV only if it offers entertainment substantially different from that already available on free television. FCC policy is seen as necessary to satisfy the program rule, as well as to protect the patronage of existing broadcasters from substantial erosion.

As noted earlier, the basic concern over STV relates to diversion of programs and audience from free TV, although the calculations presented above indicate that neither is a real threat. Past experience supplies two guides to the issue. The existing network systems are highly profitable and, according

25. See FCC, *Annual Report, 1970*, pp. 39–40.

to the Hartford results, only a small fraction of viewers are willing to pay the steep prices—about $12 monthly—that experiment charged. But even if 20 percent, rather than 4 percent, of cable homes subscribed to STV at $10 monthly, and viewed it half of the time, network audiences (and advertising revenues) would decline only by 5 percent. While such a loss would reduce profits in the network system by about one-fourth, it would still leave the industry a 45 percent after-tax rate of return on investment, significantly above average.[26] Meanwhile, the STV system would raise revenues of $720 million from subscribers and, if allowed, about $150 million from advertisers. Since no technical limit would restrict the number of such systems that could be formed, or received by a viewer, competition would cause them to multiply until profits per system dwindled to average. With costs $250 million annually at most, about four STV systems, in addition to the three existing networks, would be viable, all producing programming of roughly the current quality. Of course, the STV penetration and viewing figures assumed are very high—five times as high as Hartford. A final result much closer to the Hartford projection is a more reasonable expectation. Thus audience diversion appears to be no problem.

Substantial program erosion is also unlikely, even in a system of scrambled signals and STV advertising, which is the most favorable cable-STV environment. If 10 percent of the projected 30 million cable subscribers bought STV, and if 12 percent of these were willing to pay $1 to watch, say, an hour-long episode of the most popular network shows, the STV revenues would be only about $370,000 per episode, including advertising of about $10,000. These revenues are substantially less than the shows now generate from advertising on free network TV.[27]

The preceding analysis goes much further than is necessary to justify a permissive attitude toward cable STV. As long as cable capacity is reasonably large, and as long as a large fraction of the nation remains unwired, the alleged dangers of cable STV to the existing broadcasting system are illusory. If the estimates of the profitability of STV made here are not convincing, there is even less to worry about regarding diversion of free programs to pay TV, and an even more permissive stance toward STV development on cables is justified.

Steps short of a completely permissive attitude could be taken toward

26. See Chapter 1 for network profit figures.
27. The ten most popular television shows each week normally have audiences ranging from 14 million to 20 million households. At 3 cents per hour per home, this translates to between $400,000 and $600,000 in advertising revenues.

encouraging STV. Perhaps the minimal step would be to place STV in the hands of nonprofit public broadcasting, as suggested in Chapter 8. Presumably public broadcasters have no desire to raid the networks for existing programs; furthermore, they are most likely to undertake programming that differs from the conventional fare. Unfortunately, as Hartford illustrates, to close STV to conventional fare is to sacrifice most of the consumer welfare that might spring from its development. In fact, "highbrow" STV very probably is not commercially viable outside a system devoting considerable time to "lowbrow" programming.

The second partial step with respect to development of STV would be to ban advertising on it. Such a ban would have little effect on a Hartford-style STV system, appealing to a small fraction of the viewers, for advertising would account for very little of its revenues. But should STV prove much more successful than Hartford suggests, the ban would limit its revenues considerably. If 1 percent of 30 million future cable subscribers watch an STV program, the advertising potential is less than $10,000 an hour, but if 10 to 20 percent watch, it begins to approach that of the least popular network programs. Still, the ban on advertising, like the public ownership proposal, has a rather hollow ring. A marginal STV operation might become commercially successful only if allowed to pick up a little extra revenue through advertising; an overwhelmingly successful STV system would grow and prosper even without it. An advertiser is willing to pay very little for a half hour of a viewer's time; viewers need not pay much for viewing time to dwarf the contribution the advertiser makes to STV revenues.

CHAPTER SIX

Cable Television and Signal Importation

CABLE HOLDS THE PROMISE of all but eliminating the scarcity of channels that accounts for so many of the problems of television—restricted program choice, limited diversity, and highly concentrated control. Cable systems can provide twelve, twenty, forty, or even more channels instead of the four or five that are now typically available over the air. Yet the promise cable holds out is still just that. Cable serves about 10 percent of all television homes, largely in areas with few or even no over-the-air signals. In the top one hundred television markets, which hold 87 percent of the viewers, the Federal Communications Commission (FCC) until recently has prohibited cable from carrying the signals of stations in distant communities,[1] thus eliminating one of the incentives for subscription—a greater choice of programs—and reducing the number of subscribers to the point of unprofitability. As will be demonstrated in the first section of this chapter, carrying distant signals is a necessary condition for nationwide cable.

Even some who concede the necessity of signal importation for the success of cable fear its potential impact on existing broadcasters.[2] Bringing in distant signals, mostly from independent stations, broadens viewers' choices (presumably a good thing) but could squeeze broadcasters' profits (perhaps a bad thing). This issue involves more than a simple choice between the interests of viewers and of broadcasters. The keener competition cable offers might change over-the-air broadcasting so drastically that many viewers

1. For a description and analysis of the formulation of FCC cable policy, including rules governing signal importation, see Edward Greenberg, "Wire Television and the FCC's Second Report and Order on CATV Systems," *Journal of Law and Economics*, Vol. 1 (October 1967), pp. 181–92.

2. See, for example, Franklin M. Fisher and Victor E. Ferrall, Jr., "Community Antenna Television Systems and Local Television Station Audience," *Quarterly Journal of Economics*, Vol. 80 (May 1966), pp. 227–51.

would be worse off. We believe that such a result is unlikely. Profits of broadcasters will fall with signal importation, but the services they provide will change only slightly. The second section of this chapter spells out the basis for this conclusion, and the final section considers its policy implications.[3]

---

3. The literature on signal importation and its consequences for broadcasting is relatively extensive, despite the recent origins of this economic problem.

A steady stream of studies has been produced by the group at the RAND Corporation. See Leland L. Johnson, *The Future of Cable Television: Some Problems of Federal Regulation*, RM-6199-FF (January 1970), and *Cable Television and the Question of Protecting Local Broadcasting*, R-595-MF (October 1970); and Rolla E. Park, *Potential Impact of Cable Growth on Television Broadcasting*, R-587-FF (October 1970); *Cable Television and UHF Broadcasting*, R-689-MF (January 1971); and *Prospects for Cable in the 100 Largest Television Markets*, R-875-MF (October 1971).

Another important body of work is by Harold J. Barnett and Edward Greenberg at Washington University in St. Louis. See, for example, "Regulating CATV Systems: An Analysis of FCC Policy and an Alternative," *Law and Contemporary Problems*, Vol. 34 (Summer 1969), pp. 562–85; "On the Economics of Wired City Television," *American Economic Review*, Vol. 58 (June 1968), pp. 503–08; and "A Proposal for Wired City Television," *Washington University Law Quarterly*, Vol. 1968 (Winter 1968), pp. 1–25, reprinted in *The Radio Spectrum: Its Use and Regulation*, Proceedings of a Conference on the Use and Regulation of the Radio Spectrum (Brookings Institution and Resources for the Future, 1968).

A third group is at Stanford University. See, for example, William S. Comanor and Bridger M. Mitchell, "Cable Television and the Impact of Regulation," *Bell Journal of Economics and Management Science*, Vol. 2 (Spring 1971), pp. 154–212; Stephen R. Barnett, "Cable Television and Media Concentration, Part I: Control of Cable Systems By Local Broadcasters," *Stanford Law Review*, Vol. 22 (January 1970), pp. 221–329.

The Report of the Sloan Commission, *On the Cable: The Television of Abundance* (McGraw-Hill, 1971), discusses the issue of signal importation (see, in particular, Chapters 5 and 7), as does President Lyndon Johnson's Task Force on Communications Policy; see their *Final Report* (1968).

Important econometric work was done at an early stage by Franklin M. Fisher and his associates. See Fisher, "Community Antenna Television Systems and the Regulation of Television Broadcasting," in American Economic Association, *Papers and Proceedings of the Seventy-eighth Annual Meeting, 1965* (*American Economic Review*, Vol. 56 (May 1966), pp. 320–29; and Fisher and Victor E. Ferrall, Jr., "Community Antenna Television Systems and Local Television Station Audience," *Quarterly Journal of Economics*, Vol. 80 (May 1966), pp. 227–51.

A thought-provoking article by Ralph Lee Smith—"The Wired Nation," in *The Nation*, Vol. 210 (May 18, 1970), pp. 582–606, later expanded into a book with the same title (Harper and Row, 1972)—is also worthy of review.

For a fairly complete bibliography on cable television, see the list of sources compiled by the President's Office of Telecommunications Policy, "Cable Television Bibliography," Staff Research Paper (Executive Office of the President, Office of Telecommunications Policy, February 1972; processed).

The Economic Viability of Cable Television

Whether a cable system can meet its costs, including the profits necessary to attract the required capital, depends largely on the "penetration rate"— the percent of homes in a wired locality that subscribe to the service. The penetration rate is a key variable because in a typical system, three-quarters of the capital costs, and an even larger proportion of the operating costs, are either totally fixed or set by the number of miles wired. Thus adding another subscriber adds relatively little to costs, but makes more revenue available to cover the fixed cost of wiring a locality. A more extensive discussion of costs appears below.

Cable Penetration

The probable penetration rates for cable systems in large cities are difficult to estimate, for most systems are in markets with viewing options differing radically from those in most of the top one hundred markets. In an attempt to overcome this difficulty, separate least squares regression analyses were performed on two types of cable systems: thirty-one large systems having 10,000 or more subscribers, and forty systems whose managers report that they compete with three good over-the-air network signals. These two samples come as close as is feasible to representing the systems that will develop in the top hundred markets.

In the analysis of large systems, the traditional economic variables of income and price did not prove to be important, probably due to the absence of much variation in these variables among systems. What mattered were the differences in viewing options, as measured by stations receivable over the air and on the cable. The results of this regression, discussed fully in Appendix A, were then used to estimate the penetration rate for cable systems offering different combinations of viewing options. Penetration estimates for four hypothetical national cable systems—each representing a possible regulatory rule on signal importation—are shown in Table 6-1.

System 1 imports no independent signals and does not carry the local ultra high frequency (UHF) independent stations.[4] The only advantage it offers is improved reception of networks and of very high frequency (VHF) independents. In the large markets, where all three networks have local

4. It is, of course, purely hypothetical, since FCC rules require that all stations be carried.

Table 6-1. Estimated Percent of All Homes Subscribing to Cable Television, by Over-the-air Viewing Alternatives

Over-the-air alternatives		*Estimated cable penetration (percent)*			
Affiliates	*Inde-pendents*	*System 1*[a]	*System 2*[b]	*System 3*[c]	*System 4*[d]
3	3	9.5	35.6	47.8	65.4
3	2	9.5	40.6	52.7	67.4
3	1	9.5	47.8	59.1	70.2
3	0	9.5	59.1	67.9	74.9
2	0	59.8	74.6	78.4	81.8
1	0	78.3	83.5	85.2	86.9
0	0	87.9	89.7	90.4	91.1

Source: Derived by authors. See text for discussion.

a. Provides for all local signals plus importation of affiliated stations to provide three-network service. Estimates assume no local UHF independent is carried.

b. Provides the services in system 1, plus *two* independent signals in addition to local VHF independents.

c. Provides all the services in system 1, plus *four* independents in addition to local VHF independents.

d. The same as system 3 except that one channel of network-type programming is offered in place of one independent signal.

affiliates, the penetration rate is only about 10 percent. System 1 also provides for the importation of network signals in the smaller markets that do not have three-network service. In these markets, importing the missing networks is sufficient for high penetration. This explains why the present cable industry, comprising primarily operators located in outlying areas with limited over-the-air options, shows relatively little interest in convincing the FCC that it ought to relax its restrictive importation rules.[5]

System 2 provides three networks and two independent signals in addition to local VHF independents.[6] This system roughly approximates the extent of signal importation proposed by the FCC in August 1971, but is substantially more liberal than the November 1971 "accord," arranged by the Office of Telecommunications Policy, and the final FCC rules adopted

5. The current rules, discussed more completely below, represent an "accord" between broadcast and cable interests, and essentially freeze cable out of most of the fifty largest markets.

6. The two additional signals include local UHF independents; however, distant independents are needed to bring the total to two in all but a few markets. The two imported signals are assumed to be specific stations, chosen freely by the cable operator with the knowledge of the imported station. This permits the development of viewer habits and loyalties to the distant signal, and allows the imported station to adjust its advertising prices to account for the new audiences.

in February 1972.[7] Penetration rises several-fold, to 60 percent, in markets with only three networks, and to over 35 percent in areas with three VHF independents.

System 3 provides three networks and four independents in addition to local VHF independents. In the largest market, New York, the added signals raise penetration from 10 to 48 percent, even though this market already has three VHF independents. In markets with three networks but no local independents, importing four independent signals yields a penetration approaching 70 percent. System 3—one with considerable signal importation—will serve throughout this chapter as a benchmark to estimate the effects of a liberal policy toward signal importation.

System 4 provides three local UHF or imported independents and an additional option as popular as the existing networks—either a fourth network or an attractive cable origination (such as home games of local professional sports teams, as is provided by one New York City system). This fourth, network-quality, option would enhance the penetration rate, though not nearly as dramatically as does the step from no importation to four independent stations.

Several aspects of the estimates in Table 6-1 are worth emphasizing. First, in the absence of distant-signal importation, or some other major additional stimulant to penetration, no more than 10 percent of the television homes in most of the 100 largest markets will subscribe to cable television. Second, distant-signal importation alone is sufficient to change dramatically the likely level of penetration. Third, in the foreseeable future penetration probably will in no case exceed 70 percent, so that substantial public interest continues to lie in over-the-air broadcasting. Consequently, the impact of cable on its viability cannot be ignored.

The regression analyses of the second sample of cable systems, all of which compete with three good over-the-air network signals, are also reported in Appendix A. While the first group of systems exhibited little variation in price, the second showed very little variation in viewing options offered. Probably because all systems compete with an attractive slate of "free" stations, they all offer numerous options, including several imported signals and some cable origination. This sample did not prove fruitful for

---

7. See Chairman Dean Burch's letter of August 5, 1971, to the Chairman of the Subcommittee on Communications of the Senate Committee on Commerce (FCC 71-787), printed under title "FCC Plans for CATV Regulation," in Television Digest, Inc., *CATV and Station Coverage Atlas and 35-Mile Zone Maps, 1971–1972* (Washington: TD, 1971), pp. 27a ff. (cited hereafter as "FCC Plans for CATV").

estimating the relative importance of different types of additional signals offered on the cable; however, it did provide estimates of the importance of price and income, as well as of the time required for a newly constructed cable system to reach its maximum penetration.

According to the principal results of this analysis, (1) the profit-maximizing price for cable service is not significantly different from the price charged by the surveyed systems of roughly $62 annually (where one-fifth of the installation fee actually charged, or $1 per week, is added to the annual service fee);[8] and (2) cable systems approach the equilibrium penetration rate more rapidly than is normally supposed—a given mile of cable will reach approximately two-thirds of its expected penetration rate, on the average, within eighteen months of service initiation.[9]

Profitability of Cable

The competition for cable franchises from local governments is perhaps the best evidence that a substantial profit potential is attributed to many systems. It has taken the form of "bidding" to give local governments a percentage of the annual revenues, averaging 5 percent of gross subscription revenues, with some as high as 36 percent.[10] Much of the bidding may reflect the hope that the FCC will intervene to limit these payments, but their magnitude means an entrepreneur must envisage an above-average profit in the long run.[11] Other evidence of profitability lies in the sales prices of established systems. A common rule of thumb establishes a sales price for these systems of four times the initial investment. Expectations, not just current earnings, enter into prices, further evidence that investors view the industry as potentially profitable.

Available information on costs and revenues substantiates a bullish view of cable prospects. To estimate cable profitability, revenues were assumed to be $66 per subscriber per year, the amount typically charged by cable systems. In constructing cost estimates, cable systems were assumed to have twelve-channel capacity, which is sufficient to provide the types of service

8. More information on the calculation of the profit-maximizing price is contained in Appendix A, including the demand curve, reported in Table A-4.

9. The more conventional assumption is five years; however, the methods used to derive the longer estimate are faulty (see Appendix A).

10. "FCC Plans for CATV," p. 46a.

11. The February 1972 rule does limit local taxation of cable systems to a range of 3 to 5 percent of revenues; however, the rule is weakly stated—localities may request exceptions—so that the issue remains to be resolved. See *Federal Register*, Vol. 37 (February 12, 1972), Pt. 2, p. 3277.

hypothesized in systems 2, 3, and 4. Cost data were derived from a study by Comanor and Mitchell.[12]

Profits of cable systems vary with size and geographic location. Table 6-2 shows the steady-state profitability of several systems.[13] Assuming a 50 percent corporate income tax, the after-tax returns on capital range from 14 to 25 percent. Since cable systems can use some borrowed capital at an interest rate below the profit rate, the equity return appears to be well in excess of that for manufacturing, which, during the sixties averaged between 9 and 13 percent, after taxes, on stockholders' equity.[14] Assuming an interest rate of 10 percent and a debt-equity ratio of 1, the after-tax return to equity for these systems ranges from 25 to 41 percent.

These profit estimates should not be regarded as definitive, for both the costs and the revenues assumed in Table 6-2 can, for any particular system, be grossly in error, for any of the following reasons:

1. Profits are lower than estimated here once the course of penetration during the first years of operation is accounted for. The assumption that the current penetration of a system as a fraction of its ultimate penetration

12. William S. Comanor and Bridger M. Mitchell, "Cable Television and the Impact of Regulation," *Bell Journal of Economics and Management Science*, Vol. 2 (Spring 1971), pp. 154–212. Some minor adjustments were made to these estimates to correct for some double counting of costs and to smooth the discontinuities in the relation between costs and the size of the system. Comanor and Mitchell count disconnection as a capital cost, but they also include as operating expenses the technicians, tools, and vehicles used to make disconnections. Similarly, house drops are counted as a $20 capital cost, but only $5 of this is the hardware; the rest is service from the same technicians, tools, and vehicles. The cost estimates used here ignore the capital expense for disconnections, and the service component of "secondary" house drops, that is, additional wiring of houses for cable that does not add to total subscribers but instead offsets a disconnection elsewhere. The effects of the discontinuities and double counting in the Comanor-Mitchell study is most apparent in considering the example they used to illustrate profitability of cable systems. Had they hypothesized a system of 7,499 subscribers over 149 miles of cable, instead of 7,500 over 151 miles, profitability would have been about 70 percent higher, with an after-tax rate of return of about 19 percent instead of 11 percent.

Two other major studies of cable costs in a single metropolitan area (Dayton, Ohio, and Washington, D.C.) have produced results broadly similar to those of Comanor and Mitchell. See Leland L. Johnson and others, *Cable Communications in the Dayton Miami Valley*, Basic Report R-943 KF/FF (RAND Corporation, January 1972), and William F. Mason and others, *Urban Cable Systems* (Washington: Mitre Corp., 1972).

13. "Steady state" refers to the situation after penetration reaches the final equilibrium level. Lower profits during the early period when the number of subscribers is growing are, for the moment, ignored.

14. U.S. Bureau of the Census, *Statistical Abstract of the United States, 1971* (1971), p. 473.

Table 6-2. Revenues, Costs, Profits, Investment, and Rate of Return for a Cable Television System, on Selected Assumptions[a]

Thousands of dollars

	Top 100 markets		Outside top 100 markets	
Accounting item	*7,500 subscribers*	*25,000 subscribers*	*3,500 subscribers*	*7,500 subscribers*
Revenues	495	1,650	231	495
Operating expenses	242	657	123	228
Depreciation	93	281	44	81
Gross profits[b]	160	712	64	186
Profits as a percent of revenue	32	43	28	38
Gross investment	931	2,813	445	813
Average net investment in a ten-year period	466	1,407	223	407
Profits as a percent of net investment[b]	34	51	29	46

Source: Based on data in William S. Comanor and Bridger M. Mitchell, "Cable Television and the Impact of Regulation," *Bell Journal of Economics and Management Science*, Vol. 2 (Spring 1971), pp. 154–212, especially Tables 11 to 14 and Appendix 3.

a. The system size is the final, long-run number of subscribers. Calculations are based on the following assumptions: (1) annual revenues of $66 per subscriber with no advertising receipts; (2) 75 percent penetration with all homes on the route wired during construction; (3) systems in the top 100 markets have 10 percent of mileage underground, those outside the top 100 markets have 5 percent underground; (4) two-channel two-hop microwave system at a capital cost of $67,000.

b. Gross profits and rate of return are calculated before provision for income tax, and are based on the average value after depreciation of the system during a ten-year life.

is 40 percent after one year, 70 percent after two, 85 percent after three, 95 percent after four, and 100 percent after five years, reduces the profitability of the system by about 20 percent in the first five years.[15]

2. More than offsetting the adjustment for the lag in reaching the final penetration rate is the fact that cable systems normally have a longer useful life than the ten years used for depreciation purposes. After ten years, the entry for depreciation in Table 6-2 becomes an increment to profits. The assumption of two years of useful life beyond ten more than offsets the loss of revenue associated with the correction for the period of growth to full penetration.

3. The profit estimates of cable systems are very sensitive to changes in the assumed revenue per subscriber. While the systems that seem the most likely prototypes for those that will develop in the big cities charge about the assumed $66, the average for the entire cable industry is perhaps $5 less. A 10 percent lower price would yield roughly 25 percent less profit. But

15. This assumed growth in subscription is roughly consistent with the results reported in Appendix A, but is somewhat faster than assumed by Comanor and Mitchell and others.

even with the lower prices, big-city cable systems would still earn after-tax profits substantially above those of most other industries, and roughly double the 8 to 10 percent return typically granted to public utilities.

4. Profits are also very sensitive to the ultimate penetration rate since most of the costs of the cable system are independent of the fraction of potential customers that subscribe. For example, the 10 percentage point greater penetration of system 3 over system 2 raises the profit rate on investment by about 5 percentage points.

5. Finally, the density of homes along the cable has an important effect. The calculations in Table 6-2 and by Comanor and Mitchell assume a density of about 80 homes per mile of cable. For example, the system of 7,500 subscribers has 10,000 potential subscribers spread over 125 miles of cable. Comanor and Mitchell report that the average for all systems that they examined was 79 homes per mile outside the major markets. In our sample of large cable systems, the density is over 100 homes per mile, which is more likely to be representative of suburban areas of large cities. If the 7,500 subscriber system required only 100 miles of cable, its annual operating costs and depreciation would drop by more than $30,000 and its total capital investment by about 17 percent.

These qualifications to the estimates reported in Table 6-2 suggest that cable in big cities will have enormously large potential profits—if it is permitted to import distant signals. With penetration rates of 70 to 75 percent, all but one of the qualifications to Table 6-2 imply higher profits than are estimated. The remaining analysis of the potential of cable is based on the assumption that a system with 70 percent penetration will earn pre-tax profits equal to 40 percent of the average book value of investment, and that a cable system requires a penetration rate of 40 to 50 percent to earn profits equal to the average for American industry. These assumptions, of course, apply only in the urban centers of the top 100 markets, which can support systems large enough to capture scale economies and where, in any case, nearly all of the development of cable is likely to occur. More specifically, the Comanor-Mitchell cost data imply that a cable system in a suburb cannot fall very short of fifty subscribers per mile of cable if it is to be a viable investment.[16] This means a minimum population density of

16. Assume a residential area contains ten streets per mile, with each street having a 100-foot right-of-way. If the area contains single-unit dwellings on lots 80 feet wide, a single street will contain about 100 houses per mile. At three residents per household, this is a population density of about 3,000 per square mile. If one-third of the blocks are devoted to parks, schools, and commercial property, the density is then 2,000 per square mile. All of these figures are roughly consistent with the pattern of development in a low-density suburb.

Table 6-3. Estimated Nationwide Penetration of Hypothetical Cable Television Systems

Number of homes in millions

	(1) Homes subscribing if CATV service were offered to all the nation's homes		(2) Homes that will be offered cable service		(3) Expected homes subscribing	
*System*ᵃ	*Percent*	*Number*	*Percent*	*Number*	*Percent*	*Number*
System 1	23%	14.5	20	12.6	15	9.5
System 2	55	34.6	75	47.3	43	27.1
System 3	66	41.6	81	51.0	54	33.9
System 4	75	47.3	88	55.0	66	41.6

Source: Derived from estimates of potential cable penetration in Table 6-1 and profit estimates discussed in the text.
a. See Table 6-1 for definition of systems.

about 2,000 persons per square mile at 50 percent penetration, and of about 1,400 persons per square mile at 75 percent penetration. In dense central city areas, where both costs and potential subscribers per mile of cable are higher, minimum feasible penetration is about 40 percent.

The preceding results can be combined with the estimates of potential penetration in Table 6-1 to estimate the number of homes likely to be offered cable service under each of the four national cable systems. The first set of columns of Table 6-3 shows the percentage and number of homes that, given the opportunity, would subscribe to each system. These penetration rates were determined by weighting the rates of Table 6-1 by the proportion of homes with the relevant over-the-air viewing alternatives.[17]

The second set of columns shows the proportion of homes that will be offered cable service. No area with fewer than 350 subscribing homes per square mile is likely to have cable services under any system. We assume that these areas account for about 10 percent of the television homes, which would be about half of the rural population.[18] In the poorest sections of cities, it is likely that too few households would be able to afford the subscription fees required to cover the higher costs of operating cables. We assume also that about 2 percent of the population lives in such areas, or

17. For data on the distribution of TV homes by number of over-the-air viewing options, see Table 6-6.

18. U.S. Bureau of the Census, *Statistical Abstract of the United States, 1972* (1972), p. 17.

roughly half of the urban poverty population. Thus, even with the most attractive system, 12 percent of the TV homes would not be offered cable.

A third group would be offered cable services under all three systems. Of the population in the top 100 markets, roughly 15 percent are assumed to be in areas with problems of signal reception that make cable development profitable regardless of the number of signals broadcast. Here cable systems will reach roughly 90 percent penetration.

New York and Los Angeles—the two top markets, with 9 million TV homes (15 percent of the total)—already have extensive over-the-air options. Los Angeles has three local UHF independents whose signal can be improved on cable; however, one UHF independent is a Spanish-language station. Any cable system in Los Angeles could offer signal improvement on two UHF stations, so penetration should reach 34 percent. New York has two UHF independents, one of which is a Spanish-language station. Without importation or cable origination, penetration in New York would probably be about 28 percent. Both penetration figures are probably too low to induce cable development in all but the highest-income sections of the city. Importation of two signals brings penetration in good reception areas to about 45 percent. Perhaps half the city would be wired at this penetration figure.

The availability of cable for the remaining population depends on the extent of signal importation. System 2—with two imported or local UHF signals—will probably achieve sufficient subscriber penetration to warrant the wiring of markets ranked between 3 and 100, all but one of which have at most one VHF independent. System 3—with four imported or local UHF signals and the resulting higher penetration—will clearly achieve the wiring of those markets, and also much of New York and Los Angeles.

From these assumptions and observations, the second set of columns in Table 6-3 shows that the fraction of the households that will be offered cable service will be 20 percent for system 1, of which areas outside the top 100 markets account for 7 percent, markets 3 through 100 for 11 percent, and the top two markets for 2 percent. System 2 probably (and system 3 certainly) will cause the wiring of markets 3 to 100, which means that about 75 percent of the nation's homes will be offered service. System 3 induces the wiring of half of markets 1 and 2. Finally, system 4 leaves only rural and urban poverty areas unwired.

The inescapable conclusion from Table 6-3 is that despite the high average profits of cable systems, a nationwide system, involving subscription by more than half the homes, will not develop unless distant-signal importation is permitted on a wide scale. A few big-city cable systems may be large enough to attract viewers through cable orgination, as is now happening in sections of New York City, where cable systems broadcast home games of local professional sports teams. But, as will be discussed more thoroughly in Chapter 7, origination will prove too costly for most cable systems. Consequently, for most of the nation the hope for extensive cable development lies in relaxation of signal importation rules so that systems may offer the strong independent stations from distant large cities.

The Impact of Cable Growth on Broadcasting

The common objection to signal importation is that it might jeopardize the financial viability of over-the-air broadcasting. The danger is often stated in terms of audience losses by local stations, without recognizing that the losses are to imported signals originating with other local stations, albeit in different localities. Obviously there are gainers and losers; to assess the impact of signal importation we need to evaluate the shifts in audience and their consequences. We assume, as FCC rules have required for some time, that cable carries local stations and also that no network affiliate signal is duplicated—that is, no network signal is imported to compete with a local affiliate of the same network.

Who Loses?

For the benchmark system 3, we have estimated losses in audience for local stations for various markets classified by the number and type of over-the-air stations available. The procedures used to construct these estimates are described in Appendix A and the results are presented in Table 6-4.

In only two instances does system 3 seriously erode local audiences. VHF independents in the larger markets lose local audiences, but these stations are likely to be exported and so gain distant audiences (see discussion below). Network affiliates in single- and two-station markets suffer audience declines of 50 and 30 percent, respectively, although their losses are primarily to the imported networks. Four of the top 100 markets have two network affiliates and two have only a single affiliate. Paradoxically, of the 107 television markets of smaller size, 76 are one- and two-network markets, yet here the FCC has not significantly restrained signal importation.

Table 6-4. Effect of Penetration of Cable Television System 3 on Local
Audience of Local Station, by Over-the-air Viewing Alternatives

Over-the-air alternatives			Percentage change in local audience share		
VHF affiliates	VHF independents	UHF independents	VHF affiliates	VHF independents	UHF independents
3	3	1	*	−16.0	+70.0
3	1	1	−3.8	−24.0	+100.0
3	1	0	−3.8	−24.0	...
3	0	0	−7.6	...	...
3	0	2	−7.6	...	+145.0
3	0	1	−7.6	...	+145.0
2	0	0	−28.5	...	...
1	0	0	−50.0	...	...

Source: Derived by procedures described in Appendix A. See Table 6-1 for definition of system 3.
* Less than 0.5 percent.

The estimates presented above are roughly consistent with the observed
results of signal importation in two California cities, Bakersfield and San
Diego, that were studied in detail by the FCC.[19] In both cities cable systems import seven Los Angeles stations—three affiliates and four VHF independents. The shifts in viewing are shown in Table 6-5, which compares
viewing in cable homes with viewing in noncable homes in the same city.
While the situation is complicated by the fact that in both cities Los Angeles
stations can be received over the air with an expensive roof antenna, these
two examples indicate that the estimates in Table 6-4 are of the right order
of magnitude.

To estimate the effect on the affiliates, the audiences of Los Angeles and
local affiliates must be added since in system 3 network signals are not duplicated. Among San Diego noncable homes, network affiliates had 96 percent of the viewing; in cable homes, they had 75 percent. In Bakersfield, the
total share of affiliates fell from 97 to 77 percent. In both cases, the loss is
about 20 percentage points. At 50 to 70 percent penetration for the entire
viewing area, this would mean a loss of about 10 to 14 percent of the entire
market of both cable and noncable homes. The comparable estimate in
Table 6-4 is 7.6 percent.

The San Diego and Bakersfield examples are important because they

19. See "The Economics of the TV-CATV Interface," Staff Report to the Federal
Communications Commission, prepared by the Research Branch, Broadcast Bureau
(1970; processed).

Table 6-5. Percentage Distribution of Viewers, Cable and Noncable Television Homes, Sign On to Sign Off Time, San Diego, 1969–70, and Bakersfield, 1968[a]

City and stations	Cable	Noncable
San Diego		
4 Los Angeles independents	22.2	2.0
1 San Diego UHF	2.9	2.0
3 Los Angeles affiliates	13.7	7.4
3 San Diego affiliates	61.2	88.6
Total	100.0	100.0
Bakersfield		
4 Los Angeles independents	22.0	3.0
3 Los Angeles affiliates	16.0	3.0
3 Bakersfield affiliates	61.0	94.0
Total	100.0	100.0

Source: "The Economics of the TV-CATV Interface," Staff Report to the Federal Communications Commission prepared by the Research Branch, Broadcast Bureau (1970; processed). Figures are rounded and may not add to totals.

a. For San Diego, weighted average shares of two surveys in February and March 1969 and February and March 1970; for Bakersfield, November 1968.

provide the only two examples of signal importation into larger markets having all three networks (San Diego ranks 52; Bakersfield, 149). They demonstrate that a significant number of viewers in a major market will watch imported VHF independents, even when the three networks are available. They also provide observations to test the number that will switch to the independents.

The results from these two cities are sometimes discounted because both are said to be dominated by Los Angeles in important socioeconomic ways, so that the interests of their residents in Los Angeles stations is a special case. This explanation is wrong on four counts.

First, these cities are both over one hundred miles from Los Angeles; if the "orbit" of New York is as large as that of Los Angeles, every community from Springfield, Massachusetts, to Wilmington, Delaware, will exhibit the same "atypical" reaction to New York stations as San Diego has shown to those in Los Angeles.

Secondly, the explanation rests on a misconception of the size and historical position of the two cities. The population of the San Diego metropolitan area is well over one million, larger than Atlanta, Miami, and New Orleans. Its proximity to Mexico, to a large naval installation, and to an extensive aerospace industry, gives it a character much different from that of Los Angeles. Bakersfield is the center of the southern part of the Central Valley, one of the leading agricultural areas in the country.

Third, an impressive number of cities and towns have cable systems either importing or seeking to import Los Angeles signals. Among the places that in the spring of 1971 either applied for or received permission from the Federal Communications Commission to import the signals of Los Angeles independents were El Paso, Texas; Deming and Gallup, New Mexico; Douglas, Arizona; Fort Collins, Greeley, and Leadville, Colorado; and Scottsbluff and Alliance, Nebraska. Similarly, Deer Lodge, Montana, and Dickinson, North Dakota, have requested permission to import signals from Salt Lake City, Utah, and a microwave company in Utah seeks to deliver San Francisco signals to cable companies in its state. Nine cable systems in Delaware would like to import Baltimore stations, while the Bartlesville, Oklahoma, system wants to import virtually every station in the state, plus independents from Missouri, Kansas, and Texas.[20]

Fourth, a strong independent station does not devote itself to local interest programming. The movies, travelogues, game shows, talk shows, reruns, editorialized news programs, and even sports events that fill the schedules of the Los Angeles independents have national appeal, and cannot be dismissed as potential vehicles for increasing the viewing options available to cable system subscribers anywhere in the nation.

The only conclusion consistent with this evidence is that strong independent stations in big cities provide a valued viewing option in every community that does not have many local stations.

The effect of widespread signal importation can be roughly approximated by the existing fragmentary data. Network affiliates might lose 10 to 20 percent of the cable audience to imported independent signals. In system 3 half of the homes subscribe to cable, making the national loss of network audience—and consequently of advertising revenues—between 5 and 10 percent, with a midpoint of approximately 7 percent. Since profits as a percent of sales for networks and affiliates taken together are about 20 percent, signal importation should cause network system profits to fall about one-third, assuming no cost or price adjustments to the lower earnings. Each of the networks would lose about $10 million; the major burden of the losses, about $150 million, would be borne by affiliates—a total loss of under $200 million.

With the exception of about half of the UHF affiliates, network stations

20. See Television Digest, Inc., "1971 CATV Activity Addenda," Weekly Addenda to *Television Digest*, Vol. 11 (1971), various weekly reports.

have been enormously profitable, in recent years earning after-tax profits of 60 to 70 percent on tangible broadcast investments. The advent of nation-wide signal importation would cut in half the after-tax profits of affiliates in areas served by cable. While the affected affiliates would still be more profitable than much of American business, there would be an enormous reduction in the book wealth of station owners through a decline in the re-sale value of station licenses. That resale value, in effect, capitalizes the ex-cess returns from station ownership, and explains why licenses sell at such high figures. From the viewers' standpoint, even this reduced profitability would still be sufficient to keep the present affiliates operating. The day-to-day operations of a station are not affected by the market value of the license as long as the station shows an operating profit.

The situation for UHF independents is quite different. As shown in Table 6-4, UHF stations on cable increase their audience because the gains from signal improvement swamp the losses from increased competition. Still, with 90 percent of them operating at a loss,[21] the picture for UHF inde-pendents is so bleak that even a doubling of audience—sometimes now less than 1 percent of the market—will not pull many stations into the black. Most now operate only a few hours a day; costs would be much higher if a full broadcast day were attempted. Very large revenue increases are neces-sary to enable these stations to provide services that even approach those envisioned by the FCC in allocating the UHF frequencies twenty years ago. Signal importation, then, helps UHF independents, but not enough to eliminate the "UHF problem."

UHF affiliates should do much better, for cable will, in effect, convert them to VHF affiliates for the cable audience. Since half are already profit-able, the change is likely to make this sector financially viable.

The Audience Gains of the VHF Independents

In system 3, the four imported signals would be independents, except in the few small markets that would also import three-network service. With-out regulatory restraints, the four imported independents would be drawn primarily from VHF stations. Concentrated in the top twenty markets and having better signals than UHF stations do, these stations draw substantial audiences and thus revenues to support expensive programming. They are therefore more attractive than most UHF stations to cable operators in search of maximum feasible penetration.

21. See Chapter 4.

The twenty-three VHF independents fall into two distinct groups—(1) the three New York City, four Los Angeles, and two Seattle-Tacoma stations, and (2) the single stations in fourteen other markets. The New York and Los Angeles independents are distinguished by the competition among them, by their large market shares vis-à-vis the networks (about 25 percent during prime time in each city), and by their outstanding programming. Because satellite transmission of imported signals could eliminate geographic distance as a factor in costs, signals from these big-city independents will be no more expensive than those from nearby sources, and cost-sharing with other cable systems may make them even less so. This point is discussed in Chapter 9.

VHF independents would gain revenue from access to distant cable audiences. Of course, distant viewers are worth nothing to local advertisers, but national advertisers are largely indifferent to whether their messages reach San Diego via an imported signal or local stations, and have been the source of an estimated 70 to 85 percent of the revenues of VHF independents.[22] With signal importation, more national advertising would appear on these stations, and local advertising would shift to affiliates or UHF

22. The estimates of independent revenues were calculated indirectly by first estimating the revenues of affiliates and then subtracting that number from data for all stations. The average shares of total revenue accounted for by network compensation, sales to national and regional advertisers, and local advertisers were calculated for those markets containing only three stations, all affiliates. Total revenue for affiliates in markets with independent stations was estimated by assuming network compensation was the same percentage of total revenues as was that for affiliates in three-station markets. Affiliates' revenues from national and local advertisers were estimated by assuming they were the same proportion of total revenue as were those for affiliates in three-station markets. Estimated national and local revenue for independents was obtained by subtracting the estimates for affiliates from the market total. These estimates indicated that 86 percent of the revenue of independents was from sales to national advertisers. The source of all data was Federal Communications Commission, *35th Annual Report, Fiscal Year 1969*, pp. 140–43.

The foregoing assumes the distribution of revenue among the three sources to be the same for all affiliates regardless of the size of the market, whereas it is generally believed that stations in the larger markets—that is, the top fifty—have a greater proportion of national spot revenue than stations in smaller markets. To allow for that possibility revenue functions to explain national and local revenue as a function of audience size were estimated for affiliates in three-station markets using the FCC data cited above plus audience estimates from American Research Bureau, *1968 Television Market Analysis*. These revenue functions were then used to estimate the national and local revenue of affiliates in the thirteen markets that then had VHF independents. Subtracting these estimates from market totals gave alternative estimates of national and local revenue for independents, which indicated that 71 percent of their revenue was derived from sales to national advertisers.

stations. Indeed, eventually VHF independents may carry nothing but national advertising, but as a conservative estimate, the advertising value of a distant viewer is assumed to be only two-thirds that of a local viewer.

Even then, big-city independents should be able to make up their revenue loss in local markets by gains in distant markets. According to the model in Appendix A, the independent's share in a market with three VHF independents will shrink from 3.6 percent to 2.4 percent of the local cable homes—a loss of 1.2 percentage points—because of the importation of four independents under system 3. Its share of distant cable homes in markets without any local VHF independents would be 3.2 percent, the equivalent of about a 2 percent share in the home market. One distant cable home, then, nearly makes up for the lost audience from two local homes on cables. Specifically, an independent in a market of three VHF independents would have no loss in revenue if the number of cable homes in its distant markets were 56 percent of the number of local cable homes. Table 6-6 indicates that two-thirds of the television homes are in markets having no VHF independents, so that these big-city independents should have little difficulty in securing enough distant markets to increase their revenues.

Once they lose their advantage as the sole independent available to viewers, the sixteen VHF independents outside New York and Los Angeles will lose some local audience. Even so, they too are likely to be net gainers. Calculations made with the same procedures that were used to estimate the

Table 6-6. Over-the-air Viewing Options, by Number of Markets and Percentage of Television Homes, 1971

Viewing options			
Number of networks receivable	Number of VHF independents receivable	Number of markets	Percentage of television households
3	4	1	5.3
3	3	1	9.5
3	2	1	1.2
3	1	14	17.8
3	0	108	57.7
2	0	39	6.0
1	0	43	2.6
	Total	207	100.0

Source: Computed from data in Broadcasting Publications, Inc., *1972 Broadcasting Yearbook* (Washington: BP, 1971), pp. 12–39. Figures are rounded and may not add to totals.

effect of importation on New York and Los Angeles independents suggest that these stations would need to gain access to one distant cable home in order to offset the loss in viewing they would experience if one local home subscribed to a cable service providing system 3.

Since these stations are the strongest independents in their regions, tney should be distributed widely. Indeed, in the Midwest and South the shortage of eligible VHF candidates for signal importation means that either UHF stations or New York and Los Angeles independents would be needed to fill out system 3.

Programming and Signal Importation

It is also argued that signal importation would lead to lower quality programming, because, by diverting audiences to independents, it would rob networks of revenues and force a reduction of expenditures on programming. This result is not likely, for most of the revenue loss of the network system would be borne by profits. The competition among networks for audience would continue to restrain them in reducing program spending.

Less spending by networks and affiliates is likely only for the two program categories that are unprofitable, local originations and public service broadcasts. Both categories are carried in response to regulatory pressures, which may lose force as profits fall, or as a public service contribution, which managements may be less willing to make. Both are now a very small proportion of the broadcast schedule, for reasons explained in Chapters 3 and 4.

Furthermore, even this change would not be great. Data developed by Rolla E. Park suggest that the already limited amount of prime-time local programming would not be sensitive to declines in station revenues. Instead, the dollar amounts spent producing these programs and the non-prime-time hours devoted to them both would fall.[23]

Public service programming such as documentaries now accounts for about 5 percent of network prime time, and serious drama and music for another 2 or 3 percent. Even the most successful of these programs seldom draw an audience share comparable to that attracted by lighter entertainment.[24] Their replacement by standard entertainment fare would help restore profits at the expense of diversity.

23. According to the Park estimate, up to 20 percent of incremental revenue is spent on local programming. See Rolla E. Park, *Potential Impact of Cable Growth on Television Broadcasting*, R-587-FF (RAND Corporation, October 1970), p. 56.
24. See Chapter 3.

The effect on news programming, by both networks and local affiliates, would probably manifest itself in expenditures rather than number of hours. Regularly scheduled news programs draw audiences of respectable size, but often fail to be money makers because of the extra expense of on-the-spot coverage. A shift to less extensive coverage to preclude losses would be likely to occur.

Entertainment (including sports) constitutes the major portion of present programming and accounts for most of the viewership. Here we are concerned with the relationship of networks and stations to the programming industry, which, as Chapter 3 described, produces most of the entertainment shows.

As a result of signal importation, VHF independents would offer a more lucrative market for the program producers. Indeed, they would be, in effect, regional networks, and simultaneous sales to only a few, strategically located, big-city independents could give a program almost nationwide coverage. This would provide attractive alternatives to the networks for the first-run syndicators. Program producers would have more bargaining strength with respect to networks, and in the nonnetwork market when they could not obtain network showing.

The independents would still have a lower audience potential than the networks, limiting the competition for programs and probably forcing some degree of continued reliance on reruns of network shows. The shift of audience to independents and away from networks would raise rerun revenues, since potential and actual audience size are reflected in the syndication price, thereby offsetting some of the loss to the networks. On balance, too many factors militate against the possibility of declining program quality on networks to make it a serious threat. To the extent it did materialize, the cause would lie in the growing strength of the imported independents which would offer programs closer to network quality.

The Benefits and Costs of Cable Development

Several strands of the analysis come together in an evaluation of the costs and benefits of various aspects of cable development, which in turn leads to a set of proposals for signal importation.

The Gains

Even proponents of cable tend to minimize the welfare gains from increased choice among types of commercial fare already available. Yet most

Americans obviously like to watch present-day commercial programming, and the choice of seven rather than three channels represents a major improvement in quality. As one indication, a fifth of the San Diego cable subscribers watched the imported signals of Los Angeles independents, and thus saw programs that would have otherwise been unavailable and that they preferred to those on local stations. Another index of the value of these additional channels is, of course, that imported signals make cable sufficiently attractive to viewers that it becomes economically viable. With signal importation, many Americans would have the choice of television now visible only in Los Angeles and New York.

The model of consumer demand for television developed in Appendix A permits a very rough estimate of the change in consumer welfare brought about by system 3. For subscribing homes, cable yields a gain of about 1 percent of consumer income. If half the homes in the nation subscribed to system 3, the annual gain would be $3.5 billion. Since the cost of system 3 (including minimum profits necessary to induce investment) is about $1.8 billion, the consumer surplus—the difference between what consumers collectively would be willing to pay for system 3 and what they would actually pay—would be about $1.7 billion annually. No great significance should be attached to the precise magnitudes; the point is simply that system 3 represents a significant gain in welfare.

This gain in welfare is solely that from television regarded as a private consumption good. Yet competition in the most important mass medium also ought to be counted as a significant gain to society. With seven channels, the power of the networks would diminish, for they would face the competition of four powerful independent stations throughout the nation. More channels provide a greater opportunity for program diversity and for decentralization of programming decisions.

The potential benefits of cable are discounted only because most television reformers have little taste for commercial television. To expect them to count more commercial television as a gain is analogous to expecting those who go barefoot to applaud improved performance in the shoe industry. But most Americans wear shoes and most are avid watchers of commercial television.

The other side of this gain in consumer welfare is that its sacrifice would also forfeit development of a nationwide cable system in the foreseeable future. Without extensive signal importation, cable would serve only 10 million homes; with it, the number of subscribers rises to over 30 million, half the nation's television homes and two-thirds of the homes offered cable service.

The gains of signal importation depend on the kind of signal imported. Several proposals are designed to limit the cable operator's choice of signal.[25] Their rationale is apparently either a desire to give more stations access to the added audience, or to retain a shadow of localism by requiring importation of the "most nearly local" stations. In addition, the FCC has decided to limit the number of imported signals to two, presumably to minimize the impact of additional competition.[26]

Such restrictions compromise the benefits of signal importation. Economics, of course, will impose limits on the number of signals imported because cable operators will weigh the gain in subscribers arising from more signals against the increased cost of more importation. This is especially true beyond the first few stations, since further imports would necessarily have to be drawn from the UHF ranks, which now attract few viewers in their own home markets and would be likely to fare even worse in distant markets.

The natural economic check to importation makes it unnecessary to restrict the choice of signals to import, with one exception: when the network is represented by an over-the-air local affiliate. In this case, the gain for viewers in importing a station of the same network, which will have identical programming at the identical time, is too small—if, indeed, any exists at all—to offset the cost involved in the substantial loss of audience by the local affiliate, whose existence is essential to the welfare of the over-the-air audience. Nonduplicated programs of affiliates of the same network should be permitted, however, since they offer a distinct gain to viewers.

Apart from these strictures, the cable operator should be free to carry such distant signals as he chooses. Further, he ought to be *required* to carry three networks, public broadcasting, and at least four independents unless the costs of so doing are prohibitive. Compulsion is not needed in markets where the three networks are already available, for the additional signals are needed to enlist subscribers. Yet where they are not available off the air, simply offering all three networks can make a cable system profitable. In these areas, the system is unlikely spontaneously to bring in independent signals, for they would not add greatly to penetration rates. To allow cable operators to bring in only the three networks would merely perpetuate an existing inequality in access to commercial broadcasting that is no longer necessary.

No geographical limitations should be placed on signal importation, and

25. The recent FCC proposals are discussed below.
26. *Federal Register* (February 12, 1972), p. 3265.

leapfrogging—passing over a nearby station to import a more distant one—should be permitted. Big-city independent VHFs would, as a result, be extensively imported. Such stations have already proved to be successful both in their own markets and as imports, largely because their fare and their resources are close to those of the network affiliates. Importing these independents probably does the most for cable penetration, giving the operator an incentive to choose them over other alternatives.

The major VHF independents would then become, in effect, the regional stations the FCC rejected in the 1950s. Since several of them have common ownership, they would capture potential access to a nationwide audience. With an improved competitive position in the purchase of first-run syndications, films, and original programming, they could become more effective rivals to the networks. Metromedia is reaching this state simply through the ownership of four big-city independents, and could easily develop into the type of network DuMont envisioned twenty years ago.

This increased competition is one of the major social gains from signal importation. Fear of the alleged political power of the networks and the complaints from actors, writers, and producers about their arbitrariness stem from the insulation from competition that they enjoy. By increasing the power of the independents, cable could do much to alleviate these problems.

The Cost of Cable

Few benefits come without costs, and cable is no exception. The FCC has explicitly rejected all of the preceding analysis and proposals for widespread signal importation because of the importance it attaches to these costs. Yet if the costs to society only, and not to individuals, are considered, cable is surprisingly free of drawbacks. Wiring the nation is expensive, but subscribers will willingly bear the costs. The major potential social cost is the reputed danger to over-the-air broadcasting;[27] but cable could better the situation for VHF independents a great deal, and for UHF independents somewhat, with only the networks and their affiliates the losers.

The losses to existing networks can be viewed as the removal by competi-

27. This is the main concern of the FCC: "Clearly, cable . . . can, if permitted, provide the full television complement of a New York or a Los Angeles to all areas of the country. Although that would be a desirable achievement, it would pose a threat to broadcast television's ability to perform the obligations required in our system of television service." The FCC then forthrightly states: "We seek to minimize possible impact on local broadcasting." *Federal Register* (February 12, 1972), p. 3264.

tion of the benefits of a monopoly position. The loss, furthermore, would be in the value attached to the licenses of affiliates, with little effect on station operation. Still, losses in wealth are painful, and network affiliates are likely to put up a battle against cable expansion. They favor a ban on signal importation for the largest markets, although they would probably prefer to extend the ban to include more markets. Limits on signal importation strict enough to prevent the extensive development of cable in the big cities would sacrifice nearly all of cable's potential benefits to protect less than $200 million in network system profits.[28]

Finessing the network affiliates on the importation issue will continue to be difficult. One method would be subsidies to the networks to maintain their profits, but it would be expensive. Another solution would be to abandon the "local service" doctrine for network affiliates. In the Northeast, where they are separated by as little as forty miles, allowing affiliates of a network to combine assets to form one large station and a system of repeaters that covers a much broader geographical area would substantially reduce costs and raise profits. Unfortunately, the devotion of the FCC to the local service doctrine makes it unlikely that it would permit such consolidation, particularly while the existing stations were still at least marginally profitable. Another partial solution would be to ease the pressure on the networks to provide public service (for which read "unprofitable") broadcasting, replacing it with more popular, conventional—and lucrative —fare. This solution, too, is unlikely to win many adherents in the public sector, although, since the pressures are informal ones, it would probably eventuate in any case if network profits fell.

No way to compensate the network affiliates is really attractive and inexpensive should they continue to make an important political issue out of cable development and should their political power prove to be indomitable. In this situation, society would be much better off paying the network system $200 million annually to maintain its profits than to allow its opposition and that of its affiliates to prevent cable development. Compensation of the networks is not economically necessary, for without it they will continue to function. Furthermore, both networks and their affiliates have been very profitable in the past and, even with widespread cable development, would still earn above-average profits on their real investment. While the value of station licenses (and the return now earned on them) would fall drastically, it would remain substantial because the over-the-air channels

28. From the analysis on p. 165 of this chapter.

would continue to exist. Paradoxically, the value of station licenses is a product of regulatory policy allegedly in the public interest, yet now is the prime factor inhibiting regulators from permitting full development of a cable system that would be of great value to the viewing public.

Thus far, UHF broadcasting in general has barely escaped disaster and though cable would alleviate the problem, it would not resolve it. Cable would improve the position of UHF independents, the weakest part of the television system, but they would still be too poor to originate local programming or to purchase first-run syndications.

The FCC has hope that UHF will eventually become profitable, hope that could be strengthened by taxing cable $50 million annually to cover the losses of UHF. Should the UHF stations prove inherently unprofitable, a subsidy would become perpetual, but it would be worthwhile if proponents of UHF, notably the FCC, could thus be persuaded not to block cable development.

The final claimants for compensation are program producers, who are trying to persuade Congress to make cable systems liable for copyright payments on distant signals. They have at least temporarily lost their battle in the courts, for in 1968 the Supreme Court held that "at least under certain circumstances, the retransmission of an out-of-town signal was not a performance within the meaning of the Copyright Act, and hence did not give rise to copyright liability."[29]

One economic basis of the program producers' claim is that the program industry will lose significant revenues from signal importation.[30] Signal importation primarily shifts audiences from the networks to imported, primarily VHF, independents. The producers sell programming to both segments, with the VHF independents primarily a market for reruns. Viewed most simply, the loss from one set of customers—the networks—could be recouped from another set—the independents—by raising fees on the latter in proportion to their gains in audience. Thus, no need for additional copyright protection would arise.

There remains a persistent fear that program payments by VHF independents will somehow not reflect their distant audiences. The market now works well enough: If an independent experiences a doubling of its local

---

29. *On the Cable: The Television of Abundance*, Report of the Sloan Commission on Cable Communications (McGraw-Hill, 1971), p. 51. The Supreme Court decision is *Fortnightly Corp.* v. *United Artists Television, Inc.*, 88A S.Ct. 2084 (1968).

30. We leave aside the strictly legal arguments of the interpretation of the Copyright Act.

audience, the gain is reflected in due course in higher payments for its programs. For the same response to be forthcoming when a station is imported by a cable system, two additional requirements would have to be imposed. First, cable systems would have to be required to make relatively long-term commitments to import specific stations so that the syndicators could adjust their rates to reflect audiences in both local and distant markets. Second, cable systems would be required to take programs and advertising intact from distant stations so that these stations could realize greater advertising revenues. With these requirements, syndicators would know they were reaching both distant and local audiences in selling to certain independents, and could base their syndication fees on both kinds of audiences.

Even with these requirements, the evidence to date suggests that distant audiences have considerably less advertising value than local audiences. Thus, Chazen and Ross conclude:

> To some extent, compensation [for imported signals] already occurs because the cable circulation of the distant signal can serve as a basis for higher advertising charges by the originating station. In turn, some of these additional revenues may find their way back to the copyright owners. But this process provides only partial compensation. Many of the advertisements carried over the distant signal are local in nature or are placed by a national advertiser but keyed to a regional market. The advertiser thus gains little when his messages are heard in some distant city which he did not select. From interviews we have learned that it is difficult to sell distant circulation of a broadcast station for any price approximating that obtained for the home audience.[31]

The process Chazen and Ross describe is likely to provide much greater returns from distant audiences once the practice of signal importation is well established. As indicated above, signal importation is likely to be concentrated on the twenty-three VHF independents, making them in effect regional stations. Local advertising and advertisers preferring more selective distribution would shift to local affiliates. National advertisers that desire distant audiences and were willing to pay for such a distribution of their commercials would spend more on imported stations. In such a world, compensation for distant signals—as Chazen and Ross use the term—would be more complete.

There remains a considerable element of uncertainty concerning the market adjustments to distant audiences. Program fees are negotiated between a limited number of major purchasers, on the one hand, and, on the other, a larger number of sellers—each of which, however, has a unique product.

31. Leonard Chazen and Leonard Ross, "Federal Regulation of Cable Television: The Visible Hand," *Harvard Law Review*, Vol. 83 (June 1970), pp. 1838–39.

Outcomes in such markets are difficult to predict and one could argue for copyright fees simply as a hedge against such uncertainties as might reduce program payments. Since the audience shift is estimated to be 5 to 10 percent, the losses cannot in any case be catastrophic.

Copyrights have probably become a major issue for reasons quite different from the overall losses in program industry revenues. Unfettered signal importation would undermine the geographical exclusives, now common in the initial licensing of a program to a station, that preclude the program owner from licensing the same program or series to a second station in the same geographical market for a period that ranges between two to seven years.

These exclusives have been a puzzle to economists.[32] Such a view is recorded in the Report of the Sloan Commission on Cable Communications:

> It is difficult to see why exclusive agreements are as common as they are. They diminish the opportunity of the copyright owner to maximize his returns; they reduce the flexibility of independent stations (and network stations to the degree that they program as independents). They deprive the viewer of a large degree of choice, particularly in time of viewing. Their survival can be laid in part to inertia, and in part perhaps to the bargaining power of network affiliates and a few powerful local independent VHF stations. (They constitute, it might be added, one more burden under which UHF stations are obliged to labor.)[33]

With this view of exclusives, we doubt that public policy ought to restrict signal importation or modify copyright arrangements to insure their preservation. Yet this is what the FCC recommends in its 1972 ruling.[34] No episode of any program may be imported into any market in the top fifty if (1) the program has been in syndication for less than a year, or (2) any station in the market holds an exclusive right of any duration to any episode of the same series.

Still another basis of the copyright claim is that the greater the revenue for the program industry the greater diversity and quality will be. The analysis in Chapter 3 suggests that larger payments will show up largely as

32. For a discussion see *ibid.*, pp. 1830–36.
33. *On the Cable*, p. 52. One explanation for the existence of exclusives is that they create a market for old movies and television series reruns. With exclusives limiting access to recently produced programs, stations are forced to dip into series of the 1950s and movies of even earlier vintage to fill their schedules. Since these programs have extremely low residual costs when resyndicated, they are very profitable to the packager—if only a market can be created! From a social welfare point of view, this reasoning hardly justifies the practice.
34. *Federal Register* (February 12, 1972), p. 3286.

more income to scarce program talent—that is, as rents—and will have only a modest effect on program production.

While the case for copyright protection is not strong, modest payments are not likely to undermine cable development simply because cable is potentially very profitable. Yet we would prefer that there be no copyright liability, to avoid the risks of levels of payment and arrangements of copyright terms that will inhibit cable development.[35] Such an outcome will benefit neither producers, viewers, nor cable operators, but will leave the present system of broadcasting intact. Indeed, it could be that this prospect of gains to the networks and their affiliates has elevated the issue of copyright protection to major importance.

Perhaps the entire copyright issue has been obscured by the technological form that signal importation has taken. Suppose a new kind of home television set were invented that allowed viewers in Prescott, Arizona, to view Los Angeles stations over the air. We doubt that many would argue that either the manufacturer of that set or the Arizona viewers should make copyright payments to the producers of programs on Los Angeles stations. Yet cable is an analogous invention with similar economic effects.

This analogy is prompted by the Supreme Court's majority opinion in the Fortnightly case, which held that distant signals did not entail copyright liability. That opinion states:

Essentially, a CATV system no more than enhances the viewer's capacity to receive the broadcaster's signals; it provides a well-located antenna with an efficient connection to the viewer's television set. It is true that a CATV system

35. For a contrary view advocating copyright payments for signal importation by a group sympathetic to cable development, see Sloan Commission, *On the Cable*, pp. 52–54. We have several difficulties with this analysis. First, it holds that "program producers are entitled to a return from performances of their product" (p. 52). One can hardly take issue with the principle, but the analysis ignores the likelihood that the fees of syndication will reflect the advertising value of distant audiences. Second, it argues that copyright payments place distant signals on a parity with local origination, which now requires copyright payments from the cable operators. This ignores the initial payments for broadcast rights made by the originating station, which should reflect the value of distant cable audiences. Third, the commission does recognize our concern that copyright arrangements might inhibit cable development. They state: "Established distributors, in command of desirable product, will inevitably devise inventive ways of denying programming to such small entrants as cable installations and UHF stations as a means of retaining existing profitable arrangements. Effective enforcement of antitrust laws would minimize the damage from such endeavors" (p. 54). While we hesitate to take issue with a commission that includes several distinguished lawyers, we observe that the antitrust laws have done little to improve the access to programming by UHF stations, a record that does not augur well for their effectiveness in helping cable operators obtain access on reasonable terms to distant signals.

plays an active role in making the reception possible in a given area, but so do ordinary television sets and antennas. CATV equipment is powerful and sophisticated, but the basic function the equipment serves is little different from that served by the equipment generally furnished by a television viewer.[36]

Conclusions

We are proponents of laissez-faire with regard to signal importation, not out of ideological preconception but because the fears of injury to over-the-air broadcasting do not seem valid and because we do not believe in compensating those whose loss from technological progress is in essence a monopoly position.

Cable can make an important contribution to improving the access to commercial television and increasing competition for the networks. Signal importation would be worthwhile even if it were not necessary for cable development. Many of the strongest advocates of cable view signal importation as only a necessary condition for nationwide cable and regard its major social contribution as the new kinds of television programming examined in the next chapter. In this view, the permissible amount of signal importation turns on what is needed for cable development, and, beyond this, is of little social utility.

The FCC August letter of plans for CATV regulation reflects this minimal view of signal importation. The November 1971 accord between the broadcasting and cable industries, ratified virtually intact by the FCC the following February, implied an even more restrictive view. This accord is said to be the result of FCC and White House pressure, and reflects the sort of compromises and sacrifices of consumer welfare described in Chapter 4. Its central feature allows the importation of two signals if a market has three network affiliates and one independent station. As the calculations for system 2 indicate, this alone would make cable viable if cable systems were free to bring in high-quality VHF independents. But the accord effectively restricts this freedom:

1. If any market in the top fifty has no independent, a cable system may import three stations, provided that one is a nearby UHF. Such stations

36. *Fortnightly Corp.* v. *United Artists Television, Inc.*, 88A S.Ct. 2084 (1968) at 2089. This decision was extended in *Columbia Broadcasting System, Inc.* v. *Tele-PrompTer Corp.*, 251 F Supp. 302 (1965), in which importation of distant signals by microwave was still held not to subject cable systems to copyright liabilities. (The latter case, though filed earlier, was decided after the former.)

now have programming of low quality, and since each will be imported by only a few systems, they are not likely to experience an increase in their audiences large enough to support improved programming. These stations will be a weak inducement for cable subscription and importing them will threaten its viability. In any of the top fifty markets with at least one independent, systems can import two distant independents; however, any of these stations that are from one of the twenty-five largest markets must be from the *nearest* such market. This restriction precludes extensive importation of the strong VHF independents in the largest cities. In fact, in many areas the stations in the nearest market among the top twenty-five will be weak UHF independents. Thus *all* of the imported signals can be essentially useless to the cable operator in building subscribers.

2. Limiting signal importation as outlined in (1) above will prevent the development of present VHF independents into regional stations that could pose a modest competitive threat to the networks and to the profit levels of the affiliates.

3. Strengthening of all independents is further precluded by the provisions in the accord that protect exclusive program rights. In the top fifty markets, programs cannot be imported if a local broadcaster has obtained exclusive rights to them; furthermore, the accord sets no time limits on such rights, although in the next fifty markets exclusivity is limited to two years. This aspect of the accord will prevent importation of the best movies and first-run syndications. Many affiliates carry the prime-time staples of big-city VHF independents, such as David Frost or relatively recent movies, on daytime schedules; such showings, with their exclusivities, will black out these programs from evening time and thus sacrifice the welfare of viewers. This measure also means that imported independents frequently will be blacked out. In fact, cable operators will have to switch back and forth among several stations to fill the time on the import channels. As a result, the audience a particular station attracts on distant cable systems will be uncertain and variable, so that the imported stations will not be able to capture added advertising revenues from their larger audiences. This measure probably kills any prospect that VHF independents will challenge the networks, and prevents the use of importation as a means to make UHF independents financially viable.

4. The FCC has adopted especially stringent regulations regarding the definition of a local station, so that cable systems located in television markets where signals of stations in other markets can be received over the air will be forced to offer fewer commercial viewing options than can be re-

ceived with an outdoor antenna.[37] The FCC's rule is that a signal is "local" and, if carried, does not count against the distant-signal quota of the cable system, if (1) a reference point in the community (the post office, the studio, or the transmitter) in which the station is located is within 35 miles of all parts of the community in which the cable system operates (including parts not served by the cable system); or (2) the station is "significantly viewed" within the cable system's community.[38] With few exceptions, the second rule is the important one, for large cities separated by fewer than 35 miles are inevitably considered to form a single television market.

The concept of "significant viewing" seems reasonable enough. If a station is, essentially, never watched, the potential customers of the cable system will not care whether that station, or some other, is a distant signal on the cable. In either event, the cable system will be able to offer more channels than the viewer watches over the air. But the test of significance imposed by the FCC is so strict that many UHF independent stations would fail it *within their own market*. To be considered "significantly viewed," an independent must capture a 2 percent share of total viewing, while an affiliate must capture 3 percent. Of the thirty-seven UHF independents in the top fifty markets, sixteen—or 43 percent—are not significantly viewed in the county in which they are located. Among UHF affiliates, four of twenty fail the same test.[39]

5. The cable industry will pay some form of compensation to owners of program copyrights. Whether this is a significant aspect of the accord depends on the kind and level of copyright payments, which are still to be negotiated, but potentially it could place so high a premium on importation that it will not be worth doing.

The accord places in jeopardy the wiring of the nation—particularly in the top fifty markets that comprise two-thirds of the television homes. Our calculations cannot estimate the probable penetration of such a restricted system, since present broadcasting has no counterpart to such a hybrid. Most likely, these restrictions will stunt cable development for another decade. The February 1972 statement would even seem to agree: "We are

37. Market overlap is common, especially in the East. Baltimore-Washington, Boston-Providence, Hartford-New York, and Los Angeles-San Diego are among the pairs in which signals from one area can be relatively easily received in at least parts of the other.

38. *Federal Register* (February 12, 1972), pp. 3262–64.

39. Based upon the FCC's list of significantly viewed stations. See *ibid.*, pp. 3298–3340, and Television Digest, Inc., *Television Factbook, Stations Volume, 1970–1971 Edition* (Washington: TD, 1970).

affording cable the minimum number of distant signals necessary to promote its entry into *some* of the major television markets" (emphasis added).[40]

Even if cable systems do develop, a great part of the gain in consumer welfare that they could have fostered will fall victim to the preservation of the fundamental features of American television—extremely high profits for networks and their affiliates, limited competition, and the charade of local service. The losses in consumer welfare cannot be compared objectively with the value of maintaining the essential features of the current system. To skeptics about the value of the status quo, the sacrifice of consumer welfare achieves only a perpetuation of the current faults of the industry. This view is in accord with consumer sovereignty: The value viewers attach to the diversity provided by many commercial channels makes extensive signal importation profitable. It is also in accord with the general policy maxim of promoting competition. Unrestricted signal importation presents the networks with more competition from independent stations. It also removes the technical obstacle to the growth of group-owned independent stations into regional or even national networks.

40. *Federal Register* (February 12, 1972), p. 3261.

CHAPTER SEVEN

Cable and New Television Services

CABLE VISIONARIES DRAW their enthusiasm from the prospect that cable will offer new kinds of services, not from an expectation that signal importation will provide simply more of the fare already available on over-the-air television.[1] Indeed, echoes of this view can be found in the statements about cable of the Federal Communications Commission (FCC), in which new services are considered the prime justification for cable development.[2] This chapter examines the prospects for new cable services.

1. See, for example, Stephen White, "Toward a Modest Experiment in Cable Television," *Public Interest*, No. 12 (Summer 1968), pp. 52–66. The prospects for new services is a major focus of the Sloan Commission study, *On The Cable: The Television of Abundance* (McGraw-Hill, 1971); in particular see Chapters 6 and 8–11, and Appendix C.

Actual experiences with these services are reported in three RAND Corporation studies: N. E. Feldman, *Cable Television: Opportunities and Problems in Local Program Origination*, R-570-FF (September 1970); Leland L. Johnson, *Cable Television and Higher Education: Two Contrasting Experiences*, R-828-MF (September 1971). Two other proposed systems are described in Leland L. Johnson and others, *Cable Communications in the Dayton Miami Valley: Basic Report*, R-943 KF/FF (January 1972), and William F. Mason and others, *Urban Cable Systems* (Washington: Mitre Corp., 1972).

In addition, see *Final Report*, President's Task Force on Communications Policy (1968), and Ralph Lee Smith, "The Wired Nation," *The Nation*, Vol. 210 (May 18, 1970), pp. 582–606, later expanded into a book with the same title (Harper and Row, 1972).

2. Letter from FCC chairman, Dean Burch, to the chairman of the Subcommittee on Communications of the Senate Committee on Commerce, dated August 5, 1971 (FCC 71-787), printed under title "FCC Plans for CATV Regulation," in Television Digest, Inc., *CATV and Station Coverage Atlas and 35-Mile Zone Maps, 1971–1972* (Washington: TD, 1971), pp. 27a ff. The chairman stated, "We believe . . . that cable can make a significant contribution toward improving the nation's communications system—providing additional diversity . . . and creating the potential for a host of new communications services" (p. 27a). A February 1972 statement is stronger: "[Cable] success will depend on the provision of innovative nonbroadcast services." *Federal Register*, Vol. 37 (February 12, 1972), Pt. 2, p. 3261.

Not all of the new services are likely to be economically self-supporting (self-supporting services are those generating revenues that are at least equal to the added costs they impose on the cable system). The distinction between self-supporting and uneconomic services is not merely one of bookkeeping; it involves issues of social equity and economic efficiency. If self-supporting services are offered, no cable subscriber is worse off, since subscription fees are not taxed to meet their costs. At the same time, the social gains from cable are enlarged: Since someone voluntarily is paying for them, the added services must be providing benefits at least equal to their costs. Furthermore, in the absence of regulatory prohibitions, cable operators, animated by market forces alone, will offer self-supporting services in time.

In contrast, uneconomic or subsidy services are provided only in response to regulatory requirement: The deficit they create becomes, in effect, a tax on cable systems and ultimately on cable subscribers. The presumed public policy judgment is that the social benefits from the services exceed the implicit tax. The subsidy need not come from cable revenues; they simply happen to be a convenient new variety of taxable funds.

Channel Capacity and Supplemental Services

The number of cable channels determines the number of supplemental services that can be offered. The point can be illustrated by taking as a standard system 3, defined in the last chapter. That system had twelve channels, eight of which were required for the provision of three networks, public television, and four independent signals. (More channels would be required in areas with very high frequency (VHF) independents.) Four or fewer channels are thus open for supplemental services. To offer a wide range of services necessarily means incurring extra costs for the construction of a large system. Systems of twelve and twenty channels appear to offer the lowest costs per channel on a single cable, given present technology, although there is some hope of raising the higher number to twenty-four or twenty-five.[3] The problem is to avoid interference with over-the-air users of the frequencies around and between existing VHF channels.

3. For a discussion of costs, see William S. Comanor and Bridger M. Mitchell, "Cable Television and the Impact of Regulation," *Bell Journal of Economics and Management Science*, Vol. 2 (Spring 1971), pp. 166–74.

Few detailed studies have been made of the cost differences between a twelve- and a twenty-channel system. Comanor and Mitchell[4] have made perhaps the most detailed comparison, and their cost data are the basis for the following conclusions:

First, the principal means for obtaining at least twenty-channel capacity are (1) laying two cables, and (2) transmitting additional signals on one cable using the frequencies in the middle of the VHF band. The latter is considerably cheaper, and furthermore does not risk interference between the over-the-air and cable signals, as the dual-cable method does. The fuller use of VHF frequencies requires higher performance amplifiers, which add $300 per mile to the cost of distribution cables;[5] each home set must have a convertor costing $30.[6]

Second, the construction of twenty-channel capacity, including equipping subscribers with convertors, would increase capital costs to about 20 percent above the costs of twelve-channel systems. Capital costs are about one-third of total costs, so that twenty-channel capacity increases total costs by about 7 percent. The costs per hour of these added channels are low. To take a typical example, the 7,500 subscriber system within the top one hundred markets shown in Table 6-2 would incur additional annual costs of only 37.5 cents per subscriber per channel. This is very low compared with the costs of programming. Live broadcasting costs at minimum $50 an hour not including payments to performers and writers.[7]

Third, the costs for the twenty-channel system consist largely of the convertors that permit subscribers to receive the additional broadcasts; however, installation of the convertors can be delayed until all twenty channels are in use. This is a particularly attractive approach because if the twenty-channel capacity is built into the TV receiver at the time of manufacture, the cost falls to about $10 per set. As twenty-channel systems come into use, sets should be manufactured with this capacity, just as they now are to receive ultra high frequency (UHF) broadcasts.

Finally, the twenty-channel system must be constructed at the outset. Converting an existing twelve-channel system to twenty channels is extremely expensive; indeed, Comanor and Mitchell report that "the cost of rebuilding an existing system is often somewhat higher than the cost of

4. *Ibid.*, pp. 154–212.
5. *Ibid.*, p. 209.
6. Sloan Commission, *On the Cable*, p. 191.
7. A compendium of studies on origination costs can be found in Comanor and Mitchell, "Cable Television," Appendix 4.

constructing a new system, since service to subscribers must be maintained during the construction period."[8]

The central question is whether channel capacity should be left to market determination or dictated by regulatory action. An answer rests on the likely profitability and social utility of the new services, which are open to a wide range of uncertainty (see discussion later in this chapter).

Given the major difference in costs of new construction versus conversion and the uncertainties about future demand, a decision for twenty channels seems the correct one, although some operators may have such short time horizons that they will build twelve-channel systems even though twenty might be profitable eventually. (In fact, about two-fifths of the new CATV systems beginning operation in June 1972 had only twelve channels.[9]) Perhaps a more compelling reason for a twenty-channel requirement is that society may find uses for the extra channels, some of which are not expensive to buy. We would recommend a twenty-channel requirement, which would add about $100 million to the cost of a national system, to be passed on to subscribers.

The more visionary uses of cable require forty or more channels. Costs begin to rise sharply when multiple cables must be laid or when the single cable must be equipped to carry frequencies far outside of the VHF band (for example, in the UHF band). Barring a technological breakthrough, a requirement for many more than twenty channels would impose very high costs in search of very uncertain benefits.

Local Originations and Leased Channels

Local originations and leased channels both involve the sale of channel time, but there is a fundamental distinction between them. Leased channels are rented by cable operators to commercial and other organizations for a fixed time, perhaps only a few minutes. The lessee assumes all responsibility for programming and recovers the cost by advertising or by the sale of access to the channel. Origination means that cable operators act, in effect, as television stations, providing the programs and selling advertising. Both services are conceived of as self-supporting.

8. *Ibid.*, p. 209.
9. Television Digest, Inc., "CATV Factbook No. 42," Weekly CATV Addenda (June 5, 12, 19, 26, 1972).

Commercial Origination

Commercial, or local, origination was at one time much favored by the FCC. It appeared to perpetuate the tradition of localism, in that the cable operator would act as a local station, and the hope was that, through him, "truly" local programming would at long last be produced and aired. Thus the commission's proposed cable rules of 1970 required cable operators to originate 21 hours of programming per week.[10]

The difficulty was that such commercial originations could not be self-supporting, as the following calculations demonstrate. If the operator of a cable system of 50,000 subscribers—larger than any system now existing—had about the same advertising revenue per viewer as a commercial broadcaster and aimed to earn $2 per year per subscriber in advertising, he would need an audience rating of about 8 percent, which is in excess of that achieved by the most successful VHF independents. Yet with these revenues, a 50,000-subscriber system would have less income than most weak UHF independents. The commercial originations would lose money for exactly the same reasons that almost all UHF stations do. Faced with network competition, these stations draw small audiences and their advertising revenues are sufficient to buy nothing more attractive than old movies and fourth reruns of off-network shows. The fate of local originations on cable would be the same financial failure that awaits a UHF independent in a very small market that already has three networks and four strong independents.

Some argue that cable operators will provide more locally oriented programming and so capture much bigger audiences than UHF stations. Yet live programming is more expensive than UHF rerun fare and usually attracts fewer viewers; indeed, this is the reason why UHF independents do so little of it now.

Possible exceptions to this dismal picture for commercial origination in our view are automated time, news, and weather; ethnic television; cable networks; and program origination in very large cities.

AUTOMATED PROGRAM SERVICES. These broadcast services consist simply of time, news, and weather reports in a ticker-tape format. They are quite cheap—only a few dollars per hour—and can be bought from various service companies. About 40 percent of cable systems offer automated

10. "Second Further Notice of Proposed Rule-making, Docket No. 18397-A," *Federal Communications Commission Reports*, Vol. 24, 2d Series (August 21, 1970), p. 586.

origination, and advertising on these tapes often covers their expense.[11] Even when it does not, the cost is so low that cable operators are willing to use them anyway.

OCCASIONAL LOCAL PROGRAMMING. While the evidence is scant, the experience of some stations suggests that, in every community, some types of local programs will draw good-sized audiences. Thus certain cable operators have been successful with local high school sports, local elections, or other locally oriented programs. In larger communities, commercial sports—unavailable on over-the-air television—are often quite successful. Achieving these occasional successes is, however, quite different from drawing significant audiences for 20 or more hours a week.

ETHNIC PROGRAMMING. Two UHF independents that show a profit are Spanish-language stations, one in Los Angeles and the other in San Antonio. Among Spanish-speaking people, these stations outdraw the networks.[12] A cable system located in an area with a high concentration of, say, Latin Americans, Poles, Italians, or blacks, might be able to draw a substantial audience, and finance itself from advertising revenues, by programming for that group. The success of some ethnic radio stations, particularly the soul stations, confirms this point. Sharing taped series of ethnic programming, to create an ethnic network, cable systems in suitable areas could reduce programming costs per system and consequently increase profitability.

Another possibility is simply the importation of UHF ethnic stations. Given access to its specialized audience in several geographical areas, perhaps such a station would be profitable. Notably, the FCC encouraged the import of non-English language broadcasts by not charging the stations that originated them against the regular quota of imported signals.[13] The main failing of the ruling is its narrow conception of ethnic broadcasting, which confined it to foreign-language stations. Only the color blind would so limit the ethnic concept.[14] Indeed, a black UHF station, should the FCC authorize one, should be exempt from the importation rules. Allowing just

11. For more detailed statistics on these services, see Charles Tate (ed.), *Cable Television in the Cities: Community Control, Public Access, and Minority Ownership* (Urban Institute, 1971), p. 105.

12. These comments are based on discussions with industry sources. Data on the profitability of individual stations are not available.

13. *Federal Register*, Vol. 37 (February 12, 1972), Pt. 2, p. 3266.

14. There is considerable interest in black ownership and control of cable systems as well as black programming. See Tate, *Cable Television in the Cities*, particularly Chapters 2 and 3 and the workshop reports.

one such station to be retransmitted over numerous cable systems might well be a major innovation credited to cable.

CABLE NETWORKS AND OTHER PROGRAM SOURCES. A third possibility for a profitable new service on cable is taped programs or a direct transmission network aimed at the cable market. Several taped program services have been proposed by program syndicators and some tape libraries have been established; they feature children's programs, talk shows, instructional features, religious programs, and rock shows. Network reruns and movies are not included.[15]

These program services expect to charge the cable operator 30 cents to $1.00 per month per subscriber for about 20 hours per week.[16] Assuming that a prime-time cable viewer will have the same advertising value as an over-the-air viewer, the revenue from a viewer watching the entire prime-time 7 to 11 P.M. schedule of the cable network package is only three dollars per month. Since the charge for tapes is based on the number of subscribers, not viewers, these program services are profitable only if average audiences are between 10 and 33 percent of the subscribers, an almost impossible condition.

In a few cases packaged programs on cable have done well. Cable operators in cities without local television stations have succeeded in selling local advertising, and some systems subject to signal importation restrictions report that local origination has increased penetration rates.[17] These successes indicate that, in the long run, cable origination services might be profitable if they come into wide use, so that production costs can be spread over a larger number of subscribers and thus the price per subscriber reduced. Nevertheless, most of the interest in this kind of packaged origination arises because it would be a cheap way of meeting the requirement to originate programming that the FCC is attempting to impose on operators.[18] But the showing of taped programming produced in Hollywood or New York is hardly what the FCC hoped to achieve in its origination requirement.

15. See *Broadcasting*, Vol. 78 (May 4, 1970), pp. 23–24, for a description of some of these services.

16. Feldman, *Cable Television: Opportunities and Problems*, p. 17.

17. *Broadcasting*, Vol. 78 (May 4, 1970), pp. 23–24.

18. The FCC has tried to impose origination requirements on all systems having more than 3,500 subscribers. The origination rule was restated in February 1972 (see *Federal Register*, February 12, 1972, p. 3287), though it is not in effect, having been set aside by an appeals court decision in May 1971. See *Broadcasting*, Vol. 80 (May 24, 1971), p. 20, for a discussion of the case.

A much more ambitious form of cable-originated programming is full-scale, interconnected, advertiser-supported networks. Such networks could provide the equivalent of signal importation and, as a result, would raise many of the same issues. They would provide more options and more competition for the present networks and local stations. But they would arouse concern about financial losses of existing broadcasters that might lead to the same regulatory obstacles that have blocked extensive signal importation. An additional impediment to cable networks is their cost. As compared with signal importation, the full-scale network requires a substantial investment with uncertain prospects.[19]

ORIGINATION IN THE LARGEST CITIES. A final promising possibility for profitable commercial origination is in the largest cities, particularly New York and Los Angeles. In cities with the greatest number of over-the-air options, cable penetration will be low, and thus systems may not be profitable if cables rely simply on imported signals to generate subscribers. Commercial origination, particularly of sports events or other distinctive programming not available over the air, might add an incentive for subscription. In addition, cable may be an attractive advertising medium in the largest cities because over-the-air rates reflect the huge potential audiences of these stations and discourage advertisers who wish to reach only a relatively small geographic area. Similarly the diversity of the audience may mean good shares for some cable programs directed at certain localities. All of these conditions apply to the two largest population centers, New York and Los Angeles, where cable systems have already used origination to attract customers. They may also be present in a few other cities.

THE ORIGINATION REQUIREMENT. Our dim view of the prospects for commercial originations was confirmed by the response of cable operators to the FCC's origination requirement. The trade magazine, *Broadcasting*, reported from the National Cable Television Association convention: "most operators talk glumly about the burden of programming."[20] Shortly thereafter, several operators succeeded in a lawsuit to block the requirement of mandatory local origination, and won their point when the Eighth Circuit Court ruled that the commission did not have the authority to impose it. The commission defended its rule by pointing to the contribution local

19. The issue of a cable network has already caused concern among broadcasters. *Broadcasting*, Vol. 76 (June 30, 1969), p. 71, reports that "as a major provision (and major cable-industry concession) of the compromise agreement on CATV regulation worked out by the staffs of NAB and NCTA in May, but vetoed by the joint board of the NAB on June 20 . . . there was to be no interconnection for entertainment programs in cable's future."

20. *Broadcasting*, Vol. 78 (May 4, 1970), p. 23.

origination could make to localism and diversity, and is still attempting to find a legal way to impose an origination requirement, as is evidenced by its restatement of the rule in its February 1972 cable decision.

Experience with the local service doctrine and public affairs requirements for over-the-air broadcasting suggests that insistence on programming that is unprofitable avails little, even when the original objective is desirable. The UHF experience implies that viewers gain little from unprofitable commercial broadcasting operation as well. Compared with both public service and UHF independent commercial broadcasts, cable originations have the advantage that subscribers provide a ready source of revenue to meet any loss, but the implicit tax hardly equals the benefit. Even without a mandatory rule, some local origination experiments will be undertaken, and, in some markets, prove profitable. In the long run, as most of the nation becomes wired, various new program services spreading programming costs over many subscribers may also develop. But genuine local service is unlikely to become extensive on cable for the same reasons that now prevent its appearance over the air.

Leased Services

Leased service is distinguished from commercial origination by the role of the cable operator. With leased channels, the cable operator acts in effect as a common carrier, offering a channel to an independent customer. One major economic distinction is that the cable operator does not assume the commitment of the fixed costs of a 21-hour schedule. The other major distinction inheres in the common-carrier concept itself. The cable operator simply provides channel time for which at least marginal cost is charged, and the lessee assumes all responsibility for programming, and either advertises, himself, or sells advertising. This diffusion of responsibility and initiative for program decisions is a new departure in American broadcasting policy. A holder of a broadcasting license is responsible for all programming on his station; thus, in essence, the needs of the community are entrusted to a single individual or group. The common-carrier concept relies instead on a presumably wide mix of lessees, all with differing views. Common-carrier cable broadcasting could be an important new way to meet the problem of concentration of control and inequality of access to mass media. The FCC has been especially progressive in developing the common-carrier concept in its policy statements since early 1971.

The common-carrier concept carries with it three corollaries.

1. Rates must be nondiscriminatory, for otherwise the cable operator,

through preferential pricing, could favor one kind of programming over another. The FCC, in strongly favoring the common-carrier concept for leased channels in the cable statement of February 1972, laid down a general guideline of nondiscriminatory pricing with access awarded on the basis of first come, first served—though what that will mean in detail is still unstated.[21]

2. The common-carrier concept divorces the cable operator from program responsibility. Americans are used to burdening licensees with such responsibility, and complaining to the station management about programs they consider unpatriotic, obscene, violent, in bad taste, or simply poor. The February 1972 FCC statement deals with this problem, especially with the potential libel suits[22] which, the commission concludes, would be deflected by its regulations requiring open access. The lessee would, of course, continue to be liable for his statements.

3. At least some channels on all systems should be made available for leasing. The desire for access means that capacity should be available at a price that covers at least marginal costs. To require idle capacity would burden subscribers, but the access concept is defeated if no leased time is available. Solving this dilemma, the FCC adopted an ingenious "$N + 1$ rule" to insure expansion of cable capacity to meet demand.[23] Whenever leased channels are, for six weeks, in use for 80 percent of the time on 80 percent of the weekdays during any period of three consecutive hours, the cable operator must make an additional channel available within six months. The commission deferred the question of procedure once the full capacity of the system is utilized. We will return to it at the end of this section.

For the foreseeable future, leased channels are not likely to be extensively used. On an advertiser-supported basis, the possibilities of economic uses include (1) occasional telecasting of specific local events, such as high school sports or local political activities; (2) automated program services along the lines described in the preceding section; and (3) audio signals only, such as a cable-cast disc jockey or discussion program. In Canada, local advertising apparently makes cable FM radio broadcasts financially viable.[24] Even-

---

21. *Federal Register* (February 12, 1972), pp. 3270–71. The only exception to the first come, first served policy is that one channel must give priority to part-time users.

22. See, in particular, *ibid.*, p. 3271.

23. *Ibid.*

24. Feldman, *Cable Television: Opportunities and Problems*, pp. 6–7. These channels are not operated by the cable system but rather a closed-circuit FM operator provides the programming and covers his costs by advertising sales.

tually, as videocassettes become readily available, video jockey shows may be as common as their phonograph counterparts are now.

The common feature of these uses is the low cost of both programming and channel leasing, so that they are self-supporting despite small audiences and revenues. Other low-cost possibilities, particularly occasional local events, may arise and make a qualitatively significant contribution to program diversity. But in total, such programming is unlikely to occupy more than one or two channels.

The major possibility for profit lies in leasing channels to subscription television. In Chapter 5 we concluded that nationwide STV via cable not only might be financially viable but also might pay rates well above the costs of carrying it. In an unregulated industry, leasing of STV channels would develop even though up to the present broadcasters have not had to pay cable systems to carry their signals.[25]

Cable STV would be quite a different matter. An STV channel would not increase penetration significantly since the increment in consumer welfare arising from its availability would be substantially offset by its price. In the absence of a common-carrier rule, the cable system would therefore have to be induced to carry STV, most likely in arrangements that split profits between cable owners and STV much as they are between networks and affiliates; however, this is not a true cost, for any payment slightly above collection costs would induce cable owners to carry STV. To reimburse cable operators for STV collection costs and to allow them to share in STV's profitability, STV would have to pay higher rates than other lessees, an arrangement that would compromise the principle of nondiscriminatory rates. Since STV is likely to develop only after cable becomes more widely

25. Broadcasters have been carried free by cables for two reasons. First, regulation has largely determined the allocation of stations to systems. Second, cable owners benefit as much from the arrangement as broadcasters do. While the increased penetration of a cable system due to the third network varies according to options on the cable and over the air, the third network accounts on the average for about 25 percent of the cable subscribers, each of whom is worth to the cable owner at least $60 in gross revenues and nearly that in profits (since the costs of additional subscribers to a given system are very low). The network captures roughly 25 percent of the viewing time of all cable subscribers (see the discussion of cable viewing in Chapter 6); together with its affiliate, it receives about 2.5 cents per hour for every home viewing its signal, so that the system gains about $13 per year for each home on the cable system (see Chapter 3). The cable owner gains perhaps $50 each from one-fourth of his subscribers (that is, $12.50 on the average from every subscriber), roughly equal to the gain of the network system. Of course, in an area already served by three networks, a cable system must carry them all to capture any subscribers, and the networks have a lower audience on the more competitive cable system.

available, the first come, first served policy for leased channels may bar STV unless it is afforded access through higher rates.

Another use of leased channels is for nontelevision services. Printed-message transmission and home computer services are two possibilities, although their prospects are conjectural. The FCC has required that cable systems have simple two-way capability, through which the subscriber's set can send yes-no signals for surveys and marketing services, as well as touch off burglar alarms.[26] Whether this requirement will be self-support-ing is questionable; but the investment it involves is minimal, adding only about 1 percent to cable costs.[27]

In the long run, leased services, particularly STV and the nontelevision uses, might fill all twenty channels, and paying more than their marginal costs, might be quite profitable for cable systems. One use for the added profits is a reduction in subscription rates. The FCC puts in a strong word for the subscriber: "The public interest, as well as the cable industry's eco-nomic interest, may well be found in reducing subscriber fees and relying proportionately more for revenue on the income from channel leasing."[28] Another use is expansion of cable capacity from twenty to forty or more channels to meet the growing demand. With nondiscriminatory rates, ex-pansion is probably the preferred use. High profits and capacity utilization would indicate a consumer preference for more channels. As the source of demand, users of leased channels, not subscribers, ought to bear the full cost of expansion.

Subsidy Proposals

In the late 1960s several proposals were put forth to use cable television revenue to achieve a variety of public purposes. The high point of this kind of thinking was the commission's 1970 proposed cable rules,[29] which em-bodied these elements:

Signal-importing cable systems in the top one hundred markets would pay 5 percent of their revenue to the Corporation for Public Broadcasting.

One channel would be programmed at least 21 hours a week, with a spec-ified percentage devoted to local news and local live originations. Although

26. *Federal Register* (February 12, 1972), p. 3270.
27. See Comanor and Mitchell, "Cable Television," pp. 209–10 and Table 19.
28. "FCC Plans for CATV Regulation," p. 38a.
29. "Second Further Notice of Proposed Rulemaking," *FCC Reports* (August 21, 1970), pp. 580–89.

advertising could be sold on this channel it would, as indicated above, probably operate at a loss.

One or more free channels would be devoted to civic purposes and education.

Since proposing these rules, the FCC has realized that the subsidy burden cable can carry is limited, and that subsidies are in effect taxes on subscribers. These 1970 proposals have been superseded by the August 1971 statement and the 1972 rulings, which limit the subsidy measures; but the notion of cable as a potential source of funds for a variety of public purposes is still common.

In part, the notion persists simply because cable generates a "surplus" whose use is difficult to resist. The surplus is merely a concept used here to examine the competing claims of subsidy proposals. It is the revenues in excess of true costs that, in principle, unfettered cable development would produce. But it does not now, and will never in reality, exist, for regulation would never be so permissive as to allow a substantial surplus. But every regulation that reduces the surplus, including lower prices to subscribers, can be viewed as entailing a reduction in potential cable profits equal to the decline in the surplus the regulation occasions.

The Size of the Surplus

The surplus originates from the fact that cable is normally a local monopoly in which each area is served by one operator, usually under a franchise from the local government. The justification for monopoly franchises is the presumption that two or more competing companies will, by duplicating the expensive trunkline cable, sustain higher costs per subscriber than a monopolist.[30] Local monopoly means that prices significantly above costs will not be undercut by competition.

To estimate the size of the surplus, the starting point is the $66 annual charge used in the last chapter. At that price cable would be economically viable, and would even provide some payment to commercial broadcasting or copyright owners. Of course, if these payments were substantial, they would erode much of the surplus.

30. The "natural monopoly" argument should not be accepted without question. Some believe that, at least in large cities, parallel cable systems are not wasteful, especially if the demand for channels is high. See Richard A. Posner, *Cable Television: The Problem of Local Monopoly*, RM-6309-FF (Santa Monica: RAND Corporation, May 1970).

The profit-maximizing price for cable subscription may well be above the $66 average for the large and high-capacity systems examined in Appendix A, although no statistical evidence suggests it. Cable is a regulated industry, however imperfect the regulation. In granting franchises, local governments specify monthly fees, installation charges, and operating characteristics of the system, none of which can be altered without approval. To some degree, this practice should lead to cost-based pricing. If so, systems that are less successful in obtaining subscribers may be more successful in charging revenue-maximizing prices, for, with fewer scale economies operating, their average costs would be higher. Thus part of the negative correlation between price and penetration rate is induced by regulation, biasing the estimate of the revenue-maximizing price downward. The $66 average used here may be, therefore, somewhat conservative: Cable systems in large cities might be able to increase profits by charging somewhat more than this amount, making the estimate of the surplus derived from the $66 figure too low.

Charging a subscription price of $66, system 3 (described in Chapter 6), with its 34 million subscribers, would have annual revenues of $2,244 million. Assuming that 30 million of the subscribers are attached to large systems that capture scale economies, the total profits are about $1 billion.[31] The profit required to induce cable development is about $400 million (producing a 10 percent after-tax return on equity). In addition, approximately $100 million must be deducted for the cost of a twenty-channel system, for system 3 costs were estimated only for twelve channels. This leaves a "surplus" of $500 million.[32] This estimate is subject to considerable uncertainty, of course; its actual size could be several hundred million dollars higher or lower. It is used here simply as a best guess to compare with the costs of several subsidy services.

A point often forgotten is that the surplus is collected through prices above costs, with an inherent welfare loss to society. Higher prices do more than simply transfer money from subscribers to owners; they also discourage some potential subscribers who are willing to pay to society the costs of cable but are unwilling to contribute to the surplus. No method of paying for subsidy services completely avoids this problem, however. If, instead, general tax revenue were used to finance some of these proposals,

---

31. Calculated from Table 6-2.
32. The Comanor-Mitchell cost estimate includes about $100 million in payments to local governments, which are neglected here since the claim of local government to the surplus is to be evaluated.

the result would be welfare loss through collection costs, the disincentives income taxes would impose, or the discouragement of demand inherent in sales taxes.

Is the surplus worth collecting? An answer depends on the uses to which it would be put. We first turn to "disastrous" possibilities—disastrous in the sense that their net cost exceeds the surplus, so that requiring them would preclude the development of cable.

Disastrous Proposals

The first disastrous proposal that has been given serious attention is the suggestion that all, or virtually all, of the nation be wired, and, perhaps, that all commercial broadcasting leave the air and switch to cables. In the absence of government subsidies, cable systems could not afford to wire the nation. The unfettered cable environment leaves three areas unwired: much of New York and Los Angeles, where over-the-air options are tempting enough to discourage complete cable penetration; a few areas having high costs, because cables must be laid underground, or relatively low potential revenues, because families cannot afford subscription fees; and the least densely populated part of rural America.

A cable system cannot cover costs through subscriber revenues if the population density is less than 350 homes per square mile.[33] Even if as many as 90 percent of the households in these areas subscribed to cables, the revenues generated would be under $500 million. The cost of providing them with cable service would be outlandishly expensive. Were wiring confined to areas with a density of 50 or more homes per square mile, costs would still exceed revenues by several billion dollars.

A cross-subsidization scheme, such as has long been used to finance the wiring of rural America for electricity and telephones, will not work with cables. With costs considerably higher, the potential revenues in the system are simply not as large as those for other utilities, and thus neither is the surplus available for subsidized users.

The second unrealistic proposal is to allow each subscriber to choose his own program from a library of films and tapes. A simple experimental system in which a subscriber can have a page of a newspaper, dictionary, or other printed matter reproduced on his television screen has been developed, but the annual cost of this service, even when fully developed, is esti-

33. See Chapter 6.

mated to be $200 to $400 per subscriber.[34] Yet this service is less sophisticated, and therefore less expensive, than providing subscribers with a choice of programs. Since the size of the cable television surplus is small compared with the costs of these services, they would have to be essentially self-supporting or requiring them would foreclose cable development.

A third unrealistic proposal is for switched broadband, or "picturephone," service, allowing a telephone user to see, as well as talk with, the person he calls. One estimate places the cost of a nationwide two-way switched video system with pictures of the quality of present television at $1.2 trillion.[35]

In measuring the cable surplus against the costs of three extreme proposals, the principal point is that cable television systems cannot carry unlimited burdens to realize any technical dream heedless of cost. While $500 million is a considerable amount, it does not go far in giving reality to the more visionary proposals for cable services, nor does it bulk large against the $3.5 billion advertising revenues of the existing television industry.

Realistic Proposals

While the cable television surplus is insufficient for the fondest communications dreams, it is still ample to buy two or three ancillary items. In the following evaluation of some of the uses of the surplus, it should be borne in mind that one alternative to them is simply to permit unregulated cable development. If this approach were adopted, almost 50 percent of cable revenues would be before-tax profits of cable systems; the surplus would then be divided about equally between cable owners and government, which would profit from federal and state income taxes.

TAXATION. One obvious use of the surplus is simply its distribution to public purposes. The first such purpose is payments to educational television, as in the FCC proposed "public dividend," a 5 percent tax on cable revenues. This use would absorb a little over $100 million of the surplus. As we point out in another chapter, the financing of public television has been a continuing problem. Yet to impose its support on cable subscribers is to burden only half the television audience. Recognizing this, public television authorities have proposed that the public dividend be used solely for

34. Walter S. Baer, *Interactive Television: Prospects for Two-Way Services on Cable*, Report R-888-MF (RAND Corporation, November 1971), p. 65.
35. Sloan Commission, *On the Cable*, p. 203.

cable noncommercial broadcasting.[36] But even this modification does not avoid the fundamental inequity of taxing *all* cable viewers for any form of public television that only a small minority of them watch. The logic that even nonviewers benefit from a more informed citizenry supports general taxation rather than a specific television tax. Since the August 1971 letter of intent, the FCC has abandoned the public dividend concept.

The second tax is payments to the local government. The FCC proposes that cable systems pay 3 to 5 percent of revenues as a franchise fee to municipalities. Some fee seems justified since cable imposes local regulation costs, but the difficulty is that municipal franchise fees have reached a level that would capture much of the surplus. Recent franchise fees average about 8 percent,[37] which on a national scale, yields $175 million in revenues.

The logic for limiting cable taxation was stated by the FCC as follows:

Many local authorities appear to have exacted high franchise fees more for revenue-raising rather than regulatory purposes. Most fees are about 5 or 6 percent, but some have been known to run as high as 36 percent. The ultimate effect of any revenue raising fee is to levy an indirect and regressive tax on cable subscribers. Second, . . . high local franchise fees may burden cable television to the extent that it will be unable to carry out its part in our national communications policy.[38]

Unremunerative Services

An alternative to transferring revenue is taxation in kind, by requiring cable systems to offer unremunerative services.

WIRING POVERTY AREAS. One such proposal is to force cable systems to wire some areas they would otherwise ignore as uneconomic. In smaller communities that do not have sizable, concentrated areas of poor families that cannot afford the cable fee, the tendency is to lay cable in front of nearly all homes. Big cities, of course, do have such areas, which contain perhaps 5 percent of the homes in these cities, or 2 percent of the homes in the nation that are likely to be offered cable service. On the basis of the methods of estimating costs described in Chapter 6, it would cost cable companies about $50 million annually to extend service to these areas. If half of the households subscribed at a reduced fee of $50 annually, reve-

36. See the submission of the National Education Association, FCC Docket 18397-A, December 7, 1970.
37. Calculated from several issues of Television Digest, Inc., "CATV Activity Addenda," Weekly CATV Addenda to *Television Digest.*
38. *Federal Register* (February 12, 1972), pp. 3276–77.

nues of $25 million could be raised. Thus, insistence that cable companies wire all parts of cities would claim about $25 million of the surplus.

LOCAL PUBLIC SERVICE ORIGINATIONS. Another public service proposal for allocating the surplus is giving governments in large cities a free, live-origination channel. The least expensive form of local origination incurs an annual cost of $100,000 to $200,000 per system for an eight-hour broadcast day.[39] If the final cable network has 6,000 systems—that is, 3,500 new systems are required to serve 30 million new subscribers—this cost is between $0.5 and $1 billion. But the scheme costs much less when confined to large cities, since the cost per cable system is only very slightly dependent upon the number of subscribers. Thus, if half the cable subscribers— 17 million homes—subscribe to systems serving 50,000 homes, the cost of eight hours daily of live local origination without advertising is at most $70 million. This cost is highly sensitive to the average size of systems, since origination costs the same regardless of the number of subscribers. Serving big cities with systems of 5,000 subscribers each makes origination ten times as expensive as it is with systems of 50,000 subscribers. For this reason, the proposal to wire each neighborhood independently is probably unrealistic. Least expensive would be to interconnect one channel on all cable systems in each of the fifty largest metropolitan areas for live local originations, sacrificing the idea of fragmentation of the public service origination within each city. This plan would cost not more than $10 million.

These cost comparisons suggest that in the larger cities—those with metropolitan populations of more than 500,000—free transmission for one live local broadcast is feasible in the absence of attempts to fractionalize viewers by neighborhood and broadcast different live originations to many different areas of the city. Cities ranking in metropolitan population from thirtieth to seventy-fifth would be confined to a common program for all subscribers. The very largest metropolitan areas—New York, Los Angeles, Chicago—could afford at least fifteen independently programmed systems (assuming complete cable wiring is forced upon the first two) before exhausting the surplus of their cable systems. These fifteen, of course, would be spread over the entire metropolitan area, not available to the central city alone; all of Manhattan, for example, could probably support four or five independently programmed free channels.

ACCESS CHANNELS. The FCC has shifted its position from requiring a single free government channel, fully supported by the cable operator with programming, to requiring free access to three channels, one each for local

39. See Comanor and Mitchell, "Cable Television," pp. 205–07.

government, educational uses, and noncommercial organizations.[40] The users would provide all programming; consistent with the common-carrier concept for leased channels, the cable operator would have no control over or responsibility for program content. Programming costs would be $25 per hour or more, depending on the elaborateness of the program.

The most novel is the public access channel. Since commercial organizations would be barred, this channel is designed for those who have something to say rather than something to sell. The idea is predicated on the view that some groups have limited access to mass media and yet have information, entertainment, and points of view that should be given expression.

Cost should not deter these groups. Lecture hall rental, for example, often runs in excess of $100, and a casual inspection of the meetings and lectures offered even in a city of medium size suggests that enough demand exists for extensive use of an access channel. Television programs are not perfect substitutes for meetings with the face-to-face contact that maintains the social cohesion of voluntary organizations, but they may be a better way to generate interest among the general population.

Public access channels are not a full solution to the problem of access to the mass media and their very large audiences. Because these channels are unlikely ever to provide large audience shares in competition with commercial television, they leave the heart of the problem of access to mass media unresolved.

Although they may solve this problem in no more than a technical sense, public access channels afford the opportunity to be heard—by no matter how few. At certain crucial times and for certain organizations, even this exposure may be important, and on occasion their programs may draw substantial audiences. However limited their appeal, public access channels could make a substantial social contribution.

One problem is to ration time among noncommercial groups. While the cost of programming could discourage use, the number of claimants could easily exhaust the available time, particularly in the evening hours. The FCC has yet to develop any rules except to assert the principle of nondiscrimination. First come, first served is in the spirit of their proposals, but is an organization with ten members to have the same priority as the one with a thousand? Is every organization to have the same amount of time? How to deal with groups with a common point of view who split up in

40. *Federal Register* (February 12, 1972), p. 3270.

order to get more time? These questions only underline the difficulties that must be overcome in establishing open access.

Since the cable system provides only the channels, the costs of access channels to cable systems are nominal when compared with those for the provision of complete service discussed earlier. The Comanor-Mitchell data suggest that three channels would cost only about $30 million annually. The benefits are uncertain, but experimentation in this new way of using television is cheap. At some later date, the channels might become valuable for, say, leased services, and then the cost to subscribers in terms of valued viewing options, and to cable systems in terms of revenue forgone, might be significant. By that time, the value of these services might be better established.

Subscribers

The basis for the claim subscribers make on the surplus is that an excise tax on cable fees is not an especially equitable or efficient mechanism for subsidizing unremunerative cable services. For the vast majority of viewers, the motivation for subscribing to cable will be the expansion in conventional viewing options it will provide. Our statistical analysis of the determinants of cable penetration shows that viewers place a very high value on more network programming, a moderately high value on more commercial independent stations, and a very small value on more of the other types of stations and originations offered on cables. The Hartford STV experiment also shows that the program types for which viewers have the greatest unsatisfied demand are primarily those already available in substantial amounts on the commercial system. Wanting more conventional viewing options, most viewers will derive little benefit from the unremunerative services laying claim to the surplus. This conclusion is almost tautological: A service is unremunerative only because too few people view it to encourage anyone—advertisers, public organizations, or the viewers themselves—to pay for it.

It does not necessarily follow that the unremunerative services should never be provided. The value of some of them to society may exceed the sum of their values to individuals, expressed through private markets. Nevertheless, higher cable fees are not the best mechanism for supporting these services, since the cable excise is related neither to the benefits derived by a subscriber nor his financial ability to pay. All cable subscribers will pay the same amount for subsidizing unremunerative services, regardless of their income or the satisfaction they derive from them. The burden on lower income groups is especially heavy. Furthermore, although statistical analysis is inconclusive on the relation between cable fees and penetration rate, as discussed in Appendix A, some individuals will choose not to subscribe to cables if fees are high enough to produce a surplus of the magnitude discussed here. It would be particularly inequitable to deny some viewers the opportunity to subscribe at a price that covers the cost of the basic service because they are unwilling or unable to pay a higher price designed to support services they do not want. Thus the viewer must be regarded as a legitimate, attractive claimant for the cable surplus, and satisfying him through policies—public utility regulation, municipal ownership of cable systems, perhaps even competition among systems—that keep prices roughly in line with cost is preferable to other uses of the surplus.

The FCC recognizes the validity of the preceding argument, as the extract on page 199 makes plain. But it has all but abandoned its own argument, imposing numerous costly regulations on cable.[41] While it has backed off from some regulations that it had proposed earlier—a contribution to public broadcasting, free origination for local government, and a requirement that cable systems install a system that would allow local UHF stations to insert their commercials on imported signals—several others remain.

PAYMENTS TO LOCALITIES. Initially, the FCC proposed limiting franchise fees paid to local governments to 2 percent of revenues; however, in the February 1972 ruling it simply set a guideline of 3 to 5 percent. A local government must submit a report justifying any fee of more than 3 percent. The ruling will probably prevent the more outrageous franchise fees, but seems unlikely to hold the level much below the guideline ceiling of 5 percent. Thus, franchise fees will probably consume between $100 million and $150 million of the surplus.

41. Whether the FCC is the proper authority for deciding how many and which new cable services should be provided is a debatable point. The Sloan Commission has argued that the new services offered by a cable system should reflect the needs of the community served, and that the assessment of those needs can be made best by local governments. But the FCC has largely preempted this regulatory responsibility by allocating channels on cable systems and by preventing local governments from imposing additional rules and requirements without its formal approval. While the commission has left subscription fees to local regulation, it has essentially barred local governments from making their own decisions about the proper tradeoff between fees and unremunerative services. For more complete discussions of the division of regulatory responsibility and the role of local regulation of fees and services, see Posner, *Cable Television;* Michael R. Mitchell, *State Regulation of Cable Television*, Report R-783-MF (RAND Corporation, October 1971); Sloan Commission, *On the Cable*, especially Chapters 11, 12, and 13; and FCC cable television rules and regulations, particularly section 4, in *Federal Register* (February 12, 1972).

FREE ACCESS CHANNELS. While cable systems need not bear the entire broadcasting costs of local government as originally proposed, they will be required to provide three free access channels at a cost of about $30 million.

MANDATORY LOCAL ORIGINATION. The FCC has maintained its mandatory origination rule, insisting that all systems with more than 3,500 subscribers must operate "to a significant extent as a local outlet by origination cable-casting" and must have "facilities for local production and presentation of programs other than automated services."[42] Except in a few very large systems, the probable consequence of this regulation is the minimal programming effort that will satisfy the "significant extent" and "local production" clauses. Since the likely audience of the origination channel is on the order of that of a small UHF independent station, the programming will be no better and may even be worse since, unlike UHF stations, the cablecaster is not subject to periodic licensing by the FCC, need not compete for the rights to his origination channel, is not concerned primarily with the operation of television stations, and will be subject to more stringent rules on advertising than is a broadcaster.[43] This requirement alone will probably foreclose cable development in most large cities; were the full system 3 developed, the cost of the origination requirement would run to at least several hundred million dollars.

TWO-WAY COMMUNICATIONS CAPACITY. The FCC required a minimal two-way capability, so that the costs should be only about $10 million.

While their inexpensiveness and the prospect of a significant new service that they offer make some case for FCC encouragement of two-way communications and public access channels, there is little excuse for the positions on franchise fees and cable origination. The FCC's own eloquence on the regressive nature of the former need not be elaborated upon. As to the latter, it should pass the more direct test measuring the benefits against the expenditure of general tax money, rather than slide by on a buried tax on cable subscribers. The danger of such subsidy proposals is that they saddle cable users with measures that they and others would reject as taxpayers.

The preceding calculations of the surplus and the costs of imposing various rules upon it are, of course, based upon system 3, described in Chapter 6. System 3 has far more signal importation, and hence is more attractive to subscribers and more profitable, than the system the FCC has decided to authorize. As indicated in Chapter 6, the viability of the FCC system is doubtful even without additional regulations that would raise its costs,

42. *Federal Register* (February 12, 1972), p. 3287.
43. For example, cablecasters may not interrupt program material for advertising. See *ibid.*, p. 3288.

simply because it is likely to attract too few subscribers. Furthermore, the system is unlikely to be enhanced by the new services the commission has required. Yet these services would make even system 3, with its widespread importation, of questionable viability. Thus, if the FCC has not succeeded in seriously hampering cable development with its importation and copyright rules, it certainly has by imposing other costly operational regulations.

If, despite FCC regulations, cable does eventually develop in the larger cities, it will do so at higher costs and lower benefits to subscribers than are achievable. The underlying purpose of the FCC regulations is to protect the existing structure of the broadcast industry by imposing a high indirect tax on cable television viewers, partly in the form of higher subscription prices to cover the costs of unnecessary services and partly by limiting the access of viewers to the services they value. Congress would reject overwhelmingly a proposal to tax 34 million potential subscribing homes to system 3 $20 to $30 a year each to subsidize the extremely profitable network affiliates. Yet this is the effect of the FCC's new policy for cable television. In the words of disgruntled Commissioner Nicholas Johnson, "In future years, when students of law or government wish to study the decision making process at its worst . . . they will look to the FCC handling of the never-ending saga of cable television."[44]

The process by which the FCC reached its final resolution of the cable problem fits well the general description of commission behavior in Chapter 4. The August 1971 letter of intent, while placing more restrictions on cable development than our analysis would indicate were warranted, nevertheless was not so onerous as to prevent cable development. Systems in the top one hundred markets would have been permitted to import two distant signals—one a UHF independent from within 200 miles, the other without restrictions on point of origin—without exclusivity protections. Stations imported to achieve the minimum service standard (three independents in the top fifty markets, two in markets 51–100) would be counted against the two-import limit. The "significant viewing" test was weaker for independent stations: They would have had to capture 1 percent (not 2 percent) of the audience in an adjacent market in order to be carried without counting against the distant signal quota.[45] Finally, the August 1971 statement does not require cable systems to originate programming. Had it been the final

44. "Opinion of Commissioner Nicholas Johnson, Concurring in Part and Dissenting in Part," in FCC, "News," 82156 (February 28, 1972), p. 2 of the Johnson opinion. This document is hereafter referred to as "News."

45. According to Chairman Burch, this transferred sixteen stations in eleven cities from the "local" to the "distant" class. "News," "Concurring Statement of Chairman Burch," p. 12.

FCC position, cable would probably have been developed in most of the larger cities, according to our estimates reported here and in Chapter 6, although with no "surplus" and with less consumer benefit than would result from more liberal rules.

The FCC found the August statement unsatisfactory simply because powerful interests in the broadcasting industry found it unacceptable. The Office of Telecommunications Policy in the Executive Office of the President arranged a meeting of FCC Chairman Dean Burch and representatives of the broadcasting, cable, and program production industries to discuss cable policy. The FCC agreed to the November accord out of fear that more liberal rules for cable development would have been overturned by Congress in response to pleas from the broadcasters.[46] All the commissioners were straightforward in calling the decision on cable a compromise

46. All of the commissioners issuing statements about the February 1972 ruling agreed more or less on why the commission stepped back from the August 1971 proposal.
Dean Burch: "The ultimate answer must finally be found in legislation. . . . But the obstacle to legislation has long been the ability of any or all the contending industries— cable, broadcasting, copyright—to block any particular legislative approach with which they might take issue. . . .
"After we outlined our regulatory program in the August 5 Letter . . . broadcasters were understandably nervous that this program would go into effect. . . ." (*Ibid.*, p. 9.)
Robert T. Bartley: "The largest broadcast stations and representatives of the copyright owners have again succeeded in preventing the development of cable in most of the largest markets. . . .
"It is clear . . . that until there is copyright legislation applicable to cable, the opponents of cable can continue to prevent its growth." ("News," "Concurring Statement of Commissioner Robert T. Bartley," p. 1 of the Bartley statement.)
Robert E. Lee: "The Report and Order argues that in view of the 'consensus agreement' developed through the Office of Telecommunications Policy (OTP) with the cooperation of Chairman Burch, further comment from the public is unnecessary: The compromise must be taken in its entirety or rejected and on that issue the broad consensus among the industries makes it unlikely that further comment would be helpful. This is not persuasive. Many within and without the affected industries do not accept the compromise and they should be heard." ("News," "Dissenting Statement of Commissioner Robert E. Lee," p. 2.)
Nicholas Johnson: "Subsequent to our adoption of the August 5 letter, apparently not satisfied with the concessions made to each of them, broadcasters and copyright owners, with the support and encouragement of the White House and Chairman Burch (and the participation of cable interests), carved up the cable pie in a manner more to their liking. . . .
"The new rules graphically demonstrate what economic protectionism can do to a sound regulatory scheme. . . .
"The vested economic interests—broadcasters (who felt threatened by this new technological competitor), copyright holders (who were afraid cable systems would diminish the value of their products), and the cable industry (who felt threatened by the political power of the broadcasters . . .)—met with the representatives of the White House and

reached by the three affected industries. Some rued the fact that others who might also be affected were not permitted to take part in the development of the compromise, although Commissioners Burch and Reid defined the public interest as being essentially whatever the three major interests could agree upon. In short, the industries able to represent their cases strongly before the commission, and to threaten to do battle with the commission in the courts or in the Congress should the decision be unfavorable, had their way. They participated in the writing of the final rules, while neither any other party at interest nor six of the seven FCC commissioners were included. Rather than run the risk of adhering to the August 1971 position— which had been approved by a vote of 6 to 1—and then losing a subsequent political and legal battle, the agency chose to forecast, and then adopt, the position it felt to be the most likely political compromise. Thus, network affiliates are to be protected against the creation by cable of more network-like options; copyright owners still have their "exclusives" which guarantee a future market for their movies and reruns that can be resyndicated numerous times at virtually no cost; existing cable firms, located primarily in areas where cable does not have to offer much in the way of service in order to capture subscribers, lose little, and in fact are protected against unfavorable comparisons with new firms providing greatly expanded services in the nation's larger markets. Meanwhile, the vast majority of viewers must content themselves with a lean diet of three networks, one independent station, and one educational station, even though technology exists to offer them richer fare in both broadcast and new cable services at prices they are willing to pay, without costing broadcasters anything more than a partial sacrifice of their extremely high profits.

---

with FCC Chairman Burch and finally agreed to the compromise. . . ." ("News," "Opinion of Commissioner Nicholas Johnson," pp. 7–9.)

Charlotte T. Reid: "While I do not find myself in complete accord with each and every item set forth in the new Rules, the fact that these rules reflect the consensus agreement reached by the principal parties (cable television system owners, broadcasters and copyright owners) are far better than no rules at all. It, therefore, seems clearly in the public interest to give implementation to the compromise. . . ." ("News," "Concurring Statement of Commissioner Charlotte T. Reid," p. 1.)

Richard E. Wiley: "The choice realistically confronting the Commission, after all, was this particular program—or none at all." ("News," "Concurring Statement of Commissioner Richard E. Wiley," p. 1.)

CHAPTER EIGHT

Public Television

IN THE UNITED STATES, TELEVISION broadcasting has been dominated by commercial enterprises. Of the 1,901 separate television broadcasting assignments authorized by the Federal Communications Commission (FCC), 1,255 (or 66 percent) have been assigned to or reserved for commercial broadcasters. Of the 716 assignments in the more desirable very high frequency (VHF) broadcast band, only 123 (or 17 percent) are allocated to noncommercial broadcasting.[1]

These figures differ dramatically from those on allocations in the rest of the world. Many countries permit no commercial broadcasting at all, and even most countries that do permit it reserve a large number, if not a majority, of frequency assignments for noncommercial stations (Tables 8-1 and 8-2).[2] In Europe, for example, only Great Britain and Portugal permit private commercial television broadcasting, although a few other countries allow advertising on government stations. Over 70 percent of the television stations outside the United States, and over 80 percent of those outside the United States and Canada, are government or private nonprofit operations.

Noncommercial interests have fared much better in fixed-service television than in broadcasting. Fixed-service television refers to systems in which an audio-visual signal is sent to a relatively few points, such as all the schools in a school district. The signals, which can be received on conven-

1. Amplitude modulation (AM) radio allocations are even more lopsidedly commercial. Of 4,422 AM radio frequency assignments and reservations, only 25—less than 1 percent—are for noncommercial stations. Frequency modulation (FM) radio allocation is similar to television: Of 3,033 separate assignments and reservations, 591 (19 percent) are for noncommercial broadcasters. An up-to-date box score of the number of stations in each category that are on the air, under construction, or not yet assigned can be found in the section, "For the Record" of most issues of the weekly trade magazine, *Broadcasting*.

2. Many countries that permit commercial broadcasting severely limit the nature and extent of advertising. It is common, for example, to prohibit advertising except during breaks between programs. Britain's independent commercial television system, for example, carries much less advertising than a typical American station.

Table 8-1. Ownership and Programming of Television Stations in Countries with More Than 100,000 Television Sets, January 1, 1970

Station ownership and programming	Countries
Government and private, noncommercial	Algeria, Belgium, Bulgaria, China, Cuba, Denmark, Germany (East and West), Iran, Israel, Morocco, Norway, Poland, Saudi Arabia, Sweden
Government, commercial	Austria, Chile, Colombia, Czechoslovakia, Finland, France, Hungary, Iraq, Ireland, Italy, Malaysia, Netherlands, New Zealand,[a] Rumania, Singapore, Spain, Syria, Switzerland, USSR, United Arab Republic, Yugoslavia
Private, commercial	Hong Kong, Lebanon, Okinawa, Panama, Philippines, Portugal
Virtually all private, commercial[b]	Argentina, Brazil, Taiwan,[c] Korea,[c] Mexico, Peru, Uruguay, Venezuela
Mixed private and government, commercial	Canada, Iran, Thailand[d]
Mixed private and government, noncommercial, and private, commercial	Australia, Japan, United Kingdom, United States

Source: Television Digest, Inc., *Television Factbook, Stations Volume, 1970–1971 Edition* (Washington: TD, 1970), pp. 1028b–1065b.
a. Also government noncommercial broadcasts.
b. Fewer than three noncommercial or government commercial stations.
c. Three or fewer private commercial stations.
d. Only one private commercial station.

Table 8-2. Profit and Nonprofit Foreign Television Stations, by Countries with over and under 100,000 Television Sets, January 1, 1970

Type of station	Countries with more than 100,000 sets		Countries with under 100,000 sets	
	Number	Percent of all stations	Number	Percent of all stations
All stations	2,033	93	151	7
Profit	609	28	68	3
Nonprofit	1,424	65	83	4

Source: Same as Table 8-1, pp. 926b–1065b.

tional sets only with a special antenna and adapter, can be directed at the specific locations desiring reception, and thus require much less energy (and hence involve less expense) than broadcasting. By contrast, broadcasting signals are omnidirectional, blanketing a large geographical area, so as to be received by virtually an infinite number of television receivers. The Federal Communications Commission announced its intention to allocate twenty-eight of the thirty-one channels available for fixed service to instructional television fixed service (ITFS). Only three are reserved for operational television fixed service (OTFS)—systems operated by either private or government organizations for noninstructional broadband communication. As of January 1971, only twenty-one private users had applied for permission to construct OTFS systems, compared with 187 applications by March 1972 for ITFS, of which 139 systems were operating. That ITFS stations are rapidly approaching the number of authorized or operating noncommercial broadcasting stations (see Table 1-1) emphasizes the growing importance of a service initiated only in 1964. Considering the number of public school districts, colleges and universities, and private and parochial school systems, it is not unreasonable to expect ITFS soon to account for many more television stations than all of broadcasting, commercial and noncommercial.

The underlying premise of this chapter is that the basic commercial orientation of American television is not likely to be materially altered in the foreseeable future. Although noncommercial television will thus continue to be a supplement to the commercial service, it seems likely to grow more important in the next decade, with more stations in both the broadcasting and fixed-service bands. Public funds committed to television are likely to increase significantly. Government policy toward noncommercial television, expressed in FCC regulations and legislative limitations imposed by Congress, can affect the extent and kind of growth profoundly. Unfortunately, as is the case with any new, incompletely understood technology, government policy decisions must be made on the basis of inconclusive, often conjectural, information about the possibilities of television. The following pages are devoted to the mundane matters of defining the role of public television, describing the present system, and analyzing the choice of methods to finance it; they do not succumb to the temptation to speculate about pathbreaking innovations in public television. Also ignored is the extreme possibility of eliminating or severely restricting commercial broadcasting and switching to a primarily public system. Regardless of the merits of a primarily noncommercial system, the stakes of the commercial broadcasters in maintaining their current paramount position are too great to make undermining their position a viable policy alternative. The remainder of this chapter deals with the narrow issue of a modest expansion in the present noncommercial system. Because public broadcasting is so different from public fixed-service TV in its purposes and in the problems it faces, ITFS and the FCC policies toward it are discussed in Appendix C.

The Rationale for Public Television

The demand for a government-supported public broadcasting system originates in the realization that a commercial system with a relatively small number of competing stations will orient its programming toward a mass market. Proponents of public broadcasting argue that some provision should be made for other, smaller, audiences.[3] The prestigious Carnegie Commission on Educational Television, which proposed the formation of a federal Corporation for Public Television, expressed this view:

Television should serve more fully both the mass audience and the many separate audiences that constitute in their aggregate our American society. There are those who are concerned with matters of local interest. There are those who would wish to look to television for special subject matter, such as new plays, new science, sports not now televised commercially, music, the making of a public servant, and so on almost without limit. There are hundreds of activities people are interested in enjoying, or learning about, or teaching other people. . . .

To all audiences should be brought the best energies, the best resources, the best talents—to the audience of fifty million, the audience of ten million, the audience of a few hundred thousand. Until excellence and diversity have been joined, we do not make the best use of our miraculous instrument.

The utilization of a great technology for great purposes, the appeal to excellence in the service of diversity. . . . these are the objectives. . . .[4]

The Carnegie Commission emphasizes two dimensions of the programming goals of public television: programs that some viewers would prefer to the existing commercial fare, and high standards for programming. Al-

3. A secondary contention is that conventional options should be available without advertising and other "clutter" that detract from the pleasure of viewing. While commercial-free conventional programming is a meritorious concept, it would not appear to have a clear claim on the public treasury. It is more of an argument for subscription television that has no advertising, where a viewer could provide an alternative source of financial support for the conventional fare.

4. *Public Television: A Program for Action*, The Report and Recommendations of the Carnegie Commission on Educational Television (Bantam Books, 1967), p. 14 (hereafter referred to as the *Carnegie Commission Report*).

most every type of programming would be the legitimate domain of public television, including the sort offered by commercial networks, but of too high a quality to be supported by advertising revenues; only this type, at its current or lower quality, would be excluded.

Conspicuous by its absence is the view that public television should be solely or primarily an educational medium in the narrow sense of the term. Despite the phrase "educational television" in its own name, the commission believed that the role of public broadcasting embraced responsibilities broader than educating viewers. The record of the public broadcasting system since the adoption of the Carnegie Commission's recommendation for a federally financed programming and networking organization demonstrates that the broader view of public television has been generally accepted. Still, the commission did not go to the opposite extreme of advocating a public television system designed to serve the mass audience, as does the British Broadcasting Corporation. The commission accepted the view that the commercial system will continue to serve the vast majority of viewers.

Nevertheless, even if the problem of establishing permanent federal financial support is solved, the future of public television remains unclear. To say that public television should produce programming not available on commercial television is to offer only a vague mandate. The types of programs that public television is likely to broadcast in the future are still uncertain, and will be affected by the political forces operating on it. There are two critical questions: What constitutes a "desirable" extent and type of public broadcasting system? Will the constituency that public broadcasting can muster, after permanent financial support has been established, support a desirable system?

Before proceeding to answer these questions, it is worth noting that the experiences of the BBC, the public television system that so many Americans, particularly the better-educated and more affluent, find so attractive, are largely irrelevant to the analysis of the potential for the type of noncommercial system that is emerging in the United States. As pointed out above, the BBC is the primary source of televised mass entertainment in Britain, a position that American public television does not, and probably never will, occupy. In addition, broadcasting in Britain did not evolve under a local service doctrine. To the contrary, only in recent years has any local programming been produced on either television or radio. The following discussion examines the role of a network of independent public television stations, each serving a relatively small geographical area and operating amid several commercial competitors, *not* the general concept of noncommercial broadcasting as an alternative to a predominantly commercial system.

The Benefits of Public Television

The rationale for a publicly supported television network has two components. First, some viewers choose to watch public TV programs, evidence that they receive a direct benefit or satisfaction. Second, nonviewers may benefit from public television.

The second benefit is difficult to define and measure, and may not even exist. Public television as envisaged in the Carnegie report is, like its commercial brother, essentially a medium for conferring satisfactions upon viewers by presenting programs that some people like to watch. The premise of the Carnegie Commission is that some tastes in programming are not being satisfied. It would be presumptuous and disingenuous for the fanciers of public TV to argue that a broader social welfare is served by pleasing them. Nevertheless, public broadcasting potentially offers some benefits to nonviewers.

THE CONTRIBUTION TO CULTURAL HERITAGE. Just as drama lovers benefit from Shakespeare's plays, future generations will benefit from the endowment of culture produced in the present. Yet no generation can make its preferences for a cultural heritage known to its predecessors. If public television supports and extends the production of culture in the present, future generations will benefit; all present members of society, not just public television viewers, might be willing to purchase an increase in their collective cultural legacy. But this argument holds for *any* medium that produces culture, not television alone. In fact, television is a relatively expensive medium for augmenting the cultural legacy. Only if certain culture unique to television is highly valued would support for public television be an efficient way to increase the cultural inheritance of future generations.

THE EXPERIMENTAL VALUE OF PUBLIC TV. Because it is less dependent on its success in building a large audience, public television is expected to be more experimental in its programming and techniques. Commercial stations then might borrow both from public TV, and thereby enhance the attractiveness of their own offerings.

While such nonviewer benefits arising with programming spillovers exist theoretically, their practical importance is probably quite small. To date public television does not appear to have had any significant effect on commercial broadcasting. No American public broadcasting program has switched to the commercial system, although a few programs produced by the British Broadcasting Company (BBC) have been purchased by the commercial networks. Moreover, the commercial system has yet to copy from the American public system, although public broadcasting has offered several innovations in children's programs, serious drama, and public affairs.[5]

DIVERSITY IN PUBLIC AFFAIRS PROGRAMMING. The different constituency of noncommercial broadcasting gives it a different perspective on social issues, runs another argument for public TV. Because it seeks audience maximization, commercial broadcasting presumably has a centrist perspective on public issues, while noncommercial broadcasting, less concerned about audience size, can give other views more attention. The belief that society benefits from allowing a wider range of views to be expressed in the mass media follows from the generally held faith in the democratic process. The availability of information from more diverse sources presumably enables citizens to discriminate better between "desirable" and "undesirable" government policies and political candidates, and thereby improves the ability of the democratic process to generate "good" social policy.

Nevertheless, the principal beneficiaries of a new voice in public affairs broadcasting are likely to be the viewers of the programs. First, only viewers will receive the entertainment value of the programs. Second, if political or social change does come about because public television provides a forum to a hitherto unrepresented view, the broadcasts must have caused the distribution of opinions on the issue among viewers to shift in favor of change—presumably one that the viewers believe to be beneficial. However, since nonviewers presumably made a conscious choice not to view the programming with a new perspective and since their distribution in terms of political values and socioeconomic characteristics is unlikely to be identical with that of viewers, the two groups need not reach identical conclusions about the benefits to be derived from the social change that resulted from the new programming.

The significance of all three of the major nonviewer benefits of public broadcasting is impossible to determine with any scientific precision.

5. Public TV may have had one indirect effect on commercial TV. By providing a new comparative norm for commercial programming, it may have increased the pressure on the networks—particularly from federal regulators—to improve their own fare. One example is the influence the popularity and technical success of Sesame Street may have had on commercial children's programs.

Nevertheless, we believe it justifiable to assume that most of the benefits of public broadcasting accrue to its viewers.[6] Henceforth our investigation is confined to the problem of providing public broadcasting to these viewers in an efficient manner.

The Efficient Scope of Public TV

If most of the benefits of public television are enjoyed by its viewers and not by society generally, public broadcasting can be justified on either of two grounds: (1) The benefits to the viewers exceed the costs of providing the service, or (2) society desires to redistribute income to viewers by subsidizing their television viewing.[7]

If viewers are fully aware of the benefits of public television and of alternative ways to spend their time and income, the best measure of the value of public television to them is the amount they are willing to pay for it.[8] While there is little direct evidence on how much public television is worth

6. It is worth noting that the prestigious BBC, which long had a monopoly on broadcasting in Great Britain and which is still the dominant broadcasting organization in that country, was not set up on the grounds that it would produce widespread social benefit. Rather, the British Post Office simply did not want to take on what it regarded as the politically onerous task of choosing among competing applicants for broadcasting licenses. See R. H. Coase, *British Broadcasting: A Study in Monopoly* (Harvard University Press for the London School of Economics and Political Science, 1950), p. 21.

7. While no detailed discussion of the redistribution issue is presented here, it is not necessarily frivolous. Society generally likes to earmark subsidies, particularly subsidies of low and middle income groups. Subsidizing food, housing, and medical care is clearly preferred, as is evidenced by various tax deduction rules, regulations on spending by welfare recipients, and in-kind transfer programs such as food stamps and public housing. Just as telephones have recently moved from the disallowed to the allowed categories of expenditures for welfare mothers, so, too, might television be designated a worthy vehicle for improving the lot of specific groups, regardless of the direct costs and benefits involved. Recent proposals to devote one channel on inner-city cable systems to a job mart on which local employment opportunities are listed, or to a "shopper's guide" telling the poor how to stretch the purchasing power of their income, treat television in much the same way. Both proposals assume that low income individuals will be made better off by these types of programs than by simply giving them the funds used to pay for the programming.

8. This is the conventional view of economists that consumers are rational. Alternatively, one could take the position that most viewers do not know what they like—or what is good for them—and, therefore, that a group has to be empowered to make programming decisions "in the public interest." This view is not only elitist and undemocratic, but also permits no further examination of the proper role and scope of broadcasting. We ignore the "BBC knows best" approach simply because, as economists, we have little of substance to say about it.

to viewers, the analysis in Chapter 2 shows that viewers would be willing to pay a substantial amount to increase their options generally. And, according to Chapter 3, the costs of providing more options falls far short of the amount viewers are willing to pay for them.

As argued in Chapter 2, were it not for the limits on available spectrum space, commercial broadcasting would expand until programs, on the average, generated enough revenues to cover costs (including whatever profit is necessary to induce people to enter the business). As the number of commercial stations has increased, some broadcasters have come to orient their programming to large minority audiences, rather than opting for their share of the mass market. This phenomenon explains specialized periodicals, radio stations devoted to soul and country music, and even the Spanish-language television stations in New York, Los Angeles, Miami, San Antonio, and Hanford, California. The larger the number of commercial broadcasters competing in a given area, the fewer the minority tastes that will fail to be served.

The preceding argument casts the Carnegie Commission statement of principle in a different light. The "many separate audiences" that the commission believed ought to be served better are the groups too small to be of interest to commercial broadcasters. And the number of such groups—and hence the potential audience for public television—depends upon the number of commercial broadcasters. Specifically, if the number of commercial broadcasting options—especially the number of nationally programmed options—were to expand, the residual unserved audience would shrink.

In the next decade, cable television offers the possibility of more commercial options, particularly if regulation does not constrain its growth. Furthermore, home video playback devices, and perhaps even direct satellite-to-home broadcasting, both discussed in the next chapter, are likely to broaden viewing options. These developments raise the serious issue of the scope of public television in the future. Will there continue to be certain types of programming that produce more benefits than costs, or will the coming technological changes in broadband communications increase viewing options so much that public television will no longer serve a worthwhile purpose?

Certainly if the commercial television system remains financed solely by advertising revenues, many desirable types of programs will not be broadcast on it, even if expansion is made possible by technological and regulatory change. Because advertisers place a very low value on viewer time, commercial broadcasting is unlikely to expand much even after cable removes the technical limit on the number of channels. With two more national networks and three or four more independents available to all viewers, profits in the television industry would probably decline sufficiently to remove the incentive to entry, yet viewers would continue to value additional options sufficiently to make another national network worth its costs.

Two further aspects of the future development of the commercial system also weaken the case for public television. First, cable systems may originate some programming designed to attract and hold subscribers even though, as the preceding chapter indicates, such origination may not be extensive. A cable owner would be especially interested in providing programming for specific minority audiences if it would induce them to subscribe. Second, subscription television (STV) may be permitted to develop as one ancillary service offered on cables. Both developments would enable a small group of viewers to express intensely felt viewing preferences through a market. Both would provide an opportunity for any minority audience to obtain access to the programming it wants as long as it was willing to pay the costs of the program and of marketing a "product" that can be provided significantly more cheaply if offered free. Unless an income redistribution, or external benefit, argument is to be relied upon, the justifiable scope of public television in such an environment will embrace programs that could collect pay TV revenues sufficient to cover programming and transmission costs, but insufficient to cover, in addition, the costs of the signal scrambling-descrambling, monitoring, or billing devices peculiar to pay TV operations.[9]

Paying for Public Television

The question of the size and role of public television cannot be separated from the question about who should pay for it. We consider first the general criteria for financial support, and then three specific issues: the cost of a public broadcasting system, alternative sources of revenue, and techniques of government support.

9. The lonely shreds of evidence on the potential scope of public television, given growth in cable television and STV that is constrained only by the extent of the market, are, at best, only indicative, being derived from the past pay TV experiments conducted in a world far different from that hypothesized here. Generally three types of programming might fall into this category: (1) programs of entirely local interest (like Hartford's high school sports), which could command substantial local audiences but which would have a high cost per viewer even if total costs were much lower than those for national programs, (2) public affairs programming, and (3) a few serious entertainment categories, probably including some drama.

General Criteria

At this time, the national component of public broadcasting is financed largely through the normal congressional process, with the one minor modification that, unlike numerous other government programs, whose authorizations as well as appropriations are dealt with annually, authorizations to spend appropriations are normally made for several years. The authorizations process begins in policy-making congressional committees, where the political pressure on public broadcasting to be conformist is likely to be less than it would be in the appropriations committees. The present system offers public broadcasting some—but nowhere near all—of the political insulation that public broadcasters, the Carnegie Commission, the Ford Foundation, and the 1967 President's Task Force on Financing Public Broadcasting have all strongly recommended.

The desire to protect public broadcasting from congressional influence is worth examining, for it underlies most of the proposals for financing the system. Its rationale is that Congress will be tempted to reward or punish public broadcasting according to the content of its programs.[10] Since elected political officials tend to represent the middle of the political, social, economic, and cultural spectra, they will be inclined to judge public television on the basis of its conformance to median tastes and values. A public broadcasting system that tries to serve the "many separate audiences" will not receive as much congressional support as one that, like commercial broadcasting, is centrist in orientation.[11]

That close congressional scrutiny will tend to make public broadcasting

10. The same thing might be said as well about interference of the executive branch in public broadcasting. In fact, President Nixon has put much more political pressure on the public broadcasting system than has Congress, attempting to reduce its national programming, particularly of public affairs. See "Remarks of Clay T. Whitehead, Director, Office of Telecommunications Policy at the 47th Annual Convention, National Association of Educational Broadcasters" (delivered in Miami, October 20, 1971; processed), and his statement in *Financing for Public Broadcasting—1972*, Hearings before the Subcommittee on Communications and Power of the House Committee on Interstate and Foreign Commerce, 92 Cong. 2 sess. (1972), pp. 273–327. A summary of the debate between the CPB and the Nixon administration can be found in John Carmody, "Public TV Confrontation," *Washington Post*, April 15, 1972, or in "Politics and Public Broadcasting," a special report by National Public Radio, aired January 12, 1972. On June 30, 1972, the President vetoed a bill intended to provide increased financing for the corporation.

11. The 1923 Sykes Committee, appointed to examine the possibilities for broadcasting in Britain, reached this conclusion, noting that direct government control of broadcasting "would probably succeed in making its service intolerably dull." Quoted in Coase, *British Broadcasting*, p. 39.

less controversial and more attuned to a mass audience seems plausible. Whether that tendency is undesirable, however, is uncertain in the absence of careful specification of both the method of financing public broadcasting and the audiences that it will try to serve. There is no valid reason to prevent a group of individuals from organizing to secure collectively a good or service. Fanciers of public television, with their atypical values and tastes, should not need majority approval to purchase the television fare they desire. But this argument is hardly relevant to most of the proposals for financing public television, for rarely do they link method to beneficiaries. The proposition that, without retaining the right of review, society generally should provide financial support for television for a dissatisfied minority is on much shakier ethical grounds than the proposition that society should permit mutually beneficial transactions between viewers and program suppliers.

Should a public television system supported from universally levied taxes be subject to congressional review? Resolution of this issue requires a comparison of the costs to nonviewers with the net benefits to viewers; still, several subsidiary points seem clear. First, in the absence of benefits to nonviewers or of a social objective to redistribute income in favor of public television viewers, a method of financing that relates the available funds to viewer satisfaction is preferable to automatic, periodic payments from a widely levied tax. Second, the public broadcasting programming that is desired by nonviewers and viewers alike (such as children's shows) is a good candidate for general-revenue financing. Third, a public television system oriented to the mass audience with programming resembling commercial fare—a likely result from effective congressional control—is probably redundant. In a world of cables and satellites relatively unencumbered by regulatory restrictions, this type of public broadcasting will simply erode the audience for commercial fare, causing the marginally viable option of commercial broadcasting to disappear and thus leaving viewer satisfactions unchanged. There may be socially and politically undesirable implications in replacing a relatively independent news voice with a government-controlled one, even though both are likely to be centrist. Yet this is the system that appears now to be developing.

This last conclusion may startle some viewers familiar with present public broadcasting programs, for they obviously differ in important ways from commercial fare.[12] Yet public television is likely to become less innovative unless financing arrangements are changed. With the decline of the relative

12. Many claim, however, that the difference is not great enough. For example, the centrist, risk-avoiding stance of public broadcasting was said to be revealed in the deci-

importance of numerous independent sources of financing, congressional appropriations contribute a greater fraction of income for the public broadcasting system.[13] The influence of Congress on programming, as well as the interest of congressmen in how the money is spent, is likely to grow with greater congressional appropriations. Furthermore, as the appropriations to public television rise, it will grow less reliant on imports, especially from the British Broadcasting Corporation. And the effective control over program content that Congress can exercise will spread as grants from the Corporation for Public Broadcasting—the nonprofit private agency that distributes federal funds for public broadcasting—finance the production of more and more public television programs.

The Cost of Public TV

The cost of a national public television system is determined by three factors: (1) the number of stations, (2) the number and quality of programs, and (3) the method and extent of interconnection.

The educational broadcasting system of the late 1950s and early 1960s represented the low-cost extreme for a national system. Only a relatively few market areas were served by public television stations: As late as 1966, only 114 stations were operating, and several of these were operating as commercial stations.[14] Very few programs were available: In the same year, the Washington, D.C., public television station, WETA, televised 86 percent of the programs available from regional and national public broadcasting libraries, and still had to run some programs twice a week in order to fill its prime-time schedule.[15] Many programs were of a low technical quality, consisting of discussions or lectures taped in a plain studio containing a single camera and a few chairs. Interconnection between stations was provided by "bicycling"—using couriers and the mails to exchange tapes and films—rather than by microwave, cables, or satellites for simultaneous interconnection. This type of system is quite inexpensive, with an-

sion by the Public Broadcasting Service (the public TV network) not to broadcast a 12-minute segment of The Great American Dream Machine that was critical of the Federal Bureau of Investigation. See *Broadcasting*, Vol. 11 (October 11, 1971), p. 53.

13. A detailed discussion of financing appears below.

14. *Carnegie Commission Report*, p. 239.

15. "Report of the Task Force on Financing Public Broadcasting" (Executive Office of the President, draft, October 2, 1967; processed), Chapter 2, p. 7.

nual costs of perhaps $40 million.[16] It is also unlikely to be a very important part of the television industry. In the mid-1960s, public television probably did not account for more than 1 percent of the total viewing audience.[17]

The other extreme in quality and availability would be a public broadcasting system roughly comparable to the networks, producing both national and regional programming on a large scale. If the programs used top-flight production and performing talent at prices paid by the commercial networks, and if the stations were as extensively interconnected, the annual costs would be at least as large as a network's—about $700 million (including all affiliate costs).[18]

Most proposals for public television envision a system between these extremes. The Carnegie Commission proposed a system of 210 stations and 170 repeaters, serving about 95 percent of the population and approximating the size of each of the commercial networks. It recommended that public television produce more local and regional programming than do commercial stations, but it also believed that the costs per program would be much lower than those incurred by the commercial system. Finally, the commission proposed that the public stations be interconnected in roughly the same manner as the commercial networks. The total annual cost of the system, including annualized capital expenses, was estimated at $270 million, or, in 1972 prices, about $350 million.[19]

As of June 1972, the public television system was roughly two-thirds as

16. This amount would finance 80 stations at $500,000 each. In 1966, 113 public television stations reported annual operating costs of $34.3 million, or about $300,000 per station (*Carnegie Commission Report*, p. 241). In addition, Alexander estimates that annualized capital costs are about 20 percent of total costs, which would be $75,000 per station in 1967 (Sidney S. Alexander, "Costs of a Nationwide Educational Television System," in *ibid.*, p. 147). In 1972 prices, the total 1967 operating and capital costs per station would be about $500,000.

17. In 1965, the American Research Bureau estimated that about 9 percent of American television homes watched public television each week, and that they did so for an average of 1.4 hours a week. Since 1.4 hours is about 4 percent of the total weekly viewing per household, the average audience of public broadcasting was 0.36 of 1 percent. The A. C. Nielsen Company estimated that in 1966 public television viewing was about one-third higher, or about half of 1 percent (see *Carnegie Commission Report*, p. 251). Even a doubling of these estimates, to take account of the UHF handicap of more than one-third of the 1965–66 stations and of the fact that public TV did not serve all markets, does not bring the audience potential above 1 percent.

18. About 87 percent of all commercial stations are affiliates, and total broadcast expenses in 1969 were $2.4 billion. See FCC, *37th Annual Report, Fiscal Year 1971*, pp. 152, 158.

19. See *Carnegie Commission Report*, pp. 46–52, 75, 77, 142, for material relating to this paragraph.

large as the Carnegie Commission's proposals; 214 public television stations were broadcasting in the United States, and another 13 had been granted construction permits.[20] Perhaps sixty of these stations are "repeaters" in that not only are they parts of multiple-station systems, usually owned by state educational authorities, but they also share studio facilities with the main station in their system.[21] The annual costs of the 1971 system (including annualized capital costs) were nearly $160 million, of which about $30 million was the TV budget of the Corporation for Public Broadcasting (which supports program production) (see Tables 8-3 and 8-6) and the Public Broadcasting Service (which distributes and promotes national programming). The present arrangement costs about one-third as much as the proposed Carnegie system (though having more than half as many stations), primarily because the number and quality of programs being produced are far short of the Carnegie goal, although far surpassing the quality of public television of as recently as three years ago.

In all likelihood, the number of stations will reach about 225, with 150 more repeater stations. With the minimum annual costs of about $500,000 for a public television station, and about $100,000 for a repeater, this system will have a basic cost, for minimal programming such as that of the early 1960s, of about $125 million (a comparable base cost for the present system would be about $80 million). Network interconnection will probably cost another $10 million.

The two aspects of costs above minimum service that will determine the total cost of public broadcasting are the number and the quality of programs offered to each station. National programming, such as is now supported by grants from the Corporation for Public Broadcasting and broadcast over the public television network, is generally of higher technical quality than local programming, and therefore more expensive per program; however, because it is broadcast over more stations, it has a relatively low cost per station. Programs with only local interest are usually inexpensive—most of them cover news and public affairs, which are less expensive than entertainment—but because only one station broadcasts them, the cost per station of widespread national reliance on them is very high. Regional programs, broadcast over several stations in one or a few states, are intermediate in both per program and per station costs.

20. *Broadcasting*, Vol. 83 (July 10, 1972), p. 52.
21. See Television Digest, Inc., *Television Factbook, Stations Volume, 1970–1971 Edition* (Washington: TD, 1970), pp. 878b–919b.

Table 8-3. Direct and Indirect Costs of Public Broadcasting Licensees, Fiscal Years 1969, 1970, and 1971[a]

Dollar amounts in thousands

Type of cost	1969		1970		1971		Percent Increase	
	Amount	Percent of total	Amount	Percent of total	Amount	Percent of total	1969–70	1970–71
Direct operating cost	$72,226	75	$84,052	75	$113,242	75	16	35
Direct capital expenditure	21,476	22	23,176	21	29,596	20	8	28
Total direct expenditures	93,702	97	107,228	96	142,838	95	14	33
Indirect costs absorbed by supporting institutions	3,231	3	4,451	4	7,509	5	38	69
Total direct and indirect expenditures	96,933	100	111,678	100	150,347	100	15	35

Sources: 1969, National Association of Educational Broadcasters, *The Financial Status of Public Broadcasting Stations in the United States, 1968–69*, p. 12; 1970, 1971, Corporation for Public Broadcasting, "Public Television Financial Statistics, Fiscal Year Ending June 30, 1971" (CPB, April 1, 1972; processed), p. 7. Totals and percentages are derived from data before rounding.

a. Does not include expenditures by Corporation for Public Broadcasting, but does include grants to the licensees from CPB.

Table 8-4. Costs of Selected Public Television Programs, 1970–71 Season[a]

Dollars

Program	Producer	Average cost per episode	Average cost per hour
World Press	KQED (San Francisco)	4,500	4,500
The French Chef	WGBH (Boston)	8,750	17,500
San Francisco Mix	KQED	22,250	44,500
Realities	NET (New York)	46,000	46,000
The Advocates	KCET (Los Angeles) WGBH	50,000	50,000
Great American Dream Machine	NET	100,000	67,000
Sesame Street	Children's TV Workshop	50,000	50,000
Book Beat	WTTW (Chicago)	18,000	36,000
Easter at Boy's Town	Nebraska ETV	6,900	13,800
Hollywood Television Theatre (regular)	KCET	36,000	36,000
Hollywood Television Theatre (specials)	KCET	125,000	62,500[b]

Source: Corporation for Public Broadcasting, unpublished data.
a. Support provided by the Corporation for Public Broadcasting.
b. Hollywood Television Theatre specials have a fixed budget of $125,000 per program; the length of the production is not fixed, however, since it depends upon the play being produced. The productions are from 1½ to 3 hours in duration.

Table 8-4 shows the cost to CPB per episode and per hour of several of the programs offered during the 1970–71 season on the national public broadcasting network. With few exceptions, the hourly cost is in the general neighborhood of about $50,000, which is quite low compared with the $200,000 per hour of most commercial network programs.[22] Several factors contribute to this difference in costs between the public and commercial systems.

22. In many instances the cost differential between public and commercial programming of the same type is much larger. Weekly production costs for the movie series offered by the commercial networks, whether the movies have been made for television or exhibited previously in theaters, run between $300,000 and $750,000 (see *Broadcasting*, Vol. 80, April 5, 1971, pp. 32–33). By contrast, "The Andersonville Trial" on the public broadcasting network cost $146,000; the executive producer of the program, Lewis Freedman, estimated that the program would have had a price tag of $1 million had it been produced for the commercial system (see "TV Channels," *Washington Post*, September 5, 1971).

PROGRAM SALES. Program producers attempting to sell a new television series to a commercial network normally are required to make one episode of the series—a "pilot"—before a network will agree to purchase the series. In some cases, two pilots have been made (for example, two unsuccessful pilots shown in the summer of 1971 were based on the movie, Cat Ballou). Pilots are expensive, costing between $100,000 and $400,000 each. If the program is sold to a network, the pilot becomes the first episode; if it is not sold, it is close to a total loss to the producer. The costs of the numerous failures must be balanced against revenues in excess of costs for the successes if the program production firm is to survive. Producers of public broadcasting series rarely are required to make pilots.

PRODUCTION TECHNIQUES. Noncommercial programs are probably less elaborately produced than most of their commercial counterparts. The former are made with fewer properties and fewer out-of-studio scenes, and, in the smaller station, with less studio equipment. Retakes are also less common. This is probably the most important single factor in the differential in costs between commercial and noncommercial programs.

TALENT FEES. Star talent—writers, directors, and leading performers—charge less for participating in the production of public television programs. Many directors and performers receive only union scale wages, rather than the high fees they are paid by commercial television, the movie industry, the legitimate theater, and nightclubs. George C. Scott, winner of an Academy Award for acting, reportedly received only union scale wages for directing The Andersonville Trial.[23] Bill Cosby, who received $75,000 during the 1971–72 season for his leading role in a daily program on public television designed to teach children reading skills, probably earns three or four times that amount for his commercial television work.[24] Furthermore, public television pays lower residual rights. Actors earning union scale wages for commercial productions are paid 100 percent of the scale wage for the first rerun, which is many times the normal fee for public TV productions.

TECHNICIANS. Technical personnel are obtained at lower cost by public television stations. While wages are approximately the same as those in the commercial system, trade unions have been more lenient on work rules, such as the number of days and hours of work the station must provide each worker.

23. *Ibid.*
24. Although Cosby's earnings on his two past series on commercial television are not known precisely, fees of $5,000 to $10,000 per episode are typical for TV series stars.

EQUIPMENT GIFTS. Public television stations are given used production materials—especially studio equipment—by commercial stations or manufacturers. This is probably the least significant of the items contributing to lower production costs.[25]

Unfortunately, very little data, other than occasional unsupported claims in periodicals, exist to estimate the importance of any of the factors listed above. A rough estimate would be that, of the $150,000 per hour by which public television costs fall short of commercial costs, perhaps $10,000 is due to avoidance of pilots, $100,000 to less elaborate production, $20,000 to lower talent fees (although this is probably much larger for the dramatic specials on Hollywood Television Theatre), $15,000 to special arrangements with craft unions, and $5,000 to gifts of equipment.

The cost differential between public and commercial programs is not likely to remain as large if public financial support for public television grows substantially. During the financially pinched infancy of a national public television system, production personnel have been willing to make sacrifices to keep costs to a minimum; however, as the budget increases, they are likely to insist on parity with commercial television. Furthermore, even if the budget does not grow, some erosion of these service donations is likely to occur as the potential of public television fades into a reality that, due to inadequate financial support, falls short of the promise. Consequently, a realistic estimate of the costs of alternative levels of program quality for the national public television system should make provisions for narrowing of the present cost differential between public and commercial programs.

Alternative Sources of Revenues

Public broadcasting stations now receive financial support from numerous sources: all levels of government, private foundations, private enterprise, and viewers (Table 8-5). In fiscal year 1971, the largest single source was state government, which, directly, or indirectly through its educational system, provided 39 percent of all revenues. Local government provided 14 percent, and the federal government, either directly, or indirectly through the Corporation for Public Broadcasting, provided 17 percent, making the total government share 70 percent. Private nonprofit institutions, such as

25. The material on program costs summarizes several conversations with people in public broadcasting. We are especially indebted to Rose Blyth Kemp of Columbia College for helping us assemble this information.

Table 8-5. Sources of Income of Public Television Stations, Fiscal Years 1969, 1970, and 1971

Dollar amounts in thousands

Sources of income	1969 Amount	1969 Percent of total	1970 Amount	1970 Percent of total	1971 Amount	1971 Percent of total	Percent change 1969–70	Percent change 1970–71
Intra-industry sources[a]	4,486	5	8,194	8	14,745	10	83	80
Federal government	5,744	7	4,982	5	9,885	7	−13	98
Local schools and boards of education	20,192 }	24 }	17,509	17	17,045	12	4 }	−3
Other local government sources			3,391	3	3,107	2		−8
State boards of education	24,667 }	29 }	10,658	10	15,011	11	21 }	41
Other state government sources			19,205	18	31,673	22		65
State universities	5,154 }	6 }	9,283	9	8,844	6	89 }	−5
Other universities and colleges			459	*	646	1		41
Underwriting[b]	2,538	3	2,514	2	3,295	2	−1	31
National foundations	6,573 }	8 }	7,402	7	14,515	10	30 }	96
Other foundations			1,174	1	1,417	1		21
Auctions (gross)	2,177	3	3,453	3	3,883	3	59	12
Commercial broadcasting	187	*	599	1	342	*	220	−43
Subscribers and individuals	5,747	7	6,762	6	8,448	6	18	25
Business and industry	2,072	2	2,126	2	3,066	2	3	44
Other production contracts	2,385	3	3,512	3	3,033	2	47	−14
All other fund raising	3,006	4	2,419	2	3,026	2	−20	25
Total station income	84,928	100	103,641	100	141,982	100	22	37

Sources: Same as Table 8-3. Totals and percentages are derived from data before rounding.
a. Primarily grants from the Corporation for Public Broadcasting.
b. Money earmarked by donor (usually a private business) for a specific program or activity.
* Less than 0.5 percent.

foundations and private universities, accounted for 12 percent, businesses of various types for 4 percent, and individuals for 6 percent. The sale or rental of equipment, programs, or programming facilities was the primary source of the remaining 8 percent.

As is readily apparent from Table 8-5, nearly all of the growth in funds for public broadcasting is accounted for by state and federal government sources. The budget of CPB doubled between 1969 and 1970, and nearly doubled between 1970 and 1971, with much of the latter increase channeled to the Public Broadcasting Service to underwrite the costs of simultaneous network interconnection of public stations. Of the $38 million increase in public television income between 1970 and 1971, $28 million came from state and federal sources, $7 million from foundations, $2 million from individuals, and $1 million from underwriting.

Despite the high proportion of revenues they now provide, state and local governments cannot be expected to be an important factor in the growth of national prime-time public television. They are interested primarily in instructional programming, integrated with public education systems, and much less in the national and regional prime-time public television under examination here. Furthermore, the rapid growth in state support of public television, revealed in Table 8-5, is probably a transitory phenomenon, representing the disproportionately large fraction of initial capital costs of entry by state education offices and universities into public television. For example, in the period covered by fiscal years 1970 and 1971, university and state public television stations accounted for 56 percent of all capital expenditures of public television stations, although their income was about 43 percent of the total. Further, one-quarter of the increase in direct expenditure in fiscal year 1970 by all stations was for capital cost increases by these two types of license holders, while in fiscal year 1971 they accounted for only 8 percent of the increase in direct expenditures and community-licensed stations absorbed 9 percent of the increase.[26] These data indicate that much of the growth in total state support for public television is, in fact, due to the entry of new state-owned stations, rather than to a general increase in the budgets of existing stations.

Besides the federal government, the principal nationally relevant sources

---

26. Corporation for Public Broadcasting, "Memorandum to Public Television Station Managers" (CPB, April 13, 1971; processed); CPB, "Public Television Financial Statistics, Fiscal Year Ending June 30, 1971" (CPB, April 1, 1972; processed); Ronald J. Pedone and others, *Financial Statistics of Noncommercial Television License Holders: Fiscal Year 1970* (CPB, 1971), p. 12.

of funds for noninstructional public television are donations from corporations, grants from foundations, and subscriptions from viewers. Funds from these sources grew by $10.5 million between 1970 and 1971, an amount capable of financing about seventy episodes of the more expensive national programs on public television, including interconnection costs. In the absence of expansion in federal financing, these sources cannot do much more than cover the annual cost increases of roughly the existing level and quality of national, prime-time public television. While they were important in getting high-quality, national public television started, they cannot sustain its growth to maturity.

All of the nonfederal sources of public television financing have provided, in essence, the basic public television system mentioned above—a system of stations reaching nearly all of the national television audience, but with only the least expensive, most rudimentary programs. A few underwriting donations from businesses and grants from national foundations provide a few programs above minimum quality. The amount of federal support essentially determines the quality of most of prime-time, national public television.

Techniques of Federal Support

The problem of devising a channel for federal financial support to public television has two parts: raising revenues and distributing funds.

Raising the Revenues

The two leading advocates of federally supported public television, the Carnegie Commission and the Ford Foundation, have investigated exhaustively alternative sources of tax revenues to finance the $100 million federal contribution that they proposed. The Carnegie Commission recommended a manufacturers' excise tax on television sets beginning at 2 percent and rising to 5 percent.[27] The Ford Foundation proposed that part of the costs of public television be offset by allocating to it some of the cost savings of a domestic communications-satellite system.[28] Both examined

27. *Carnegie Commission Report*, pp. 68–70.
28. Ford Foundation, "Public Policy Issues: Reply Comments of the Ford Foundation in Response to the Commission's Notice of Inquiry of March 2, 1966, and Supplemental Notice of Inquiry of October 20, 1966," submitted to the FCC as part of Docket 16495 (December 12, 1966; processed), Vol. 1, accompanying letter, p. 2.

numerous methods of raising revenues for public broadcasting besides the techniques they recommended, including a license fee for television sets (which Great Britain uses), advertisements on public TV, a pay or subscription public TV service, a tax on commercial television profits, a user charge for electromagnetic spectrum rights, a sales tax on broadcast revenues, and a sales tax on revenues of the entire communications industry.[29]

All of these methods have essentially the same rationale: They provide an independent source of revenue that facilitates a trust fund arrangement and thus insulates public television from annual congressional budgetary review, and they are borne by either the beneficiaries of public television or those who benefit from other government communications policies, such as spectrum allocation or support of communications research and development.

The first point has some historical validity in that numerous federal programs that avoid the annual appropriations process are trust funds tied to a specific tax. In the cases of social security, highway construction, and unemployment insurance, for example, a specific federal tax funds a program in which, without annual appropriations, expenditure commitments can be made on the basis of the program authorization. Even in the cases of these trust funds, however, the appropriations committees play some role, for they must approve the total expenditure commitment by the executive agency before the disbursements can be made. This approval, though, is virtually automatic. Many other programs financed by general revenues are essentially as insulated from the annual appropriations process as are the programs financed by special tax trust funds. For example, the portion of Medicare that pays for physicians' services is financed in part by general revenues and is paid in the same manner as the remainder of the program that is financed by the social security payroll tax. Another example is public assistance. Congress has established formulas by which states are reimbursed for a fraction of their expenditures in various welfare programs. The total federal expenditure, paid out of general revenues, is then determined by decisions states make about the size of benefits and the requirements for eligibility, and by the number of individuals falling into poverty. In similar fashion, loans to foreign governments to pay for the purchase of military equipment from the United States can be committed on the basis of the authorizing legislation. While the appropriations committees must approve of

29. For a discussion of several of these alternatives, see Joseph A. Pechman, "Possible Tax Revenues for Non-Commercial Television," in *ibid.*, pp. 35–47. The development of the British system is described in Coase, *British Broadcasting*, pp. 34–36.

public assistance and military loans before the checks are actually mailed, the process has always been essentially as automatic as the approval of disbursements from, say, the highway trust fund. Thus, whether a program is formally connected to a trust fund that is financed by a special tax is not the critical factor in insulating it from close scrutiny by the appropriations committees of Congress. Of far greater importance is whether the legislation that establishes the program confers upon some specific group a right to a specific amount of federal money. Once Congress creates such a right, the appropriations committees have little choice but to ratify the expenditures that have been committed.

The second reason for a special tax for public television also has little justification. Both an excise tax on television sets and a license fee for using them would fall on all viewers, which is inequitable if public broadcasting benefits primarily those who desire programming distinctly different from the commercial fare. This argument is much more important in evaluating the financing of public television in the United States than it would be in assessing the tax on television sets imposed in Britain to finance the BBC, for the BBC occupies two of the three television channels operating in Britain and is expected to serve the mass audience. Similarly, a tax falling heavily on consumers—a sales tax on all communications, or on broadcasting revenues, that would be passed on in part through higher prices—taxes all to pay for a service benefiting a minority. Taxing the high profits of broadcasters, who benefit from the channel scarcity resulting from FCC policies on spectrum allocation, has an equity rationale—that government should capture the monopoly profits that its policies create—but there is no good reason to tie these revenues to public broadcasting rather than to general federal purposes. Furthermore, a still better policy would be to avoid monopoly inefficiencies altogether by allowing more competition in broadcasting. A tax on broadcaster profits would perversely promote the financial health of public television through blocking innovations such as high-capacity cable television systems or satellite-to-home broadcasting. The possible erosion of the monopoly profits of broadcasting, and the consequent weakening of public television, could be used as arguments to oppose these innovations.

Assigning public broadcasting some of the cost saving from satellite technology is subject to the same criticism, but the argument against it is perhaps less convincing. A tax on satellites to recoup government investment in the technology has some equity justification, but it is inefficient. The incremental cost of satellite communications does not include the sunk cost of development. If someone is willing to pay the incremental cost, society is no worse off for permitting him to do so. To set a higher price—one that covers development costs but that no one is willing to pay—is to sacrifice all the fruits of development because, in retrospect, their total cost was not worth their total benefit. Nevertheless, the imposition on broadcasters of a price higher than incremental costs will probably have little if any effect on their utilization of the satellite. Satellites are so much cheaper than terrestrial systems for interconnection that even a tax of as much as 40 percent on satellite services is unlikely to deter their use (a point explored more fully in Chapter 9). Furthermore, the demand by the commercial networks for interconnection probably does not depend on price; it is determined primarily by the number of delayed transmissions required for squeezing the evening programming into prime time in all time zones (see pages 247–49).

The potential subsidy for public broadcasting available through satellites could be made available in two ways. First, as many have proposed, the domestic satellite owner could be required to provide free service to the public broadcasting system.[30] To offer essentially the same interconnection service to public broadcasting by satellite as the networks now have on the ground would cost about $10 million (see Chapter 9). Second, a tax on satellite revenues could be imposed, and the proceeds allocated to public television. The amount of the tax could be as high as $25 million to $30 million without making satellites more expensive than the ground system for network interconnection. The second approach is slightly preferable to the first in that it gives public broadcasting more freedom in allocating its budget; however, since network interconnection is desired by public broadcasters in any event, whether it comes free or at a cost to be paid for by a $10 million tax on satellite revenues makes little difference to the result.

A final channel for subsidizing public television is public subscription

---

30. In fiscal year 1971 PBS paid $2.0 million for network service subject to interruption by AT&T. The FCC has determined that CPB should bear the incremental costs of network service, and, recognizing CPB's budgetary problems for an interim period, proposed a fee schedule:

Fiscal year	Total Bell System charges to CPB for year (millions of dollars)
1972	2.0
1973	3.0
1974	4.0
1975	4.9

These charges are for a less extensive service (only a 110 point network in 1973) than commercial networks now have or than a future satellite will provide. See FCC, Memorandum Opinion and Order (Docket 18316), adopted June 3, 1971.

television. Some programs would be offered on a subscription basis, with the profits used to defray some of the costs of free programs. There are several means for offering a public STV system: (1) Charging a monthly subscription fee, a second public television service could be offered full time on cable systems; (2) a few public television programs could be broadcast over the existing stations with scrambled signals, much as commercial STV stations do; and (3) the second public broadcasting channel assigned to several large cities could be used exclusively for pay TV.

Any of the above proposals could be either a substitute for or a complement to commercial STV. Because of the high costs of denying an STV signal to nonpaying viewers, the complementary approach is advantageous for the second and third public STV possibilities, because (1) the greater number of STV options would increase viewer interest, and (2) the high cost of monitoring systems could be spread among more STV channels. Given the substantial demand for STV, examined in Chapter 5, these two factors probably would act to outweigh the market-dividing effect of additional competing STV channels, particularly since the noncommercial STV option is likely to be permitted to broadcast some types of programs—new movies and "adult" programs, for example—not allowed on commercial STV.

The public STV proposal has two main advantages. First, free public TV would be supported in a direct, recognizable way and, to a greater degree than is true of the other proposals, by those who benefit most from it. Second, fears that unfettered STV would siphon off free commercial television programs would be allayed. Restrictions on programs permitted on STV could be removed, allowing regular series (such as The Forsyte Saga or the special productions of Hollywood Television Theatre) to be broadcast for a fee without any risk that popular commercial programs might switch to public pay television. It is possible that only the public television system would be allowed by the Federal Communications Commission and the Congress to exploit the potential of STV.

The disadvantage of the proposal is that it imposes the same "excess burden" involved in other methods of tying support for public television to a specific tax. If STV must cover not only its own costs but an extra $100 million to support free public television, its prices will be artificially high, thus discouraging its growth to the socially desirable extent. To exclude anyone from viewing STV who is willing to bear his share of the costs of the system is to sacrifice consumer welfare whose value to the consumer is greater than its cost. This argument is less strong in the case of public STV than with respect to the other earmarked public television taxes since, because of regulatory restrictions, the relevant alternative may be little or no STV, rather than STV under rational pricing.

Of all the methods of raising revenues for public television, we conclude that the best is to follow the precedent of public assistance by providing automatic general revenue funds by formula and with virtually automatic appropriations. Congress could then alter the financial support to public television by changing the formula, but would not subject the public TV budget to discretionary review in the annual appropriations process. One advantage of this approach is that, because it avoids a specific tax on a specific industry—broadcasters, the telecommunications industry, or television receiver manufacturers—no special interest is unnecessarily aligned against public TV.

Another advantage of general-revenue support is that it creates a smaller efficiency problem. Since the beneficiaries of public television cannot be isolated and taxed to support the service they value, it makes sense to avoid discriminatory tax burdens by drawing on the general revenue structure which, in principle at least, is designed with income distribution objectives in mind.

Not far behind general-revenue financing in their attractiveness are free interconnection on domestic satellites and STV on the public television system. For the reasons given above, neither is likely to create serious equity or efficiency problems.

Trailing far behind these three proposals in desirability are all of the special taxes. In addition to creating efficiency problems by distorting prices, they have equity effects that are strong arguments against them. The part of these taxes that is passed on to the consumers in the form of higher prices on consumer goods is, like most sales taxes, regressive. Consequently the incidence of these taxes satisfies neither of the generally accepted criteria—benefit or ability to pay. The part that is not passed on to consumers is borne largely by a specific industry. While it is progressive, by being highly focused it also strongly antagonizes a special interest, thereby diminishing the likelihood that the desirable extent of support for public television will be forthcoming within a reasonable time period.

Distributing the Subsidy

The second major issue regarding the technique for supporting public television is the manner in which the subsidy is to be distributed.

The present mechanism has two components, one of which is far more important than the other. First, the Department of Health, Education, and Welfare provides a few million dollars a year in seed money to public television stations, to defray part of the capital expenditures of a new or expanding station. Second, the Corporation for Public Broadcasting, with federal appropriations of $23 million in fiscal 1971, finances various operating costs of public television. It provides roughly $7 million to the Public Broadcasting Service; makes grants to program producers, usually public broadcasting stations, and purchases rights to programs initially produced for some purpose other than exhibition on the public broadcasting system (for example, from BBC). With about 20 percent of its budget, it also provides some general-purpose money to individual stations. A functional breakdown of the budget of the corporation and PBS is shown in Table 8-6.

The present structure is designed to promote a public television system very similar to the commercial networks. Although individual stations can reject any program provided by the network, in reality most carry nearly all of the national programs. Beyond that offered over the network financed by CPB, very little programming is or will be available to the financially strapped public television stations at low or no cost. If they do not accept the national programming, their only feasible alternative is very inexpensive programming combined with a much shorter broadcasting day. Hence, providing federal funds through CPB entails program decision making by a single, national entity, just as is the case with the commercial networks.

To diffuse programming decisions, more financial support must go directly to individual public television stations. A national public broadcasting network would then have to rely on charges levied on stations, which would have the means to tap other sources of programming, and thus would have to gear its programming decisions more to their wishes.

The relative merits of the two alternatives—supporting a national programming entity like CPB or local stations—depend in part on the relative abilities of national organizations and local stations to serve the tastes of viewers. Centralized programming is subject to the criticisms that it produces a homogenized product, that it does not permit enough experimentation or give expression to a wide enough cross-section of political, social, and cultural ideas. Among individual noncommercial stations lies a wide variety of management philosophies, so that increased financial support to stations would ensure at least some market for almost any type of programming. In addition, as a single direct recipient of federal support for public

Table 8-6. Budgets of Corporation for Public Broadcasting and Public Broadcasting Service, Fiscal Years 1970 and 1971

Thousands of dollars

Budget item	1970	1971
Corporation for Public Broadcasting		
Income		
Federal appropriation	15,000	23,000
Grants and contributions	1,185	5,824
Interest	251	235
Total income	16,436	29,058
Expenses		
Administrative	1,816	2,237
Programming grants and awards, total	9,294	17,637
Program production grants, TV	4,897	9,902
Program production grants, radio	151	1,085
Operating grants, TV	2,623	3,188
Operating grants, radio	717	1,034
Training and fellowships	376	51
Development of program quality	498	222
Program promotion	...	2,054
Library and archives	30	100
Miscellaneous	2	...
Interconnection grants	957	6,950
National Public Radio	...	175
Public Broadcasting Service	...	6,775
Programs administered by CPB	3,857	1,224
Total expenses	15,925	28,049

television, a centralized programming authority is more vulnerable to political pressure.

The complaint against control of programming by local public television stations stems from the fact that one half are operated by educational systems. This is said to give them a bias toward educational programming, which viewers do not favor. The fear is that too much of any increase in the financial resources of these stations would go to locally produced programming of low quality featuring educators as lecturers and discussants on panels.

Regardless of the validity of this fear (a point to be examined below), one way to allay it is to tie the federal support of stations to some measure of viewer approval. This could be accomplished by basing payments on

Table 8-6. Continued

Budget item	1970	1971
Public Broadcasting Service		
Income		
Grants	...	7,716
Miscellaneous	...	14
Total income	...	7,731
Expenses		
General and administrative	...	598
Network operations	...	5,103
Network communications	...	235
Network interconnection	...	1,928
Network origination	...	459
Time zone delays	...	428
Distribution of public affairs specials	...	93
Tape duplication and distribution	...	1,313
Salaries, expenses, and other	...	648
Programming department	...	208
Planning and research	...	50
Public information	...	1,042
Advertising	...	712
Salaries, expenses, and other	...	330
Total expenses	...	7,001

Sources: *Annual Report of the Corporation for Public Broadcasting, 1970,* and *Annual Report . . . 1971;* Price Waterhouse & Co., "Public Broadcasting Service, Report and Financial Statements and Supplementary Information, June 30, 1971" (PW, 1971; processed), Exhibit II and Schedule 2. Figures are rounded and may not add to totals.
a. PBS began operations in 1970, and is responsible for interconnection previously handled by National Educational Television, Eastern Educational Network, and CPB.

private contributions (which excludes other levels of government and private foundations), or simply on individual contributions (which excludes business as well), or on the audience reached by the station.

As shown in Table 8-5, about 6 percent of the revenues of noncommercial television stations come from individuals and another 4 percent from business. To provide the present federal support of public television directly to stations, a formula could be adopted giving every station roughly $5 for every $1 raised through individual contributions, or $3 for every $1 of total private contributions. The advantages of such a system are (1) that it makes the amount of federal support nearly automatic, like public assistance, thereby avoiding discretionary annual appropriations; (2) that it permits the intensity of viewer response to determine the success of a public television station; and (3) that, by giving so much leverage to individual contributions, it offers a substantial incentive for private support for public television. The main disadvantage is that it increases the ability of a relatively small number of viewers, especially in smaller cities, to buy the programming they desire by making very large contributions. Since some stations rely quite heavily on private contributions, a high-leverage grant formula could give a handful of contributors control over a substantial proportion of a station's budget.

While some stations may become dependent on a few large private donors, this is not likely to be a pervasive problem, particularly if only individual (not business) contributions figure in the formula. Even a modest noncommercial station has a budget of several hundred thousand dollars, so that an individual contribution would have to be on the order of $10,000 to be a significant factor in a broadcaster's budget. Furthermore, the budget of a station must be considerably larger than a few hundred thousand dollars to permit it to produce a substantial amount of its own programming. Even if a smaller station were controlled by a few large contributors, to fill its schedule it would still have to rely to a great extent on programs produced elsewhere and rented to many other stations. Contributor influences over the selection of such programs would, of course, remain.

Basing financial support for noncommercial stations on the extent of viewership raises several issues. First, the audience of the station has to be measured, a task ordinarily not undertaken by the commercial audience surveys, principally because no one will pay for it. To insure reliable audience measurements, public broadcasting stations would probably have to pay for audience surveys. Second, the incentive to appeal to a large audience, the pervasive influence in network programming, would be strongly injected into public television. It would be diverted from the goal of serving intensely felt minority tastes and toward the attempt to provide a little satisfaction to a large number of people, just as the commercial stations do.

Several special problems must be dealt with in deriving an equitable formula for distributing federal revenues to stations. Perhaps the most important is the decision on the extent of "equalization" in the formula. A formula based solely on contributions will provide relatively more funds to populous, high income areas, which also are better able to finance public television locally. It also means that stations in these areas will be able to produce more of their own programming, while others will have to rely on programs produced centrally or by large stations.

Because bigger cities have more resources for program production and because the costs they face in producing local programming are spread over more viewers, they would produce relatively more programming, both for purely local broadcasting and for broadcast on other stations. All stations would have an incentive to consider relative costs of programming options, and the cost per viewer of local programming is very high in sparsely populated areas. Since program rental fees are in proportion to potential audience, stations in less populous areas would face program rentals that are relatively low compared with production costs for local programs. To base financial support on the size of the market served forces stations in smaller markets to rely relatively heavily on rented programs unless they can produce programs that other stations will rent from them. This is probably an equitable arrangement for two reasons. First, scarce resources for public television will create more benefits if they are allocated directly according to the satisfactions of viewers rather than to the number of stations. Second, local programming on public TV, in addition to being cheaper per viewer, is also more likely, because of the structure of the broadcasting industry, to be the additional programming option that is most highly valued in large population centers. In the relatively television-starved smaller communities, which sometimes have less than a complete lineup of networks and rarely have even one independent, national programming is a highly prized option. But in the biggest cities, many options for national programming are already provided by all three networks and several strong independents.

Equalization by income is an equity issue with little if any consequences for the efficiency of the public broadcasting system. Since public television is to be supported from revenues paid by the general public and is intended to serve minority tastes of all income classes, a larger payment to stations in lower income communities seems appropriate. Then two stations providing equally valued services in two different communities, one rich and one poor, would be about equal in financial health, and thereby would have about equal voice in determining the programming produced for noncommercial television.

Another factor that must be considered in the formula for supporting stations is whether the station is UHF or VHF. Because UHF stations have access to a smaller audience, they are likely to generate fewer individual donations from the community. Since the type of frequency assignment a station has is a policy decision by government, it seems unreasonable to penalize further the viewer of a UHF public TV station with a subsidy that is lower by very virtue of the UHF handicap. The factor in the formula reflecting this handicap should be related to the audience lost because of it, which is only part of the over-the-air potential audience. As a local area is wired by cable systems, the UHF disadvantage should decline, a fact that should be reflected in the financing formula.

An important unresolved issue is how individual stations would respond if they were directly given a substantial share of the public support for noncommercial broadcasting. The existing patterns of programming by noncommercial stations give no indication that they would substitute low quality local programming for national programming on a massive scale. Table 8-7 shows the number of hours per week of programming offered by the Public Broadcasting Service that was not carried by local stations, grouped according to station ownership and operating budget. Stations operated by educators do show a marked tendency to broadcast less national programming. School district stations reject about 15 percent of the PBS programs, while university and state systems (the latter usually run by state educational authorities) reject about 6 percent. Community stations, which have fewer connections to educational interests, carry all but 5 percent of the PBS programs.

For the purposes of this analysis, the most important aspect of these data is that in none of the groups is there a tendency for stations with larger budgets to broadcast fewer PBS offerings. In fact, stations with the larger budgets reject fewer PBS programs than the average for the group. Thus, a subsidization system that gives a few hundred thousand dollars to stations with budgets of average size seems unlikely to alter substantially the distribution of programming that they offer.

The reason for the preceding results is to be found in the economic advantages of national programming. As pointed out above, a good national program costs less to produce per station than a relatively poor program distributed to one or two stations. The amount of direct subsidy to stations contemplated here is simply not enough to permit stations to make a massive shift from national to local or even regional programming. Stations with higher budgets continue to broadcast primarily the PBS schedule because that still is all they can afford. National networking would have economic advantages for noncommercial as well as commercial broadcasters, for reasons discussed in Chapter 3.

The diffused system of financial support will not determine primarily who originates most of the programming. Rather, its main effects will be in the following forms:

• Stations will have a greater voice in the programming decisions of CPB and PBS since they will be an important source of revenues for the national programmer.

• A few program producers will succeed in selling some national programming that has been rejected by the central authority to some noncommercial stations, just as occasionally a commercial network affiliate will now carry a syndicated program.

• Stations will devote substantially more resources to the direct cost of simply staying on the air for an entire broadcast day.

• Stations—especially stations with high budgets in big cities—will spend some of the increased revenue on local programming, but because many hours are now devoted to either reruns of network programs or simply dead air, this expenditure is unlikely to induce a significant change in the fraction of PBS programming that is carried.

The case for giving a substantial fraction of the federal support for public television directly to the stations is strong. In a public television system supported outside the normal annual congressional appropriations process, financial dependence on affiliated stations is the only important check on the performance of the national programmer. Furthermore, only through a system like that described above can public television be directly responsive to the tastes of viewers.

This does not mean that all federal support for public television should be provided through stations. Programming that is regarded as serving a national purpose, such as children's programs, should be directly financed and made available at no cost to public TV stations. Furthermore, for reasons explained elsewhere, free or low-cost network interconnection and authorization of public pay TV should be part of the total federal assistance to public television.

Since a sudden switch in the method of supporting public television could bring on a chaotic adjustment period, prudence suggests that the contribution-matching formula initially should be relatively small, such as one federal dollar for every dollar collected from individual contributions. The $8 million now being collected by stations from individuals probably understates the federal cost this method will incur, for many stations, particularly those supported by state and local government authorities, now make little or no attempt to raise private funds,[31] but would be stirred by a federal matching grant to do so. Assuming that all public stations could be as

31. In fiscal year 1970, only 0.1 percent of the revenues of state-operated public television stations came from individual contributions; for university and local school district stations, the figures were 0.5 percent and 0.9 percent, respectively. Yet community-owned, nongovernment stations collect nearly 14 percent of their revenues from individual contributions. *Financing for Public Broadcasting—1972*, Hearings before the Subcommittee on Communications and Power of the House Committee on Interstate and Foreign Commerce, 92 Cong. 2 sess. (1972), p. 297.

Table 8-7. Weekly Hours of Programming of Public Broadcasting Service Not Carried by Local Stations, by Ownership of Station and Size of Budget, Fall 1971

Ownership of station and size of operating budget (thousands of dollars)	Number of stations	Average operating budget (thousands of dollars)	Population served (thousands)	Hours of programming not carried, by type						Total hours of PBS programs	Total hours first-run PBS programs
				Cultural	Public affairs	Musical variety	Non-musical variety	Family and children	Total not carried		
Community station											
0–200	13	100	387	0.09	1.19	0.70	0.00	0.25	2.23	32.60	23.12
200–400	8	310	1,027	0.14	0.88	0.04	0.00	0.05	1.12	33.55	24.36
400–700	12	532	1,590	0.10	1.14	0.28	0.04	0.03	1.59	37.20	23.82
700–1,000	4	842	1,525	0.23	1.02	0.39	0.00	0.00	1.63	36.42	23.81
1,000–2,000	3	1,603	3,130	0.11	1.31	0.13	0.00	0.10	1.65	41.30	23.80
Over 2,000	5	3,263	8,085	0.13	1.08	0.10	0.02	0.01	1.34	42.57	24.20
Total or average	45	770	1,961	0.12	1.10	0.34	0.02	0.10	1.67	36.02	23.76
University station											
0–200	14	115	225	0.25	1.22	0.63	0.02	0.08	2.20	33.84	23.22
200–400	9	280	557	0.23	1.00	0.30	0.00	0.18	1.72	35.46	23.78
400–700	9	543	806	0.21	1.33	0.61	0.00	0.10	2.24	33.17	23.23
700–1,000	4	870	1,106	0.22	0.70	0.05	0.00	0.00	0.96	37.33	24.43
1,000–2,000	0	…	…	…	…	…	…	…	…	…	…
Over 2,000	0	…	…	…	…	…	…	…	…	…	…
Total or average	36	347	551	0.23	1.13	0.48	0.00	0.10	1.95	34.46	23.49

School district station

0–200	5	96	335	0.70	2.02	0.75	0.35	0.96	4.78	28.62	20.64
200–400	5	360	377	0.62	1.16	0.61	0.22	3.31	5.92	27.40	19.53
400–700	5	491	802	0.27	1.52	0.23	0.07	0.32	2.41	32.70	23.02
700–1,000	1	999	16,024	0.40	1.15	2.00	0.50	0.00	4.05	24.30	21.80
1,000–2,000	0	...	...	...	...	...	...	...	...	...	...
Over 2,000	0	...	...	...	...	...	...	...	...	...	...
Total or average	16	358	1,475	0.52	1.54	0.62	0.23	1.43	4.35	29.25	21.11

State station

0–200	3	115	1,269	0.63	1.96	0.33	0.33	0.17	3.42	28.51	22.10
200–400	1	329	1,195	0.20	1.30	0.50	0.10	0.05	2.15	33.05	23.30
400–700	2	442	1,155	0.02	0.75	0.50	0.35	0.15	1.78	44.00	23.68
700–1,000	3	960	1,160	0.12	0.62	0.03	0.00	0.00	0.77	37.29	24.69
1,000–2,000	2	1,604	3,112	0.34	1.43	1.58	0.06	0.00	3.41	29.24	22.03
Over 2,000	3	2,196	2,313	0.00	1.17	0.76	0.00	0.00	1.94	32.49	23.52
Total or average	14	1,017	1,711	0.23	1.21	0.57	0.07	0.06	2.24	33.89	23.26
Total or average, all stations	111	604	1,402	0.23	1.19	0.45	0.06	0.29	2.22	34.27	23.23

Source: Public Broadcasting Service, unpublished survey of affiliated stations, fall 1971. Figures are rounded and may not add to totals.

effective as the community stations in obtaining individual donations, the cost of a dollar-for-dollar matching formula would be about $15 million in the first year, but probably quickly would grow to about $25 million as the leverage of individual donations on station revenues from the federal govment affected the willingness to donate.

The device of relating federal subsidies for public television to individual contributions could also be used for providing support to the national programming entity, the Corporation for Public Broadcasting. Since a large part of the impact on viewers of public television is likely to be through national programming, there is some connection between viewer contributions to stations and the success of the national programming authority. In addition, funding CPB in this automatic manner has the same advantage of avoiding discretionary annual appropriations without affording complete escape from congressional oversight.

A Proposal for Public Television

In the long run the public broadcasting system should receive most of its federal support through automatic matching grants, a financing mechanism patterned after federal public assistance programs. A substantial share should go directly to the stations, rather than to the national programmer. Assuming that $125 million in additional support should be provided, the final arrangement could be that CPB gets one dollar for every dollar contributed by individuals to any part of the public television system, that each station is paid $3 for every dollar it receives in individual contributions, and profits of $25 million earned by national public STV are used to offset some national free public TV costs.

This system would provide an estimated $50 million to CPB, and $75 million to the stations. Direct, untied financial support for stations would climb from the present 20 percent of CPB's budget to 60 percent. While CPB undoubtedly would recoup much of these funds in fees for the national programming it supplies, some would undoubtedly support more and better local or regional programming than would be forthcoming if all federal support went directly to CPB. And probably some would also finance productions turned down by CPB, but of interest to some stations. A second national public TV network might be formed, operating on an intermittent, more restricted basis, and providing a few of these "underground" programs to interested stations as an alternative to CPB offerings. Since these developments would occur only in response to viewer support, they would be healthy, vitalizing forces within noncommercial broadcasting, allowing it to escape the homogeneity inherent in a centralized system.

CHAPTER NINE

The Economic Consequences
of New Television Technology

THE PRECEDING CHAPTERS HAVE EXAMINED the probable pattern of television broadcasting and program diversity under continued use of the technologies now widely employed—over-the-air broadcasting and cable television, in both "free" and "pay" modes. Limited spectrum space and reliance on commercial support mean that programming that appeals to mass tastes is likely to be the primary product of the over-the-air medium. Minority tastes will remain largely unsatisfied by these stations; but, in combination with a public television system, cable television, if not prohibited by regulation, would go a long way toward solving this problem.

Another hope for greater diversity lies in the widespread use of new technologies. In this chapter, satellites and videocassettes, two imminent technological advances, are examined to determine their potential effects on the structure and performance of the television industry as now constituted and on a television industry oriented primarily toward cable.

Satellites

The satellite has two uses in the television industry: (1) to transmit signals from program sources to points of retransmission, either over-the-air stations or cable systems, and (2) to transmit signals directly from program sources to home receivers.

Satellite Interconnection

The technology of satellite interconnection is already well established. Signals are sent from the program studio to a nearby ground station, then transmitted via satellite to another ground station and then to either a cablehead or an over-the-air station that transmits it to the home TV receiver. Overseas television transmission began in the early sixties, and satellites now routinely carry news programs and sports events abroad to American stations.

In the mid-sixties the national television networks became interested in satellite service for interconnecting program sources and stations in the United States. In 1966 proposals by the Ford Foundation and the American Broadcasting Companies (ABC) envisaged satellite transmission of network signals from program origination points to local stations throughout the nation, replacing the American Telephone and Telegraph Company (AT&T) land lines and microwave relay systems. The costs of this service were estimated at one-half to two-thirds the current rates for comparable cable or microwave relay service.[1]

At the same time, the potential use of satellites for other types of domestic communications was also visible in the international telecommunications system already in successful operation. Proposals to use satellites for long-distance voice and record communications were put forth by AT&T, Comsat, and General Electric.

After exploring the possible role of a domestic satellite system, a presidential task force concluded that the Ford Foundation and ABC cost estimates were roughly accurate, and that broadcast interconnection was one of several communications services that might be provided more efficiently on such a system.[2] The task force urged the FCC to authorize a "pilot" of a multipurpose domestic satellite system, jointly owned by all of the firms then interested in such a development (primarily AT&T, Comsat, and the television networks). The satellite and its earth stations would be used on an experimental basis for all types of communications services, including some (but not all) of the interconnection needs of television networks. The task force believed that a pilot system could be operational by 1971, assuming prompt FCC approval.

The logic behind the pilot system is worth examining because it relates to the technical and economic realities of satellites as means for television interconnection. On the cost side, satellites are subject to significant scale economies: The larger the satellite, the lower the cost per communications circuit. On the demand side, the task force was not certain that a large market for satellite services existed. Although, if the cost estimates were correct,

---

1. See submissions by Comsat and AT&T to the Federal Communications Commission's Report and Order adopted March 20, 1970 (Docket 16495; FCC 70–306).

2. *Final Report*, President's Task Force on Communications Policy (1969).

network interconnection was quite likely to be switched to satellites, other communications services might not find such transmission so attractive unless they were placed on the same system with the networks and thus faced lower costs per channel.

In early 1970, the FCC formally announced that it would consider applications for the construction of a domestic satellite system.[3] Neither accepting nor rejecting the proposal for a pilot system, it suspended judgment on criteria for the best domestic satellite system until all of the proposals were in. The commission explicitly stated that it was not committed to any particular number of satellite systems nor to any particular ownership arrangement, clearly indicating that it might authorize several competing systems instead of relying on the historical pattern of monopoly for regulated public utilities. The docket for applications for the first generation satellite system was closed in March 1971, but even then the FCC reiterated its intention to be continually receptive to applications as soon as decisions were reached with regard to those pending.[4]

Of the applications to construct various types of domestic satellite systems, some covered special-purpose systems: AT&T and Comsat jointly proposed a system devoted solely to long-distance transmission of voice and record data within the existing AT&T telecommunications system; and the Hughes Aircraft Company initially proposed a similar system of long-distance transmission of voice and record data within the independent telephone systems, primarily General Telephone and Electronics Service Corporation (GT&E), and to interconnecting cable television systems (Hughes is the third largest single stockholder in the nation's largest cable television company, TelePrompTer). As the proposals accumulated, the economic and technical evidence supporting multipurpose systems became impressive. After the docket had closed, it appeared that three applications had a good chance of approval. Only one, the AT&T-Comsat proposal, was for a single purpose, and that was viable only because of the magnitude of AT&T's telecommunications needs. The other two, one by Comsat and one an amended proposal by Hughes, aimed at serving several purposes, including the interconnection of both network and cable television systems.

The requirements of the television networks for satellite interconnection are extremely complex, and inevitably lend a strong advantage to a multipurpose system. All three commercial networks and the public broadcast-

3. *Federal Communications Commission Reports*, Vol. 22, 2d Series (March 24, 1970), p. 86 (FCC 70–306).
4. *FCC Reports*, Vol. 34 (March 17, 1972), p. 1 (FCC 72-229).

ing system use interconnection in four ways.[5] First is the simultaneous broadcast of the same program throughout the nation; while this is the most obvious use, it is also the least frequent. Second, and also obvious, is the regional time-delay system. Normally a television program is broadcast simultaneously in only the eastern half of the nation (the Central and Eastern time zones). The same program is then broadcast to stations in the Mountain time zone two hours later, and to stations in the Pacific time zone three hours later. The networks achieve this so-called time delay by recording and rebroadcasting each program in Denver and Los Angeles. Even a live broadcast originating in Los Angeles normally is treated in the same manner. The live performance is transmitted from Los Angeles to the Denver time-delay center and to the "loop" in the eastern half of the nation, where individual stations receive and broadcast the program immediately for its only truly live broadcast. Two hours later the recorded broadcast is then transmitted to the western intermountain stations, and three hours later it is delivered to Pacific stations—including the Los Angeles station where the program originated.

The third use of interconnection is to break up the national audience into regions for other than time-delay purposes. Most common is the telecasting of professional football games. On a typical autumn Sunday, as many as eight different football games are televised simultaneously to different parts of the country. The public broadcasting system also devotes some prime time to regional programming.

The fourth use of the interconnection system is program assembly, which is especially important to the nightly news programs. Newsworthy events are filmed by the network affiliates in the localities in which they occur, then transmitted to New York or Washington for incorporation into the network's national news program. Between 4:30 and 6:00 p.m. (Eastern time), this is the primary use of the network interconnection system.

In total, these demands for interconnection produce a very uneven time pattern of demand for interconnection circuits. Most of the time the commercial networks have a peak demand for about nine channels; given the intentions of the public broadcasting system to practice the same time-delay pattern as the networks in the near future, the over-all peak demand for interconnection channels on a satellite will be twelve channels. But the peak will last only a few hours during the afternoon and evening, leaving most

5. Network interconnection needs can be deduced from complete network time schedules, after accounting for time-delay needs. See *Broadcasting*, Vol. 80 (January 11, 1971), pp. 50–51, for an example.

channels of a satellite built solely for broadcasters idle the rest of the time. Obviously, the cost of providing interconnection service to television will be lower if others can be found to rent these circuits in off-peak periods. The most interesting of several possibilities is to devote at least part of the excess capacity of the primary and back-up satellites to feeding programs directly to cable television systems, which will video tape them for later broadcast.

Satellite interconnection of both the network stations and cable systems is only a few years away. When it comes, it will have four effects on the television industry.

INTERCONNECTION COSTS. The interconnection costs of nationwide networks will fall. Currently the networks each pay about $20 million annually to AT&T for the terrestrial microwave and cable interconnection system.[6] As discussed in Chapter 8, the FCC proposed a fee schedule for public broadcasting of $2.0 million for fiscal year 1972, with higher fees scheduled for succeeding years, reaching $4.9 million in fiscal year 1975.

Judging from preliminary analyses by several companies who have applied for FCC approval to launch a domestic satellite, the costs of satellite interconnection would be about $13 million annually for the networks—in essence, half the current amount.[7] The proposed satellite prices include some explicit and implicit subsidies. For example, some of the applicants, either in their public statements or in private negotiations, have said they would give public broadcasting, without charge, two full-time satellite channels, and on a preemptible basis, as many other channels as are available. One proposal includes program origination capability in thirteen cities with two origination sources in New York City, and reception capacity in sixty-four cities.[8] (The last provision falls far short of interconnecting all of the affiliates of public broadcasting—a more realistic number would be 125 or 150—but these needs pose no serious problems since reception capability is the cheapest component of the satellite system.) The firm proposing this configuration has estimated that 12.5 percent of the cost of the satellite system can be attributed to providing free interconnection to public broadcasting. But this estimate is based on the average cost of a channel in the system. Because of scale economies in a satellite system, to

6. FCC, *37th Annual Report, Fiscal Year 1971*, p. 157.
7. See proposals in FCC Docket 16495, Vol. 14 (March 1, 1971). Some of the information in this paragraph has been revealed to the authors on the condition that the firm be kept anonymous, so that we cannot give a complete list of references.
8. Submission to FCC Docket 16495.

construct one scaled to commercial networks would save very little compared with the costs of the system that would, in addition, serve public broadcasting.

None of the proposals submitted to the FCC would provide free of charge as extensive an interconnection service as public broadcasting desires, even assuming the provision of an adequate number of receiving stations. Still, at the "supplemental rate" one firm has suggested that for occasional service, the public broadcasting system could purchase for a total annual cost of under $2 million essentially the same interconnection capability as the commercial networks would have.[9] This is still substantially less than the cost of the less extensive terrestrial system that AT&T has offered.

Fundamentally, lower interconnection costs simply increase the profits of commercial networking. The reductions are not large compared with the total costs, including programming, of operating a network; not even the public broadcasting system, with its low budget of about $35 million for network operations, will find its financial position profoundly altered. Thus satellites will not overcome the other barriers to the formation of additional commercial over-the-air networks.

THE EXTENT OF NETWORK INTERCONNECTION. The terrestrial interconnection network is a point-to-point system, joining only cities on the microwave or cable links. Several network affiliates, and about fifty public broadcasting stations, including all stations in Alaska and Hawaii, are excluded.

Satellites are like a broadcasting station, beaming a signal over a wide geographic area. At no additional cost a satellite system can be designed to spread its transmissions throughout the United States and Canada. Then, for only a few hundred dollars, any locality can construct a receive-only earth station and rebroadcast network programs either over the air or through cables.

From the standpoint of the commercial networks, nationwide interconnection is an advantage, but not an important one. To generate a larger audience and consequently greater advertising revenues, many public affairs and sports programs must be broadcast immediately. Yet the vast majority of network programs—and consequently the largest source of advertising revenues—are taped long before broadcast. The advantage of

9. According to this proposal, for $13 million annually the basic network service includes two full-time channels plus 81 hours a week on other channels, compared with two channels plus preemptible back-up service for public broadcasting. The supplemental rate is $444 an hour per satellite channel. Thus, the network service differential would cost $1.87 million if purchased by the Public Broadcasting Service at the supplemental rate.

simultaneous nationwide service here is negligible, except to match the service of a competing network.

Of the few stations that are not interconnected, most are in sparsely populated areas; Honolulu is the sole metropolitan area with a population exceeding 500,000 in this group. Network-interconnected stations serve all but 3 million of the homes with television receivers.

For public broadcasting, the nationwide interconnection that satellites would make possible is much more crucial. PBS interconnection is now "interruptible"—that is, AT&T can switch the circuits to other users whenever they desire. Serious preemption problems have arisen, particularly on service to the Pacific Northwest, the Southwest, and the South. In the long run, as negotiations between AT&T and PBS for permanent service are concluded, this problem will dissolve. Nevertheless, the terrestrial system will interconnect a smaller fraction of public broadcasting stations than of commercial network affiliates. This is a major drawback for the public system, which, reflecting its noncommercial nature, puts heavy emphasis on serving the smaller markets as well as it serves the larger ones.

To the vast majority of viewers, satellite interconnection will not change the existing television service noticeably. For a sizable portion—perhaps 25 percent—satellites will permit interconnection of local public broadcasting stations, which then probably will carry many more national public affairs programs. To a smaller portion—perhaps 5 percent—satellites will bring commercial network interconnection. The most important consequences for these viewers will be access to live sports events and to the network nightly news, both of which are among the more popular programs. Satellites will offer them a substantial increase in the welfare they derive from television.

CABLE SIGNAL IMPORTATION COSTS. Satellites will have three important effects on signal importation costs. First, for signals imported more than 500 miles, satellite circuits will be cheaper than terrestrial circuits. Second, since satellite-circuit costs are not dependent on the distance the signal is transmitted,[10] a cable system will save nothing in importing relatively near signals, once the 500-mile limit of terrestrial-system advantage has been

10. AT&T prices for transmitting television signals are based on the air-route distance between source and receiver, regardless of the actual transmission route. Although a transmission from Washington to Phoenix will probably be routed through both Los Angeles and New York, the price charged will be lower than that for transmission between the latter two cities. It is, of course, possible that AT&T will not continue this pricing practice after satellite competition becomes a reality.

passed. Thus a cable system in Montana will find signals from Chicago, Los Angeles, and New York equally expensive.

Third, and perhaps most important, satellites offer cable operators a significant incentive to band together to import the same distant signals. Just as satellites offer nationwide network interconnection of over-the-air affiliates at little additional cost, so, too, do they offer nationwide distribution of a single imported over-the-air station. For perhaps $5 million annually (based on Comsat's rate proposal), including reception costs, a single independent station can be transmitted to every cable system in the nation. This is a total annual cost of under $1 per cable subscriber. As Chapter 3 reported, a viewing home is worth about $50 a year to broadcasters. A strong independent should capture at least 4 percent of the market, or $2 per TV home. With 6 million cable subscribers, these figures mean that in advertising revenues alone the value of national satellite distribution of a strong independent should be more than double the interconnection cost, even at today's relatively low rate of cable penetration. Once the effect of the practice on cable subscriptions and on viewer welfare through greater program diversity is added to the calculation, the use of satellites for national distribution of independent station signals appears extremely worthwhile to all concerned. And it is this realization that underlies the Hughes and TelePromptTer proposal to devote substantial capacity of a satellite system to cable system interconnection.

PROGRAM DIVERSITY. The effect of satellites on cable interconnection costs could spur the emergence of a new television network comprising a few big-city independent stations and the existing cable systems. At present cable systems are widely dispersed, to a great extent in remote areas, making the cost per subscriber of microwave interconnection prohibitively high. At the same time, microwave interconnection of big-city independents, at a cost of at least $15 million annually, is far too expensive to be worthwhile. A reasonable estimate of the total revenue of the largest independent in each of the twenty largest cities is about $40 million. Satellites will allow these two groups to interconnect at a cost that is low compared with the $350 million total revenues of a big-city independent and all cable systems. Coupling these figures with the economic reality of an enormous unsatisfied demand for more commercial network programming, we conclude that satellite interconnection of cables and big-city independents will occur very shortly after satellite service is begun—assuming that FCC regulation does not prevent it.

Lower interconnection costs will also promote the growth of a national network subscription service, particularly since it would require access to audiences on the two coasts. The reduction in transcontinental interconnection costs will be especially large when satellites are put into use, thus opening up, at little extra cost, cable systems as a market for pay TV.

Satellite-to-home Broadcasting

As a way to send signals directly from the program source, satellites offer another revolutionary possibility. Networks could send signals from their New York or Los Angeles studios directly to the viewer's set without utilizing either local stations or cables.

The use of direct-broadcast satellites would also overcome the spectrum shortage that now restricts the number of channels. At this time, only 3.7 to 4.2 gigahertz (GHz) of the technologically usable spectrum below 15 GHz is used, while potentially usable frequencies as high as 1,000,000 GHz are not now used because the necessary technology has not been developed. High frequencies are not utilized now because atmospheric conditions make long-distance ground-to-ground transmission of a relatively interference-free signal very difficult. Satellite-to-ground transmission reduces the distance signals must travel through the troublesome atmosphere, since most of the transmission to and from the satellite is through the upper atmosphere, which has very low density. As a result signal attenuation is less of a problem.

Signal attenuation due to rain is severe in the upper reaches of the spectrum, but the problem can be circumvented in several ways. Ground stations could be located in areas with low rainfall or distributed in such a way that the probability of all being out of operation at the same time would be very small. Or, satellite beams could be focused and electromagnetic energy concentrated more precisely over the area to be served. What is most striking is the availability of enough usable spectrum in the range from 15 to 100 GHz alone to provide 100 times the spectrum space now available.

Direct satellite broadcasting will require new types of receivers. Hughes claims to have developed a rooftop antenna that would allow existing sets to receive satellite broadcasts at 4 GHz. Although the cost of receive-only antennas is still highly uncertain, some engineers believe that they might cost as little as $80 for reception at 4 GHz, if produced in large quantities, while for the upper reaches of the electromagnetic spectrum, the costs of a reception device might not exceed $150 per set.[11] These figures make direct broadcasting via satellite a feasible and fairly economic means of expanding the number of channels at a cost probably lower than that of creating a nationwide cable television system. Yet cable offers fewer problems of signal impairment.

The difficulty with satellite-to-home television is the small incentive for the necessary institutional change, the same problem UHF television faced a decade ago. Viewers, of course, have no reason to make the expenditure for set modifications, since the networks are not now broadcasting via satellite. Neither existing nor potential networks, in turn, have an incentive to begin broadcasting via satellite since there are no viewers. One gain of direct satellite broadcasting would be alleviation of spectrum scarcity as the networks switched to one national channel each. But since they, in turn, are not charged the scarcity value of the spectrum they now use, they would not gain by using less spectrum; indeed, they would suffer from increased competition. Furthermore, to free spectrum requires that *all* viewers purchase a satellite receiver, for all local network stations would have to be totally eliminated.

Some engineers foresee the possibility, after 1985, of satellite-to-home broadcasting over the unused UHF channels, without the attachment of special satellite receivers to present sets. This would represent a major technical change, for new network-like companies could broadcast over wide areas without establishing local stations.

Unlike cable TV, direct satellite-to-home broadcasting will prove a serious threat to local stations in the long run. Only to the extent that viewers preferred local to national, or even regional, programming would the local station survive. This is perhaps the telling point in the forecast for this technology. As shown in Chapter 4, the strongest single motivation in FCC broadcast policy throughout its history has been the local service doctrine. Cable development, regional over-the-air stations, and even pay TV have all stumbled on the roadblocks the FCC placed because it saw in them some threat to free local programming.

Without regulatory intervention, the outcome of the competition between cable television and satellite-to-home broadcasting might be too close to predict. The former would offer more specialized locally oriented

11. The cost of terminals for both sending and receiving satellite broadcasts is now under $2,000, as Hughes has agreed to provide five such stations to the National Institutes of Health at prices somewhere between $1,000 and $2,000 each.

services and a picture of better quality; the latter would be less expensive to viewers and would provide much more nationally oriented programming. With regulatory intervention, satellites probably have no chance. In the absence of substantial political support (which appears unlikely to materialize), the FCC is unlikely to abandon the local service doctrine. And since substantial cable development can be permitted without great violence to the present over-the-air system, the FCC will probably favor cables over satellites should it decide to permit widespread use of either technology.

Videocassettes

Videocassette systems are now being heralded as a communications breakthrough rivaling the printing press and surpassing television itself. Marshall McLuhan predicts that videocassettes will affect "every aspect of our lives—will give us new needs, goals and desires, and will upset all political, educational and commercial establishments." *Life* had euphorically christened videocassettes the "good revolution."[12] An executive vice president of RCA, Chase Morsey, Jr., has said: "If you want to calculate the market for video playback, just add up the collective market for movies, books, records, audio cassettes, adult courses, encyclopedias, business magazines and fairy tales."[13] And an Arthur D. Little, Inc., study forecasts that the videocassette industry will reach $1 billion in sales on a world-wide basis by 1975.[14]

Rather than outline the social revolution that videocassettes might bring, the following discussion seeks to describe the technological options, estimate the likely costs and markets, and give a rough idea of the effects videocassettes are likely to have on the television industry.

The Technical Alternatives

The videocassette concept is simple. A "program" can be recorded off the air either commercially or at home, and like a phonograph record, played back through a home television set or a similar video screening device.

As of 1971 at least twenty-five companies were developing various types

12. See Edward Kern, "A Good Revolution Goes on Sale," *Life*, Vol. 69 (October 16, 1970), pp. 46–53.
13. Television Digest, Inc., *Videocassette Sourcebook* (Washington: TD, 1971), p. 2.
14. *Ibid.*

of video playback systems, nearly all of which are mutually incompatible technically. Some of the systems and their characteristics are listed in Table 9-1. Inevitably, only a few systems can survive, for the development of a mass market in videocassettes—the purchased or rented program packages—requires that a large number of homes be able to play a single type of cassette.

Two basic approaches to videoplayer systems are currently being pursued. Optical film systems, the first, are in essence inexpensive movies with sound tracks. In all of these the video portion of the encased program is recorded on 8-millimeter film and the audio portion either on a sound track on the film or on synchronized magnetic tape. Some of these systems, called programmed film systems, reduce the amount of film by varying the speed at which it is advanced, showing credits, titles, and animated portions very slowly.

One programmed film system, developed by Retention Communication Systems, will be priced under $200, including display. The cost of materials for the combined film-tape cassettes (which does not include the cost of the program) will be between $3 and $10 for one hour of programming.

The second basic approach is to encode information that can be translated by a player into a broadcast signal, which is then fed to a normal television receiver. The principle is essentially like a phonograph or tape recorder. Among the media used for encoding are film, vinyl tape, vinyl discs, magnetic tape, glass, and plastic. Encoded systems are already being produced, although not yet for the home entertainment market. Playback systems now cost about $800, and the materials of their encoding media cost between $25 and $40 an hour (exclusive of programming costs). The costs of both players and cassette materials are expected to fall dramatically within a few years, as the table shows.

One encoded system, Columbia Broadcasting System's electronic video recording (EVR) system, has been promoted as a replacement for business and school instructional films. While the costs of its cartridges appear high for home use, they are about one-third lower than the least expensive alternative for high-quality pictures, sixteen millimeter motion pictures. For example, Motorola has marketed a series of twelve 16-millimeter films by former coach George Allen and several Los Angeles Rams football players on how to play football, at a price of $1,495; for the same price, Motorola will sell the series on six EVR cassettes, with an EVR player included.[15] EVR has also been a potential claimant for the home video market, but the

15. *Ibid.*, p. 15.

Table 9-1. Characteristics of Selected Videocassette Systems, May 1971

Type of system and major developers	Cassette medium	Cassette playing time (minutes)	Materials cost of cassette (dollars per hour of playing time)	Price of equipment (dollars)	Remarks
Optical Film, constant frame speed (Eumig [Austria], NordMende [Germany], Vidicord Holdings [U.K.], Eastman Kodak, GTE Sylvania)	Super-8 film	30	110	480–270	Video recording component extra
Optical film, programmed frame speed (Philips [Holland], Retention Communication Systems)	Super-8 film	60	3–10	189–375	Playback only
Encoded film (CBS)	Silver halide 8.75 mm film	25 (color) 50 (black and white)	37.50 (color) 23.10 (black and white)	795 (now) 300 (future)	Playback only
Encoded nonmagnetic tape (RCA)	½-inch vinyl tape	30	4–6	400	Playback only; laser holographic system
Encoded magnetic tape (Ampex, Avco, Philips [Holland], Sony, RCA, Arvin, Japan Victor, TEAC [Japan], Matsushita [Japan])	½-inch iron oxide or chromium dioxide tape	30–120	10–30	500–850	Several systems can record off the air at no extra cost; general recording capability about $500 extra, including camera
Encoded disc (Telefunken [Germany]-Decca [U.K.]-Teldec)	Thin-foil poly-vinyl chloride disc	5–12	2.75	120 240 (with changer)	Playback only; longer playing time expected within a few years at little extra cost
Encoded disc (Philips [Holland], MCA, Thomson-CSF [France])	n.a.[a]	n.a.[a]	n.a.[a]	n.a.[a]	…
Encoded disc (3M)	Glass or plastic disc	n.a.	n.a.	n.a.	…

Source: Television Digest, Inc., *Video Cassette Sourcebook* (Washington: TD, 1971), last page. a. In experimental or developmental stage. n.a. Not available.

decision of CBS to withdraw from the production of players and cassettes, leaving the market to its licensees, probably indicates that the company no longer expects EVR to be the dominant home system.[16]

Most firms have investigated magnetic tape systems, which have several important advantages over other systems. First, their technology is the most highly developed. Television stations have used commercial varieties of videorecording and playback systems for many years. Only the optical film systems can build on as much related prior development. Second, videotape, at least at present, is by far the least expensive mode if home-recording capability is to be included. Color videotape recording capacity and color video playback (not including the television set or other display device) is already available for $1,000, and the price may fall to as little as $500 within a few years. A color camera, necessary for recording anything beyond off-the-air broadcasts, will cost $500 extra, and a black-and-white camera as little as $200. Videotape also has the advantage of extremely long playing capacity—up to two uninterrupted hours. Its principal disadvantage is that it is quite expensive if a user wants only playback capacity.

For playback only, the most promising types of systems appear to be nonmagnetic tapes and discs. The RCA "Holotape," based on the use of lasers, has relatively long-playing—thirty-minute—cassettes whose materials cost around $5 per hour. The Telefunken-Decca polyvinyl chloride disc plays for only twelve minutes at the most, but costs only about $3 an hour. The playback device sells for only $120, or $240 with an automatic changer.

Programming

A number of firms have been accumulating rights to videocassette programming. The development of a programming industry is, of course, critical to the success of video playback systems. Furthermore, in a pattern analogous to that in other entertainment media, the programming part of the industry is likely to be both more important and more profitable than the manufacture of playback devices, because the latter invariably becomes relatively competitive, while the former does not. Hardware designs and systems may confer short-term monopoly rights on developers by virtue of the greater experience they have with the new technology and of their patent protection. But within a few years the first advantage dissipates and

16. *Broadcasting*, Vol. 81 (December 27, 1971), p. 16.

the second erodes. (Even if the patents prove to be effective protectors of the technology, antitrust action often prevents the developer from collecting the full monopoly rent.)

Probably the most completely developed programming package has been put together by Cartridge Television, Inc., a division of AVCO Corporation. It has concentrated on two types of entertainment—video music, the counterpart in videocassettes to the long-playing record or the audio tape cassettes, and old movies. As of mid-1971, Cartridge TV had, ready to be marketed, approximately 200 music tapes, with playing times of thirty minutes to two hours; their price per minute of programming was expected to be roughly the same as that of a long-playing record,[17] even though the materials cost alone ($12 to $17 an hour) exceeds record prices.

AVCO's movie library is even more extensive, containing about 300 films, nearly all of which have been previously exhibited[18]—and many of which are "adult" fare.[19] Several other companies believe that "adult" fare will be a big part of the videocassette market. Grove Press, for instance, has announced that it will produce a monthly 90-minute videocassette version of *Evergreen Review* for a $100 a year subscription price.[20]

On all of the systems with long-playing capability, the materials cost of a movie-length cassette will be at least $25, and on several it will be over $100. For all but relatively high income families, owning a library of favorite movies will not be economically feasible, and as a consequence, program producers expect to create a network of rental shops. A videocassette with a lifetime of about 100 plays, and a cost of somewhere between $100 and $200 including programming, would be rented for twenty-four hours at a fee of a few dollars. At $3 or $4 per rental, $200 in profits would be left to be divided among the retail store, the distributor, and the cassette manufacturer.

Whether the price of the cassettes will depend on content (like books) or will be relatively standardized (like records or first-run theater admissions) is still in doubt. Since the prime competitors of videocassettes are records and theaters, it seems more natural that standardized pricing will develop.

To date the programming ideas of the videocassette manufacturers seem

---

17. Television Digest, Inc., *Television Digest with Consumer Electronics*, Vol. 10 (August 24, 1970), p. 9; for a description of AVCO offerings, see *Television Digest with Consumer Electronics*, Vol. 10 (July 6, 1970), p. 9.

18. *Videocassette Sourcebook*, p. 23.

19. *Television Digest* (July 6, 1970), p. 9.

20. *Television Digest*, Vol. 11 (February 1, 1971), p. 9.

more prosaic than revolutionary. Preview showings of nearly completed systems have featured conventional television fare: musical performances, moon landings, sports events, animated cartoons, commercials, instructions on how to use an electric tool, a tour of an art museum, and an explanation of the effects of a new drug. Since most of the systems apparently must rely on relatively expensive cassettes at least for the first few years, programmers are concentrating on markets with very large dollar demand —the large audience for movies and popular recording artists and certain smaller audiences that can afford very high prices, such as institutions and businesses.

The exciting programming ideas, quite naturally, are more closely associated with the technologies promising an inexpensive cassette, the nonmagnetic tape and disc systems. Telefunken-Teldec, with its cheap discs, expects some market for video disc giveaways: for example, video highlights of the previous day's sports events as part of a newspaper, sound-and-motion pull-out advertisements and stories in magazines, video instructions accompanying home-assembled furniture and toys, and the like.[21] Telefunken's system also is the most developed of those that have any serious hope of matching, within the next few years, the price of long-playing records for an audio-video combination.

The Potential Market

Videocassettes undoubtedly will be the next major home entertainment medium. The only issue in doubt is the time required for a relatively small number of systems to achieve dominance, permitting standardization, mass production, and low costs. Since similar processes in long-playing phonograph records, television sets, and audiotape decks took only a few years, it seems reasonable to predict that within the same period a video playback system priced under $500 and with programming available for not more than $20 an hour will be mass marketed.

At $500, videoplayers will cost about the same—in terms of constant purchasing power—and absorb less than two-thirds the proportion of real disposable personal income as a 1950 television set priced at $300. And despite the expense, in 1950, 9 percent of the nation's homes had television and by 1954 penetration had risen above 50 percent. In 1960 color televi-

21. *Videocassette Sourcebook*, p. 11.

sion was almost nonexistent; by October of 1971 50 percent of the nation's homes had color sets.[22] Furthermore, the comparison with color TV may understate the prospects for videocassettes, since color TV is more a quality improvement of an existing medium than a basically different one. Even more telling, audiotape equipment is already outselling conventional record player equipment two to one, demonstrating how quickly it has captured the market[23] as well as the greater attractiveness of an active medium—in this case, one that permits people to record programming of their own choice—compared with a passive one.

Because the products under consideration are normally considered luxury goods—for which demand increases rapidly with income—per capita income data are also relevant. From 1950 to 1971, per capita disposable income rose from $1,646 to $2,660 and consumer spending per capita on household durable goods from $106 to $170 (all data in 1958 dollars).[24]

The economic consequences of videocassettes are likely to be far-reaching, but less so for television than for audio recordings and theaters. Videocassettes will offer a far better product than an audio recording at no more than twice the price (and perhaps at the same price), and the same product as movie theaters at a much lower price. The effect on both could be devastating. It is, in fact, conceivable that neither audio recordings nor motion picture theaters will survive the coming of mass-marketed videocassettes.

Television, on the other hand, will continue to have one enormous advantage over videocassettes: It will be free. Even the monthly cost of cable subscription will be far lower than that of viewing videocassettes extensively, unless a viewer were content to watch the same program day after day. Because of the added visual dimension of entertainment, videocassettes will probably be played somewhat more frequently than phonograph records or audio tapes, but their replay frequency still seems unlikely to be so great as significantly to erode the audience for commercial television, particularly if cable is given the opportunity to multiply free viewing options. Videocassettes may thwart the development of subscription television.

---

22. Calculations for purchasing power and real disposable income are based on data in *Economic Report of the President, January 1972*, pp. 213, 247. Television penetration data are from Television Digest, Inc., *Television Factbook, Services Volume, 1970–1971 Edition*, p. 60a; National Association of Broadcasters, *1971 Dimensions of Television* (NAB, 1971), p. 11; and Broadcasting Publications, Inc., *1972 Broadcasting Yearbook* (Washington: BP, 1972), p. 71.

23. The audiotape market is only about five years old, while long-playing records have been around for over twenty years.

24. *Economic Report of the President, January 1972*, pp. 198, 207, 213.

Viewers who are willing to pay substantial sums for diversity may find cassettes a more flexible and no more expensive alternative to STV. Cassettes can offer a greater choice of programs, and, if they become widely used, can be made convenient to obtain by marketing them through numerous retail establishments—supermarkets, pharmacies, department stores—much as is now the practice with phonograph records. Furthermore, if the popularity of cassettes is great enough to warrant widespread retailing, demand will also be sufficient to permit the industry to capture economies of mass production. Videotape rentals would then be about $1 per program, which is roughly the price that has been charged in past STV experiments. Thus, customers with special interests, whether in opera, rock concerts, or Humphrey Bogart movies, could easily turn to videocassettes. The most devoted might even build up extensive video libraries, particularly since they might wish periodically to rerun what they regarded as classics.

Videotapes for the home, for either large or specialized markets, could also be a source of programming for cable operations. Some taped programs, particularly those now syndicated, might be withheld from the home market to protect potential revenues from syndication on broadcast television. Yet many might be made available to both homes and broadcasters (over-the-air or cable), for either original showing or rerun. This dual market could attract significant new program resources. It could make new, more specialized material available to cable operators in the same way that the record industry's home market has made a wider variety of music available to radio stations. The video disc jockey, playing a series of short, inexpensive cassettes, could prove an attractive and inexpensive source of cable origination, or even of programming for the struggling UHF independent. Cable operators might use such programs to cater to minority tastes.

The most likely outcome of videotapes seems to be the fulfillment, outside the structure of the commercial television industry, of some part of the specialized viewing demands. While this outcome will have some effect on the audience for commercial television, its principal consequence will be to moderate the pressure on commercial television to serve such viewers. By offering alternatives for the small minorities, it will solve, at least partially, the dilemma an essentially mass medium faces in attempting to serve all its potential audience. The innovation will serve primarily those now ignored by commercial and even public television. Doing so, it will not alter significantly the kinds of problems or the prospects discussed in other chapters, except those of STV.

Other Technical Possibilities

While videocassettes and satellites loom nearest on the technical horizon, numerous other innovations have been widely discussed within the industry, if not subjected to extensive research and development. Skimming through a few issues from the technical trade press—*TV Communications, Television Digest with Consumer Electronics, Broadcast Management/Engineering*, and *Proceedings of the IEEE*—gives an impression of the many potential improvements in television. Two that deserve special notice are the high-resolution picture and solid-state display.

High-resolution Picture

The resolution of a television picture depends upon the amount of frequency assigned to a television station. In the United States, each station is assigned a bandwidth of 6 million cycles per second, or 6 megahertz (MHz). For example, a station on channel 2 operates in a range of frequencies from 54 to 60 MHz. Of these 6 MHz, about 4.5 are used for picture transmission.

A television receiver creates a video picture by electronically scanning the luminescent coating inside the picture tube. The quality of picture that a television set is capable of producing is heavily dependent upon the number of scan-lines. (American television employs 525.) The more scan-lines, the greater the picture detail that can be broadcast and received. The number of scan-lines severely limits the maximum size of the picture, just as photographic enlargements are limited because graininess increases with size. To have more scan-lines requires more bandwidth per channel.

The commitment to the 6 MHz, 525 scan-line system was made when the typical television set was a black-and-white, twelve-inch screen. As technological progress has made large color screens economically attractive, this technical decision has become very constraining.

If channels were assigned 12 MHz, for example, and if the same 1.5 MHz were reserved for spacing and for transmitting the sound portion of the program, about 1,200 scan-lines could be used. This would make possible a television screen about 4 feet square (a 70-inch screen) that would have the same picture quality as a present 23-inch set. Looking at his TV set in his living room, a viewer would perceive roughly the same quality and detail as he would sitting about two-thirds of the way back in a motion picture theater.

High-resolution television sets are no great trick to manufacture. European countries have always used systems with more scan-lines than ours; the French system uses 819.[25] Systems using as many as 2,000 scan-lines have been proposed for the broadcast of texts and for other applications that require detail. Military applications have led in the development in the United States, where high-resolution systems of over 1,000 scan-lines are used in weapons delivery and satellite photography. The major problems are the additional costs of the picture tube (which will be, perhaps, three or four times as expensive as the current tubes) and the regulatory problem of finding wider bandwidth assignments for the high-resolution stations.

The second problem could be resolved through cables and, to a lesser degree, through use of the UHF assignments. The part of the spectrum between channels 4 and 5 and between channels 6 and 7 that is assigned to other users could be used on cable systems by television if certain precautions were taken against interference. Thus, channel 2 could begin in the range of the spectrum below the allocation to television (allocated over the air to land-mobile motor-carrier communications), filling the spectrum from 48 to 54 MHz as well as 54 to 60.[26] Cable origination channels could then broadcast high-resolution signals, or over-the-air local stations could feed cable systems a high-resolution version of the picture being broadcast over the air.

Unlike VHF, the UHF band is a continuous stretch of the electromagnetic spectrum; but it is relatively uncrowded. In many localities adjacent UHF channels could be assigned to the same station, which could then broadcast a high-resolution picture.

The only significant technical obstacle to the development of high-resolution television relates to compatibility. Since most television receivers will, for the foreseeable future, be of the less expensive, low-resolution type, high-resolution television must be developed so as to mesh with the existing system. This requirement means either that high-resolution receivers be capable of receiving conventional broadcast signals, or that low-resolution receivers be capable of receiving some version of a high-resolution broadcast.

Compatible high-resolution receivers have been developed and demonstrated, but their cost is still very high. Because most of the cost lies in the

25. *World Radio-TV Handbook* (Soliljevej, Denmark: WRTH, 1970), p. 278.
26. A plan for putting high-resolution television on cables was worked out by Edward W. Herold, "A Compatible High-Resolution TV System for Cablecasting," *Proceedings of the IEEE*, Vol. 58 (July 1970), pp. 1013–15.

picture tube, a breakthrough in television display devices would hasten the broad availability of the high-resolution picture. In any event, the theater-quality, large-screen television system is almost certain to be technically and economically feasible within the next decade, and to increase the attractiveness of television in relation to other entertainment media, especially motion pictures. Furthermore, if spectrum is added to UHF stations, the high-resolution picture might prove to be the vehicle the FCC has long sought to make UHF broadcasting viable. To confine broadcasting of high-resolution pictures to UHF stations would give them an important technical advantage that might more than offset the disadvantages they now suffer.

Solid-state Display

The most expensive component of a television receiver is the picture tube. It is also the component that governs the size of the television receiver; as anyone who has ever pried off the back of his television set knows, a receiver is essentially an empty box for protecting the picture tube.

The cost and size of the picture tube are serious impediments to constructing large-screen systems, and hence present the most important barrier to ideas like the high-resolution picture. The principal hope for overcoming this problem is to replace the picture tube with a flat semiconductor device, just as some manufacturers have done for every other tube in the receiver. A receiver then could be hung on the wall like a painting and, indeed, even be hidden behind a Picasso.

The effect of the development of solid-state displays on the price of television sets is difficult to predict, for the complexity required in the semiconductor substitute for a picture tube is still unknown. Nevertheless, if the historical cost advantage of these devices over the components they have replaced is repeated,[27] the introduction of a semiconductor should reduce the costs of the picture component by at least 90 percent, and of the entire television receiver by 25 to 50 percent.

Conclusions

Because television has become so much a part of American life, it is easy to overlook the relative infancy of its technology. This chapter has sug-

27. See John E. Tilton, *International Diffusion of Technology: The Case of Semiconductors* (Brookings Institution, 1971), for a discussion of the growth of the semiconductor industry.

gested some of the innovations that, within a generation, might change television and its social and economic impact as profoundly as any previous development, including nationwide network interconnection and color. All of these innovations have implications for the quality and diversity of the medium, as well as the more mundane matter of cost to the viewer. Satellites, videocassettes, high-resolution pictures, and solid-state display all could offer more diversity in programming options if the institutional environment permits their full exploitation. They also supply impressive evidence that the socioeconomic importance of television will be, if anything, augmented by the development of television technology in the intermediate future.

CHAPTER TEN

Policies for Improving Television

FOUR CRITICISMS ABOUT TELEVISION were enumerated in Chapter 1. This chapter uses the results of the analysis in this book to evaluate the validity of these criticisms, the efficacy of present policies in meeting them, and the means available for improving television. The final section considers the likely response of the present regulatory organization to these means. Although the views expressed here rest heavily on the analysis of the preceding chapters, we do not present a detailed summary of our findings. In exchange for the resulting brevity, we hope that readers will bear in mind the dependence of this chapter on its predecessors.[1]

Evaluation of the Criticisms

Each of the four criticisms can be restated as an objective. Without question, it is good to have television that educates and informs (the cultural criticism); that is not controlled by a few individuals (the concentration criticism); that provides many types of entertainment programs (the wasteland criticism); and that offers multiple options (the Lawrence Welk show criticism). The question turns, rather, on the relation between costs of improvement in these four dimensions and their benefits. In none of these dimensions can either the costs or the benefits be quantified with exactness. Yet even imperfect information permits delineation of feasible alternatives and reasoned judgments about them. In this chapter we set forth both the alternatives, as we see them, and our choice among them.

1. Thus our view on the need for more options in television rests on the analysis in Chapter 2, pessimism about the future of ultra high frequency on Chapter 3, our skepticism about the regulatory process and localism on Chapter 4, and our reliance on cable with signal importation on Chapters 6 and 7. Our views on public broadcasting and new technology are based on the discussions in Chapters 8 and 9.

The Cultural Role of Television

Expanding the broad educational role of television (apart from direct instructional television) is probably the improvement whose benefits are most uncertain, while its costs are potentially very great. The fundamental difficulty is that most Americans look to television for light entertainment, not for education and information. To muster large audiences for educational programming, as the British Broadcasting Corporation (BBC) did in its early days, would require imitating its original, one-program policy, which essentially offered a choice between Shakespeare and nothing. Confidence in the ability of television to mold a culturally uplifted society could warrant subscribing to this view. But its triumph can come only at the price of utter defeat for the goal of wider options. And while many Americans might rest comfortably on the notion that "BBC knows best," others believe the viewer knows best.[2] And the viewer wants more entertainment options.

Even the more modest remedy of dividing scheduling between serious programming and standard fare would, if implemented through the networks, mean curtailing light entertainment. And the record suggests that serious programming would be a significant share of network schedules only if mandated by regulation, for it is unlikely to supplant standard fare by popular demand. Such a mandate would reduce the entertainment options of the majority and thus the revenues of the commercial system, stirring a conflict with the objective of wider options and the principle of viewer sovereignty.

The most restricted version of the call for more serious programming relies on the old-fashioned type of "educational" public broadcasting. Here, the issue remains who should pay for such stations—particularly on a scale of program quality and availability comparable with the commercial system. These programs attract only small audiences if required to compete with light entertainment programs. Hence, to support them with public moneys is to tax the majority for the sake of a tiny minority. Yet to implement a payment mechanism, such as those offered in Chapter 8, that relies on viewer support creates incentives to satisfy majority preferences.

2. The BBC philosophy toward programming was developed by its first general manager, J. C. W. Reith, who expressed his own views in 1924 in his book, *Broadcast Over Britain*. According to Reith, "It is occasionally [pointed out] to us that we are apparently setting out to give the public what we think they need—and not what they want, but few know what they want, and very few what they need." Quoted in R. H. Coase, *British Broadcasting: A Study in Monopoly* (Harvard University Press for the London School of Economics and Political Science, 1950), p. 47.

Concentration of Control

Concentration of control is clearly a critical issue. The contention that concentration is minimal because there are so many stations misstates the situation. In fact, only a few stations operate in any one area and, more importantly, significant program decisions are concentrated in three separate sources, for affiliates are largely conduits for their networks. Three firms can be vigorous rivals, but even so, a triopoly is too narrow to foster many centers of innovation or a wide range of views among the controlling group. If it produced a prosaic product, television would stand out as a highly concentrated industry. Yet, paradoxically, a country uniquely dedicated to promoting competition seems to accept concentration in its most important mass medium.

Concentration intensifies concern about fairness in news and public affairs broadcasting. Even if network leadership is always public-spirited and wise, the traditional American rhetoric emphasizes decentralization and broader competition. Given the economic advantages of networks, concentration can be diluted only by the introduction of effective competitors —strong very high frequency (VHF) independents, other networks, or independents with access to regional audiences. Of course, the aim, instead, could be rules that restrain the use of power, such as historically the Federal Communications Commission (FCC) has attempted to devise; but the persistence of the debate over concentration makes manifest the failure of this approach.

Diversity in Programming

Perhaps the most frequently heard of the four criticisms centers on television's failure to allow for diversity in its programming. The lament is that one detective series follows another, or that, in some time periods, movies appear on every network. This wasteland criticism raises the same issue as the cultural criticism—the relative weighting of majority and minority preferences. One detective series follows another because that is the diet the majority prefer. Given the present number of channels, increasing diversity necessarily means depriving the majority. This difficult choice could be mooted by an increase in the number of channels, which would enable minority tastes to be met with less loss of conventional fare.

The Scarcity of Conventional Options

Insuring the satisfaction of minority tastes through the market decisions of commercial television calls for a very large expansion indeed, simply because new facilities would respond first to the much larger audience that demands more options among the standard fare. This unfulfilled demand constitutes the least well recognized of the four criticisms, and yet its intensity, as measured by price and number of viewers, makes it the one of greatest economic significance. Having low regard for conventional fare, television reformers would find little solace in a proliferation of the programming that sparks their criticisms. But all subscription television (STV) experiments and the past experience of cable systems indicate that the greatest unsatisfied demand is, in fact, for more of the same.

The last three criticisms can be ameliorated in the same way—expansion of the television industry. Better television requires more television. More television can permit more competition, more diversity, and, most obviously, more options.

Present Policies

While government policy has responded to each of the four criticisms, its efforts have been constrained by the desire to preserve the structure of the industry. Since each of the criticisms touches the fundamental nature of the medium, tinkering at the margins has not satisfied, and in all likelihood will not satisfy, television's critics.

Public policy has looked to the development of ultra high frequency broadcasting (UHF) to expand television and thus broaden options and diversity and reduce concentration. To this end the FCC has been willing to impose the prime-time access rule and to insist that the two imported signals on large-city cable systems be from nearby cities. But it has been unwilling to undertake disruptive policies—such as deintermixture[3] or banning VHF networks—that might give UHF some chance for success. And even if such policies were adopted, economic realities suggest that most of

3. Deintermixture would make the stations in each market either all VHF or all UHF so that no station has a signal disadvantage in comparison with its competition. The proposal is discussed in Chapter 4.

the nation would still be served by a relatively small number of stations—certainly fewer than are now enjoyed by residents of Los Angeles and New York. Without fundamental change in broadcast policy, UHF television is not likely to expand to anywhere near the extent envisioned in the FCC's station allocation plan.

Public policy has favored a national public broadcasting system. This system supplies another viewing option; but, under the political pressures to which it is bound to be subject, it is apt, especially in its news and public affairs programming, to become essentially another conventional network. Centralized financing through the Corporation for Public Broadcasting, rather than more diffuse direct support of stations, will strengthen the conventional orientation of public broadcasting. Viewers who value standard fare will not find this outcome inherently bad. But, in this form, public television is unlikely to alleviate the criticism of the social and political role of the medium.

Finally, the Congress and the FCC together have promulgated numerous rules intended to diffuse control of programming and to improve news and public affairs broadcasting. The equal-time rule, the fairness doctrine, and the various restrictions on ownership of television stations are all attempts to guarantee "balanced" presentation of politically controversial issues and greater consciousness among broadcasters of their own importance to the political system. Even the doctrine of localism is this kind of policy, for it envisages local broadcasting as a vigilant watchdog over the local political system. That this collection of policies has had little impact is obvious from the paucity of serious television journalism, particularly on local issues, and from the rising chorus of complaints that television does not give voice to a sufficient variety of political views.

The failure of existing policy stems from failure to recognize the relationship between the economics of television and the performance of the industry. The essence of the problem is the lack of viewing options of every type. Yet UHF, whose promotion is the only policy oriented toward augmenting the number of options, is burdened by technical inferiority and by the economic albatross of local service.

The final irony is that present public policy has successfully forestalled several new developments that might ameliorate all four problems because they threaten both the existing system and the policies currently being pursued. Cables, STV, and satellites have been hampered by restrictive rules and costly regulatory procedures, yet they represent the best hopes for improving the medium.

Future Policy

We see little hope that a television industry that solves the problems embodied in the four criticisms can evolve out of evolutionary change. Bolder policies are required. Each threatens the present structure of the television industry, though most do little more than reduce the high profits of broadcasters.

Cable

In the next few years, cable offers the best hope for greater diversity, more options, and less control over program content by the networks. At the same time that it brings to the rest of the nation television of the quality and quantity available in Los Angeles or New York, cable can, relatively inexpensively, serve some minority tastes through common-carrier channels.

The key to the development of a nationwide cable system in the near future is distant signal importation. To attract enough subscribers to support themselves, cable systems must offer significantly more conventional viewing options. In a few areas, improving the signal on local stations, particularly UHF stations, may be enough to assure viability. In a few large cities, cable originations—especially of local sports events—could be enough. But if cable is ever to be a nationwide force for expanding television, distant signal importation is a necessity.

According to our analysis, the recent FCC decision on distant signals will permit cable development in only a few large cities, and will also severely limit its potential benefits where it does develop. First, cable penetration will be substantially lower than it would be if more importation were permitted. Second, cable subscription fees will only barely cover costs, eroding the possibility of financing additional capacity, public access channels, and channels for local government. The new rules will foster some increase in options, but not for most of the nation, nor in great enough degree so that diversity, which has the next claim on expanded capacity, will also grow.

The rules will also prevent the development through cable of the regional stations that were vetoed by the FCC twenty years ago. To prohibit these stations is to sacrifice the principal hope for building more effective competition to the three networks.

Unfortunately for the viewer—whether his criticism turns on options, diversity, or political representation—the beneficial consequences of the new rules fail to realize cable's true potential. Allowed unlimited signal importation, adjacent cable systems in the top 100 markets would probably band together to import no more than a half-dozen distant signals, as has recently been done in the Plains states. This development would mean that several independents would obtain regional or national audiences. It would mean that cable penetration would be deep enough to make viable such innovations as access channels and some cable origination. But it would also mean abandoning the hope that the unclaimed UHF assignments in smaller cities will eventually go on the air—a hope that is, according to our analysis, probably forlorn.

STV

In the next ten years, a nationwide STV system offers a good prospect for solving at least some of the diversity problems. Past pay-TV experiments reveal that some programs geared to minority tastes are so prized by their adherents that they could be profitable ventures on STV, even though they are not on free commercial television.

To achieve viability, STV must have access to a large potential audience. Lower collection costs would also enhance its prospects. Over-the-air STV does not appear feasible on a national basis because of the difficulty of obtaining enough station assignments and because of the costs of sending, receiving, and monitoring scrambled over-the-air signals. Only in the very largest cities would STV be likely to succeed, and even then the prices would be so high that only a few percent of all potential viewers would participate.

With relatively high channel capacity and less expensive monitoring alternatives, cable offers the best mechanism for developing STV. A national cable system should be able to generate an STV audience large enough to support expensive programming at reasonable prices to viewers.

STV has been mistakenly identified by broadcasters, the Congress, the FCC, and much of the public as a serious threat to free television. The fear rests on a sound premise: If commercial television were to shift to STV, the result would be very little change in programming but a substantial reduction in viewer welfare. Because technical factors limit expansion, an over-the-air, all-STV system also would offer roughly the array of options now available, so that the principal result would be more revenue for broadcasters and program producers. Cable STV, which is free of technical limits would, through increased options, derive only normal profits, but would be inefficient in that the cost of serving one more viewer, which is zero, would always be less than the STV price. Since STV also would be somewhat more sensitive to the intensity of viewer tastes, it is impossible to state which system—all-free TV or all-cable STV—is preferable. Yet this question is academic, for an all-STV system is not politically feasible. In any case, mass audience programs will remain on free TV, for their best opportunities for profit—with a few exceptions, notably sports—probably lie there.

In any event, the mixed system is probably more beneficial to viewers than one that is wholly free or wholly pay. The mass audience can continue to enjoy its preferred programming at no cost. With cable development, they can also get substantially more conventional fare at a low price. Finally, those with intensely felt, but minority, tastes can buy what they want. Though minority tastes that are mildly felt will remain unsatisfied and some resources will be "wasted" in collecting STV fees, both inefficiencies will be minimized to the greatest feasible extent through a mixed system on cable.

New Technologies

Direct satellite-to-home broadcasting and videocassettes can contribute further to all of the television goals. The first will greatly expand the technical and economic limits on networking, and could eliminate the problem of concentration of control over the mass media by making a multiplicity of networks economically feasible. Videocassettes could provide infinite diversity at a very low cost. Both represent fundamental challenges to the television industry because they would make virtually unlimited choice of programs available to everyone. It is conceivable, although not necessarily likely, that television could become a medium like magazines, in which mass audience ventures were less successful and less important than specialized ventures. Or, more likely, it could evolve into a medium like books or records, in which mass audience and specialized ventures were both significant. At a minimum, it would offer enough options to constitute an essentially competitive industry.

Can Change Occur?

As advocates of viewer sovereignty, we believe that public policy should permit the development of all the major new television innovations—cable, STV, satellites, videocassettes. Of course, had viewer sovereignty been paramount in the eyes of policy makers, the case for these innovations would not be so strong. Regional stations would have been permitted, and the majority of stations would not have been handicapped with the technically inferior UHF allocations. Today everyone would have many more viewing options, and the present criticisms about television might be muted.

Past trends in policy afford little comfort to the proponents of expansion in television. After fifteen years of pleadings before the commission, cable and STV are still hindered. And after ten years of technical and economic feasibility, a domestic communications satellite is not yet in place. While restrictions on new developments are slowly being relaxed, we see no reason to believe that public policy will ever carry the process far enough to allow the expansion in television that is economically warranted. A new legislative mandate for broadcast regulation is necessary if the goals of greater diversity, more options, and decentralized control of programming are to be achieved.

One element of the new mandate would divest the FCC of its concern for program quality and content, putting broadcasters on the same legal footing as printed media. The FCC's record of broadcast licensing reveals that it has not succeeded in promoting the programming it desires, while, in the effort, it has imposed significant costs on viewers by restricting options. If the Congress believes that a limited common-carrier status should be imposed on broadcasters (with respect to political access, for example), the details of that status should be spelled out by legislation; however, we believe such limitations will prove unnecessary in an expanded television system.

Second, the primacy of competition as the means for achieving better television performance should also be formally established, relegating localism to a much lower priority. Viewer tastes should be relied on to determine the number of options and the mix of local, regional, and national stations. Specifically, the mandate for competition should favor full development of signal-importing cable, cable STV, and broadcast satellites.

In the arena of licensing, the FCC, in our view, should be concerned primarily with the engineering or technical aspects of spectrum management. In a restructured, substantially expanded television system, restrictions on station ownership should be reconsidered. Certainly, if viewers have access to numerous viewing options, the need for restrictions on station ownership is less. And, with more stations, cost savings through pooled ownership might become more significant as station profits were reduced through competition. More experience with the new environment might show a need for controls on station ownership; however, we suspect the issue will become relatively unimportant.

A substantial reduction in regulation of television will be of significant benefit to viewers. With the possible exception of cable delivery of signals,[4] television is by no stretch of the imagination a natural monopoly to be regulated as a public utility. Viewers' demand for programs and advertisers' demand for viewers are adequate to justify a substantial expansion and diversification in television options. In the past, public policy prevented this growth by imposing technical restraints through spectrum allocation policies. Now new technologies have removed the spectrum constraints, and policy has responded by direct prohibitions of certain types of services that consumers are willing to pay for and that business is willing to provide. All this in the name of two myths: that free television is a delicate industry that can easily be destroyed, at tremendous cost to viewers, and that the public reaps enormous benefits from local service. But localism in broadcasting has produced little local programming while exacting a cost in restricted viewing options. The high public stake in free television is precisely the reason why the survival of the industry is unlikely to be endangered by changes in policy and technology. What would be threatened by a significant increase in competition within the television industry is that part of the wealth of station owners attributable to the broadcast license—a license whose value is due in large measure to government policies. We are not persuaded by the argument that undesirable government policies cannot be changed because to do so sacrifices some of the wealth of those who have benefited from those policies. While we understand the broadcasters' opposition to changes in policy that would reduce their wealth, we also believe that the public interest in broadcast policy should not be sacrificed on their behalf.

4. Even this is debatable. See Richard A. Posner, *Cable Television: The Problem of Local Monopoly*, RM-6309-FF (Santa Monica: RAND Corporation, May 1970), especially pp. 3–4.

The Value of Viewing Options, the Demand for Cable Subscription, and the Impact of Cable on Broadcast Audiences

CABLE OR COMMUNITY ANTENNA television systems (CATVs) constitute the only means through which individuals can express the intensity of their demand for viewing options by their willingness to pay for the opportunity to expand the number or increase the quality of television signals they can receive. Consequently, the experience of cable systems provides a reasonable basis from which to infer the value of viewing options. The first part of this appendix describes one way of making such inferences from data on cable systems, and presents estimates of the value of viewing options derived by analyzing a selected sample of systems. The second part discusses the difficulties inherent in obtaining reliable estimates of the determinants of demand for cable television, particularly in markets with a wide selection of strong over-the-air signals.

The Value of Viewing Options

Cable systems offer viewers improved clarity of television reception plus the ability to receive signals from stations too distant for direct reception. The prices charged for these improvements vary from system to system with the options offered, the incomes of the subscribers, and the choices of over-the-air programming. These variations in turn lead to intersystem differences in shares of potential subscribers so that data are generated that permit inferences about consumer valuation of the quantity and quality of television programming.

A Model of CATV Subscriber Behavior

The quality of service offered by a community antenna television system may be defined as a function of the number of viewing alternatives and its signal clarity. The quality of over-the-air, that is, free, television is a function of the same two variables. The amount an individual is willing to pay for a CATV subscription depends upon his income, his utility function, and the comparative quality of service offered by the two kinds of systems.

The relationship among these three parameters is shown in Figure A-1, which portrays a typical viewer's indifference map between income—as a proxy for other goods—and television viewing quality. A viewer with income Y will be on the indifference curve I_2 when the quality of over-the-air viewing is Q_f. The maximum this viewer would be willing to pay to subscribe to a CATV service offering viewing quality Q_c is given by the distance on the income axis denoted as S^m. This is the maximum because at any

Figure A-1. Relationship between Amounts a Television Viewer Is Willing to Pay for CATV and Income, Utility Function, and Quality of Service Offered[a]

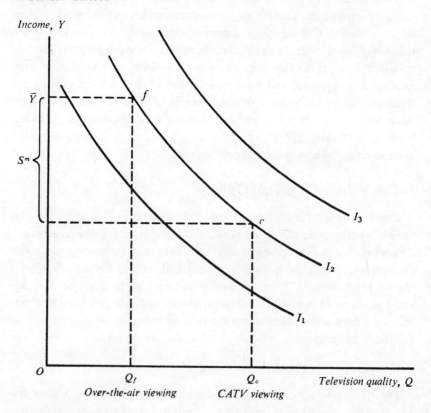

a. See discussion in text.

higher subscription fee the viewer could not attain the indifference curve I_2, and would therefore be worse off than if he had not subscribed.

The demand curve for subscriptions facing the management of a CATV system is simply a ranking, from highest to lowest, of all potential subscribers by their maximum subscription fee. Since the last, or marginal, subscriber pays his maximum fee, the total number of subscribers to a system depends upon the actual fee charged, the number of potential subscribers, and their distribution with respect to their maximum subscription fees.

To proceed beyond these general statements requires specific assumptions about the forms of the relationships. The first assumption is that the typical viewer's utility function is a multiplicative function of television viewing quality, Q, and all other goods and services. If the cost of television quality is denoted by S, all other goods can be represented as $(Y - S)$, for a viewer with income Y. Thus, for the ith viewer in a given market

$$U_i = \alpha_{i0}(Y_i - S_i)^{\alpha_{i1}}Q^{\alpha_{i2}}. \qquad \text{(A-1)}$$

In particular, if Q_f is the quality of over-the-air viewing and Q_c the quality of service offered by a CATV system, the viewer's utility, if he does not subscribe, will be

$$U_i^f = \alpha_{i0} Y_i^{\alpha_{i1}}Q_f^{\alpha_{i2}}. \qquad \text{(A-1a)}$$

If he does subscribe, his utility will be

$$U_i^c = \alpha_{i0}(Y_i - S_i)^{\alpha_{i1}}Q_c^{\alpha_{i2}}. \qquad \text{(A-1b)}$$

And the maximum subscription fee for this viewer, S_i^m, is the fee that equates U_i^f and U_i^c. Thus, combining (A-1a) and (A-1b) and rearranging gives

$$S_i^m = Y_i\left[1 - \left(\frac{Q_c}{Q_f}\right)^{-\gamma_i}\right], \qquad \text{(A-2)}$$

where

$$\gamma_i = \frac{\alpha_{i2}}{\alpha_{i1}}.$$

If all potential subscribers to a given CATV system have the same income $\bar{Y}$ and the fee charged by the system is $\bar{S}$, (A-2) can be written as

$$\bar{S} = \bar{Y}\left[1 - \left(\frac{Q_c}{Q_f}\right)^{-\bar{\gamma}}\right],$$

where $\bar{\gamma}$ is the value of γ for the marginal subscriber. Rearranging and taking logarithms gives

$$-\bar{\gamma} = \frac{\ln [1 - S/\bar{Y}]}{\ln \left(\dfrac{Q_c}{Q_f}\right)}.$$ (A-3)

Equation (A-2) shows that, under the assumption made so far, the distribution of potential subscribers to a given CATV system with respect to their maximum fee depends only upon the distribution of potential subscribers with respect to the parameter γ. Assume that the distribution of potential subscribers to any CATV system with respect to γ is an exponential distribution with density function $f(\gamma)$, given by

$$f(\gamma) = \mu e^{-\mu\gamma} d\gamma.$$ (A-4)

Equation (A-3) shows that the value of γ for the marginal subscriber, $\bar{\gamma}$, is determined by the income of the representative subscriber, the fee charged, and the quality of service offered relative to that available over the air. Given these parameters, for any actual subscriber, $\gamma \geq \bar{\gamma}$ as defined by equation (A-3). Nonsubscribers will be those viewers for whom $\gamma < \bar{\gamma}$. With N_s the number of actual subscribers and N_p the number of potential subscribers, the number of nonsubscribers is $N_p - N_s$, which is given by

$$N_p - N_s = N_p \int_0^{\bar{\gamma}} \mu e^{-\mu\gamma} d\gamma.$$ (A-5)

Evaluating the integral and rearranging gives

$$\frac{N_s}{N_p} = e^{-\mu\bar{\gamma}}.$$ (A-6)

Taking logarithms gives

$$-\bar{\gamma} = \frac{1}{\mu} \ln \left(\frac{N_s}{N_p}\right).$$ (A-7)

Finally, combining equations (A-7) and (A-3) gives

$$\frac{\ln (1 - S/\bar{Y})}{\ln \left(\dfrac{N_s}{N_p}\right)} = \frac{1}{\mu} \ln \left(\frac{Q_c}{Q_f}\right).$$ (A-8)

While all of the variables on the left-hand side of (A-8) are observable, those on the right are not. Consequently, the final step is to specify a stochastic relationship between quality and some observable magnitudes.

An important determinant of viewing quality is the number of stations, or viewing alternatives, available. The total number of stations may, however, be an inadequate basis for determining quality since viewers are unlikely to consider that all stations offer equally desirable viewing alternatives. The typical viewer probably makes different assessments of stations affiliated with the major television networks, independent stations, and educational television stations (ETV). Furthermore, the total number of network-affiliated stations available is a poor basis even for determining the contribution of the class to viewing quality. Since their primary differentiating feature is their provision of programming originated by the networks and since a substantial amount of their programming may be identical, the ability to receive more than one station affiliated with the same network may add little to overall viewing quality.

Consequently, it is desirable to distinguish between the number of *network* alternatives available and the number of network-affiliated stations available in determining the quality of viewing.

Taking account of these considerations, a reasonable specification of the relationship between the quality of service offered by a CATV system and the numbers and types of stations it delivers might be

$$Q_c = \beta_0^c (1 + N_A^c)^{\beta_1}(1 + N_I^c)^{\beta_2}(1 + N_E^c)^{\beta_3}(1 + N_D^c)^{\beta_4}u_c,$$

where N_A^c = the number of primary network alternatives offered

N_I^c = the number of independent stations offered

N_E^c = the number of educational television stations offered

N_D^c = the number of duplicate network-affiliated stations offered

u_c = a random disturbance.

Similarly, the quality of over-the-air viewing can be specified as

$$Q_f = \beta_0^f (1 + N_A^f)^{\beta_1}(1 + N_I^f)^{\beta_2}(1 + N_E^f)^{\beta_3}(1 + N_D^f)^{\beta_4}u_f.$$

Combining these relationships with equation (A-8) gives

$$Z = \lambda_0 + \lambda_1 \ln X_A + \lambda_2 \ln X_I + \lambda_3 \ln X_E + \lambda_4 \ln X_D + w, \quad \text{(A-9)}$$

where

$$Z = \frac{\ln (1 - S/Y)}{\ln \left(\dfrac{N_s}{N_p}\right)}; \qquad \lambda_0 = \frac{1}{\mu} \ln \left(\frac{\beta_0^c}{\beta_0^f}\right);$$

$$\lambda_i = \frac{\beta_i}{\mu}, \text{ for } i = 1, 2, 3, 4; \qquad X_i = \frac{(1 + N_i^c)}{(1 + N_i^f)}, \text{ for } i = A, I, E, D;$$

$$w = \ln(u_c/u_f).$$

Thus, assuming that the parameters β_i are the same for all systems, the

λ_i in equation (A-9) can be estimated from a regression of Z on the X_i for a sample of CATV systems.[1]

While it might be desirable to have estimates of the β_i because they are measures of the weights assigned by the typical viewer to the various types of station alternatives in arriving at a measure of the overall quality of viewing availability, they are impossible to obtain since there is no way of determining the value of μ. Nevertheless, estimates of the λ_i are sufficient for estimating the value of viewing options.

When television is provided free to an individual, the maximum price he would pay for the quality of viewing available rather than go without is a measure of his welfare gain from free television of that quality. Thus, for a very small group of viewers, dN_s in number, all with maximum fee S_n^m, total welfare derived from free television is given by

$$dW = S_n^m \cdot dN_s.$$

This can be written as a function of γ by substitution from equation (A-1) as

$$dW = \Upsilon\left[1 - \left(\frac{Q_c}{Q_f}\right)^{-\gamma_n}\right]dN_s;$$

furthermore, from equation (A-4),

$$dN_s = -(\mu e^{-\mu\gamma}d\gamma)N_p.$$

Therefore,

$$dW = -N_p\Upsilon\left[1 - \left(\frac{Q_c}{Q_f}\right)^{-\gamma}\right]\mu e^{-\mu\gamma}d\gamma. \tag{A-10}$$

From equation (A-7)

$$-\gamma = \frac{1}{\mu}\ln\pi, \tag{A-11}$$

where

$$\pi = \frac{N_s}{N_p}, \text{ or system penetration;}$$

consequently

$$d\gamma = \frac{-d\pi}{\mu\pi}. \tag{A-12}$$

---

1. Estimation by ordinary least squares requires the further assumption that the random error terms w have mean zero and constant variance σ_w^2 for all systems.

Substituting these into (A-10) and rearranging gives

$$dW = N_p \bar{Y}\left[1 - \left(\frac{Q_c}{Q_f}\right)^{\frac{1}{\mu} \ln \tau}\right]d\pi.$$ (A-13)

Now consider a situation in which the number and types of free channels available are given compared to a situation where none are available. Obviously this is equivalent to a comparison between a CATV system that offers the same alternatives at a zero price while nothing else is available. Thus, the relevant measure of (Q_c/Q_f) is

$$T(x) = \frac{\beta_0^c}{\beta_0^f} (1 + N_A)^{\lambda_1}(1 + N_I)^{\lambda_2}(1 + N_E)^{\lambda_3}(1 + N_D)^{\lambda_4},$$

except that (β_0^c/β_0^f) should be set equal to unity rather than to e^{λ_0}, because in the situation assumed viewers do not receive the advantages of improvement in signal clarity offered by CATV. Once estimates of the λ_i are obtained, the value of $T(x)$ can be estimated for various levels of over-the-air reception capability. Finally, for over-the-air television, it can be assumed that all potential viewers will accept the service, so that the upper limit of π is unity when the subscription fee is zero.

Thus, from equation (A-13) total welfare generated by providing some level of free television whose quality is designated by $T(x)$ is given by

$$W(x) = N_p \bar{Y}\int_0^1 [1 - T(x)^{\ln \tau}]d\pi.$$ (A-14)

Evaluation of this integral gives

$$W(x) = N_p \bar{Y}\left[\frac{\ln T(x)}{1 + \ln T(x)}\right].$$ (A-15)

Equation (A-15) permits the computation of the share of income that viewers would give up in order to obtain a given level of free television programming, and hence provides a measure of the value of viewing options.

Estimation of Consumer Valuations of Viewing Alternatives

A sample of thirty-one CATV systems having at least 10,000 subscribers in 1969 was used to estimate a variation of equation (A-9). The specific equation estimated was

$$Z = \lambda_0 + \lambda_1 D_1 + \lambda_2 D_2 + \lambda_3 D_3 + \lambda_4 \ln X_A + \lambda_5 \ln X_I + \lambda_6 \ln X_D + w,$$
(A-9a)

where

$$Z = \frac{\ln [1 - \bar{S}/\bar{Y}]}{\ln \left(\dfrac{N_s}{N_p}\right)} ; \qquad X_i = \left(\frac{1 + N_i^c}{1 + N_i^f}\right) \text{ for } i = A, I, D,$$

and D_1, D_2, and D_3 are dummy variables. Many CATV systems offer one channel devoted to continuous broadcast of time, news, and weather reports in addition to regular broadcast stations. For systems in the sample offering this service the value of D_1 was unity; otherwise it was zero. A few systems also originate some regular programming of their own. The value of D_2 was unity for systems in the sample that offered this service; for systems that did not the value of D_2 was zero. To compute $\bar{Y}$ for each observation, per capita annual income for 1966 for the relevant city was multiplied by 3.28, the national average number of persons per household in 1967.[2] Thus, $\bar{Y}$ is an estimate of household income in 1966–67 for potential subscribers to each system. CATV systems typically impose both a monthly subscription fee and an installation fee. Thus, to obtain a measure of $\bar{S}$ these charges were converted to an annual fee. To do so the monthly fee was multiplied by twelve and added to one-fifth of the installation fee. The rationale for this procedure is that roughly 20 percent of the population changes residence each year. The number of subscribers in 1969, N_s, was taken from data in the *Television Fact Book*. The same source provides the number of homes "in front of the cable" already laid by the system, which was taken as a measure of N_p in 1969.[3]

The number of stations of various types carried by each CATV system is also available from the *Television Fact Book*. The numbers and types of stations available over the air should ideally be determined by surveying viewers in each locality. However, for this part of the study the stations receivable without CATV service for each locality were taken as the stations within whose grade A contours the locality was situated.[4]

The variable D_3 took on the value of unity only if the CATV system of-

2. U.S. Bureau of the Census, *Statistical Abstract of the United States*, editions for 1969 and 1971, pp. 863–915 and 36, respectively.

3. Television Digest, Inc., *Television Fact Book, Services Volume, 1969–1970 Edition* (Washington: TD, 1969), pp. 79a and 363a–591a, respectively.

4. A station's grade A contour is defined as the curve enclosing all locations estimated to be able to receive an acceptable signal at least 90 percent of the time for at least 70 percent of the locations within the contour. An attempt was made to obtain more accurate information on the quality of over-the-air viewing alternatives by a mail survey of the operators of the systems used. The response rate was, however, far too low to provide a usable sample.

fered at least one more educational television station than was available over the air. Differential educational television service was accounted for in this way because few systems in the sample offered more than one additional educational station and because there tends to be little difference in programming among such stations.

One other problem requires discussion. The model developed here involves the determinants of subscriber equilibrium. For that reason it should be estimated from a sample of systems in equilibrium, that is, those in which subscribership can reasonably be expected to remain unchanged so long as the values of the variables in the model are the same. Yet some of the younger systems in the sample may not yet have reached equilibrium, a process whose duration is unknown.

On the other hand, CATV systems appeared first in localities with the poorest quality of over-the-air reception. The procedure of basing the quality of over-the-air reception on the stations within whose grade A contour a system is located is only an approximation and the difference between this approximation and actually prevailing situations is probably directly related to the age of a system.

The failure of the regression equation to take account of these phenomena not only reduces its explanatory power but also creates a possibility that the residual variance will be related to system age. If the first phenomenon predominates, one might expect the residual variance to be inversely related to system age; while if the second phenomenon is predominant, the residual variance would probably be directly related to system age. The initial regression results tended to confirm the predominance of the second phenomenon and to allow for it the observations were deflated by the square root of the age of the system. Results of the undeflated and deflated regressions after reflation are presented in Table A-1.

The results for the deflated regression are generally encouraging except for the negative sign on the educational television dummy, D_3. The coefficients on X_A, X_I, and X_D not only are positive and significant, but their relative magnitudes are initially appealing. The coefficient on X_A is by far the largest, which accords with the popularity of network programming and its quality relative to the reruns of network programs, original syndications, and old movies typically offered by independent stations. Likewise, the appeal of duplicate network alternatives lies in their nonnetwork programming which tends closely to parallel that of independent stations outside of prime time. Thus it is not surprising that the coefficient on X_D is smaller yet insignificantly different from that on X_I.

Table A-1. Coefficients of Consumer Valuations of Television Viewing Alternatives[a]

Type of equation	Dependent variable[b]	Constant	Dummy variables[c]			Comparative service[d]			Coefficient of determination R^2
			D_1	D_2	D_3	Primary network X_A	Independent X_I	Duplicate network X_D	
Undeflated	Z	0.0092	-0.0142 (0.0099)	0.0161 (0.0107)	-0.0271* (0.0096)	0.0571* (0.0111)	0.0099 (0.0073)	0.0067 (0.0065)	0.563*
Deflated[c]	Z	0.0031	-0.0053 (0.0071)	0.0077 (0.0077)	-0.0216* (0.0078)	0.0385* (0.0093)	0.0098* (0.0053)	0.0086* (0.0046)	0.520*

Source: Derived from equation (A-9a), based on a 1969 sample of thirty-one cable television systems having 10,000 or more subscribers.
* Significance at the 5 percent level or better on a one-tailed test.
a. The figures in parentheses are standard errors.
b. $Z = \dfrac{\ln[1 - \bar{S}/\bar{Y}]}{\ln\left(\dfrac{N_t}{N_p}\right)}$, where $\bar{S}$ = annual television fee, $\bar{Y}$ = per capita household income of potential subscribers, N_t and N_p = number of actual and potential subscribers, respectively.
c. See text for description of the dummies and the deflator.
d. $X_i = \dfrac{(1 + N_t^i)}{(1 + N_p^i)}$, for i = primary network alternatives A, independent stations I, and duplicate network affiliated stations D, where N = number, c = cable television, and f = free television.

While the coefficients on both D_1 and D_2 would be expected to be positive, the negative coefficient on D_1 is not particularly disturbing since it does not approach significance. The insignificance of the coefficient on D_2 is also not surprising in view of the limited amount of local origination that CATV systems in the sample offered.

The negative and highly significant coefficient on D_3 is, however, rather disturbing. An ETV coefficient insignificantly different from zero would not have been surprising in view of the small audiences that free ETV typically attracts. But these results imply that a CATV system that offered the same advantages relative to over-the-air reception plus additional ETV service would command a lower fee. Since viewers are not forced to watch ETV there is no reason why, other things equal, they should in essence demand a discount for systems providing it.

The finding that viewers apparently do demand such a discount might be nothing more than a statistical mirage if, within our sample, systems that offered additional ETV service tended to provide fewer additional commercial television stations than those offering only the basic ETV service. However, the ETV dummy D_3 is positively correlated with the other quality variables and is also positively correlated with the total number of stations offered. Thus it is not true that systems that provide ETV serivce do so at the expense of commercial television service.

Another possible explanation of the negative ETV coefficient arises from the probable errors introduced by using grade A contours to determine reception quality without CATV service. Systems in the sample can be divided into two categories according to whether they are situated within standard metropolitan statistical areas (SMSAs). Since most stations are in SMSAs, viewers in those areas undoubtedly have better over-the-air reception than viewers outside them even though the latter may be within the grade A contours of the same stations. This suggests, other things equal, that viewers outside SMSAs would be willing to pay more for CATV service. At the same time, studies of ETV audiences show that they are composed largely of viewers with education and income above the average. This raises the possibility that viewers in SMSAs might value ETV service more highly than other viewers. A tendency for the ETV dummy to be positive primarily for systems outside SMSAs might explain the negative coefficient on the ETV dummy.

To test these hypotheses regressions were run allowing for a different intercept for non-SMSA systems and allowing the coefficient on D_3 to differ between SMSA and non-SMSA systems. The results of the first of these alternatives indicated no significant difference in the intercepts, while the coefficient on D_3 remained negative and significant. Allowing the coefficient on D_3 to differ between SMSA and non-SMSA systems also failed to improve the results. In that formulation the coefficient for SMSA systems was significantly negative while that for non-SMSA systems was negative but insignificant.

Thus, the negative coefficient on D_3 remains a mystery. It is probably due to the omission of some variable that would more accurately reflect the quality of over-the-air viewing, but what the true variable is is not apparent.

In view of these problems some skepticism as to the reliability of the estimates of the other coefficients is warranted. However, if these problems are overlooked, estimates of the welfare viewers derive from free television can be made. Such estimates are presented in Table A-2 for various levels of free television service. In all cases the welfare measure, or consumer surplus, is the percentage of total income viewers would give up to obtain the stated level of service rather than have no service at all.

The results can be summarized as follows:

(1) Network programming is highly valued compared to the programming of independents.

(2) Welfare increases, although at a rapidly diminishing rate, with the addition of either networks or independents.

Table A-2. Estimated Consumer Surplus from Selected Levels of Free Television Service, by Type of Station[a]

Percent of total income

Number of stations	Affiliated stations		Independent stations	
	Total surplus	Marginal surplus	Total surplus	Marginal surplus
1	2.60	2.60	0.67	0.67
2	4.06	1.46	1.07	0.40
3	5.07	1.01	1.34	0.27
4	5.83	0.76	1.55	0.21
5	6.45	0.62	1.73	0.18

Source: Derived from equation (A-14). Note that the surplus for combinations of affiliates and independents cannot be obtained simply by adding the relevant surpluses from this table. For example, the surplus for a situation involving three networks and one independent station is given by,

$$W = \frac{1.3863 \times 0.0385 + 0.6931 \times 0.0098}{1 + 1.3863 \times 0.0385 + 0.6931 \times 0.0098} = 0.0568,$$

or 5.68 percent.

a. Consumer surplus is the percentage of total income that television viewers would give up to have the stated level of service rather than no service.

Demand for Cable in the Top 100 Markets

Evaluation of regulatory policies toward cable television systems depends on an assessment of prospects for the growth of such systems in the 100 largest markets. For this reason a number of attempts have been made to estimate the determinants of demand for cable television and the shares of homes in the 100 largest markets that, given the opportunity to do so, would be likely to subscribe to cable systems. This section points out the difficulties encountered in predicting this demand and offers some explanation for differences in predicted penetration of cable systems.

Chapter 6 presented predictions of ultimate penetration for systems that offered three networks plus four independents in addition to VHF (very high frequency) independents receivable over the air. These estimates were derived from the model presented earlier in this appendix, as follows:

For given levels of cable and over-the-air service, equation (A-9) can be rewritten as

$$\frac{\ln(1 - S/Y)}{\ln\left(\dfrac{N_s}{N_p}\right)} = \theta, \qquad (A\text{-}16)$$

where the value of θ can be computed for any level of cable service relative to over-the-air service by using the estimated coefficients presented in Table A-1. Rearranging (A-16) and exponentiating gives

$$\frac{N_s}{N_p} = (1 - S/Y)^{\frac{1}{\theta}}.$$

In the sample employed to estimate equation (A-9), the mean value of $(1 - S/Y)$ was 0.993. Thus ultimate penetration was estimated by calculating relevant values of θ and then computing

$$\frac{N_s}{N_p} = 0.993^{\frac{1}{\theta}}.$$

Alternative estimates of the determinants of penetration have been made by Comanor and Mitchell and Park.[5]

---

5. William S. Comanor and Bridger M. Mitchell, "Cable Television and the Impact of Regulation," *Bell Journal of Economics and Management Science*, Vol. 2 (Spring 1971), pp. 154–212; Rolla E. Park, *Potential Impact of Cable Growth on Television Broadcasting*, R-587-FF (Santa Monica: RAND Corporation, October 1970), and Park, *Prospects for Cable in the 100 Largest Television Markets*, R-875-MF (RAND, October 1971).

Analyzing systems similar to that discussed in Chapter 6, the Comanor-Mitchell study produced estimates of ultimate penetration in the 100 largest markets that are only slightly below the predictions derived from the model employed in the present study. On the other hand, estimates of ultimate penetration based on the Park studies are on the order of two-thirds (*Potential Impact*) to one-half (*Prospects for Cable*) of those presented in Chapter 6.

All three studies—Comanor-Mitchell, Park (1970), and that presented here—estimate the demand curve for cable subscriptions from data on systems that provide additional viewing options, generally outside the 100 largest markets. The virtue of this procedure stems from the considerable variance in over-the-air viewing options among these smaller markets. This variance permits the separate effects on cable subscription of differences between over-the-air and cable viewing alternatives to be estimated with a reasonable degree of confidence. However, this virtue may be purchased at the expense of accuracy in predicting cable subscriptions in the 100 largest markets, which tend to have more and better over-the-air alternatives than do the smaller markets.

Beyond this basic similarity, the models have little in common except that all attempt to explain cable penetration in terms of the additional viewing options subscribers enjoy relative to over-the-air options, subscription fees, and household income of potential subscribers. The demand equation used in the present study is the only one that is built from a basic utility-maximizing model of decision making by the individual potential subscriber. While doing so required making some simplifying and, to some degree, unrealistic assumptions about the shape of individual utility functions and about the ways in which they differ among potential subscribers, the resulting demand equation is at least consistent with the assumption of utility-maximizing behavior at the household level. In contrast, Comanor-Mitchell and Park specify ad hoc linear relationships between cable penetration on the one hand and the price, income, and quality variables on the other, and there is no way of telling whether such a formulation is consistent with reasonable assumptions about the nature of subscribers' preferences.

A second major difference among the models is that, unlike the one employed here, those of Comanor-Mitchell and Park attempt to account explicitly for the fact that ultimate penetration is not reached instantaneously. While this attempt makes sense, its outcome is irrelevant if the time required for penetration is short relative to the age of systems in the sample used to estimate the demand equation. Furthermore, at least two reasons argue for discounting the estimates Comanor-Mitchell and Park present of the impact of system age on penetration.

Both studies enter as an explanatory variable some simple transformation of system age as measured by the number of months elapsed between the date the system first began operations and the date on which the observation on penetration was taken. Penetration is measured as the ratio of actual subscribers to the number of homes in front of the system's cable. Using elapsed time from system start-up to measure the impact of time on penetration is, therefore, valid only if total system size—that is, miles of cable and homes in front of the cable—has remained constant over the period. For most, if not all, systems that assumption is completely unfounded. The typical development pattern involves first wiring a portion of the community and then expanding the system sequentially as penetration on the initial cable segments rises. As a result, it is possible to observe relatively "old" systems with low penetration primarily because they have recently expanded capacity. This phenomenon means essentially that the procedures Comanor-Mitchell and Park follow can substantially underestimate the speed with which penetration occurs.

The introduction of system age or a transformation of it directly into the demand equations raises additional problems, especially when there are relatively old systems in the sample. The first, that is, oldest, cable systems were built in areas with exceptionally poor over-the-air alternatives, those in which local station signals were obscured by hills, buildings, or unusual interference problems. All of the studies under discussion used relatively crude measures of the quality and availability of over-the-air viewing options, and the difference between actual and measured over-the-air quality is probably greater the older the system. Consequently, a variable that is equal to system age or a transformation of it is to some extent a proxy for the quality of over-the-air reception. Thus, the direct inclusion of system age in the demand equation leads to a biased estimate of the effect of time on penetration and also, perhaps, to biased estimates of the other variables in the equation.

The third major difference among the studies under consideration is that Comanor-Mitchell and Park use much larger samples of systems than that used here. While large samples are normally desirable, their merit in this instance is dubious. Here, a large sample is achieved by including a great many very small systems that are very similar to each other. Their addition thus adds little or no information and hence does not lead to more reliable coefficient estimates. Furthermore, loading the sample with observations on systems operating under conditions very unlike those that prevail in the largest markets compromises a demand equation whose major purpose is to predict behavior in those markets.

In summary, then, it seems that there are no strong reasons to prefer the Park (1970) or the Comanor-Mitchell estimates to those presented here. All three suffer from using data that are not representative of conditions in the 100 largest markets. Subject to that qualification, however, the estimates presented here have the advantages of being based on a fully specified regression model and of being free of the problems associated with inclusion of system age as a determinant of penetration.

The only way to counteract the problems inherent in basing estimates on data from the smaller markets is to select a sample in which over-the-air alternatives are very similar to those prevailing in the largest markets. This means including in the sample only systems operating in localities with three strong network signals available over the air. But when this is done there is very little intersystem variation in the cable viewing options relative to over-the-air options so that the impact of added viewing options cannot be reliably estimated.

Table A-3 presents, for example, an estimate of equation (A-16) based on data from a selected sample of 40 cable systems. The sample was obtained by mailing a questionnaire to each of the 400 cable systems operating within the grade A contour of affiliates of all three networks. Of the 60 respondents to the questionnaire, 40 submitted information complete enough to be useful in statistical analysis and indicated that at least 50

Table A-3. Coefficients of Cable Television Penetration in 100 Largest Markets[a]

| Dependent variable[b] | Constant | Dummy variables[c] | | | Comparative service[d] | | | Coefficient of determination $\bar{R}^2$ |
		D_1	D_2	D_3	Primary network X_A	Independent X_I	Duplicate network X_D	
θ	0.0095*	0.0033	−0.0020	−0.0032	0.0065*	−0.0030	0.0019	0.062
	(0.0045)	(0.0038)	(0.0026)	(0.0030)	(0.0036)	(0.0022)	(0.0017)	

Source: Derived from equation (A-16), based on responses to a 1971 mailed survey by forty cable television sytems operating in markets with good over-the-air viewing options.
* Indicates significance at the 95 percent level on a one-tailed test.
a. The figures in parentheses are standard errors.
b. $\theta = \dfrac{\ln(1 - S/Y)}{\ln\left(\dfrac{N_s}{N_p}\right)}$, where S = annual cable fee, Y = per capita household income, N_s and N_p = number of actual and potential subscribers, respectively.
c. See text for description of dummy variables.
d. See Table A-1, note d.

percent of their subscribers could receive all three networks by investing no more than $25 in an outside antenna. Of these 40 systems, 22 indicated that 100 percent of their subscribers could receive all three networks over the air; on the average for all 40 systems, 89 percent of the subscribers received all three networks over the air. Thus, this sample can be taken as highly representative of the availability of viewing options in the top 100 markets and of cable systems in those markets that will need to compete with a fairly extensive menu of free, over-the-air stations.

The general pattern of coefficient estimates in Table A-3 is similar to that in Table A-1 except that the coefficient on the additional independent signals offered on the cable in the former is negative. The principal difference in the two estimates is that in Table A-3 only the coefficients on the intercept and on the increment to network options are statistically significant by conventional standards. The overall explanatory power is also very low, with an $\bar{R}^2$ (corrected for degrees of freedom) of only 0.06. The source of these highly inconclusive results is the lack of variation in viewing options either over the air or on the cable offered by these systems. Nearly all systems competed extensively with the three most important viewing options, the networks, and nearly all systems filled an entire twelve- to fifteen-channel cable system with a full array of network duplicates, independents, public broadcasting stations, and even one or two cable origination channels.

Respondents to the survey questionnaire were also asked to estimate the typical quality of the picture received over the air by their subscribers, rated good, fair, poor, or none, again assuming a $25 investment in an antenna. Attempts to incorporate gradations of signal improvement as explanatory variables also proved unsuccessful, but again nearly all systems reported all three network signals as good (the remaining systems typically reported two good and one fair signal from network affiliates). While these results increase the confidence one has that the sample is representative of conditions in the top 100 markets, they also prevent an assessment of the true significance of various increments to viewing options when these conditions prevail.

Park (1971) has also attempted to derive penetration estimates by estimating a demand equation from a sample of sixty-three systems operating in areas that, on the average, were within the A contour of four stations and the B contour of six stations. While this sample is reasonably representative of conditions in the 100 largest markets, it has little variance in cable relative to over-the-air viewing options. To introduce additional variance

Park assumes that all stations within whose B contour a home lies are not equally receivable over the air. Instead, he assumes reception quality to be lower for UHF (ultra high frequency) than for VHF stations and he assumes that reception quality of both declines with distance from the station's transmitter. While these are surely legitimate assumptions, their inclusion in the model complicates its estimation and makes the results heavily dependent upon the handling of these features.

The inclusion of the distance and signal-type considerations (as well as system age) in the model means estimating three nonlinear parameters. This rules out the direct application of ordinary least squares in favor of a complicated procedure for choosing values for the nonlinear parameters that minimize the sum of squared residuals when the remaining, linear, parameters are estimated by direct application of ordinary least squares.

Such a procedure renders the final results of questionable reliability. The choice of values for the nonlinear parameters, which measure the quality of UHF reception relative to VHF reception and the effect of distance on reception quality, strongly influences the measured sample variance in the variables reflecting the quality of cable relative to over-the-air service. Choosing the values of these parameters that minimize the sum of squared residuals amounts to nothing more than choosing a particular member of a set of transformations that maximizes the sample variance of the quality variables. In addition, the attempt to measure the impact of time on penetration is subject to all the problems discussed with respect to the Comanor-Mitchell and Park (1970) studies.

The importance of these considerations is illustrated by the results presented in Table 2 of Park's study. It contains estimates of his model under alternative sets of constraints on the coefficients and nonlinear parameters. The table demonstrates that the sum of squared residuals is *maximized* relative to alternative formulation when distance from the transmitter is assumed to have no effect on reception quality. Table 3 of the same study suggests that distance from the transmitter is by far the single most significant explanatory variable in the model in terms of the proportion of explained variance for which it accounts.

In a sense this result is not very surprising. It says, in effect, that if distance from over-the-air transmitters is the characteristic of systems that shows the greatest variance in the sample, it will be the characteristic that will account for most of the variance in subscriptions among systems in the sample. The result also indicates, as suggested above, that a sample that exhibits this property may not provide very good estimates of the impact of other service variables on subscribership. Indeed, one way of assessing the reliability of a model is to compare its implications with judgments as to "reasonable" properties of the estimates.

Park's model, like the one presented here, finds primary network service to have the largest measured impact on subscribership. This result is "reasonable" in the sense that the typical television viewer in fact watches network-affiliated stations much more frequently than he does other stations. However, Park estimates the coefficient on independent station service to be only one-fifteenth as large as the coefficient on primary network service, in contrast with the model presented here, in which the comparable relation is about one-fourth. That this is the major source of difference between Park's estimates of penetration and those presented in Chapter 6 can be seen from the following exercise. Park estimates that penetration of a system offering three distant independents in addition to three VHF affiliates and a UHF educational station available over the air would average about 25 percent of homes, depending on distance from the over-the-air transmitters. This estimate can be recalculated using a value of 0.8 for the coefficient on independents so that the size of the independent coefficient relative to the primary network coefficient is approximately the same for the model presented here. When this is done estimated penetration turns out to be 68 percent, or not substantially different from the prediction of the model used here. Thus, the question of which estimates to rely on comes down, in practice, to the question of which estimate of the coefficient on independent station service is more believable.

There is some reason to believe that Park's procedure underestimates the impact that the provision of independent stations has on the demand for cable television. Specifically, Park finds the coefficients on independent station service and educational television station service to be insignificantly different from each other, implying that subscribers are indifferent as between equal percentage increments in the two. This implication does not seem reasonable in view of the audience shares that VHF independents gain over the air relative to the audiences for educational VHFs.

Single independent VHFs garner audiences ranging from about 3 to 11 percent and averaging 6 percent of television homes. As a group the three VHF independents in New York attract 15 percent of television homes, as do the four in Los Angeles. On the other hand, educational stations attract at best less than 3 percent of television homes, and the more typical share is

0.5 to 1.5 percent.[6] Thus, at least when they are free, independent viewing options appear to be valued much more highly than educational station options.

One factor that could account for the Park result in the face of the above observations is that the distant independents offered by systems in his sample may be predominantly UHF independents. While Park's procedure allows for difference between UHF and VHF stations of all sorts over the air, UHFs of a given type on the cable are treated as equivalent to VHFs of the same type on the cable. Yet the two do not offer equivalent viewing alternatives. Rather, UHF programming systematically attracts smaller audiences, for reasons that have been discussed extensively in Chapter 3. Since UHF independents do not get much larger audiences than educational stations do, it would not be surprising to find that potential cable subscribers found the two equally attractive.

The preceding discussion implies that very little about the relationship between the demand for cable service and the availability of over-the-air service can be learned by studying markets in which neither the characteristics of the cable service nor the number and variety of stations available over the air exhibit much variation. In these circumstances other factors, such as price, income, and alternative available entertainment options, are likely to be the important sources of intersystem differences in penetration rates. This conclusion is confirmed by the estimated demand equations for cable service shown in Table A-4.

The equation was estimated from the same sample survey data used to estimate Table A-3—forty systems competing with a number of stations available over the air. In addition to price and income variables, the equation contains variables measuring the total number of options offered on the cable relative to the strong signals available over the air, a dummy variable equal to unity for systems located within the SMSAs of the cities that are the centers of the top 100 television markets, and the age of the system. Only the relative number of viewing options is not statistically significant by conventional standards—and even that is positive with about 85 percent confidence. Variables disaggregating the viewing options into classes of stations were, as in Table A-3, not statistically significantly important in explaining penetration rates.

The SMSA dummy variable was used to correct for special conditions that might prevail in the top 100 markets. While all of the systems were

6. American Research Bureau, *1968 Television Market Analysis* (New York: ARB, no date), pp. 9–11, 50–53.

Table A-4. Determinants of Penetration for Cable Systems Competing with Three Strong Over-the-air Network Signals[a]

		Independent variables				
Dependent variable	Price[b]	Household income (thousands of dollars)	Top 100 SMSAs	System age	Increment[c] to viewing	Constant
Penetration rate[d]	−0.013 (4.36)	0.078 (3.22)	−0.113 (2.30)	0.042 (3.39)	0.059 (1.10)	0.565 (2.10)

$$R^2 = 0.659 \qquad \bar{R}^2 = 0.600 \qquad \text{standard error} = 0.122$$

Source: The basic data for this regression are from a 1971 mailed survey of cable systems. Of the forty systems responding that they competed with a full complement of good over-the-air network signals, five were deleted from the sample because they did not supply complete historical information about the number of potential subscribers, and thus made impossible computation of the mean period a potential subscriber has had the opportunity to subscribe—the measure of system age used in the analysis. The basic income data, from U.S. Bureau of the Census, *County and City Data Book, 1967* (1967), are 1960 Census figures for the county in which the cable system is located.

a. The figures in parentheses are *t*-statistics.

b. Twelve times the monthly fee plus one-fifth of the average installation charge actually made.

c. This variable was measured as log $[(1 + C_s)/(1 + G_s)]$ where C_s is the total number of operating channels on the cable (including cable origination) and G_s is the total number of over-the-air signals that, according to the manager of the cable system, his customers could receive with "good" picture quality by purchasing an outside antenna costing no more than $25.

d. The number of subscribers divided by the number of potential subscribers as of January 1, 1971.

located in areas in which over-the-air viewing options approximated those in large markets, some were in smaller communities in which nontelevision entertainment options obviously would be far more limited than in metropolitan areas. Thus, the coefficient on the SMSA variable should be interpreted as measuring the competition cable systems have from other forms of entertainment in bigger cities.

The age variable was computed from annual data on the potential number of subscribers to each system since the system began operation. Each cable system indicated the number of homes in front of the cable as of January 1 for each year since the cable system was constructed. The increment to the number of potential subscribers during a given year was assumed to have had, on the average, six months to subscribe by the January 1 measuring date. The variable used to estimate the equation in Table A-4 was the average length of time that all current potential subscribers had had the opportunity to subscribe. While most of the systems in the sample had been operating for five to seven years, the average duration of potential subscription for all homes in front of the cable was much lower—about three and three-quarter years. This measure of the age of the system significantly affects the estimated speed with which the system approaches its equilibrium number of subscribers. Using the equation in Table A-1 to estimate ultimate penetration rates, the equation in Table A-4 indicates that cable systems reach 50 percent of ultimate penetration in the first year.

The equation in Table A-4 also indicates that, at current prices, total revenues could probably be increased by cutting prices; the elasticity of demand at the mean is estimated at 1.95. Thus, current prices are consistent with profit maximization if the marginal cost of adding a subscriber is roughly half of the price, about $30. Most analysts believe that marginal cost is below this figure, perhaps about $10 to $20 (including amortization of capital costs). This marginal cost would imply a profit-maximizing price of between $47 and $56 annually, which is not significantly different from the actual average. Put another way, for the average price in the sample—$62—to be profit-maximizing at a marginal cost per subscriber of even $10, the estimated coefficient on price in Table A-4 would have to be −0.0093, which is not significantly different statistically from the actual estimate. Thus, the hypothesis that cable systems charge profit-maximizing prices cannot be rejected.

The income data used in estimating Table A-4 were 1960 Census figures on per capita income for the county containing the system. Household income is per capita income times the number of people per household. Though out of date, these data were used because several systems were located in very small communities for which income information that is available only from the decennial census has yet to be published for 1970. With the coefficient translated into 1972 prices, the equation indicates the penetration rate will increase by about 0.05 if income per household rises about $1,000. This makes cable penetration remarkably sensitive to income if the cross-section results prevail through time in a given locality, for then the equilibrium penetration rate, given the growth in real income, grows about 1 percentage point per year.

The linearity of the estimated equation requires some defense, for the equation does not have convenient asymptotic properties when independent variables take extreme values. For sound theoretical reasons, the "true" relationship cannot be strictly linear. Nevertheless, the linear approximation provided a better statistical result than did other functional forms. Given the nature of the sample, this should not be surprising. The sample contained one observation on a system less than two years old, and one observation on a system more than seven years old, using the period since the beginning of operation as the measure of age. Or, considering the age variable used in the regression—the mean time a potential subscriber had had the opportunity to be hooked up to the cable—only two systems were more than six years old. Thus, the sample did not contain observations that would permit estimation of either asymptote of the relation between penetration and time. The proper conclusion is that in the middle of the range of system age—from, say, two and one-half to five years—the relationship is approximately linear.

Alternative measures of the time variable were also tried: the natural logarithm, the inverse and the square of the inverse of the mean age of subscriber, and transformations of the chronological age. All produced much less significant results.

The Audience Share of Stations

The share of homes that view a given station will depend upon the quality of the station's programming and signal and both the quality and number of alternative signals available to viewers. This study uses affiliation status—American Broadcasting Companies (ABC), Columbia Broadcasting System (CBS), or National Broadcasting Company (NBC) affiliate; or independent—as an indicator of average program quality, and frequency assignment—VHF or UHF—as an indicator of signal quality. Competing stations are taken to be all stations assigned to a given market area. Audience shares are average number of homes viewing a station during prime time divided by the total number of television homes in the station's area of dominant influence (ADI).[7]

The effects of affiliation status, signal quality, and number and type of competing signals were determined for network affiliates by least squares estimation of the following equation:

$$S_A = \alpha_1 D_1 + \alpha_2 D_2 + \alpha_3 D_3 + \alpha_4 U + \alpha_5 \ln(1 + N_A) + \alpha_6 \ln(1 + N_I),$$

where S_A is the share of ADI homes viewing an affiliated station, N_A is the number of *competing* network affiliates in the same market, and N_I is the number of independent stations in the market. The other variables are dummy variables defined as follows:

7. Areas of dominant influence for a market have been determined by the American Research Bureau by allocating all the homes in each county to the single market whose stations receive the largest share of total viewing by homes in the county.

$D_1 = 1$ if the observation refers to an ABC affiliate;
0 otherwise.
$D_2 = 1$ if the observation refers to a CBS affiliate;
0 otherwise.
$D_3 = 1$ if the observation refers to an NBC affiliate;
0 otherwise.
$U = 1$ if the observation refers to a UHF station;
0 otherwise.

For independent stations the equation estimated was

$$S_I = \beta_0 + \beta_1 U + \beta_2 \ln (1 + N_I),$$

where S_I is the share of homes viewing an independent station, U is defined as above, and N_I is the number of competing independents. The number of network affiliates competing with the independent station does not appear in the equation because there are always exactly three such stations. As a result, the estimate of the constant term β_0 is the average share of ADI homes that view a VHF independent station in markets in which there are three affiliates and one VHF independent.

The equation for affiliates was estimated using a random sample of sixty-five network affiliates, approximately equally divided among the three networks. The equation for independents was estimated using a sample of forty-six observations, the number for which the necessary data could be obtained. All the data used were taken from the 1968 edition of the American Research Bureau's *Television Market Analysis*. The results are presented below.[8]

$$S_A = 0.427 D_1 + 0.445 D_2 + 0.420 D_3 - 0.036 U - 0.209 \ln (1 + N_A)$$
$$(0.027) \quad (0.029) \quad (0.029) \quad (0.030 \quad (0.028)$$

$$- 0.014 \ln (1 + N_I);$$
$$(0.027)$$
$$R^2 = 0.915;$$

$$S_I = 0.051 - 0.041 U + 0.0009 \ln (1 + N_I).$$
$$(0.007) \quad (0.006) \quad (0.005)$$
$$R^2 = 0.604.$$

The equation for affiliated stations was used to estimate a share of cable subscribers and a share of the over-the-air viewers that affiliated stations would attract under various circumstances. The cable share was multiplied

8. The figures in parentheses are standard errors.

by the share of homes subscribing and the over-the-air share was multiplied by the share of homes not subscribing. The sum of these two magnitudes provides an estimate of the total share in the presence of cable television. The difference between this "after-cable share" and the estimated "before-cable," or over-the-air share, was expressed as a percentage of the before-cable share to provide the estimates shown in Table 6-4.

The same basic procedure was used to obtain estimates of the impact of cable penetration on independent station audiences. However, the independent station equation reported above was not used to estimate the cable and over-the-air shares.

Note that the estimated coefficient measuring the impact of increased competition on independent station audience size is positive but not significantly different from zero. We believe this to be an unreasonable estimate of the actual impact of increased competition that can be explained in two ways: (1) In only two markets, New York and Los Angeles, was there more than one VHF independent until the early seventies (Seattle-Tacoma's second VHF independent went on the air in 1970); and (2) UHF independents get such small audience shares regardless of the degree of competition. As a result data are insufficient to support a good estimate of the effect of increased competition on independent station audiences.

The estimates that appear in Chapter 6 were derived by assuming that the impact of increased competition from independent stations on independent station audiences is the same as the impact of competition from independent stations on affiliated station audiences. Thus, the share independent stations have of the audience on the cable was estimated by using the relationship,

$$S_I = 0.051 - 0.014 \ln (1 + N_I).$$

Since affiliates have much larger audiences than independents, it is likely that an additional independent will attract more viewers from affiliates than from competing independents. Consequently, the estimated loss on the cable to local independents due to more competition from imported independents is probably overstated. Nevertheless, it is adopted to assure that the estimates will be less likely to understate the potential damage of cable to local independents. The conclusion in Chapter 6 that VHF independents need be imported in only a relatively small number of distant markets to make up for local audience loss due to the installation of cable in the home market is, then, based on an estimated audience loss at home that is probably too large.

A Model of the Economics of Networks

THIS APPENDIX provides a formal analysis of the economic relationships among networks, affiliates, and program suppliers that were discussed in Chapter 3, and presents estimates of some of the parameters of those relationships. The model is based on two simplifying assumptions: (1) The value of audience for a given broadcaster is the same for all programs within some block of time—say, the prime evening hours; and (2) broadcasters are offered, or can produce themselves, some set of half-hour program units, with each of which is associated an (expected) audience size and a price.

Assuming the value of audience to be equal for all programs broadcast in prime time is equivalent to assuming that the demand curve facing individual broadcasters is a function only of audience size and that programs do not differ in the extent to which audience size is sensitive to the amount of time devoted to broadcasting commercial messages. Under these assumptions the ratio of commercial time to program time would be the same for each broadcast period during prime time. Taking half-hours as the units of broadcast time, these assumptions imply a constant revenue per viewer per prime-time half-hour.

The assumption of half-hour program units is merely a convenience and does not render the model unsuitable for analyzing behavior when programs are of different length provided it is assumed that audience size and costs can be expressed in half-hour equivalents. The assumption that a program unit is defined by its expected audience size and cost ignores program quality. Although this concept of quality is sometimes useful in theoretical discussions, it is difficult to deal with empirically. If the quality of a program alters the receptivity of an audience to advertising, then, along with expected audience and costs, it is of interest to the profit-maximizing broadcaster.[1] Finally, expected audience size for a given program unit is not in-

---

1. This statement requires some modification, for the broadcaster must also consider the possibility that a program might offend regulators or viewers and reduce the audience of other programs that he might broadcast. Similarly, a program may create good will

dependent of the overall program mix of a broadcaster or of the program choices of his competitors. But to take account of these factors would greatly complicate the following analysis without changing the essence of the conclusions to be drawn from it.

Under the assumptions of a given revenue per viewer per program unit and a given expected audience size and cost per program unit, expected net revenue generated by broadcast of any program unit, r, is simply given by

$$r = va - f,$$

where v is revenue per viewer, a is expected audience size, and f is the cost of the program to the broadcaster. The above relationship can be conveniently rewritten as

$$r = va(1 - e),$$

where $e = f/va$ and denotes the share of total broadcast revenue extracted by the owner of the program. This restatement of the definition of net revenue to the broadcaster is useful since program charges are typically determined by negotiation and represent the program owner's share of the rents that the broadcast of his program generates.

Now consider a network owning broadcast rights to a set of m programs that, if broadcast over a nationwide system of local stations, would attract audiences $a_i, i = 1, 2, \ldots, m$. For convenience it is assumed the programs are ranked by audience size so that $i < j$ implies $a_i \geq a_j$. If broadcast over the affiliate system, the programs would generate gross revenues of

$$\sum_{i=1}^{m} va_i,$$

but in the absence of the network's ability to command the affiliates to carry its programs, the network must make carriage of its program lineup economically attractive to the affiliates. This it can do most easily by allowing them to share in the potential revenue that the programs will generate.

The share of revenue from the ith program, c_i, that the network gives up to its affiliates—the condition that must be satisfied in order to guarantee that affiliates will clear the full network lineup—stems from the availability of nonnetwork programming to the local stations. The set of nonnetwork programs available can be characterized by (1) the expected audiences

---

with regulators or viewers and have favorable spillover effects on relations with regulators or audience size for other programs. We abstract from these features in the interest of simplicity.

of the programs α_i, $i = 1, 2, \ldots, n$, where by assumption $n > m$ and the programs are ordered so that $i < j$ implies $\alpha_i \geq \alpha_j$; and (2) the shares of potential broadcast revenues demanded by the suppliers of these programs, η_i.

In order to induce affiliates to clear the full network lineup, every network program must be more profitable to them than carriage of the most profitable nonnetwork program. Thus, in general

$$c_i v a_i \geq (1 - \eta_i) v \alpha_i, \qquad \text{for all } i,$$

or

$$c_i \geq (1 - \eta_i) \frac{\alpha_i}{a_i}. \tag{B-1}$$

Two observations may be made at this point. First, the share of revenue that must be given up to affiliates will be minimized, other things equal, if $a_i \geq \alpha_i$ for all i; that is, if networks monopolize broadcast rights for the most popular programs. Second, minimization of the share of revenue given up to affiliates requires a different sharing proportion for each program. It may, therefore, be very costly to implement a structure of sharing ratios that minimizes the share of revenue given up to affiliates since that would require renegotiating the sharing proportions with each affiliate every year as programs and their audiences changed. In addition, the finely tuned exercise of network monopoly power that such negotiation demands would be likely to incur regulatory wrath. These considerations suggest the prudence of a simpler, though perhaps less efficient, structure of sharing ratios. Mathematically this means that the condition stated in (B-1), above, is likely to be satisfied as an inequality for some programs while minimization of the share of revenue given up to affiliates would require (B-1) to be satisfied as an equality for all programs.

Thus, the major means by which a network can hold down the share of revenues that it must yield to affiliates is the superior audience appeal of its programming relative to that available from nonnetwork sources. A network can always offer a program owner more favorable terms than he could obtain by dealing with stations independently because of savings in transactions costs it affords. This means that networks can obtain programming with greater audience appeal than will be available from nonnetwork sources and can do so at prices that reap some profit for the network. At a minimum this profit would equal the savings in transaction and distribution costs that networking provides. But a potential for profits beyond this amount exists and its magnitude can be influenced by the terms upon which networks compensate their affiliates for clearing network programs.

Consider a network offering its affiliates a set of m programs with audiences a_i, $i = 1, 2, \ldots, m$. Assume that the total revenue that any one of these programs would generate is va_i whether it is offered as part of the network lineup or on a syndicated basis directly to local stations. Transaction and distribution costs aside, the owner of any program will offer it to the network so long as his share of program revenues is as large as he could obtain by syndicating it.

If the owner of the ith program were to withdraw his program from the network lineup, the network would replace it with some program with expected audience a_r. Affiliates would continue to clear all of the previous network programs but would clear the replacement for the withdrawn program only if their net revenue from carrying it were at least as great as their net revenue from broadcasting the program that withdrew. Affiliates would clear the replacement rather than broadcast the syndicated program so long as

$$c_m va_r \geq (1 - \eta_i)va_i,$$

where c_m is the maximum share of revenue that the network gives up to affiliates. Canceling v and rearranging gives the condition

$$\eta_i \leq 1 - c_m\left(\frac{a_r}{a_i}\right),$$

where η_i is the maximum share in broadcast revenue that a program owner could extract in syndication. In syndication, however, the program owner will incur distribution costs. Distributors typically charge a share of gross revenue for their services and if this share is given by d, then the maximum share a program owner could ever extract from a network is limited by

$$e_i \leq (1 - d)\left\{1 - c_m\left(\frac{a_r}{a_i}\right)\right\}. \tag{B-2}$$

Thus, the maximum share a network would have to offer a program owner increases as audience size increases but decreases with the share of program revenues that networks give to affiliates. This establishes the assertion made above that the terms of affiliation agreements partially determine the share of broadcast income that will accrue to program owners.

While the need to provide an economic incentive to carry network programming establishes a lower limit on the share of revenue that networks must yield to affiliates, equation (B-2) provides no indication of an upper limit on the maximum sharing proportion c_m. Such a limit is, however, provided by the economics of program production. Obviously, a network must be willing to pay program producers at least the opportunity cost of resources used in program production. Consequently, it would be fruitless for a network to set c_m so high as to make it impossible for a program producer to recover these costs. Given the uncertainties of program production, it is obviously not in the interest of a network to set c_m so high that program producers can do no better than recover their real resource costs.

While so far the analysis has implied that potential audiences for programs are well known to all parties, in practice considerable uncertainty surrounds the audience that any individual program will attract, particularly programs that have yet to be broadcast. One device for dealing with these uncertainties is the program series in which the cast of characters and general themes are relatively constant from episode to episode. Another is the practice of ordering a limited number of episodes of a series after judging the potential audience on the basis of a pilot film of a typical episode. The use of pilots and the practice of ordering limited numbers of episodes both facilitate sequential decision making in the face of uncertainty. The audiences attracted by each set of episodes provide information on which to base the decision to produce further episodes.

A producer of a potential network series thus faces uncertainty about whether his series will be ordered into production, that is, whether his pilot will be accepted or rejected. If it is accepted, he faces additional uncertainty as to the size of audience it will attract and the length of the series' network run. In the presence of these uncertainties the decision to invest in the production of a pilot must be based on an estimate of the expected return that rests heavily on the historical experience of established programs, which, in turn, results partly from the shares of broadcast revenue that producers have been able to command. Producers will invest in new pilots only if the present value of expected returns is at least as great as the cost of pilot production. Since networks are interested in promoting new pilots, they must consider the impact of the terms on which they deal with the producers of current programs on the future supply of pilots and hence of new series.

That these considerations impose an upper limit on c_m can be demonstrated as follows. Pilot production will be a profitable investment if the present value of expected returns exceeds the cost of pilot production or if

$$(1 - t)\theta_n[e_n V_n + (1 - \rho)\theta_s e_s V_s - K_n] > P, \tag{B-3}$$

where

V_n = present value of expected broadcast revenue of an accepted pilot during the network run

V_s = present value of expected broadcast revenue of an accepted pilot in off-network syndication

K_n = present value of the opportunity cost of producing the expected number of episodes of an accepted pilot

P = cost of producing a pilot

e_n = program owner's share in broadcast revenue from network run

e_s = program owner's share in revenue from off-network syndication broadcast after payment of distributor's fee

t = profits tax rate

θ_n = probability a pilot will be accepted by networks

θ_s = probability that an accepted pilot will be released into off-network syndication

ρ = network's share in profits from off-network syndication.

Obviously, the networks would like, if possible, to set e_n so that (B-3) is satisfied as an equality since program costs would then be minimized and profits maximized. With (B-3) rearranged, the optimal value of e_n from the network's standpoint, e_n^o, can be expressed as

$$e_n^o = \left\{1 + \frac{\mu}{\theta_n(1-t)}\right\}\frac{K_n}{V_n} - (1-\rho)\theta_s e_s\frac{V_s}{V_n}, \qquad \text{(B-4)}$$

where $\mu = \dfrac{P}{K_n}$.

The value of ρ has no influence on expected network profits. This is easily demonstrated by noting that under the assumption that all programs receive exactly e_n^o of broadcast revenue, expected network profits from a new program (before taxes) can be expressed as

$$\pi_n = (1 - \bar{c})V_n - e_n^o V_n + \rho\theta_s e_s V_s,$$

where $\bar{c}$ is the average share of broadcast revenue given up to affiliates. Substitution of (B-4) in the above expression gives

$$\pi_n = (1 - \bar{c})V_n + \theta_s e_s V_s - \left\{1 + \frac{\mu}{\theta_n(1-t)}\right\}K_n,$$

which does not depend on ρ.

The relationship between e_n and ρ is illustrated in Figure B-1. The line $\pi\pi'$ with slope equal to $-\theta_s e_s V_s/V_n$ represents equation (B-4). Combinations of e_n and ρ corresponding to points below $\pi\pi'$ are ruled out by the requirement that the expected profitability of pilot production must be non-

Figure B-1. Relationship between Program Owner's Shares in Broadcast Revenue from Network Run and in Profits from Syndication

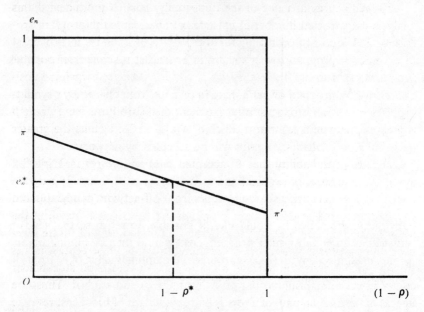

Source: Derived from equations discussed in the text.

negative. All points along $\pi\pi'$ result in equivalent and maximum expected profits for the network. Thus, if networks do not share in profits from off-network syndication their preference would be for $e_n^o = \pi'$ in Figure B-1. As noted earlier this would be achieved by allowing all programs to earn exactly π' of their actual broadcast revenue on their network run.

Without sharing in syndication profits the network is unlikely to be able to keep down to the level π' the actual shares of broadcast revenue that program producers claim. Equation (B-2) indicates that owners of programs that attract audiences no greater than the expected audience for the replacement program cannot force a network to pay them a share of broadcast revenue larger than $(1 - d)(1 - c_m)$. This suggests that if networks were to set c_m close to $(1 - \pi')/(1 - d)$, they would insure that the average program would earn no more than π' for its owners. However, programs that drew above-average audiences would be able to bargain for shares of broadcast revenue greater than π' and the expected share of broadcast revenue that program producers could expect to earn would rise above π' to, say, e_n^* in Figure B-1, where expected network profits are not maximized if ρ is zero. But if networks can obtain shares in off-network syndication profits to the extent of ρ^*, they can offset completely their inability to restrict network run shares of above-average programs to the network profit-maximizing level.

Although networks may not be able actually to employ this device, this analysis suggests that it is useful to them in bargaining with program producers. The level at which the maximum share of affiliates in broadcast revenue is set places an upper bound on the share that owners of popular programs can command; but they are in a much stronger bargaining position vis-à-vis the network than is the producer of a new pilot. By negotiating a share in syndication profits at the time when their bargaining strength is greatest, networks provide themselves with a hedge against the greater bargaining power that accrues to owners of established programs.

Estimates of the parameters of equation (B-4) are present in Table B-1 along with estimates of required and actual values of the share of program owners in broadcast revenue over the period 1960–68. The procedures and data sources used to derive these estimates are described in detail in the notes to the table. In making the estimates all discounting of future revenues and costs was carried out at an annual rate of 12 percent, which is slightly greater than the average after-tax rate of return on stockholder equity in manufacturing corporations over the period studied. Thus, the figures in the final column of Table B-1 are the shares of broadcast revenue on the network run that, if paid to program owners, would have set the expected after-tax rate of return to investment in pilots at 12 percent per year, provided networks did not share in profits from off-network syndication.

The theoretical analysis presented above indicated that although networks have a preference for a high value of the maximum sharing proportion for affiliates, this preference would be tempered by their interest in encouraging investment in the production of pilots. Specifically, a likely upper bound on the maximum sharing ratio for affiliates was argued to be given by

$$c_m \leq 1 - \frac{e_n^o}{1 - d}. \tag{B-5}$$

In view of the role of c_m in determining the maximum share of broadcast revenue that established programs can extract, as expressed in equation (B-2), one would expect c_m to be set quite close to its upper bound as calculated from (B-5). The average of the estimated values of e_n^o in the last column of Table B-1 is 0.313. If, then, the value of d is approximated by the average fee charged by program distributors over the same period—that is,

0.383—the estimated upper bound on c_m is 0.493. This value compares with an actual value for c_m of 0.420.

Column 5 of Table B-1 shows actual shares of network run broadcast revenue that program owners have earned on the average. These figures, which were obtained by dividing the average price paid per half-hour episode by the average revenue received per episode, demonstrate that, on the average, the networks have not completely offset the bargaining power of program owners even though they have obtained shares in profits from off-network syndication. Over the 1961–68 period the share of revenue paid out

Table B-1. Estimated Values of Parameters of the Network-Packager Relationship, 1960–68

$Year\left\{1 + \dfrac{\mu}{\theta_n(1-t)}\right\}\dfrac{K_n}{V_n}$	$\dfrac{\theta_s e_s V_s}{V_n}$	Average network profit share ρ	Program owner's share Required e_n^o	Actual e_n	Estimate of e_n^o if $\rho = 0$
	(1)	*(2)*	*(3)*	*(4)*	*(5)*	*(6)*
1960	0.345	0.019	0.284	0.331	0.316	0.326
1961	0.338	0.024	0.272	0.321	0.336	0.314
1962	0.339	0.029	0.249	0.317	0.351	0.310
1963	0.328	0.036	0.222	0.300	0.353	0.292
1964	0.352	0.044	0.221	0.318	0.350	0.308
1965	0.360	0.054	0.251	0.320	0.362	0.306
1966	0.378	0.067	0.252	0.328	0.398	0.311
1967	0.388	0.080	0.231	0.327	0.438	0.308
1968	0.441	0.099	0.224	0.364	0.406	0.342

Note: Symbols used in this table are defined as follows:

$\mu = P/K_n$ were P = cost of producing a pilot and K_n = present value of the opportunity cost of producing the expected number of episodes of an accepted pilot

θ_n = probability a pilot will be accepted by the network

t = profits tax rate

V_n = present value of expected broadcast revenue of an accepted pilot during the network run

θ_s = probability that an accepted pilot will be released into off-network syndication

e_s = program owner's share in revenue from off-network syndication broadcast after payment of distributor's fee

V_s = present value of expected broadcast revenue of an accepted pilot in off-network syndication

e_n^o = program owner's minimum required share with networks sharing in syndication profits.

e_n = program owner's share in broadcast revenue from network run.

Sources: Derived from equation (B-4) discussed in the text. Except as noted all estimates are based on data in reports prepared by Arthur D. Little, Inc., *Television Program Production, Procurement and Syndication: An Economic Analysis Relating to the Federal Communications Commission's Proposed Rule in Docket No. 12782* (1966), Vol. 2, and a supplement published in 1969, *Television Program Production, Procurement, Distribution and Scheduling*. These are cited below as ADL-1966 and ADL-1969.

Estimates of V_n and K_n (column 1) are based on an estimated expected network run of 2.2 seasons and assume that 26 episodes are produced each season with each episode receiving one winter and one summer broadcast in prime time. The expected length of network run was estimated from data giving the number of seasons that each series introduced from 1954 through 1966 remained on the networks (*Television Magazine*, Vol. 24, September 1967, p. 47). From these data the probabilities of cancellation after a given number of years were estimated and then used to calculate the expected year of cancellation for any series. Both episode costs and revenues were assumed to begin one year after investment in the pilot and the expected length of run defined the time profile over which revenues and costs were discounted. Costs for each season were estimated at 26 times the average episode cost of new half-hour entertainment series introduced in that season (ADL-1969, Table 15, p. 41). Annual revenue was estimated as follows. Average network revenue per prime-time half-hour in the months of November, April, and July for the 1960–61, 1963–64, and 1967–68 seasons was computed from data in ADL-1969, Table 16, pp. 43–45. Average annual revenue from a first and from a second network showing of 26 half-hour episodes was estimated as the sum of (i) 26 times the November average revenue; (ii) 13 times the April average revenue; and (iii) 13 times the July average revenue. Since network commercial time averages 0.837 of total commercial time, each of the estimates was divided by 0.837 to give an estimate of *total* broadcast revenue for a 26 half-hour episode series. To obtain revenue estimates for intervening years, the growth in average revenue between 1960–61 and 1963–64 was assumed to have been at a constant annual compound rate of 4.6 percent, the growth rate for the total three-year period. Similarly, estimates between 1963–64 and 1968 were based on a constant annual compound rate between 1963–64 and 1967–68 of 4.8 percent.

Average pilot costs are the cost of half-hour pilots each year as reported in ADL-1969, Table 14, p. 39. The value of θ_n—the probability a pilot will be accepted by the networks—was estimated to be 0.63 by dividing the sum of all new packager-licensed series introduced in the years 1960–64 by the total number of pilots produced in those years. The data appear in ADL-1966, Table 22, pp. 66–68, and Table 25, pp. 77–78. The value of the profits tax rate t was taken to be 0.5.

The first step in the estimation of $e_s V_s$ (column 2) was to make an estimate of the expected length of time a series would stay in syndication and the time profile of its earnings in syndication. The data on which the estimates were based were drawn from American Research Bureau, *Syndicated Program Analysis* (SPA) (Fall 1968), which gives the coverage for each off-network series carried in at least five markets in November 1968, that is, the percent of total national television homes situated in the markets in which the series was being broadcast and the dates of previous SPAs in which the series was covered. Analysis of these data showed that series in the first year of syndication received an average coverage of 17.5 percent; those in the second, 35.9 percent; those in the third, 4.4 percent; and those in later seasons, 12.5 percent. Since no data were available on the actual number of years a series had been in syndication, series in their fourth year were assumed to have earned all syndication revenues in the first four years following release into syndication. The time distribution of syndication revenues was assumed to be related to the distribution of coverage.

Data in the 1968 SPA essentially permitted an estimate of the coverage received in 1968 by series released in each of the years 1965–68. Coverage received each year by series released that year and the immediately preceding three years was estimated by deflating the 1968 figures. The deflation was based on the fact that the percentage of television homes able to receive an independent station grew at an average rate of 2.5 percent per year from 1958 to 1968. Since independent stations constitute the major outlet for off-network syndications, especially in prime time, it seems reasonable that the demand for such programming, and hence the coverage achieved by the typical series in syndication, would have been growing at a similar rate over the period. Thus to obtain estimates of the changing coverage distribution the 1968 figures were deflated by 2.5 percent appropriately compounded. The result of these calculations was a matrix showing estimates of the coverage attained in each of the first four years following release for a typical series released in each of the years 1958 through 1968.

Estimates of the share of total revenue in any year due to series released in that year and the previous three years were made by multiplying the annual coverage figures by the equivalent number of half-hours released that year. The number of off-network half-hours released was taken from ADL-1969, Table 43, p. 95. With these shares, total revenue from off-network syndication (both foreign and domestic industry sales) was allocated by release dates and the resulting allocations were divided by the number of titles released. The revenue data were taken from ADL-1969, Table 45, p. 108, the number of titles released from ADL-1969, Table 44, pp. 99–107. The result of this operation was, for example, an estimate of syndication revenues during the first year of syndication for a typical series released in the years 1960–67. Likewise, a set of estimates of second-, third-, and fourth-year revenues by release date was generated. A semilogarithmic plot of these data indicated a 29 percent average annual growth rate of syndication revenue for a typical syndicated series.

Interpolation from these plots gave a revenue profile for a typical series introduced into syndication in 1963. This profile was assumed to be the one on which a producer investing in a pilot in 1963 would have formed his expectations of future syndication revenue. However, since his expectation would have been for a network run of 2.2 seasons, the syndication revenue would have been earned four to seven years in the future. Discounted on this basis at 12 percent per year, the estimated present value of syndication earnings for a pilot produced in 1963 that in fact got into syndication comes to $1,124,000. The average fee charged by distributors, as estimated from ADL-1969, Table 31, pp. 62–63, is 38.3 percent. Consequently, the estimate for $e_s V_s$ for pilots produced in 1963 is $694,000.

It is widely acknowledged in the industry that a series must have at least two seasons on a network before syndication is feasible. Consequently, the value of θ_s was taken to be the estimated probability of an accepted pilot resulting in a network run of at least two years. This probability, estimated as described above, is 0.415. Thus, the estimated value at $\theta_s e_s V_s$ for pilots produced in 1963 was $288,000. Values for other years were estimated by applying the estimated growth rate of 29 percent per year, appropriately compounded, to the 1963 figure.

The values of ρ in column 3 are average domestic profit shares taken from ADL-1969, Table 25, p. 56.

Values of e_n (columns 4, 5, and 6) are the average prices paid per half-hour for regularly scheduled entertainment series divided by average revenue per half-hour. Average cost per half-hour for new and continuing series was computed for 1960–64 from data in ADL-1966, Table 25, pp. 75–76. For later years average cost was computed from data for the 1965–66 through the 1968–69 seasons appearing in the annual "Telecast" article provided by *Television Magazine*. In both cases the reported figures were inflated by 5 percent to allow for rerun fees. Average revenue was estimated as explained above.

for the typical program has exceeded the minimum required share by approximately 5 percentage points on the average. Prior to 1966, the excess share averaged about 3.5 percentage points, while it was about 7 percentage points during 1966–68. Looked at in a slightly different fashion, comparison of columns 4 and 5 of Table B-1 indicates that from 10 to 20 percent of the amounts actually paid for regular series entertainment programming represents rents extracted by program owners, that is, payments in excess of those necessary to cover the opportunity cost of resources devoted to program production.

A detailed examination of prime-time programming in the 1967–68 season reveals, however, wide variation in the shares of broadcast revenue extracted by different series. While the overall average share was 0.403 the average share for new series was 0.438 and that for continuing series was 0.382. Shares for new series ranged from a low of 0.377 to a high of 0.491 but more than two-thirds fell within the narrow range of 0.425 through 0.451. For continuing series the shares ranged from 0.261 to 0.559 and almost three-fourths fell between 0.350 and 0.450.

With equation (B-2) and the estimate of the minimum share of broadcast revenue consistent with an expected after-tax rate of return of 12 percent, and with the ratings actually obtained in the previous season, it is possible, for continuing series, to estimate the maximum share program owners could have extracted (e_n), and the minimum share (e_m) that would have been required, given the program's rating, to provide the owner a 12 percent rate of return. If the actual share is denoted $\hat{e}$, a measure that reflects the relative bargaining strength of the program owner vis-à-vis the network can be defined as follows:

$$\beta = \frac{\hat{e} - e_m}{e_n - e_m}.$$

The simple average value of β for continuing shows in the 1967–68 series was 0.520, while the average value of β weighted by shares of total audience was slightly lower at 0.502. This figure suggests that, on the average, program owners have been able to extract only slightly more than one-half of the quasi-rents generated by the broadcast of their programs. Once again, however, there was considerable variation about the mean, with values of β ranging from a low of 0.171 to a high of 0.975.

A regression analysis relating β to the relative audience size of programs gives a significantly negative relationship:

$$\ln \beta_i = 0.002 - 2.472 \ln (a_i/a_r).$$
$$(0.184) \quad (0.556)$$
$$R^2 = 0.463; \, F = 19.788.$$

The numbers in parentheses are standard errors.

In summary, then, it appears that the networks have been able to bargain rather effectively in procuring entertainment series programming. Nevertheless, this analysis suggests that a considerable proportion of the payments they make to program owners—as much as 20 percent of the total in recent years—constitute rents.

Instructional Television

THE RATIONALE FOR INSTRUCTIONAL TELEVISION is simply its effectiveness as an educational technique. Audio-visual instruction is already well established. The educational 16-millimeter films of the past are rapidly being replaced by television. There are three quite distinct television systems: (1) the daytime instructional programs of the public television station; (2) the new instructional television fixed service (ITFS); and (3) the even newer videocassettes.

Comparisons of Alternative Instructional Systems

The choice among alternative video classroom aids is a matter of comparative costs and system flexibility. Public television broadcasting is less expensive per school because the station's signal covers a broad geographical area and because the ultra high frequency (UHF) and very high frequency (VHF) broadcast bands present less technical difficulties. Its disadvantage is the shortage of broadcast spectrum so that usually only one, or at most two, channels in the VHF and UHF bands are available for educational use. All the area's schools, regardless of level and of sponsorship, must rely on one or two signals to satisfy their varied demands. If the local public television station broadcasts specialized instructional material on a specific subject for a particular age group, most children will benefit from the medium only rarely. Conversely, if instructional television aims to give all children frequent viewing opportunities, the programming must be of a generalized "enrichment" character that has a small role in normal instructional activities. Furthermore, enrichment programs are less useful the higher the level of schooling.

ITFS opens up considerably more spectrum space for instructional use, with twenty-eight channels reserved exclusively for educational purposes.

Note. Susan Nelson is a co-author of this appendix.

In addition, because the ITFS signal is directionalized, different programs can be broadcast simultaneously to separate locations in the same metropolitan area. With the potential for as many as one hundred simultaneously broadcast educational programs, gearing programs to the specific needs of a particular classroom becomes possible. The counterbalancing factor is that ITFS is expensive, partly because specialization per se raises per school costs and partly because of the poor propagation characteristics of the ITFS spectrum. A detailed description of four ITFS systems and their problems is contained in the supplement to this appendix.

Individual classroom video systems, such as films or videocassettes, offer the greatest flexibility, but at the highest cost. To be effectively integrated into classroom activities, these systems require large libraries of films or cassettes in each school to avoid delays and uncertainties of program distribution. In addition, sophisticated video equipment is vulnerable to operating errors that result in equipment breakage and to misplacement of components. Many of the problems of teacher-operated systems are likely to be solved eventually as inexpensive, relatively simple videocassette systems become available; for the foreseeable future, however, few if any educators are likely to find extensive use of these systems attractive. Furthermore, both broadcasting and ITFS offer advantages that teacher-operated systems can never match: opportunities for live programming and for two-way communications. These kinds of programming substantially increase the effectiveness of video methods, as well as allowing schools to make available to all students teachers with specialized talents or particular appeal.

Instructional television is obviously becoming an important part of the American educational system. Whether this development is beneficial is beyond our competence to judge, for that depends on the educational effectiveness of widespread use of video techniques. It is up to educators who have experience with the new technology first to fill the current void of scientific evaluation of its contribution and then to argue it merits. Meanwhile, for purposes of further analysis, we assume that instructional television has enough merit to warrant substantial future growth, and turn our attention to its various techniques.

Over-the-air public television seems well suited to instructional programming for very young children, for whom generalized enrichment is in order. The lower cost of broadcasting, coupled with the ability to reach children out of school as well as in, should encourage public television to provide considerable amounts of daytime programming of this type. Over-the-air broadcasting is also suited to large-scale adult education; Julia Child's The French Chef belongs in this category, its obviously high entertainment value a welcome extra. The basic courses for a University of the Air also could be broadcast, enabling a student to complete much of his undergraduate education at home. Lower-level classes in basic composition, history, literature, and other required courses are often so large that meaningful interaction between teachers and students is impossible. Little would be lost, therefore, if a student viewed a lecture in these courses on television, rather than in person (some universities now use closed-circuit television systems to broadcast lectures to overflow classrooms). As students specialize, smaller classes and the greater feasibility and value of classroom discussion make broadcasting both less necessary and less desirable. If any video technique is suitable for these courses, it is a two-way closed-circuit or ITFS system.

Instruction over public television is now widespread. Indeed, one of the most innovative activities of public television is the development of enrichment programs for young children. With many public television stations operated by educational institutions, its use for instructional purposes seems likely to expand.

ITFS, however, represents the major growth potential for educational television, since it can reach small specialized audiences and since, of all closed-circuit techniques, it is the least expensive. The next best alternative is a cable system, but using a cable to provide many program options requires either numerous channels or several independently programmed subsystems serving only part of the area, either of which raises cable costs substantially above ITFS costs.[1] Cables seem practical only as a means of providing a few more channels of essentially the kind of instructional television offered by public TV stations, appealing to a widely dispersed and relatively large audience.

ITFS has raised many unresolved issues of public policy. In fact, its development has been chaotic, inefficient, and probably seriously retarded by the inability of the Federal Communications Commission (FCC) to devise a coherent policy toward it. The commission has influenced the development of ITFS in two ways: through channel allocations and through actions on matters relating to the operation of ITFS systems.

1. For a detailed discussion of the comparative costs of ITFS, cable, and private microwave systems, see William J. Kessler, "Instructional Television Fixed Service: An Assessment of Technical Requirements" (National Education Association, 1967; processed).

The FCC and ITFS Operations

The FCC's policies with regard to ITFS operations have been very similar to those toward commercial broadcasting; the relevance of broadcasting policy to ITFS, however, is dubious.

Technical Standards

One major problem among the earlier ITFS systems was equipment that did not measure up to the specifications claimed. Apparently, ITFS technology had not progressed as rapidly as had demand by educators for the service. The FCC authorized ITFS, even though aware that research and experimentation were in the early stages. An experimental system in Plainedge, Long Island, had proven that ITFS was practicable, although it operated on a frequency different from that the FCC had allocated to ITFS. That example and manufacturers' assertions were regarded as sufficient proof of viability to warrant authorization. Neither the authorizing process nor the tests conducted to type-accept equipment were able to save sponsors of the original systems from choosing ineffective equipment, although type-acceptance is essentially an endorsement by the FCC. The FCC apparently sought to protect potential users by setting minimum performance standards—the type-acceptance procedure—but at least in the early years it failed to accomplish this purpose.

The seriousness of equipment problems is illustrated by the Marysville school district ITFS system, discussed more fully in the supplement.[2]

A paramount goal of FCC technical standards is to prevent interference, but most of the regulations are intended to insure minimum signal quality. These latter standards accomplish no constructive good: They do not prevent the technical complications that plague many systems and constitute a prevalent complaint among ITFS users. ITFS systems with the least technical trouble set standards far above those the commission has laid down. Furthermore, ITFS does not serve public viewers whose interests need protection, as is the case in broadcasting. Since neither the public nor the ITFS

2. This system was delicately dependent on continuation of government funds, which were withdrawn when implementation of the system was delayed. To some extent the FCC contributed to the delay by requiring more complex licensing procedures than had been anticipated; concerned only with minimum assurances of selected aspects of performance, the FCC did not review the feasibility of the system as a whole, and failed to caution about or discourage the especially ambitious technical plans the system drew up.

system is aided by FCC rules, the requirements represent no more than unnecessary paperwork. For marginal systems, they can turn an otherwise successful operation into a failure. A rational FCC policy toward the development of ITFS would abolish technical standards other than those necessary to prevent spectrum interference.

Financing Requirements

The FCC's protective attitude is also illustrated by its financial requirements. The application form for an ITFS system requires financial information—the cost of the system, sources and amounts of funding—to insure that the applicant can finance the project and operate for one year. Once that is determined, the FCC ends its concern for financing, as it does in licensing commercial broadcast stations. But money for education is much more uncertain than money for business operations. While the revenues of a commercial station depend on the amount of time it operates, the reverse is true of educational stations, where revenue commitments are made before operating decisions. Since the first year of ITFS operation is nearly always experimental, the FCC financial requirements bear no relation to the long-term ability of the licensee to operate his system.

The FCC's disclosure rules add significantly to the expense of an ITFS application. They do not, in exchange, assure reasonably full use after a station is authorized. If the FCC aims to serve the public interest through efficient use of the spectrum—the premise for setting standards other than noninterference as a condition for receiving an allocation—that aim is not furthered by financial requirements that do not guarantee operation of channels at anywhere near full capacity.

Continued funding for an ITFS system is a product more of the general condition of the school budget than of one year's operation that is invariably experimental. The FCC standards take no account of this reality in the life of an ITFS system and are, therefore, unrelated to the factors that determine its continued financing. Although these requirements might serve a minor protective function, on balance ITFS development would probably be enhanced if they were eliminated, simply by the removal of one more ineffective procedural hurdle.

Use of Licenses

The FCC has limited its scrutiny to minimum technical and financial standards, with little attention to the planned use of the system and the actual programming. Licenses may be granted only to "educational" institutions and broad-based community groups for educational purposes. ITFS applications must include a tentative programming schedule, although it need bear little relation to what is actually broadcast. Perhaps when the FCC establishes criteria for license renewals, programming considerations will be included, as they are for commercial broadcast license renewals. Until then, there is no federal monitoring of ITFS stations, nor are they required to keep program logs, as are commercial stations, nor even to inform the FCC whether they are actually operating. Furthermore, the commission provides no assistance in programming and no advice for creating programs locally.

In 1965 the FCC realized (1) that current and potential ITFS users were requesting information regarding the service that the commission did not have available, and (2) that coordination by region "in making efficient use of available frequencies" might be helpful to the development of ITFS.[3] Thus the Committee for the Full Development of the Instructional Television Fixed Service was established by the FCC, composed of people working with ITFS systems, mainly educators and FCC officials. Regional committees were set up subsequently to coordinate local plans on an informal and unofficial basis. These national and local committees were the FCC's only attempt to assist in the development of ITFS, primarily through coordination of channel allocations to prevent unnecessary congestion and through supplying information to help systems operate efficiently.

The committee, now known as the Committee for Instructional Television Fixed Service, is generally considered unsuccessful.[4] The vast majority of systems have developed without assistance from or coordination with national or local ITFS committees.[5]

Summary of FCC Policy

The commission has seen its role in the growth of ITFS as one of permitting the service to exist if largely irrelevant technical and financial stan-

3. Federal Communications Commission, *ITFS: Instructional Television Fixed Service—What It Is . . . How to Plan* (National Education Association, 1967), Foreword.
4. See supplement.
5. Specifically, the four San Francisco area systems discussed in the supplement report that they received little or no help in developing their operations from ITFS committees. The local meetings serve mainly to keep systems informed of each other's operations and plans. The problems of equipment, financing, utilization, and programming would have been less severe had an effective communications system been instituted, but the ITFS committees were unable to perform that service.

dards can be met, but not of actively encouraging its development. Its failure to provide information on how to find technical, program, or financial assistance in more depth than its one superficial booklet[6] indicates that the commission feels little responsibility for the success or failure of ITFS systems. The implication is that ITFS operations should remain totally independent of the government, creating their futures according to their own decisions and abilities. The FCC seems to have confidence in "survival of the fittest" as the most efficient method of choosing ITFS systems that deserve to operate.

The policy of independent development for ITFS systems is inconsistent with the protective attitude reflected in the technical and financial specifications. The refusal to give any kind of meaningful assistance indicates that the commission is not especially interested in whether channels are used efficiently while, at the same time, the financial and technical standards suggest that it does not want these stations to fail. It seeks assurance that channels will be able to operate marginally, but it does nothing to encourage efficiency.

Also inconsistent with the FCC's desire for independent development is its attempt to apply one set of standards to all types of ITFS operations. ITFS has many uses to fit the specific needs and circumstances of each educational situation. Complex regulatory standards impose an unnecessary homogeneity on a diverse set of users. The assumption behind this attempt to protect school districts from themselves is that administrators are likely to plan a system they do not want. Since the FCC has no competence in judging the merits of an educational system, its protective attitude seems unwarranted. There might be merit in the FCC guaranteeing that manufacturers live up to the specifications they claim, but that is not the effect of the requirements.

Thus the FCC's role in relation to the development of ITFS systems is ambiguous. The commission has tried, though ineffectively, to save school districts planning ITFS systems from avoidable errors that their inexperience might lead them to make. But the commission has made a conscious policy decision to let growth occur independently, and not to provide assistance to systems or to bolster the effectiveness of the Committee for ITFS. Thus ITFS growth has been marked by protectionism too great to allow independent development but too meager to be effective. A choice should be made between these conflicting roles.

6. *ITFS—What It Is . . . How to Plan.*

ITFS Allocation Policies

The FCC's "first come, first served" method of allocating channels to ITFS systems reflects the same conflict between the desire to protect and the desire to foster independent growth. The commission's responsibility in allocating the spectrum can be divided into two aspects: allocation between ITFS and commercial users, and allocation of channels among individual ITFS stations.

In authorizing ITFS on July 25, 1963, one step was taken toward setting a coherent policy for allocating channels between educational and other users. This was to permit only educational interests, with minor exceptions, to apply for new licenses in the 2500–2690 megahertz (MHz) frequency range for the first three years of the authorization. The FCC had apparently concluded that educational use of the channels needed to be protected from competition with commercial interests. After three years an evaluation of educational use of the frequencies would be made to determine whether this protection should be continued. No evaluation was ever made.

Subsequently the commercial freeze was unofficially lifted. Licenses were granted in the 2500–2690 MHz to systems operated by Dow Chemical, United Airlines, the St. Louis Police Department, and numerous other noneducational users. In June 1970, the FCC issued a Further Notice of Proposed Rule Making[7] that proposed permanently setting aside twenty-eight of the thirty-one channels in this band for the exclusive use of ITFS and restricting ITFS to that area. One year later, in FCC's Second Report and Order, the twenty-eight-channel reservation was permanently adopted, thus protecting ITFS from competition, although the potential extent of ITFS operation was decreased by three channels, or 10 percent. The three channels were allocated to the operational fixed services on an exclusive basis.[8]

The first come, first served method of allocating channels among ITFS systems seems to have been chosen to avoid policy decisions rather than to promote long-run efficiency. Regional ITFS committees, although they have no authority, are supposed to inject some coordination into local planning by reviewing all applications for systems in their areas and mak-

7. FCC 70-640, Docket 14744, published in *Federal Register*, Vol. 35 (June 26, 1970), pp. 10462–63.
8. FCC 71-600, Docket 14744, published in *Federal Register*, Vol. 36 (June 16, 1971), pp. 11585–88.

ing recommendations to the commission. The FCC apparently seeks to avoid imposing its conception of what is best for an area.

So far this method has occasioned little outcry because demand for ITFS reservations has been low enough that allocation has become a crucial issue in only a few areas. When, in Los Angeles and Cleveland, the FCC's allocative process confronted an initial demand for more channels than could be authorized, the commission threw the problem back to the local level by refusing to make a decision. In Los Angeles, channels were then allocated by a locally originated plan, which apparently achieved a rational distribution that would not have been possible had the principle of first come, first served been adhered to. In Cleveland, lacking any criteria on which to judge them and refusing to decide among the last group of competing applicants, the commission declined to grant any more construction permits until it was presented with a unified plan that would take into account the conflicting proposals. The plan, which took one and a half years to devise, was a metropolitan ITFS system operated as a common carrier by an agency composed of all the interested groups. No member would have its own channel among the sixteen authorized, but would buy time according to its needs and to the amount available. Although the channels were granted in 1969,[9] broadcasting on more than a demonstration basis did not begin for two years. The local educational TV station, not the regional ITFS committee, took the lead in organizing the ITFS interests.

The absence of congestion in other regions is not evidence that the FCC is allocating ITFS channels efficiently; rather, it demonstrates that demand is not strong enough so far to create conflicts. If ITFS continues to grow as the commission and educators hope, other areas will soon be faced with competing demands for the limited resources of the ITFS spectrum. Resolving disputes and achieving efficient allocation will be more difficult where most of the channels are filled with strong operating systems that will not readily relinquish channels they have been using. In Cleveland and Los Angeles, the systems that had been granted channels and the very few that were on the air experimentally when attempts at regional coordination began sacrificed little to comply with the cooperative effort. Such will not be the case if the FCC continues to expect voluntary coordination to solve allocative conflicts. In San Francisco, the directors of two strong ITFS systems already operating have agreed that, if and when congestion becomes a problem in their area, they will not voluntarily give up channels

9. Education Products Information Exchange, *Instructional Television Fixed Service*, Educational Product Report 31 (New York: EPIE, 1971), pp. 29–32.

they are using efficiently, even though they favor regional coordination in theory. The FCC's first come, first served approach is short-sighted, for even if regional ITFS committees functioned more effectively, efficient allocation between existing ITFS systems and new applicants would be close to impossible.

The commission's current policy toward allocation for ITFS comprises two distinct attitudes. The FCC has implicitly decided that education cannot successfully compete with business and that ITFS deserves to be protected in this unequal contest; and to do so it has acted on the precedent set by educational reservations in the UHF frequencies. To date no evaluation has been made of the educational effectiveness of ITFS nor, therefore, of the propriety of its use of the spectrum that is—like personnel, land, buildings, typewriters—simply a resource that can have educational uses, but that has others as well. Continuation of the commission's policy of protecting ITFS should hinge on a showing by educators that the service merits protection and special encouragement.

The other half of the commission's policy toward ITFS is, essentially, a failure to have a policy for allocating channels to ITFS systems. Its allocative method provides no mechanism for choosing among competing ITFS applicants; it simply grants channels to any system that is deemed "qualified" while verbally encouraging local coordination.

At least three other methods could be used for allocating channels. Each implies a distinct regulatory philosophy, just as the current first come, first served policy, combined with the commission's incoherent role in the development of ITFS, embodies an ambiguous attempt simultaneously to protect and to foster independence. The alternative policies reflect various degrees of federal control and of confidence in federal decisions to produce efficiency.

Alternative 1

A scheme that would carry the implication of nearly total confidence in federal decisions would imitate the present method of allocating spectrum for broadcasting stations. A table of ITFS allocations would balance commercial versus educational needs in the 2500 MHz spectrum, perhaps reserving a certain number of channels for private and parochial school use, for colleges and universities, and for public elementary and secondary schools. The commission could decide among competing ITFS applicants as it does for broadcasting, allowing the expense and delay of the process to encourage compromises among the applicants. After all the channels were assigned, newcomers could be accommodated either by challenging stations at renewal time, by convincing the FCC that they deserved to share time with the existing stations, or by competing with commercial users for the noneducational allocations. If few educational channels were in use, the FCC could make exceptions to allow commercial applicants for those channels.

This method assumes that the FCC can define efficient allocation. It assumes either that a federal agency has perfect knowledge of how a region wants its spectrum space divided among competing interests, now and in the future, or, more realistically, that its imperfect decisions and the resultant inefficiency are the minimum costs necessary to protect the public interest. The latter is the rationale offered with respect to broadcasting allocations intending to save channels for educational and small town stations, goals specifically considered desirable by the FCC.

The public interest aspect of ITFS is not as clear. First, there has been no determination that ITFS is educationally effective and thus worthy of protection. Second, ITFS is a closed system in which sender and receiver are part of the same organization; ITFS does not serve the community at large. The public benefit in giving spectrum space to the San Francisco Medical Center rather than to American Airlines is not easy to identify.

Since the public interest involved in ITFS is indefinite, the inefficiency caused by the federal method of allocation for ITFS is not justified and argues against applying to ITFS the procedures used for allocating broadcast channels.

Alternative 2

A system in which the FCC would not grant construction permits for ITFS stations except as part of a comprehensive regional plan would allocate spectrum according to local instead of federal decisions. Within this method, which is essentially the Los Angeles plan, the FCC's role would be administrative, not decision making. It would insure that proposed stations would not interfere with each other or with ITFS systems in nearby towns in adjacent planning areas. Renewals, newcomers, and choice among competing applicants could be handled however the local planners wanted. If this system were to rely totally on local decisions, the demands for spectrum by commercial as opposed to educational interests would also have to be balanced on the local level.

The advantage of this system would be that decisions would be made by the people most affected by the outcome and that at least some thought and planning would be given to future as well as present needs. Problems would arise in determining what group the FCC would recognize to make the binding decisions, for the process of selecting representatives to decide who can and who cannot have an ITFS system would have to be more rigorous than the method of choosing an informal ITFS advisory committee. This method of "enforced cooperation" would not solve the inefficiency caused by delegating an economic decision to a political body. No political group could balance the costs and benefits of ITFS systems to the individual schools, particularly if the issue were complicated by requests for licenses for commercial operations. The conflict between protectionism and independence still would not be resolved. In this method the commission would allow totally independent development except that "independent development" must embrace regional coordination of widely diverse groups.

Alternative 3

The final alternative to the current system would have the FCC adopt a market mechanism to allocate ITFS. The case for a market system for all spectrum allocations presented in Chapter 2 is applicable to this specific case. Until a public interest aspect to ITFS has been shown, there is no justification for seeking to override market decisions and thereby to sacrifice economic efficiency, even if such a public interest is believed to exist in other spectrum rights.

A market mechanism could be applied to ITFS allocation in the following manner. Rights to ITFS channels in specific areas of a city would be granted one by one to the educational user that would pay the most for them. School systems could combine and operate a system on a time-sharing basis if they wanted. Where the demand for channels was equal to or less than the number of channels available in an area, systems would pay nothing for ITFS grants. Where demand exceeded supply, the price system would be invoked to insure efficient allocation. School systems would be willing to pay a price for channels equal to the difference between the cost of an ITFS system and the next best alternative, and channels would be awarded to the one that valued ITFS most highly. The rights purchased would apply only to program control; system operators would not be allowed to broadcast scrambled signals that losing bidders could not receive, and would be required to make programming schedules public. Nothing would prevent another school system from using the winning bidder's programs. This would, of course, encourage cooperation rather than competition over licenses.

Once a channel had been assigned, the authorization would last for a specific number of years, perhaps five. At the end of that time the license would come up for renewal and competition would again be invited. If none developed, channels could be retained for another five years, but this time without fee. The five-year lease offers some security to the licensee in the interests of encouraging efficient operation. If within the five-year lease a system failed to operate any channel for a given period—say, three months —bidding for its use would be reopened though the lease had not ended.

If the FCC should no longer desire to protect ITFS from competition for spectrum, a market system involving competition between commercial and educational users could be developed. Rather than totally restricting the twenty-eight channels for education and three for other undertakings, all fixed service allocations would be open to everyone. Even if protection of ITFS continued, commercial applications should still be accepted for systems in areas with no threat of congestion. This approach would be consistent with ITFS protection but also would ensure that channels for which a demand existed did not stand idle.

Should competitive bidding for ITFS assignments ever drive the price of ITFS channels so high that they become an important source of FCC revenue, the FCC should regard it as a sign to allocate more spectrum to ITFS. One result would be lower prices. The remaining revenues might be returned on a per-student basis to local schools and colleges, or added to federal support for education, so as to avoid the complaint that an efficient method for allocating ITFS channels transferred resources out of education.

A combination of alternatives 2 and 3—a local common carrier for ITFS —should be seriously considered by educators and federal regulators. Even if competition between educational users and others is not to be permitted, it makes sense to sell ITFS rights on a common-carrier basis through a local ITFS entity, such as was planned in Cleveland. Each potential ITFS user is forced to consider the true opportunity cost of ITFS spectrum space in deciding upon its most effective educational strategy. The greater flexibility and narrower instructional target provided by ITFS would be assigned a more realistic cost when compared to the costs and benefits of other alternatives, such as children's broadcasts on public television, other video methods (such as cassettes and films), and traditional classroom activities.

If regional or local authorities are to be set up, the best method for allocating channels among diverse groups such as parochial schools, universities, and public schools would be a market mechanism. Otherwise, serious
inequities are almost certain to arise.

Four Profiles of ITFS Systems

Susan Nelson

The numerous instructional television fixed service systems operating throughout the nation vary widely in use and extent of success. The following descriptions of four systems in northern California provide some sense of this variety. These profiles illustrate in greater detail some of the problems—and some of the potential—of ITFS described more generally in the main text.[10]

Marysville Public School System

Marysville is a town in the predominantly agricultural California Central Valley, located about 50 miles north of Sacramento. The Marysville ITFS system is operated by the local public school district. The system was licensed in November 1969, and began operation in September 1970. It operates on two ITFS channels for about eight to ten hours a week, and serves sixth-grade students in two elementary schools with programs leased from national sources or purchased for permanent addition to the library. There is no live program production, and the production of tapes by the system has been abandoned, at least temporarily, because the quality was generally poor.

Planning for the Marysville ITFS system began in the spring of 1966. The local educators were seeking a television system within their budget that would enhance classroom lessons and that would permit "random access" —the ability of a teacher or a student to request that any tape in the library be broadcast when he desired, rather than according to a published sched-

10. The information contained in this supplement was provided through personal interviews and correspondence with operators of the four systems. The author is grateful to the following individuals for their valuable assistance: Thomas L. Banks, Coordinator of Educational Television, University of California, San Francisco Medical Center; Kenneth S. Down, Administrative Manager, Stanford Instructional Television Network; Father Pierre DuMaine, Assistant Superintendent of Schools, Archdiocese of San Francisco; and Leonard E. Larson, Assistant Superintendent of Instruction, Marysville (California) Joint Unified School District.

ule. ITFS and closed circuit connections through the telephone lines were the two major techniques considered, but the latter was ruled out by the $40,000 annual cost of using the telephone to connect the most distant school. Since school budgets are always unpredictable, an attractive feature of an ITFS system was that, after the initial capital investment, minimal operation could continue on a low budget.

Most of the problems that plague the system had their roots in the planning stage. The most serious was lack of money. Funding was originally received from both state and federal sources to conduct studies, buy equipment, and begin operation. Much enthusiasm was generated in planning sessions and teacher workshops that discussed integrating the system into the district's overall educational schemes. The aim of random access presented the first major obstacle. Essentially, Ampex Corporation custom-made the Marysville equipment. The school's officials had seen the Ampex laboratory models, but none was in field operation. Because of the experimental nature of the equipment, numerous technical problems developed at the beginning, more than in most ITFS systems. Teacher enthusiasm naturally rose and fell with the operational state of the system. Compounding these technical difficulties were procedural obstacles imposed by the FCC. The school officials thought that obtaining an ITFS license involved merely submitting a simple application. They were quite surprised to find that the form was so complex that they were expected to hire a consulting engineering firm to complete it, to retain Washington lawyers to shepherd the application through the FCC, and finally to get congressmen to apply pressure in order to shorten the FCC's response time to four months. They attribute fully a year's delay in beginning operation to the necessity of revising applications to comply with complex FCC rules and to the long delays in responses from the FCC.

The most serious result of the delays due to technical problems and the FCC procedure was that financial support was withdrawn by the time full-scale operation was finally possible. The reason for the withdrawal is not completely clear. The State Department of Education was probably too strict in charging Marysville with failure to live up to the plan for which they had been given support by going too deeply into research on uses of TV in the classroom and inadequate follow-through on their plans. Thus he funding was ended six to eight months prematurely and not renewed as had been expected. The system in operation today is barely more than the system in its experimental phase when state government financing stopped. Local money for the schools is quite tight, so the operating budget amounts to little more than salary for a full-time operator—the licensed engineer who must be present any time the system is on the air.

Utilization of the system is very low, primarily because the selection of tapes that teachers can request is limited. Besides tapes that were accumulated before the funding cut-off, one leased series of one to three tapes is generally available each week. The libraries in the two schools are equipped with twelve individual receiving sets on which students can dial their programming requests. After two requests have been filled, other students and teachers must either wait their turn or watch the previous choices. Random access, however, remains feasible since there are so few requests.

The reaction in Marysville to ITFS is quite favorable, and would probably be even more so if a realistic budget were available. The teachers believe that ITFS makes teaching easier because students are attentive to nearly anything put on television. The administrators see the ITFS as "broadening the classroom experience." Now that the technical problems apparently have been resolved, officials are interested in implementing some of the plans that limited funds have thus far made impossible: expansion of current operation to cover more grades and schools; incorporation of an existing high school class in TV production with ITFS; extension of coverage to Yuba College and perhaps installation of two-way response; rehiring of a director and the addition of staff to work on program creation; coordination with vocational schools in the region.

No solution for the money crisis appears in the near future. There even seems to be a chance that the ITFS system might stop operation because of financial pressures on the school system.

Archdiocese of San Francisco

The parochial school system of the Archdiocese of San Francisco has operated a four-channel ITFS system since September 1970. Three of the channels are fully programmed, operating five or six days a week for six or seven hours a day. While the system is also used for religious instruction and adult education, its primary use is in the instructional program of fifty-eight elementary schools in the parochial system. Five high schools also have been equipped with receivers, but programming for high school courses has not yet been started. The reach of the system is exceptionally far, as three sets of repeaters carry ITFS programs to schools 100 miles apart. Nearly all of the programming is obtained from outside sources, with less than 10 percent produced by the archdiocese.

Many Roman Catholic school districts have made a concerted effort to develop effective ITFS systems. Soon after the FCC authorized ITFS in 1963, the national organization of Catholic educators began informing dioceses of the commission's actions and of the potential for use by the Catholic schools. Dioceses were urged to apply for construction permits as soon as possible. As a result many dioceses filed applications, and were granted construction permits. (Three of these, including the large Baltimore and Washington, D.C., dioceses, still do not have adequate funds to execute their plans, and the channels they have been assigned remain unused.) Beyond initially encouraging schools to adopt ITFS, the national organization continued to serve as a clearinghouse for technical and programming information, specifications necessary to pass the FCC requirements. Diocesan systems have banded together to improve the terms of purchasing and rental agreements by dealing in larger quantities. They also have formed a network to exchange programming produced by their members.

The Archdiocese of San Francisco was among the districts that developed an operational ITFS system. It operates a good, well-organized, if not very experimental, ITFS system, now used primarily for enrichment, but gradually expanding into teacher supplement services as a partner in team teaching. In the elementary schools receiving ITFS service, two courses, middlegrade math and upper-grade music, are now heavily reliant on ITFS series.

Currently, nearly all the programming for the normal classroom use consists of videotape from national sources, including other archdioceses that have begun to produce programs. The teachers periodically visit the diocese's educational television (ETV) center to preview series and to choose those they want for their classes. The system operates with a master schedule for the semester with notification of additions, changes, and specials sent out each week. Programs are repeated frequently in an attempt to fit individual schedules, and requests for special showings of a program during free time periods are encouraged. One teacher at each school is designated the ETV coordinator to receive comments and complaints, to attend meetings at the diocesan ETV center, and generally to provide communication between the schools and the ITFS administrators.

Less educational experimentation with ITFS has taken place than had been hoped, primarily owing to inadequate money and staff. Because of arrangements such as the ETV coordinators and the previewing sessions for teachers, the system, though new, seems to be functioning efficiently. Naturally, the administrators are enthusiastic and consider the undertaking well worthwhile; however, its effectiveness is uncertain. No survey has been made of the extent of utilization of the system or of academic improvements attributable to it. At the end of the first year of operation, the diocese planned to undertake an evaluation of the effect of the ITFS system on the students.

The director of the ETV center credits diocesan organization with providing the only substantial outside help in the development of the ITFS system, and this only in the planning stages. After plans were drawn up, the archdiocese's ITFS system developed independently of even the national Catholic organization except for joint rental contracts and program exchanges. Even the funding came from within the diocese: Students pay a small fee each year which, when all schools are eventually served by the ITFS system, will cover operating costs. The FCC acted as no more than a gate that had to be passed through to gain a license; its regional ITFS advisory committee apparently did nothing.

As part of a nationwide system of parochial schools, the archdiocese received valuable technical and legal advice during the critical early stages of planning and development. It thereby avoided the predicaments in which the Marysville system found itself. The archdiocese also faces lower programming costs through agreements with other Catholic school systems. Although these advantages of association with other ITFS systems are not responsible for all of the success that the archdiocese of San Francisco has achieved, it undoubtedly improved the probability of success.

Stanford University

The Stanford University ITFS system began operations in 1969. It occupies four channels, transmitting college courses to private businesses where employees are enrolled as part-time Stanford students in a daytime release program, since no evening courses are offered by the university. All channels are on the air between seven and ten hours a day, five days a week. Course offerings fall into two groups: the Honors Cooperative Program, providing forty-seven graduate engineering and science courses for students in the graduate School of Engineering, and the program of the Association for Continuing Education (ACE), providing thirteen courses in business administration, rapid reading, shorthand, and other academic and technical areas for employees interested in continuing education of all kinds. The membership of ACE comprises companies and organizations that participate in the Stanford graduate program. About 300 students employed by twenty-nine organizations participate in each of the two programs.

The Stanford ITFS system has several unique features. Perhaps most impressive is that it was almost independent financially after two years. Participating organizations assume three separate financial obligations. They pay part of Stanford's initial development, design, and construction costs; they equip their own receiving classrooms; and they pay a television surcharge, which is intended to cover day-to-day operating expenses. These fees are offset by saving to the organizations through recapturing time lost by employees who previously traveled to Stanford to attend classes. One large company alone estimated that before ITFS was installed it was losing 2½ man-years annually in student travel time to and from the campus.

ITFS at Stanford was developed to fill a specific existing need. The Honors Cooperative Program had already operated successfully for fifteen years, with over 1,000 graduate degrees having been awarded under the daytime release plan; however, the time lost in traveling to and from campus made the program somewhat inefficient. ITFS made the program more efficient for those already participating and feasible for some who were prevented entirely from enrolling because of distance, and, in the long run, saved money for the participating organizations. With a specific efficiency goal and with its services sold in a market, success is easier to achieve and to recognize than in systems with more nebulous aims like "enrichment" and indicators of success like "improved education." So far the Stanford effort has apparently been worthwhile, for users are happy to bear the costs.

Utilization of the Stanford system is extensive. Stanford courses fill the school day and ACE courses use some of the available channel time before work, during lunch, and from 5:30 to 7 p.m. Offerings could be expanded since the system is idle over the weekends and in the late evening hours. Demand for the engineering program has been more consistent than that for ACE courses, whose program is not as clearly defined and whose courses are scheduled at less convenient times. Furthermore, ACE participation is probably more likely to be affected by external economic factors, for tuition support is not provided for all ACE offerings by all member organizations, as is generally the case for Stanford honors cooperative students. Stanford hopes that utilization of the system will be increased as other educational institutions in the San Francisco Bay area begin participating in the program.

Stanford was the first system to use frequency modulation (FM) response talk-back. Two-way audio was integrated into the original system plan, although the FCC rule allowing FM response talk-back was not promulgated until June 1969. Two-way capability was essential to the success of the system since the opportunity to make comments and ask questions is a necessary condition for a course to be offered for credit in the Stanford engineering program. The two-way system enables students in remote locations to communicate with anyone in their class, on or off campus. In Stanford engineering courses, in which a majority of the students are in the campus classroom, remote participation apparently neither hinders nor encourages class discussion to any significant degree. Some people are less hesitant to comment than they would be in a classroom, because they remain anonymous to the professor and to the majority of the class. Others would prefer to be in the live classroom than use the two-way talk-back system. It is significant, however, that both the faculty and students know that they can interact if and when they wish. ACE courses generally involve an instructor who lectures only to remote students. In this situation the response station talk-back system is the only vehicle for two-way communication.

In designing an ITFS system, Stanford had available the services of staff members with expertise in technical areas related to ITFS systems. Although an outside firm assisted with preliminary studies and with system installation, members of the School of Engineering staff cooperated closely. University lawyers provided necessary legal assistance on local matters, while an outside firm was used to coordinate legal matters with the FCC in Washington. Thus Stanford encountered no serious problems in activating its plans for ITFS, either from the FCC or from technical complications. All the resources of a prominent university were available to insure a sound, business-like result.

University of California San Francisco Medical Center

The University of California Medical Center in San Francisco, a medical school in the University of California system, operates a two-channel ITFS system that is on the air about three hours a day, four days a week. The system serves the medical school campus and several area hospitals affiliated with the school. All of the programming is live and produced by the medical center.

The University of California at San Francisco was the first medical school in the country to apply for an ITFS system and the first applicant of any kind in the San Francisco area. It sought the ITFS license to broaden the range of its existing closed-circuit system (which linked buildings of the medical school campus) so third- and fourth-year students could view lectures without returning to campus from the hospitals where they spent a large part of their time. The system is now used very little for this purpose; direct instruction is broadcast only occasionally. The major function now is broadcasting "Grand Rounds"—staff meetings (approximately six per week) at which a visiting specialist presents a paper. Students, residents, and practicing physicians all view the Grand Rounds, which are designed to keep doctors informed of new ideas in their fields. The operators believe that a significant benefit of ITFS is that it provides professors with the option to televise lectures to students who cannot return to the campus, even though the option is seldom used.

Thomas Banks, the ETV coordinator, admits that the ITFS system is underused. The resources available are concentrated on the campus closed-circuit part of the ETV system, limiting ITFS use; in addition manpower is insufficient for ITFS to expand much. Thus, integrating an ITFS system into an existing ETV system apparently can hinder the growth of ITFS as well as advance it. An experienced staff was already assembled; professors had become accustomed to teaching over television; some of the same equipment could be used. After ITFS was installed, the old system continued to receive most attention and use, probably because there was more need—or at least custom—for connecting the campus buildings. The small number of classes being broadcast would indicate that even at the outset there was less need than the planners identified for a link to the hospitals. Its use for Grand Rounds was not part of the original scheme; it turned up ex post, as a means of utilizing an existing system. But these uses appear less than adequate to justify adding ITFS to the closed-circuit system.

Underutilization of the system is attributable simply to the internal structure of the medical school, rather than any outside force. The development of the system progressed smoothly. While the first set of equipment was returned to the manufacturer because it failed to meet the specifications attributed to it, the resulting delay was not considered a serious setback. Similarly, the medical school was inexperienced but not inept in dealing with the FCC, which also presented no obstacle to its plans. As did Stanford, the medical school benefited from affiliation with a university. For example, it was not even necessary to hire a consulting engineer—a member of the university was used. No single incident in the development process appears to have discouraged use of the system. Perhaps with more money, a demand could be created for ITFS, but apparently little need currently exists.

Index

ABC. *See* American Broadcasting Companies
Advertising, television: alternative support systems, 43–44; and audience size, 10, 35–36, 41, 45, 60; believability, 14, 40; and CATV, 167–68, 176, 189; collection costs, 42, 44; discounts, 37–39; diversity effect, 10; expenditures, 1, 15, 42; income level effect, 40–44, 56; and market competition, 37–40, 56; and network-affiliate relations, 5, 15, 59–63; "participations," 38; and station ownership, 104–05; and STV, 132, 147, 149–50; supply and demand factors, 34–37, 56; viewer minutes, 35–37, 61
Affiliated stations: and audience size, 80; CATV effect, 163–66, 174–75; local service doctrine, 174; in market structure, 74; network relations, 5, 15–16, 59–63; 106; profits, 17; UHF, 7, 166, 181. *See also* Independent stations; Local stations; Networks; Ultra high frequency stations; Very high frequency stations
Agnew, Spiro, 2
Alexander, Sidney S., 90n, 91n, 221n
All-channel receiver law (*1962*), 89, 103–04, 126
Allen, George, 256
American Broadcasting Companies (ABC), 5, 52, 68, 109; deintermixture proposal, 102; satellite system proposal, 246
American Civil Liberties Union (ACLU), 127
American Telephone and Telegraph Corporation (AT&T), 59, 62, 246–47, 250–51
Audience: and adjacency, 131; and advertising, 10, 35–36, 41, 45, 60; and CATV, 217; children, 13, 241; mass, 49–53, 56; minority, 11, 49, 52–53, 82, 211–14, 216–17, 262, 273–74; public television, 211–14, 216; STV, 273–74; UHF, 82; videocassettes, 262. *See also* Diversity; Options; Programming

AVCO Corporation, 105, 259
Averson, Richard, 14n

Baer, Walter S., 198n
Barnett, Harold J., 9n, 152n
Barnett, Stephen R., 152n
Bartley, Robert T., 206n
Baumol, William J., 21n, 28n
BBC. *See* British Broadcasting Corporation
Bell Telephone Hour, 82
Blake, Harlan M., 37n
Blank, David M., 38n, 62n, 130n
Blum, Jack A., 37n
Bonanza, 48
Bradford, David F., 21n, 28n
Broadcasting and Film Commission (National Council of Churches), 127
British Broadcasting Corporation (BBC), 212, 220, 231, 235, 268
Buchanan, James M., 120n
Burch, Dean, 127, 155n, 183n, 205, 206n, 207

Cable television (CATV), 7, 13, 43, 80, 275; access channels, 200–02, 204, 273; and advertising, 167–68, 176, 189; affiliated stations effect, 163–66, 174–75; automated program services, 187–88, 192; cable networks proposal, 189–90; cable penetration, 153–61, 272–73; channel capacity, 184–86, 194; and copyrights, 175, 177–79, 181, 205, 207; demand function, 22–23, 29–30, 32, 203–04; and diversity, 127, 171; economics of, 153–62, 173–79, 272; ethnic programming, 188; and FCC, 107, 122, 125, 154–56, 162–63, 172, 179–82, 272; future of, 8, 272–73; and income level, 24, 160–61, 202–03; independent stations effect, 162, 164–65, 173; interest groups, 127; leapfrogging, 173; leased channels, 186, 191–94, 201; and local government, 203–04; local origination, 29, 186–91, 200, 204, 217, 273; local sta-

337